"The authors present an extensive *tour d'horizon* surveying relevant issues and recent discussions. This setup greatly enhances the book's orientational value for teachers in the field, while also making it a helpful introductory text for students specializing in moral philosophy and the philosophy of education. The emphasis on the human person in this book provides a vantage point from where one could develop a moral philosophy pertaining to professional training, which until now had been sorely lacking in Christian higher education. In this important respect, *Practice and Profile* fills a gap."

—Sander Griffioen
Professor Emeritus of Christian Philosophy,
VU University, Amsterdam

"An important book for faculty who seek to integrate faith and profession in the classroom. PISA—practice-minded, integral, spiritual, and answerable—is a superb template for pursuing such integration."

—Alec Hill
President of InterVarsity Christian Fellowship,
Madison, Wisconsin

"This book is highly recommended for its fundamental reflection on Christian higher education. The authors go into depth on the possibilities and opportunities encountered in the training of Christians who find themselves called to work as professionals in our pluralistic culture. The focus on the formation of future Christian leaders is rightfully set on the development of a deeply rooted spirituality and disposition of integrity."

—Jan Hoek
Professor of Systematic Theology,
Protestant Theological University,
Kampen, the Netherlands;
Evangelical Theological Faculty, Leuven, Belgium

"Educators wanting to prepare students for broad service in every square inch of God's kingdom will appreciate *Practice and Profile*. The four-part model reflects the original purposes of Christian higher education in contrast to today's Western context, where professional service often divides our hands from our hearts and minds. An excellent and example-rich encouragement for moving teaching and advising further toward holistic student development."

—Nick Lantinga
Executive Director of the International Association for the Promotion of Higher Education, Sioux Center, Iowa

"Hegeman, Edgell, and Jochemsen have carried out a much-needed and well-researched examination of higher education. Highly publicized failings in banking, business, healthcare, and other professions raise questions about the ethics training provided students. This book provides a welcome opportunity to reflect deeply on what third level education is all about. The authors provide a vision for higher education that is exciting and invigorating, yet they present it with humility and grace so that it is challenging, not overwhelming. Reading *Practice and Profile* left me excited to revisit my role in teaching ethics and reflect more deeply while rereading their significant book."

—Dónal O'Mathúna
Senior Lecturer at Dublin City University, Glasnevin, Ireland

"Professionals in Christian higher education ought to study this book seriously. It concerns the heart of their work: enabling the formation of (young) Christians for their vocation. Discussion of PISA in institutes for Christian higher education will surely be fruitful for the analysis as well as enrichment of their own training concept."

—Rens Rottier
President of DrieStar Educatief University,
Gouda, the Netherlands

"The PISA model forms a good basis for the analysis of professional performance. It also offers essential elements for the direction of moral formation in learning processes. This work deserves to be studied and to be applied. It certainly will very much benefit the quality of the professional practices and the education leading to performance in practice."

—Jacob Schaap
President of Gereformeerde Hogeschool University of Applied Science, Zwolle, the Netherlands

"Rarely have I read a monograph that so thoroughly and soundly covers the nature and the scope of moral formation in higher education. While reading the book, it becomes apparent that the authors aim for an actual renewal of moral formation, involving educational policy as well as curricula and the basic practice of mentoring. Neither instructor nor trainer, modern or Christian professional, or institute for vocational schooling can do without this study!"

—Jan Lucas van der Wolf
Pastoral counselor and diaconal supervisor, theologian, ethicist, former university student pastor, Amsterdam

Practice and Profile

Practice and Profile

Christian Formation for Vocation

JOHAN HEGEMAN, MARGARET EDGELL,
AND HENK JOCHEMSEN

WIPF & STOCK · Eugene, Oregon

PRACTICE AND PROFILE
Christian Formation for Vocation

Copyright © 2011 Johan Hegeman, Margaret Edgell, and Henk Jochemsen. All rights reserved. Except for brief quotations in critical publications or reviews, no part of this book may be reproduced in any manner without prior written permission from the publisher. Write: Permissions, Wipf and Stock Publishers, 199 W. 8th Ave., Suite 3, Eugene, OR 97401.

Wipf & Stock
An Imprint of Wipf and Stock Publishers
199 W. 8th Ave., Suite 3
Eugene, OR 97401
www.wipfandstock.com

ISBN 13: 978-1-61097-091-4

Manufactured in the U.S.A.

All scripture quotations, unless otherwise indicated, are taken from the New King James Version®. Copyright © 1982 by Thomas Nelson, Inc. Used by permission. All rights reserved.

Contents

List of Figures Tables, and Sidebars xi
Foreword xiii
Preface xv
Acknowledgments xxi
List of Abbreviations xxiii

1 The Quest for a Moral Profile in Vocation 1

2 P: Being Practice Minded 53

3 I: Being Integral 99

4 S: Being Spiritual 153

5 A: Being Answerable 213

6 Putting PISA into Practice 267

Bibliography 281
Name Index 297
Subject Index 303

List of Figures, Tables, and Sidebars

Figures

1. The normative reflective practitioner model 70
2. Experiential learning and Learning Style Inventory 146
3. Core reflection 234

Tables

1. Presence Profile 95
2. Marcia's Four Identity Statuses Related to Exploration and Commitment 244

Sidebars

1. Vignette on the Ethical Formation of Young Business Professionals 13
2. Bildung at Calvin College 24
3. An Example of Professional Profiles 40
4. Competence-Based Learning in Europe 58
5. Indicators for Professional Performance in Labor Situations 60
6. Example of a Reflection on Personal Capability in the Competency Profile of the Church Worker or Pastoral Worker 64
7. The Constitutive Side to Competencies 77
8. Believing Scripture but Playing by Science's Rules 102
9. Double Goods in CBL 110
10. Reflection Tools in the Practice of Professional Education 139

11. Personal Proficiencies in CBL: The Case of a Business School 141
12. The Need for an Integral Balance in Professional Learning 148
13. Application in the Business Discipline: Moral Management Development in the Secular Management Literature 170
14. The Personal Relationship with God 182
15. John's Story: John Finds His Callig 198
16. Mike's Defining Moment 199
17. Susan's Legacy 200
18. Competencies for Nurses Providing Spiritual Care 207
19. Personal Branding: How Can I Best Sell Myself? 226
20. Do We Want Amoral Supervision? 232
21. Core Reflection 234
22. Difficulties in Identifying Moral Issues in Reflection 240

Foreword

Preparing Students for Practice

For the past several decades, scholars involved in Christian higher education have engaged in a lively and at times intricate discussion concerning the relationship between faith and learning. If one surveys the voluminous literature that has emerged from this conversation, it quickly becomes apparent that much of available energy has been applied in particular directions, with comparative weak spots in other areas. Despite the fact that the majority of Christian institutions of higher education have a central emphasis on teaching—and commonly claim to offer a type of education designed to form students spiritually and morally as well as intellectually—the attention paid to how formation actually takes place has been relatively slight compared to the central focus on the relationship between Christian beliefs and various ideas, concepts, and theories in the academic disciplines. We have spent more time debating the contents of the Christian mind than examining how the Christian self is formed during our educational programs. Perhaps for related reasons, it has been easier to find substantial accounts of the nature of Christian learning in disciplines such as philosophy, theology, history, and literary studies than in professional programs, despite the significant role that professional programs play at many Christian colleges and universities. Key questions about how Christian higher education can prepare students for a life of Christian practice remain underexplored.

This book, then, sets out to fill a significant need. Its authors have done educators a considerable service in providing not only a precise and detailed account of how moral and spiritual formation takes place in the context of preprofessional study but also a systematic program that can guide the efforts of those who educate future professionals. While *Practice and Profile* addresses underexplored questions, it does more than provide an initial foray. The book balances careful, informed consideration of necessary theoretical questions with the provision of concrete examples and practical models that both reveal the authors' own experience in this area and suggest concrete ways forward for educators in professional programs. Critical questions surrounding moral formation in higher education are examined—how, for instance, is moral formation compatible with student self-determination and critical thinking?—and relevant ethical theories receive their due. Key related ideas are thoughtfully explored—one of the book's merits, for instance, is that it offers an account of spirituality in education that does not reduce it to a vague cluster of inner feelings and aspirations but grounds it in a more holistic and integral sense of how belief, experience, and practice tie together. And all of this background reflection is brought together in descriptions of specific moral and spiritual profiles that could shape the vocational trajectories of students and deeply enhance their professional service.

If Christian higher education is to live up to its own aspirations regarding the formation of students not just as Christian minds but as Christian practitioners within their various callings, then accounts such as this one are sorely needed. Johan Hegeman, Margaret Edgell, and Henk Jochemsen are to be thanked for the labors represented here; the rest of us are invited to think and act along with them in the interests of making our own professional practice as educators more intentional, integrated, and Christian.

David I. Smith
Director of the Kuyers Institute for Christian Teaching and Learning
Professor of German, Calvin College, Grand Rapids, Michigan
Editor, *Journal of Education and Christian Belief*

Preface

In European societies, more and more people are adopting a strong pluralism with regard to the worldviews of others, and this pluralism challenges all professionals to be able to deal with opposing worldviews, as well as a plurality of faiths. Christian students who want to enter the professional world will face this potent pluralism. One of the strongest challenges facing Christian students is to be spiritually authentic, not only in their school setting, but also in their profession. After graduation, they must maintain their integrity as Christians in an increasingly pluralistic and postmodern working environment. These young professionals will enter a world where they are urged to "sell themselves on sight," meaning they are enticed to choose a profile of a type of person who is all flashy portfolio and slick résumé. What prevents their adopting a profile commonly referred to as the "empty suit" or the "designer personality"? Even in highly professional vocations, young people may feel compelled to engage in impression management in order to survive. How do Christian educators prepare students to face these onslaughts on the integrity of their character, once they are employed as professionals?

In this book, the authors look beyond getting a diploma to the qualities required in the professional practice for which students are preparing. Our reason for doing this is that almost all vocations have a strong tradition—and as we point out later—an ethical basis. Over against the modern emphasis on the individual as an autonomous individual, we place the young professional as an individual within the normative confines of practices. Our basic philosophy is that their command of such norms is crucial for the success of their choice of direction in professional life. We argue that their choice of a profile in a profession must therefore reflect more than just their worldviews. Their choice must also reflect the normative basis of the profession. In short, we urge them to seek a proper spiritual and moral formation in the vocational context.

Where do students entering professional fields gain the required moral formation if not in the place that trains them? Surely, moral formation is not merely something left to the devices of students. We believe that educators must be involved to the point where they have a significant role in coaching young professionals. They must stimulate the student to make a committed choice as a Christian to adopt a calling and aim for a livelihood in a certain professional practice. We advocate instructors becoming engaged with the deep reflection done by students on that choice. In this book, we consider such a choice of a moral profile neither as a random occurrence nor as an event that takes place on only one occasion in the learning career of the individual student. The students' choices are based on the trust each student gives to a Christian college or university to prepare them adequately for their calling in life as a Christian, which goes beyond just getting a diploma. This trust is the most important asset stewarded by educators during these times.

Traditionally, Christian colleges and universities have emphasized understanding a Christian worldview as an important instrument for moral formation. The Christian faith has a trusted message that applies to the whole of life. Teaching and studying Christian worldviews help many faithful students understand how their spirituality plays a role in the workplace. We realize that such knowledge is quite experiential. It must be understood personally in a practical situation. Fortunately, new educational developments create openings for recognizing how personal spirituality and morality play their roles in practice. Because of this, we see strong possibilities for moral formation that goes beyond learning Christian worldviews to reflect on spirituality in practice. This does not replace their worldviews, but it meets the challenges posed by new educational developments that require students to engage in moral formation.

The steep rise of new educational developments, such as competency-based learning, constructivist learning practices, student mentoring and supervision involving extensive reflection, portfolio learning, and digital learning, creates new demands for moral formation. Many institutions of higher learning struggle with these demands because they require new learning environments and new moral competencies.

This leads to the current concern: Are educators (particularly Christian educators) equipped sufficiently to guide the new style of moral formation? Our response is that if there is not a distinct moral formation strategy involved, we are not so sure. The strategy must capitalize on a renewal of what has been traditionally called *Bildung* in the European context. At the same time, it must take into account that curricula were redesigned to meet both a strong emphasis on the workplace and a strong focus on competency learning found in professional studies. This strategy requires a regeneration of existing moral formation strategies in higher education. It means answering questions about the nature of professional practices and the requirements for being integral, spiritual, and accountable in higher education as well as in vocational practices. In particular, the strategy must allow us to provide clear direction for the phenomenal rise of reflection activity in professional studies, where already much effort is undertaken to form students for their entry into the marketplace.

What does all this mean for Christian higher education? How can we help students to bridge the gap between their Christian worldviews and their commitments to be good professional practitioners? In terms of educational practice, the question becomes, which special competencies would Christian students need to perform well as Christian professionals?

In this book, we respond to these challenges by offering a renewed moral formation strategy. We studied explicit knowledge as found in literature and documents of educational institutions. We also studied the empirical phenomenon of moral formation as found at several Christian professional universities in the Netherlands. We also engaged in empirical analyses of various faith formation models in CCCU colleges in the United States. Finally, we studied the tacit knowledge that many practitioners of good practices of moral formation have imparted to us. Our strategy for moral formation approaches the heart of the actual performance of practitioners in moral formation practices in Christian higher education.

Our scope is broad, as it covers many aspects of Christian higher education. Yet, it is also modest, in that our moral formation strategy does not presume to define that practice as such. Our aim is to point out the standards of excellence we have found to be conditional for moral formation and how they are used. At the same time, we have discovered that moral formation lies at the core of all new modern developments of education. In this respect, we hit upon the fundamentals of the nature of higher education, Christian practices in particular.

This book is to our knowledge the first modern attempt at disclosing the explicit and implicit knowledge of moral formation at Christian universities of professional education. At the same time, our own experiences in teaching at research universities at undergraduate, graduate, and professional levels in the Netherlands and North America tell us that the issues of moral formation in general higher education do not significantly differ from moral formation at professional schools as such. Neither the theories and models we have studied, nor our empirical evidence proves us wrong on this. For these reasons, our strategy can be applied in all realms of higher education, including liberal arts education.

Application of our model by Dutch colleagues training practitioners in the field prompts us to see its utility in more than just tertiary schooling. Also, its usefulness in training new faculty members at Christian colleges in the Netherlands has proven its worth. Therefore, we see good application of most elements of this model in actual professional training programs on the job.

This book has as its audience all professionals involved in higher education. Aside from teachers and mentors involved in student formation practices, it also includes managers of institutions, trustees, and professionals involved part-time in service to students. We also consider this book a required read for students in the stage of their schooling career when they have reached the point of needing to choose a distinct moral profile for their career. Finally, we emphasize that politicians, government and para-government officials, education journalists, and special-interest groups in higher education can use this book to come to better appreciate the intricacy of the faith-bound learning system. In a society that presumes the separation of faith from public performance, this book demonstrates that for education and many professions, this belief does not hold. We hope to convince skeptics that the moral formation flowing from our strategy of Christian spirituality is at the core of the legitimacy of Christian higher education—and, moreover, that it therefore needs protection and development.

In many respects, this book demonstrates the great vulnerability of Christian higher education in the pluralistic societies of the twenty-first century. Its environment is one of vast disintegration of shared values and norms in civil society, along with a strong rise of government-induced change. Without a clear and coherent strategy that arises from the very nature of Christian thought and Christian practices of education, irreversible moral fragmentation could come to beset Christian higher education. The deep moral crisis that became evident during the year 2008 in the financial world has already reached the educational realm. We discuss in this book the many instances of alarm at the failure of venerable institutions of higher learning to inculcate the required morality for responsible professional performance in students. Without an explicit effort at moral formation, which is the most valuable asset of Christian higher education, those individual men and women who entrust their professional formation to Christian institutions of higher learning may be failed simply because moral formation is a very complex, difficult task. We hope and pray this will never become our liability.

Acknowledgments

WRITING A BOOK ABOUT the practice of higher education involves practitioners and professionals of all stripes. We are grateful for the distinct privilege of having profited from significant interaction with many highly dedicated persons in the course of researching and writing this book. Their inspirational practices of moral formation, often remarkably good and sometimes even excellent, as well as their openness to discussing weaknesses, contributed to our conviction that a book on this theme would be possible.

The initial research for this book began in the research group (Dutch: *lectoraat*) of the Ethics of Care as instituted by the three Christian universities of applied sciences in the Netherlands: the Christelijke Hogeschool Ede, the Gereformeerde Hogeschool Zwolle, and the Driestar Educatief Christian University for Teacher Education at Gouda. From 2002 to 2006, Henk Jochemsen served as lector and Johan Hegeman as associate lector in this project. Johan then served in the Research Group on Education and Identity of the Driestar Educatief. We recognize the support of our colleagues from Gouda: Bram de Muynck, Issac Kole, and Evert Roeleveld; from Zwolle: Jan Hoogland, Roel Kuiper, and Pieter Vos; and from Ede: Hans Borst, Bart Cusveller, Gert Hunink, Wim van Ieperen, Nicolien de Jong, Tirza van Laar, Rene van Leeuwen, Anne Pals, Anke Penning, and Jan Carel Vierbergen. We thank the president of Christelijke Hogeschool Ede, Kees Boele, for his support over the years.

Margaret Edgell thanks the Business Department of Calvin College for time to crunch her data. Shirley Roels, director of the Lilly Vocation Project at Calvin College, provided unstinting inspiration, as well as funding, for her research on student faith formation. And she gives special thanks to the many students who participated in her research.

This book is unique in being a collaboration between practitioners working in Christian higher education in the Netherlands and in the United States. Through the International Association for the Promotion of Christian Higher Education (IAPCHE) the authors became acquainted with each other's work, which led eventually to partnership on this manuscript. Although the bulk of the research originated in the Netherlands, Margaret's research proved amenable to the basic model of moral formation. We are quite pleased our respective work fits together so well.

Nick Lantinga, director of IAPCHE, and Joel Carpenter of Calvin College introduced our work to David I. Smith, director of the Kuyers Institute of Calvin College. We are grateful for the support of the Kuyers Institute for Christian Teaching and Learning for making the publication of this book possible. We thank David for kindly and thoroughly commenting on an earlier version of this manuscript and stimulating the further development of the book.

The Board of the Stichting Steunfonds of the Christelijke Hogeschool Ede we gratefully thank for their financial support in the last stages of publishing this book.

The committed involvement of the Wipf and Stock editors, copy editors, marketing personnel, designers, managers, secretaries, and many others involved in making this book a reality is highly appreciated—a fine Christian practice!

List of Abbreviations

BaLaMa	Bachelor Labor Market
CBL	competence-based learning
CCCU	Council of Christian Colleges and Universities
CHE	Christelijke Hogeschool Ede
CoP	communities of practice
IAPCHE	International Association for the Promotion of Christian Higher Education
LSI	Learning Style Inventory
NKJV	New King James Version
NRP	normative reflective practitioner
NRPM	normative reflective practitioner model
PISA	practice minded, integral, spiritual, answerable
SCM	student career mentoring

1

The Quest for a Moral Profile in Vocation

1. THE QUEST

WHAT DOES A CHRISTIAN student need to do to become moral in a vocation? After writing this book, we would answer: follow your dream; reflect deeply; be virtuous.

That, more or less, is the short answer to the incredibly complicated and confusing question of what students should do in order to be morally formed. The long answer is even more than what this book can contain. It is living to the glory of God in the comfort of faith. In between, there are many quests that educators, together with students, embark on to arrive at these answers. In this book, we deal with one venture, which we call a quest for a moral profile. The quest for a moral profile leads to further choices for virtues, dreams, and personal reflection on a life *coram Deo* (before the face of God) in professional studies.

What are the typical requirements of the Christian quest to become moral? What is so special about this spiritual quest? We assume that, as Christians, we want to serve God by following our *calling* in life (traditionally speaking). For students, this calling may at first consist of no more than their choosing a college and a course of study. Eventually, through trial and error, and hopefully through career mentoring, they may come to choose an occupation. Typically, when starting a career, they must have a *vocation*, or a strong belief in their suitability to work in a particular career or occupation. This belief in their efficacy must become part of their dream to be "someone" in life. How do they gain this belief? There are many paths, the learning of worldviews being the most trusted and traditional one, often accompanied by training in spirituality and ethics. In this book, we assume that colleges already lead students on these paths. We go on to point to a specific quest that we call moral formation with the use of deep reflection.

To begin our discussion of moral formation, we define terms. *Moral formation* is the process of gaining the morality required by one's spirituality and ethics. In this book, we treat as development that which activates ethical knowledge, skills, and attitudes to become moral in practice, based on personal spirituality. Such development may involve explicit cultural and social formation. We assume that this development takes place in education, as we explain in detail in this chapter.

We define *deep reflection* as reflection or contemplation on the core of one's identity, core beliefs, spirituality, and narratives. This mode of reflection goes beyond simply learning worldviews in class and applying them in student mentoring. It assumes the adoption of worldviews and spirituality to focus on just how one applies these in certain practices, most importantly in professional vocations.

Deep reflection is a learning strategy for moral formation. Moral formation and deep reflection complement each other quite well. Moral formation tells students why and what they are to become and do. Deep reflection forms a learning strategy for achieving that purpose by actually manifesting their moral profile in the new practice they hope to enter. Deep reflection builds on existing moral formation to increase awareness of the image of themselves in a profession. We term this image a *vocational profile*.

What do we mean by a profile? The *New Oxford Dictionary* tells us it is "an outline of something, especially a person's face, as seen from the side." A profile is how we appear in a certain way—we could say, how we wish to be seen from one side—in this case, our moral side. We can speak similarly of having a professional profile, or a spiritual profile, or a psychological profile, and so forth.

We are interested how we choose a profile, because a moral profile is needed in the professions, especially in competence-based learning. Professional vocational training requires having a certain successful appearance or profile before entering a licensed practice, such as medicine. More often, students are asked whether their identity fits a certain competency profile, or a certain vocational profile, or a given practice profile. They are put under pressure to shape themselves to a certain professional mold. That shape is their profile. Will any profile do? No, professional practices require of their practitioners quite specific knowledge of norms, values, and virtues for performing well. Professional training requires knowledge of one's self and what it is like for that self to perform according to standards of excellence. Performing as a good practitioner entails knowing whether the virtues belonging to the proficiencies of being professional in that practice fit one's view of self. That is, there must be a match between what professional practice requires in terms of a profile and one's own image of doing so. In order to integrate their moral profile in competence-based learning, students must first become aware of what being moral is in practice.

To develop a professional moral profile, deep reflection on personal spirituality is needed. This is a matter of personal identity and thereby of spirituality. Without guided deep reflection on how personal spirituality functions in the achievement of the right identity for professional practice, many a career dream may be sadly lost because of students' mediocre attempts at being good practitioners—their work will be good, but not good enough to keep the job, or even worse, not good at all.

To develop moral profiles, students rely on educators. Here we define educators broadly beyond higher education to include practitioners in the professions: supervisors, mentors, coaches, and trainers. We reason thusly: do students rely only on teachers for gaining a moral profile? No. Hence, we broaden the category of educators to include coaches, mentors, professional supervisors, and others in private practices involved in training and guiding learners seeking spiritual and moral formation. In this book, we explain from the context of higher education what moral formation is, but we do so realizing that this model can be applied beyond the strict borders of academia.

To meet this need, a revitalization of mentoring for moral formation is necessary. We therefore believe that all educators must become involved in the way students arrive at their beliefs about their suitability to a particular career and at their understanding of its required virtues. At the same time, current expectations demand that students be the sole agents of their own moral development. We are far from optimistic that students make a proper choice of a moral profile by themselves before entering a profession. Although the involvement of schools of higher education in moral formation is historically and sociologically warranted, modern social liberal views deny this. At any rate, given current evidence of many failures in moral formation, the need to reinvigorate moral formation is serious.

The quest for a moral profile must be infused across the curriculum. The great challenge of moral formation requires mentoring to the extent that deep reflection must not be limited to supervision during internships. Nor is a widespread use of reflection tools enough. Moral formation must be an integral part of the whole curriculum in higher education. Long past are the days that we believed that a solid ethics course, or simply an improvement on already excellent worldview training, could do the trick. We contend that all educators in all courses have a responsibility to aid students in deep learning. This is of necessity a broad view of the role of moral formation in professional training. This book is essentially a study of the conditions for moral formation in a curriculum involving the responsibility of educators as well as students. Such a curriculum has at its core the students' personal quests for a moral profile in their desired profession.

The quest must be a shared responsibility. In this first chapter, we introduce the reasons for this shared responsibility to engage in moral formation with deep reflection. We also introduce the main conditions for the ethics of shared responsibility. Our central argument is this: educators need to rediscover moral formation and adopt it as their moral responsibility to students. Students for their part need to engage in moral formation and to be initiated in deep reflection leading to moral proficiencies.

The quest is fulfilled by students who meet five major conditions. These five major conditions hold moral formation with deep reflection as premises for our argument in this book:

- Students wanting to become professionals must choose their moral profile within their professional practice. That choice is guided by educators in a strategy followed by both student and educator (see below in chapter 1).

- The professional practice requires knowledge of the basic values, norms, and virtues that form an identity in that profession (see chapter 2).

- Students need to discover what it is to be integral in "head, heart, and hands" before entering the professional practice (see chapter 3).

- When they choose a moral profile, students need to call on their personal spirituality and accept coaching on this (see chapter 4).

- Students must be able to account for their choices through deep reflection (see chapter 5).

These conditions are reintroduced and described at the end of this chapter as part of a strategy of moral formation.

Now we discuss the shared responsibility between educators and students. In the remainder of this chapter, we deal with the basic contours of the role of educators and thereby the roles of institutions of higher learning in relation to the role of students in their moral development.

1.1. Moral Formation, Worldviews, and Deep Reflection

Moral formation using deep reflection does not replace other forms of development. There are many ways to discover which *direction* one must take in life. In this book, we assume worldview learning and moral formation are excellent ways to find direction. This includes learning which beliefs, values, and norms drawn from one's worldview should come into play in order to practice "the right way." Below, we explain why this is the case in education. We go on to examine how the educational tool of deep reflection improves on this learning. We can explain this best by reviewing how most educators do this.

1.1.1. Worldviews

We explain in chapter 2 that beliefs regulate actual performance in practice. An example of this would be that a teacher at a medical school chooses a regulative belief when dealing with the issue of integrity in a professional practice, say regarding medical malpractice. Traditionally, dealing with this issue has been understood in an ethical sense. At times, worldviews were called upon to guide ethical choices. Dilemma analysis has also been applied in training students to make rational choices. But what next? What happens in actual practice after the ethical choice is made? In our approach to moral formation, we do not stop by urging students to be confident about their choice. We go farther, to try to understand what actually happens at the performance level within a real practice field such as nursing, church work, or business.

Not just any belief counts as professional competence. What counts is having the beliefs proper to the profession. For Christians, how we see ourselves as Christians flows together with our beliefs that determine our performance. For example, Christian nurses may choose to decline becoming involved in certain practices that violate their conscience. Thanks to their faith and moral formation, their beliefs provide direction, but the manner in which they put these into practice count very heavily. It has everything to do who they are and how they image themselves as performing properly. Their image of themselves as nurses and their beliefs must be congruent. We believe that they learn to be competent nurses by what we call deep reflection.

Beliefs regulate how we perform in practice. Because we are interested in how practitioners apply their beliefs in practice, we focus on the regulative beliefs that guide practitioners when performing in that practice. We expect practitioners to be able to reflect on their performance in terms of their beliefs. For teachers and students engaged in nursing education, the teacher must explain how his or her beliefs regarding malpractice figure in the ethics of that practice and in its performance. The teacher's beliefs regulate the teacher's nursing practice. To learn how to do this judiciously and wisely requires a competent understanding of moral formation. Professionals who bring elements of their worldview to the work floor in appropriate ways display such competence. In such a case, we would say that the sharing of a worldview-related belief functioned successfully.

Here we hark back to a basic understanding of how the choices and beliefs of people function as *control beliefs*, as found in the worldview approach to learning.[1] Control beliefs are evident when a practitioner becomes reflective. We consider discerning direction to be a product of reflection. Discerning direction depends on exercising personal spirituality. For Christians, direction refers to the manner and extent to which a person deviates from normativity—understood as God's creational law—and renewed conformity to it in Christ.[2] By attempting to conform to norms, we come close to the metaphor of traveling the road of faith, or walking it in practice. At the same time, the concept of direction as applied to Christian life implies being aware that one's basic commitments in the walk of life relate to the context of the culture and its influence on one's discernment during that walk.[3] Related is the call for "direction discernment" by seeking shalom, or public justice,[4] a basic approach to moral formation followed at many colleges that entails a strong program of formation.

---

1. Wolterstorff, *Educating for Responsible Action*; Wolterstorff, *Reason within the Bounds*.
2. Wolters, *Creation Regained*, 73.
3. Griffioen, *Moed tot Cultuur*.
4. Wolterstorff, *Educating for Life*; Wolterstorff, *Educating for Shalom*.

Discernment also depends on our social imaginaries, or what we share with others regarding what makes our world intelligible and meaningful. In a recent, well-publicized work, James K. A. Smith puts forward a remarkable argument to step away from the worldview approach and prioritize the "social imaginary" approach for Christian higher education.[5] A social imaginary is the way we collectively imagine, even pre-theoretically, our social life in the contemporary Western world, Charles Taylor tells us.[6] The basic idea is that the required understandings needed by Christians to perform as Christians are not so much the application of doctrines, ideas, and formulas, but the social imaginary, that is, "an affective, non-cognitive understanding of the world" shared with others.[7]

We appreciate James Smith's work as it addresses the place of emotions/affect/heart as motivator for moral development; his concept comes close to the communal piety we practice as Christians. It also complements the development triad often described as head, heart, and hands in Christian literature (a concept that we treat extensively in chapter 3 of this book). Smith proposes to develop the "heart" through explicit liturgies in all of life experience. Such liturgies reflect the power of social imaginaries. Liturgies are an experiential way of understanding one's faith practice that one shares with others, as Taylor puts forward.[8] We agree with Smith that this aspect of spirituality needs our attention. (In chapter 4, we go into this matter in more depth.)

Yet, regarding ecclesial and nonecclesial liturgies, we are not convinced of the potential strength of connections between liturgy and professional practice. Yes, fasting together while serving in a food bank is a powerful experience, but how is this applied in accounting? We found that applying biblical principles in personal finance by setting up a personal budget that glorifies God to be a powerful hands-on experience (or liturgy) that enhances the understanding of stewardship, and that the lessons from personal finance can be applied to stewardship in economics and business courses. But such a social imaginary is not yet good business. It is a spiritual understanding that one may share with others or not. Only with a very keen understanding of the relationship between one's spiritual understanding and professional performance can such a

5. J. Smith, *Desiring the Kingdom*, 63–72.
6. Taylor, *Secular Age*, 146.
7. J. Smith, *Desiring the Kingdom*, 68.
8. Taylor, *Secular Age*.

consciousness be applied in business. There is a distinct gap between experiencing a social imaginary and actual performance. Much more is required than just having a desired liturgical experience. We return to this issue in chapter 4 when dealing with spirituality, and in chapter 5 when dealing with mentoring.

In higher education, we need worldviews as well as social imaginaries. It is doubtful whether James Smith's attempt to prioritize social imaginary over worldview in higher education is correct. Taylor, the source for Smith, distinguishes between two central elements of Western modernity, which he calls "the modern moral order" and "the social imaginary."[9] The moral order is an explicit set of ideas about how we should act, and about why the social world is arranged the way it is. Worldviews reveal the moral order and critique them—these are the functions of worldviews. The social imaginary, on the other hand, is a more elusive set of self-understandings, background practices, and horizons of common expectations that are not always explicitly articulated but that give a people a sense of a shared group life.

We have no reason to believe that Taylor requires us to choose one above the other in higher education. It is clear to us that cognitive ideas and beliefs as found in the moral order need a complement in the social imaginary. In order to make sense of our experiences in a particular practice, we need "some notion of a moral or metaphysical order."[10] For this reason, we cannot do without worldviews, or for that matter, doctrines, theories, and other types of formalized knowledge.

We argue that setting a contrast between metaethics and morality, or between church doctrine and actual faith, or between worldviews and social imaginaries is invalid for higher education for the reason that we ought to use both. We do agree that for control beliefs to have legitimacy, it certainly does not suffice if these are based exclusively on formalized knowledge. Such a serious limitation would constitute a faulty educational practice. Moral formation is very much an experiential matter—on this Smith is correct, but we believe that gaining direction is also very dependent on knowing the proper worldviews. As educators, we know all too well that a stringent catechism of certain beliefs may be one of the most effective ways of learning how to use worldviews well. On the other hand, knowing the catechism by rote does not guarantee a life of faith.

9. Ibid., 157–71.
10. Ibid., 172.

We agree with Charles Taylor and James Smith that social imaginaries are a key part of discerning direction in moral formation. Yet, discerning direction must be learned and continually relearned in the interplay or dialectic between the explicit belief structures and the imaginaries people have. This interplay is demonstrated in social practices, as we discuss at length in chapter 2.

We therefore assume that the practitioner knows how to take into account other values and norms in the broader social and political moral order of that practice. The reflective practitioner must be able to transcend his or her own social imaginary in order to grasp the ruling moral order. An example is how family physicians in Europe takes into account how the particular laws and political ethos surrounding abortion on demand function in that society when they determine their spiritual direction on that issue. But they do so not without cognizance of how their faith community and Christian peers regard the issue of abortion on demand, and, in particular, cognizance of how their own spirituality regulates their stance, or their social imaginary. Being reflective on pertaining norms means knowing how to position oneself as a practitioner within the bounds of worldview and spirituality. We call a person involved in practice who is aware of this normativity the "normative reflective practitioner" (as copiously explained in chapter 2). We therefore are quite interested in exactly how the reflective practitioner actually reflects and thereby performs well.

1.1.2. Deep Reflection

The call to apply social imaginaries is for us a clear support for reflection practices in higher education and most particularly the practice that we call deep reflection. Reflection is the interpretation or reinterpretation of experience, knowledge, and beliefs. Reflection tools allow participants to think actively and consciously about their experiences, actions, behaviors, choices, and views. Most curricula of professional schools in the Netherlands (and increasingly its academic universities) use reflection tools to help students reflect on themselves, on their method, and on society.[11] The daily practice of students during field trips or internships is the usual focal point for reflection. Students focus on their own behaviors, attitudes, emotions, and convictions. Training in reflection can be done on several levels. It is most preferably done in practice, the customary, habitual, or expected procedure for doing something.

11. Benammar, *Reflectietools*.

Reflection plays a major role in discerning direction. Reflection is a broad category of experiential learning that allows for what Patricia Benner, Molly Sutphen, Victoria Leonard, and Lisa Day, in their landmark study on professional education, qualify as "moral imagination."[12] According to them, moral imagination is a type of social imagination, as discussed above. Benner et al. call for a renewal of professional nursing education through the development of a critical moral stance. "Through engagement with clinical problems and particular patients and patient populations, students broaden their moral imagination, just as they broaden it by literature, nursing knowledge, bioethics and ethics of care and responsibility."[13] What Benner et al. refer to as "ethical comportment"[14] is best done by stimulating professional students to reflect about their performances in light of the complexity and harshness of the real world. This means involving all types and levels of reflection.

One could say that in the first level of reflection the pertinent question is, do I do *it*—the performance in professional practice—properly? *Properly* is meant in the sense of meeting required proficiencies, understood as rules that govern behavior. This we call stage one reflection. Reflection must move on to a second stage by dealing with the question, do I engage the proper *values* with which to perform properly? Answers for this are sought in the context of the professional practice and what does or does not belong to the required competence of the professional involved. We formulate these two questions by making use of a common understanding of the double loops of reflection as popularized by Chris Argyris, Robert Putnam, and Diana McClain Smith in 1985, and later by Chris Argyris and Donald Schön in 1996.[15]

Deep reflection assumes that we follow both loops of reflection. Deep reflection as a learning tool goes one step further to enquire whether one reflects properly. In this added step, one reflects on one's reflection, thereby examining how one uses worldviews, imaginaries, and morality in relation with one's self-image. This is a reflection on

---

12. Benner et al., *Educating Nurses*, 165–67.

13. Ibid., 167.

14. Ibid., 28–29, 167.

15. We are referring here to the basic distinction in learning developed by Chris Argyris and Donald Schön *Organizational Learning II* as introduced in Chris Argyris, Robert Putnam, and Diana McClain Smith, *Action Science*, 80–102, as single- and double-loop learning. Many applications exist; a good Dutch example is Baets and van der Linden, *Hybrid Business School*. In chapter 3, section 5, we further discuss this model.

one's frame of reference. As a manner of reflection or contemplation on the core of one's being, one's core beliefs, spirituality, and worldviews, it requires knowledge of what is right but now in the sense of being morally right. Deep reflection is a type of meta-reflection on the appropriateness of how one reflects. It deals with the questions of how students see their own reflections and how they involve their worldviews, their spirituality, and the moral demands of a profession in the ways they reflect. They must reflect on who they are as moral persons and how they regard themselves as performing in a certain profession. Deep reflection reaches a level of understanding that requires students to know and choose their vocation or calling. In line with our explanation above, the question for deep reflection becomes, *why* and with *what profile* of myself do I perform properly?

Deep reflection is intentional learning that requires knowledge of one's deepest motivations. These motivations may (consciously or not) influence behavior as well as reflection on behavior. In other words, deep reflection is on the beliefs and motivations that bring professionals to act as professionals in a certain practice. Deep reflection confirms that behavior is truly professional and offers an explanation for why it is deemed professional. It requires students to account for and justify their moral choices. In this sense, it is more than finding grounds for believing that one is a good professional because certain beliefs warrant one's action. It goes to a level deeper, to determine how one's spirituality or religion influences one's sense of vocation, in a personal sense. In deep reflection, we are interested in knowing how spirituality functions for a person in his or her respective practice and what this motivation means. Deep reflection challenges one to exhibit the deepest religious sources from which one wants to live and behave. We call listening to each other on this level *deep listening*.[16]

Deep reflection is normative because it requires us to analyze our performance level against the moral competencies that hold for our chosen profession. As an overt type of normative thinking, deep reflection builds on worldview education as well as ethics education. It comes close to what James Smith sees as social imaginaries in education[17] because it takes in the experiential side of coming to understand reality. We point out below that deep reflection is a type of learning found in cur-

16. Jochemsen, *Opdat het Gras Weer Bloeie*.
17. J. Smith, *Desiring the Kingdom*.

rent practices of education coming from strong historical roots. In the course of this book, we explain how deep reflection can be placed within the bounds of moral formation as currently practiced in serious educational enterprises. In our final chapter, we conclude that deep reflection requires moral competencies.

A discussion of deep reflection implies that there are surface approaches we want to avoid. Distinguishing between deep and surface approaches is not all that easy in practice, but it serves as a powerful impulse to examine the qualities of regular reflection and learning. To be sure, deep reflection is not juxtaposed against broad learning. Deep reflection often involves a wide and critical analysis of new ideas, by linking them to known concepts, principles, and practices. Deep reflection remains deep in the sense that it centers in the personal performance of the professional. Thus, we reasonably expect deep reflection to lead to better understanding of professions, better long-term retention of normative concepts, and better awareness of how students profile themselves in practice. We do not expect such results from surface learning or reflection. Surface reflection may fit the current cultural behavior of multitasking quite readily, but it does not produce the highest quality of professional performance.

1.2. Making a Choice of a Moral Profile

Using deep reflection in moral formation, we come to know who we are and what we want to be in a profession. Our thesis is that we make a choice as to who we want to be as a person in that profession before choosing a professional profile. We call this first choice the choice to have a moral profile because we choose based on our understanding of who we are as a moral person and of what our desired professional practice requires of us in terms of professional ethics. Our career is thus limited by our sense of our moral capabilities. For example, students shy away from medical school if they feel that they lack the confidence to conduct medical ethics every day. In this way, our choice of a moral profile is couched in how we see ourselves as moral persons. We are saying here that any student seriously intending to be a good professional aims to be a moral person in that profession, and the latter constitutes choosing a moral profile.

A more serious example is a nursing student who does not believe that her moral profile allows her to take an internship at a medical institution that requires her to assist with abortions on demand. This realization about her moral profile may cause her to doubt whether she should pursue a vocation as a nurse. A positive example would be a social work student involved in church outreach who discovers that his success with immigrant youth generates so much positive notice by peers that he makes a committed choice to become a religious worker in a large city. In these examples, the moral profile chosen is the most important part of the reflection that the students engage in when making their choice of vocation. Through this decision, they become aware of their involvement in a quest to find out if they fit the professional grade.

Negative examples, where the choice of moral profiles goes wrong, are familiar. The urgent need for proper direction is illustrated by the case below, on the morality of starting professionals in Dutch businesses, as reported by the KPMG—the leading audit, tax, and advisory service company in the Netherlands and Europe (see sidebar 1).

SIDEBAR 1. VIGNETTE ON THE ETHICAL FORMATION OF YOUNG BUSINESS PROFESSIONALS

Businesses in the Netherlands find the moral formation of students at universities seriously wanting. Research by KPMG in 2009 shows that many companies find that "young high potentials" have too little concern for values and norms. They are driven too much by profiles involving having fast-changing careers, high income, and status. In particular, many young starters lack basic virtues such as adequate levels of accountability and respect. Stark differences between age groups and genders are notable in the KPMP study. Almost 40 percent of the companies studied indicate that young managers are less strict concerning ethical issues than their older colleagues. Female managers are stricter in ethical matters than their male counterparts. Forty-two percent of the companies researched indicate having terminated the employment of "high potentials" because of a lack of proper values and norms. KPMG concludes that a clear discrepancy exists between the degree to which graduates perceive the desired ethics and the morality needed in businesses. KPMG challenges universities to improve on the education of ethics in their curricula. Their support extends to providing learning materials.[18]

18. Wallage, *Achtergrond*.

The KPMG study makes clear that achieving high proficiencies (as well as possessing ample male hormones) do not guarantee that young starters will choose or maintain high moral profiles, even in elite positions of society. This trend is not caused by mere cynicism—many students believe that strategic abilities and blatant assertiveness are the most desired profiles for excellent performance. Although many starting professionals may choose better profiles, we must interpret the results in sidebar 1 as a serious signal that seeking, finding, and maintaining a student's direction—in particular for male, high-potential starters—is a serious challenge for educators. This diagnosis is buttressed by a growing base of research indicating that moral formation for excellent performance in practices is not a task at which most universities and professional schools excel.[19]

The above illustrations fit a pattern of poor moral training found in higher education. We explain throughout this book that moral training is not a matter to be considered lightly; it is guided by students' views of the ethics to be expected in a certain professional practice, their ability to integrate this in their learning, their spirituality, and their way of accounting for the process. Moral training is a very fundamental, deep, and meaningful type of learning. Indeed, if the choice of a moral profile is the most important part of preparing for a professional vocation, then educators must understand their role as coaches supporting students' deep reflection.

1.3. The Pedagogical Paradox

We reaffirm that the pedagogical paradox continues to be relevant because it explains the measure of difficulty educators face. We hope that this discussion also revitalizes the sense of real need that educators address.

It is reasonable for an educator to respond to our claims thus far with: "Now wait a minute! Is not the moral formation of my students far too personal for me to get involved in? Is it not their own spiritual quest? After all, I am not their pastor!" This rejoinder states a longstanding issue in higher education: isn't it up to the students if and how they make the right choice of a moral profile in their quest? Such objections reflect Western ideas of autonomy and the call for moral self-education. This case is strengthened if the student is an adult, the educator works part-time or through digital learning, or they do not meet students face-

---

19. See for a thorough analysis Bok, *Underachieving Colleges*.

to-face. Should educators be bothered? Because we know this refutation is not without merit, let us go on to examine how controversial the role of a moral coach is in these modern times.

We open by agreeing with the educational philosopher Steven Garber that true educators want the best moral formation for their students.[20] This statement hits the core of the pedagogical paradox, *Führen oder Wachsen lassen* (lead or let grow). On the one hand, it is inherent to formation that learners are initiated into a given tradition and culture, with corresponding spiritual and moral values. On the other hand, the goal of formation is to realize the independence or "self-responsible self-determination" of the formed person, so that the pedagogue may become dispensable.[21] Aware of this paradox, the true pedagogue explores how much leadership to exert while still allowing students to make a self-governing choice of their moral profile. It is precisely this delicate balance that often makes Christian educators uneasy.

Their concern arises from the reality that educators in professional schools cannot avoid the pedagogical paradox. They are required to exercise influence. At the same time, modern society demands autonomy. In addition, educators involved in preparing students for the professions *cannot but* inculcate in their students whatever is required for them to achieve the required proficiencies. Competence-based learning demands such an ethos of educators. Their goal is more than just finding employment. They expect their students to persevere in their jobs after their apprenticeships in their new occupations have ended. We measure the success of a vocational choice when, after the required initiation, graduated apprentices are considered right for their jobs by their employers years after graduation. We observe that this success can be achieved by educators working within the pedagogical paradox who provide substantive leadership.

Leadership requires active involvement in the life the student. In this book, we will discuss such involvement in our discussion of deep reflection. Although deep reflection is performed by the student, educators share responsibility for its successful enactment. Educational institutions already address the challenges of the pedagogical paradox by organizing types of reflection and supervision. We postpone the description of that

20. Garber, *Fabric of Faithfulness*.
21. Vos, *Tussen Vage Waarden*. We thank Pieter Vos for bringing this to our attention.

enterprise for now, in order to hark back to very basic notions of the desired outcome of professional reflection—gaining a proper identity for a profession. We provide a modern example of this approach, which stresses the ethics of choosing a moral profile.

1.4. Professions Require an Ethics of Vocation

In this book, we investigate and appraise the ethics of moral formation needed in higher education with a view to devise an ethics of vocation. We certainly are not the only educators doing so. Throughout this book, we point out many lodes of knowledge mined by educational philosophy, moral philosophy, social science, and the practice of higher education. We acknowledge that we stand on the shoulders of many pioneers in moral formation and deep reflection.

We acknowledge in particular a sophisticated approach in the tradition of moral philosophy, which emphasizes the roles of narratives and virtue theory in moral formation. These approaches have influenced professional studies, such that modern educators in professional studies recognize the power of narratives, images, and metaphors in professional training. It takes little imagination to realize how useful such approaches can be in reflection practices, if done well.

Central to our approach is that the student, as an aspiring professional, makes a committed choice to be someone in that profession. We term this choosing a moral profile. In many respects, this choice concerns the notion of *vocation*, the strong feeling of suitability for a profession. We agree with Timothy Wineberg that the matter of vocation is one of deep reflection on one's identity: "Vocation is not only a call to public service, its deeper significance is its personal dimension—especially the sense of personal creativity, venturing, and fulfillment, which engage one's emotional, intellectual and moral life and shape one's agency and identity."[22] Arriving at an understanding of one's personal worldview is also essential to finding a moral profile. Thus, the ethical requirements for choosing a moral profile are a knowledge of worldviews and a sense of vocation.

Timothy Wineberg reminds us that profession and vocation are not the same. He emphasizes that adopting a vocation requires a sense of identity and fulfillment. This "sense of vocation" Wineberg describes

---

22. Wineberg, *Professional Care*, 3.

as "the strength of one's character and one's capabilities, as well as one's self-knowledge."[23] This idea of assessing strength accords well with modern reflection practices drawing from moral psychology (we treat this aspect in chapter 5). Our analysis thus far acknowledges that choosing a moral profile requires an understanding of the notion of vocation as well as engaging in the rigors of self-understanding. But more than self-understanding is implied. Our analysis includes the exercise of a studied reflection.

From Wineberg we learn that studied reflection on images, metaphors, narratives, and worldviews not only shapes our character and self-understanding as professionals, but it also requires an ethic of professions. This Wineberg calls "an ethic of professional care." Cultivating an ethic of professional care requires contemplation, since the quality of professional care (read: exercise of vocation) is "inescapably related to what we are as persons—our character."[24] Wineberg unambiguously requires excellence of moral development in the professional, thereby implying an ethic of responsibility to do so, which is a further moral requirement.

We question whether a focus primarily on ethics is sufficient. If command of such a morality only calls for reflection without cognizance of the deepest levels of oneself (what we call spirituality), then a shallow grasp of vocation and moral profiles may be the result. We need to examine how the mission of faith integration plays out in the area of student faith formation, particularly in the processes by which faith enters practice.[25] Regrettably, Wineberg does not expand on this.

Nonetheless, Wineberg sets certain standards for an ethics of professional development imperative to moral formation in modern professional education. We summarize his conditions as follow:

- Students entering practices need an image, a metaphor, or a profile to guide them in professional life.
- Students need to recognize the ethics belonging to the profile they choose, as well as the moral costs involved. They must be able to reflect on them.

---

23. Ibid., 4.
24. Ibid., 5.
25. Edgell, "Preparing Business Students."

- No serious moral profile can develop without a sense of vocation in the profession.
- No serious moral development can develop without an ethic that supports such development.

In the following, we will engage in further examination of such an ethics of moral development as relevant for modern professionals. Our expectation is that Christian higher education could be effective in cultivating such moral development in students. We do well to ask whether this expectation is warranted, not only in terms of desirability, but also in terms of feasibility.

In the remainder of this first chapter, two questions relating to the ethics of moral formation by educators will be probed: (1) what is moral formation in the context of higher education? (section 2), and (2) what are the challenges to moral formation in higher education? (section 3). Answering these questions will point out that moral formation must meet a range of demands drawing upon historical as well as modern developments. After dealing with these matters, we will spell out our strategy for moral formation.

2. WHAT IS MORAL FORMATION IN HIGHER EDUCATION?

2.1. The Tradition of Bildung

Our response to the first question (what is moral formation in higher education?) relies on a latent yet practicable historical custom in education called *Bildung*. Bildung is the German term for the phenomenon of a general humanistic cultural and moral formation of adolescents and young adults, which has been undertaken in Western European education since the Middle Ages.

Bildung is a concept with a rich history in German intellectual tradition, which the philosopher Hans-Georg Gadamer reviews in the opening chapters of his major work, *Truth and Method*.[26] Gadamer traces the development of the concept of Bildung through the work of Herder, Von Humboldt, Hegel, and others.[27] Gadamer highlights the point that Bildung is a verbal noun that refers to practices of formation within a culture. From

---

26. Gadamer, *Truth and Method*, 9. Gadamer defines Bildung as "the properly human way of developing one's natural talents and capacities."

27. Ibid., 8–16.

its very old roots, it still influences current practices of human learning, which become increasingly refined, nuanced, and self-sustaining.[28]

2.2. Modern Forms of Bildung

Currently, Bildung stands for a kneading, shaving, and shaping of young people in a general cultural and moral manner for their participation in modern Western society. Bildung today is mainly demonstrated in how modern humanistic moral formation finds its practical conclusion in the educational practices of young people. The image here is of a student entering the university as an active subject, able to be a creative self. This view of the student fits the concept of the autonomous yet culturally developed individual as originally conceived in the Renaissance and further developed by the German thinker Von Humboldt.[29] The practice of Bildung is still quite recognizable in the pedagogical strategies employed by modern educators to ensure that their students are well-formed as citizens.[30] Much of current use of the term Bildung, however, refers to nothing more than learning certain vocational skills.

Most prevalent among the Bildung strategies for moral formation are those strategies teaching virtues via narratives, including using the Socratic method. This approach focuses more on cognitive elements of solving dilemmas and less on developing emotional intelligences regarding problem solving. At many Dutch universities, the dilemma-solving strategy that flows from this approach is fashionable for teaching rudimentary moral problem solving, but this technique is unsuitable for serious character building.

A second strategy is that of mentoring, whereby relationships develop between teachers and students that nurture the development of the students. This can take the form of vocational mentoring as well as character mentoring. Developing such relationships are highly valued in professional programs (such as business schools) but are difficult to organize and to monitor. For this strategy to be more effective, attention must be focused on professional ways of mentoring that follow well-devised moral reference points.

---

28. Gadamer, "Education Is Self-Education," 537.
29. Lechner, *Bildung Macht Frei*, 104.
30. Hill and Stewart, "Character Education."

A third pedagogical strategy is that of collaborative learning, particularly in small groups. This approach is part of the didactics of learning competencies in vocational training emphasizing "new learning." New learning calls for the possession of specific agogical skills,[31] such as leadership, trust building, communication, and conflict management. Drawbacks are often found in the necessarily group-bound assessment, where collective development of character is difficult to determine.

A fourth strategy not found often in European schools is that of service learning, whereby (often young) students are led into confrontational situations, resulting in positive effects to their personal values and commitments. Success of service learning depends on how far this type of Bildung is integrated in the curriculum.

The fifth strategy is a combination of professional supervision, "intervision" (cooperative reviews among colleagues), and methodical reflection. These form the pedagogical strategy most used in the Netherlands. The focus is on psychological and sociocultural aspects that come to the foreground in confrontational experiences arising during student internships. These strategies require high reflection skills. They are often combined with collaborative learning strategies.

Each of these modern efforts at Bildung attempts to give students a sense of coherence, purpose, meaning, and interconnectedness in their studies. Bildung also develops their sense of citizenship, so that they can perform effectively as members of society.

Bildung is deeply ingrained in European institutions of higher education. We recognize Bildung as a historically developed, institutionalized social practice involving the formation of students according to mainly neoliberal models of humanity. Despite the utilitarian practice of Bildung in the Netherlands (often reduced to making sure young adults are useful in society), it is still fair to say that Bildung refers to a practice that calls for a general moral profile for all those involved in formation and education. This profile is the personal responsibility to achieve a cultured self-education that fits the needs of citizenship in society.[32] It supposes an expressive humanism, or "human development in its richest diversity."[33]

---

31. *Agogical* refers to those sciences relating to the personal, social, and cultural welfare of people and groups.

32. Gadamer, "Education Is Self-Education."

33. Taylor, *Secular Age*, 397.

2.3. Christian Roots of Bildung

Western European Christians also practiced Bildung traditionally, but they have not done so in a distinctly Christian fashion. If the latter is our concern, then we must point to the historical Christian roots of Bildung in the Middle Ages. The philosopher Hans-Georg Gadamer reminds us of the fact that, in the early European Middle Ages, achieving the image, or *Bild*, of Christ was one of the primary concerns for educators.[34] It is precisely this element that warrants our attention.

It may come as no surprise that the medieval concept of Bildung originally included the idea of *imago Dei*. The concept of *imago Dei* assumes that humans were created in the image of God, but lost this image to a large degree through disbelief and disobedience. Along these lines, the aim of education is to support the individual's development towards this original profile. The crux here is that even though we are created in God's image, we are called to become like Jesus Christ (*imitatio Christi*) through our own faith. This calling reminds us of the pedagogical paradox: if one has the possibility to become what one already is, an image of God, is it then not by one's own activity that one literally forms oneself? The answer was sought in medieval pedagogy. It pointed to a lost aspect of Bildung.

The mystical theologian Meister Eckhardt (1260–1328) was the first to use the pedagogical meaning of the word Bildung.[35] His idea of Bildung was that God created humans in the divine image and that subsequently humans were called to recreate and actualize the image of God that they carry in themselves. Bildung, then, was actively undertaken during the Middle Ages in order to become Christlike, even in learning.

During and after the Renaissance (fourteenth-century Italy to early seventeenth-century Europe), the term Bildung was used in the sense of the full, almost supernatural, realization of human potential. After that, we see Bildung used to refer explicitly to the "rising up" (German: *Emporbildung*) of humanity. In the practice of science and education, this was known as a specifically human way to "come into one's own" (German: *Ausbildung*) through enculturation. The crux here is understanding how Bildung influences the innermost being of the person.

---

34. Gadamer, *Kleine Schriften*, vol. 1; Gadamer, *Truth and Method*; Weinsheimer, *Gadamer's Hermeneutics*.

35. Lechner, *Bildung Macht Frei*, 18.

Charles Taylor points out how "Humboldtian Bildung supports openness to experience, the subjective response, the elevation of the aesthetic, the exploration of my own potential."[36] At the same time, it required a conscious choice of the person to live a moral, disciplined life. That could very well bring about a tension between aiming at authenticity (as present students still idealize) and living a purposeful life (as required by mores, customs, and ethos).

Indeed, to the original concept of Bildung belongs the idea that the person learns to detach from the culture he or she has been raised in and goes on to seek something new, possibly even conflicting with his or her original values. The quote from Gadamer's *Truth and Method* is well known:

> To see one's own in the alien, to become at home in it, is the basic movement of spirit, whose being is only to return to itself from what is other.... Thus, what constitutes the essence of Bildung is clearly not alienation, as such, but the return to oneself—which presupposes alienation, to be sure."[37]

Young people even may come to divorce themselves from their original tradition. Such experiences of alienation cause individuals to return to their roots, and thereby to make a definite choice for the good belonging to their original background. Gadamer uses the parable of the prodigal son to explain this.[38] He uses the concept of "self-alienation" as the starting point in learning about oneself. For Gadamer, this process is one of the roots of the *Geisteswissenschaften* (the liberal arts):

> In this structure of excursion and return we discern the circular structure of hermeneutic understanding. Already we can see why it is not a vicious circle in which the mind just spins its wheels. The spirit consists in movement—first in its departure from its home into the strange and unfamiliar, the otherwise. If the move is complete, the spirit finds a home, makes itself at home in the other, so that its new home is no longer alien.[39]

In this early sense of Bildung, the learning person lets go of the obvious and secure in order to uncover deeper truths, particularly about the self.

---

36. Taylor, *Secular Age*, 397.
37. Gadamer, *Truth and Method*, 13.
38. Luke 15:21–32.
39. Cited in Weinsheimer, *Gadamer's Hermeneutics*, 70.

In order to discover oneself in the alien it is necessary to try to become at home in that strange habitat. According to Gadamer, this struggle is the fundamental movement of the spirit in the formation of a person. In the effort to be other, the spirit returns to itself. This is more than a circular process; it consists of a movement of turning away, turning around, and turning back. Through such development, one climbs upwards.

Such a Bildung experience is a spiritual development whereby the learning person comes to know the self. It is first a "coming into one's own" in the sense of discovering one's own misery (limitations, weaknesses, and prejudices). Second, it is also a "coming back to the Father" as the parable of the prodigal son relates. This latter sense means a discovery within oneself that one wants the values and goods belonging to the household of the Father, our "true" image. It is only by "losing" ourselves that we can become our true selves.

This description not only fits the medieval version of Bildung; we still encounter examples of it today. Steven Garber provides these in his wonderful book, *The Fabric of Faithfulness*. Here is his summary of impressive examples of Bildung in students:

> (1) early struggles as a young student to make sense of life as he faced the challenge of new ideas and new relationship, (2) beginning to choose which ideas and relationships "made sense" given his developing understanding of the world and of his place in it, and (3) finding a few significant relationships with older friends—a professor and campus pastors—who both stimulated and nourished him in the meaning system he was beginning to call "mine."[40]

In modern days, Bildung has become so strongly secularized that the original pietistic meaning devised by Meister Eckhardt, redeveloped by Von Humboldt, and recently rediscovered by Gadamer has all but disappeared. The closest we come to such spiritual elements in Bildung are found in Christian liberal arts education. There we see the rise of service learning,[41] where students may experience a type of spiritual development that Gadamer calls for in Bildung. Emphasis on the Christian roots of Bildung can be found in attempts to "Christianize" the general cultural and moral formation of students. A prime example is given in a

---

40. Garber, *Fabric of Faithfulness*, 149.
41. Gunst Heffner and DeVries Beversluis, *Commitment and Connection*.

nutshell by Claudia DeVries Beversluis at Calvin College in the following sidebar.

> **SIDEBAR 2. BILDUNG AT CALVIN COLLEGE**
>
> - How do we move students into greater *self-authorship* and still help them know the supreme author of their lives?
> - How do we move students into the *decentering* process and still keep them connected to the center of the universe?
> - How do we *disorient* and still help students know who they are?
> - How do we help students *integrate* the head and the heart and the hands—their thinking and heart direction and active lives of service—even when it feels like these are going in opposing directions?
> - How do we dare go beyond just good practices and good habits, and encourage active, *critical reflection* on those habits and practices?
> - How do we *liberate* through the liberal arts and yet keep them firmly tied to the one who is our only comfort in life and in death?
> - How do we set students *free* to choose, and pray that they choose what we have chosen?[42]

These questions require answers that are fully Christian, yet they also adhere to current ideals of integral learning as found in Bildung: self-authorship, decentering, disorienting, critical reflection, liberation, freedom. The result is a Christian version of Bildung, including the profile of the Renaissance man or woman implied thereby. In this profile, the person is "Bilded" or imaged as multicompetent; open to new developments in art, science, and culture; progressive and yet highly spiritual. The profile is still quite expansive, yet it includes a certain quality that we generally consider to be virtuous, which fits well in modern society.

---

42. DeVries Beversluis, *Community as Curriculum*. (Emphasis added.)

2.4. Bildung and Spirituality

Our relays into the history of Bildung and its current practice tell us that our efforts to bolster the moral formation of students stand on solid historical ground. We can rightfully say that moral formation remains a noble calling for educators having the highest expectations for their students in all facets of their learning, including their spirituality. We believe an essential element of deep reflection is having educators guard the integrity of learning.

Engaging with the wider culture to transform individuals and cultures in the image of Christ is a strong and shared theme for Christian institutions of higher education that is based on biblical theology.[43] Much of the ideals and practices of Bildung are incorporated in what is called "faith formation" as part of student development. In this book, we are particularly interested in how students with an applied approach to their faith formation employ it in the context of their professional disciplines.[44]

If we believe that such an idealistic "rising up" is limited to highly religious, orthodox Christians, we are in for a surprise. We read more often reports of college students in all sorts of institutions of higher education, typically taking highly idealistic spiritual quests in their learning and development in college. We also read reports of how their spirituality influences their expectations of and preparation for work and community life beyond college. Jon Dalton makes an excellent argument that spirituality is an important feature of character building in higher education, since spiritual practice is one of the important ways that one enriches the inner life, transcends self-centeredness, and moves toward an undivided life.[45]

At the same time, even the most experienced educators deal with the spirituality of students no more than obliquely, for they perceive that their main calling is to ensure that students gain the right knowledge and skills. The core of their job is to give students the best educational

---

43. Edgell, "Preparing Business Students."

44. Examples covered in this book are American business students (Edgell, "Preparing Business Students"), Dutch student nurses (Van Leeuwen, *Towards Nursing Competencies*; Hunink et al., "Moral Issues"), Dutch student social workers (Borst and van der Veer, *Christelijke Hulpverlening*; Borst, *Temptatio et Gaudium*), Dutch student church workers (Landelijk Overleg Opleidingen Theologie, *Professsional met Diepgang*), and Dutch primary school teachers in actual practice (De Muynck, *Goddelijk Beroep*).

45. Dalton, "Career and Calling," 24.

opportunities and coaching that they can muster. At most, they try to create the best conditions for the moral formation of learners. They also, in many cases, continue to open windows of opportunity to remain involved in the lives of students.

Good pedagogues understand that their students must choose the right moral profiles through their own moral activities—with or without God's assistance.[46] In this way, educators take the high road when they urge their students to be moral, while they also prompt them to exercise responsible self-determination in choosing a moral profile—here we perceive the thin line of the pedagogical paradox.

Christians walking the high road as they seek the right Christian identity know, ironically perhaps, that one's own experiential walk on that high road leads to the discovery that moral development is not solely a spiritual matter. We deal with this issue in chapter 5. Choosing a profile for a professional career is a multifaceted struggle for each and every student. It generally takes many years of concerted effort and involvement by many people to achieve proper formation. A great deal of this struggle is done in connection with other spheres in life, which makes it a real-life quest, involving many profiles chosen and rejected. Therefore, our ethics of moral formation focuses on the integration of spirituality within the entire process of realizing a Christian vocation. And although this constitutes the age-old moral formation practices in Western European higher education, called Bildung, we may still wonder, is it feasible?

3. CHALLENGES TO MORAL FORMATION IN HIGHER EDUCATION

The tradition of Bildung is attractive. Its utility in a strategy of moral formation needs adjustment to the situation of higher education, in particular to factors encountered in moral formation. These factors are not all negative. Some clearly support our model.

Despite the great advantage of being able to build on the tradition of Bildung for an ethics of moral formation, we do well to note other factors that contest the soundness of moral formation in higher education. These factors may serve as handicaps to—as well as facilitators of—deep reflection. We focus in this respect on those challenges that center

---

46. Hare, *Moral Gap*.

around the basic notion of deep reflection, thereby allowing us to bring forward grounds for an assessment of the viability of our strategy for a renewal of moral formation in higher education.

3.1. Challenge 1: Can We Meet the Modern Call for Self-Determination in Moral Choice?

Modern developments have challenged our views on what morality is, and they have affirmed the need for virtue theory. It is no secret that Christian educators may find it hard to engage in moral formation if they take modern developments in education seriously. The cultural norms of both modern and current educational practice stipulate that educators must concentrate on coaching students in competence-based learning and leave moral choices fully to students.[47] Today, influential philosophers of education want us to believe that educators should focus on student demand, or students' self-determined perception of their learning needs. Only if a student invites a teacher to join him or her in the quest for a moral profile is it then considered legitimate to exercise guidance or influence on the student. Otherwise, a student's moral formation is self-directed formation, and preferably so. Can we meet this modern call for self-determination in moral choice?

We have reason for caution in our response. We realize that the agenda of moral formation is currently defined by the "pull" of learning needs as experienced by students, instead of the "push" of educators teaching Christian holiness. This tug of student demand leads many educators to shy away more and more from judging a student's quest for moral excellence (or the student's lack thereof), as well as from judging its spiritual dimension. The same holds for judging the "right" worldview; such matters are privatized in postmodern education. Reducing such quests to a personal choice is more than an easy way out; it serves to actuate Enlightenment ideals of independent thinking and performance. This route has the added attractiveness of allowing postmodern varieties of moral experience to prompt individual choice. This is a consequence of the easy way out: leaving it to the student to search for and choose what type of moral person he or she wants to be. We end by capitulating with a false sense of neutrality.[48]

---

47. Dalton, "Career and Calling."
48. Floyd, "Humility."

Such an easy way out of addressing student moral development must be challenged on the premise that morality is not an ordinary preference. Our statement is not based only on our awareness of being moral in a biblical sense with reference to the Decalogue and the new commandment. It is in the sense pointed out by Alasdair MacIntyre in his book *After Virtue*:

> In Latin, as in ancient Greek, there is no word until our word *moral* is translated back into Latin. Certainly *moral* is the etymological descendent of *moralis*. But *moralis*, like its Greek predecessor *ethikos* . . . means "pertaining to character," where a man's character is nothing other than his set disposition to behave systematically in one way rather than another, to lead one particular kind of life.[49]

As Steven Garber also points out in his book, *The Fabric of Faithfulness*, being moral is itself about the formation of character. It is about developing dispositions "to behave systematically in one way or the other"; it is "being a teacher whose purposes and passions ignite a student's moral imagination."[50] We say that it is opening one's heart to students so that they in turn open theirs to deep reflection. We therefore believe that modern developments certainly challenge our views on what morality is in the classroom, while they also affirm our great need for virtue theory. And they raise the question, just how involved should educators be in the way students choose their moral profiles?

3.2. Challenge 2: Can We Meet the Moral Call for Excellent Schooling?

We reaffirm the purpose of higher education as contributing to the formation of students. In order to foster the moral formation of students, the reformation of higher education must include an ethics and a strategy of moral formation that meets the need for virtue theory.

Involvement by educators is already high on every higher education agenda. If formal schooling is incompetent, then students run serious risks of being ill-prepared for their careers in "the real world." They are hit with a double whammy: they fail in schooling as well as in gaining a good start in their new practice.

---

49. MacIntyre, *After Virtue*, 38; also cited in Garber, *Fabric of Faithfulness*, 149.
50. Garber, *Fabric of Faithfulness*, 155.

Perhaps for this reason, the indictment of a poor quality of teaching in American undergraduate education in the year 2006 made by the past president of Harvard University Derek Bok caught a great deal of attention, not only in the USA, but also in Europe.[51] Because Bok's book builds on vast resources of empirical research, we treat his results as representative of a greater sense of dissatisfaction in the Western world regarding the quality of undergraduate higher education.

Interestingly enough, Bok focuses his attention not only on the notoriously low competency levels of the didactics of college teachers. He also specifies six "irresponsibilities" for which he holds faculty members as well as their institutions accountable.[52] In chapter 3 of this book, we will examine several of these problems to treat an integral perspective on education. At this juncture, we state that Bok's indictment has a strong moral overtone that supports our call for a moral formation strategy.

Bok takes college administrators and faculties to task because they "do not merely claim to train the minds of their students; they also promise to build their character," yet they do not fulfill the latter promise.[53] One of the main causes, according to Bok, is "a studied disregard of the research of student development in college," which he ascribes to a neglect of pedagogy.[54] This complaint, we duly note, concerns the best schools in the United States.

Bok's central thesis is that undergraduate education must begin by making clear what it is that colleges are trying to achieve. "Lacking adequate criteria of purpose, we do not know how well our higher education works in practice or even what working well would mean."[55] He calls for educators to aim at a variety of purposes that help young people grow and develop during this formative period in their lives.[56] In our evaluation,

---

51. Bok, *Underachieving Colleges*; Brush, "Fixing Undergrad Education."

52. See Bok, *Underachieving Colleges*, 34–54. These problems are: (1) differing perspectives on the role of universities, (2) traditional independence of professors and their departments, (3) neglecting purposes of education, (4) the fixation on general education, (5) the neglect of pedagogy, and (6) the neglect of extracurricular. In chapter 3 we go into factors 3 and 5 of this list in detail.

53. Ibid., 41, 59.

54. Ibid., 50.

55. Ibid., 58.

56. See Bok, *Underachieving Colleges*, chapters 4 to 11. These purposes of higher education are to help students (1) develop the ability to communicate, (2) learn critical

these purposes must include moral formation. Hence, along the lines of Bok's analysis, we argue the need for a pedagogy of moral formation involving worldviews and ethics, in order to be adequate to the task.

In a manner that recalls our treatment of the tradition of Bildung, Bok calls for a rediscovery of the normativity—meaning the whole of values, norms, and rules—of the practice of higher education. Social practices in education and in other professional fields should embody the normativity that students need for developing moral profiles. This involves more than just being practice minded. It calls for being oriented toward the constellation of norms that a certain social practice embodies on a societal or macro level. By heeding the morality of being a good student on the curricular or institutional level, students begin their training to become virtuous in their new careers.

For these reasons, we conclude that professor Bok provides strong arguments for having a formation strategy that meets the call for virtue theory. He also reaffirms the purpose of higher education as contributing to the formation of students.

3.3. Challenge 3: Can We Hold on to the Ideals of Formation?

Although many educators adhere to the ethical purposes of forming students, they are aware that moral formation is difficult to realize. We acknowledge that the moral formation of students is a challenge to achieve. We now treat several studies that point this out. We also treat several new attempts at moral formation that seem to fail in the light of poor moral behavior by graduates. Lofty ideals seem to flounder in the educational practice itself. Apparently, the moral training provided is on the whole insufficient to meet the demands of modern society.

Key influences of moral formation are economic in nature. The current practice of higher education in Europe, including professional education, follows a trend toward specialization and commercialization.[57] This affects not only the organization of curricula but also the profile of the student. Students are viewed as consumers who regard education as

---

thinking, (3) build moral character and learn moral reasoning, (4) prepare students for citizenship, (5) learn to live with diversity, (6) learn to live in a more global society, (7) acquire a breadth of interests, and (8) prepare students for a career. In section 2 of this chapter, we attribute all these qualities to Bildung.

57. Boele, *Overtuigend Anders*.

an investment of time and money in order to achieve future economic benefits.[58]

In many respects, learning in higher education may come to take on the ethos of the corporate model—be cunning and calculating! In order to be successful in a commercial environment, the student needs a profile that embodies being individualistic, technically inclined, and morally disinterested. Clearly, this corporatist or consumer profile fits poorly with the practice of traditional moral education. Simultaneously, as we point out below, the new competence-based learning (CBL) models set new standards that challenge the calculating profile.

This problem of the changing view of the student is already part of Western culture. The traditional and historical purpose of higher education has always been that the formation of students, seen as young adults, culminates during their final formal educational experience. After a groundswell of general orientation, we expect students to make smart career choices. Well-known studies by the erstwhile American civil servant and educational philosopher Ernest Boyer on the goals and purposes of higher education challenged this new view of the student.[59] Boyer's ideal was to promote the right scholarship of teachers for furthering the commitment of the student to moral and civic ideals, which is reminiscent of Bildung. Colby reminds us that Boyer's findings on educational practice in American colleges still hold:

> What today's college is teaching most successfully is competence—competence in meeting schedules, in gathering information, in responding well on tests, in mastering the details of a special field. . . . But technical skill, of whatever kind, leaves open essential questions: *Education for what purpose? Competence to what end?* At a time in life when values should be shaped and personal priorities sharply probed, what a tragedy it would be if the most deeply felt issues, the most haunting questions, the most creative moments were pushed to the fringes of our institutional life. What a monumental mistake it would be if students, during the undergraduate years, remained trapped within the organiza-

---

58. Colby, "Whose Values"; Bok, *Underachieving Colleges*.

59. Boyer, *College*; Boyer, *Basic School*; Boyer, *Collected Speeches*; see also McDonald, *Creating Campus Community*; and Jacobson, "Theology as Public Performance," and further material provided by the Boyer Center at Messiah College, Grantham, Pennsylvania. We thank John Bechtold of Messiah College for bringing us into contact with the works of Ernest Boyer at the Boyer Center.

tional grooves and narrow routines to which the academic world sometimes seems excessively devoted.[60]

Through large-scale surveys of faculty and students and extended site visits at twenty-nine colleges and universities, Boyer and his colleagues concluded by the end of the 1980s that by and large undergraduate education was not meeting the challenge of going beyond competence to commitment. Commitment here is the code word for moral formation. Since Steven Garber also devotes a chapter in his book to the topic "Education for what purpose? Competence to what end?"[61] we may assume that undergraduate education has not yet resolved this problem. Where Boyer may have thought that educators needed a good reminder, it now seems that educators vacillate in their commitment to ethics in education.

At the start of the twenty-first century, this pattern of wavering loyalty of educators to ethics in the conduct of higher education has apparently not changed much at American universities. Derek Bok calls emphatically upon American universities to engage overtly in building the character of their students. Despite the increase of courses offered on moral issues at American schools, Bok sees very little result in society of these educational efforts. Bok cites a study by the accounting firm Ernst and Young, which estimates that companies lose $600 billion every year from employee fraud and theft. He links this data to the finding of the philosopher Alan Wolfe that "the defining characteristic of the moral philosophy of the Americans can be described as the principle of moral freedom—meaning that individuals should determine for themselves what it means to lead a good and virtuous life." Bok concludes that difficulties learning the right moral profile may be a national (American) problem.[62] But more studies show that the problem goes beyond American borders.

Several startling studies show how students can achieve great moral reasoning skills (or thin morality) and even demonstrate moral sensitivity in class yet make a dramatic misuse of these moral competencies in actual practice. Businesses in the Netherlands find the moral formation

---

60. Boyer, *Collected Speeches*, 283; cited in Colby, "Whose Values." (Emphasis added.)

61. Garber, *Fabric of Faithfulness*, 76–99.

62. Bok, *Underachieving Colleges*, 149–50.

of students at universities seriously wanting.[63] As we noted in sidebar 1, research by the leading European accounting firm, KPMG, in 2009 indicates that many new employees lack concern for values and norms. Out of a serious concern for students' moral formation, KPMG is now providing learning materials to support the process.

We follow Bok closely in his indictment. He pleads convincingly for better teaching of moral reasoning and character building in undergraduate education. Should we therefore assume that Boyer's ideals can be realized, if educators will put their minds to it?

3.4. Challenge 4: Is Moral Formation at All Feasible?

At this point in our analysis of the situation, we wonder seriously: suppose Bok's indictment is valid for most of undergraduate education. Would it not be better to simply assume that moral formation cannot be carried out feasibly?

Our response is mixed. Yes, it appears that it can be done, but no, not easily so. In their well-known major review of the effects of college—now seen as a social practice—on students, Ernest Pascarella and Patrick Terenzini devote much attention to moral development in the college years.[64] Their conclusion is that moral development during higher education is carried out, but that courses regarding moral formation are mainly content oriented (instructivistic) or focus strongly on civic education in the form of service learning. After doing extensive case studies in moral and civic education, Anne Colby also arrives at the conclusion that much is done but not much profit is reaped from the efforts of moral training in American higher education.[65] This is confirmed in a study by Patricia King and Matthew Mayhew on the development of moral judgment by college students.[66] They show that dramatic gains in moral judgment during the course of a study are possible, but apparently these gains are more associated with extracollegiate participation than with the ethics courses followed, even after controlling for age and entering level of moral judgment. The implication is that there apparently is not a one-to-one relationship between following a good course of ethics and

---

63. Wallage, *Achtergrond*.
64. Pascarella and Terenzini, *How College Affects Students*.
65. Colby, "Whose Values." Not only North America, see for the Netherlands, Munk, *Ethiek in Zorgopleidingen en Zorginstellingen*.
66. King and Mayhew, "Moral Judgment."

being morally formed. Thus, there may be good reason to believe that the regular practice of higher education somehow has difficulty teaching morality effectively on a meso or institutional level. There is no reason to assume it is different in Europe. Clearly, we need far more than just a good ethics course.

A much more extensive attempt at moral formation is required, which agrees with newer educational developments. The point made by the above recent studies, in particular by Bok, is that teaching on the undergraduate level as such does not necessarily do a good enough job of moral formation. Apparently, other social practices must be engaged in higher education for bringing about the successful formation of students. We know by now that extracurricular activities (for instance service learning) can strongly support the moral development of participating college students.[67] The newer forms of didactics in new learning clearly emulate these extracurricular activities. Hence, we may expect some improvement in moral formation on a didactical level.

Before dealing with didactics (below), we clarify that the will of educational institutions to want high quality moral formation must be beyond doubt. Obvious recognition by management that they want to make moral formation feasible is a prerequisite to didactic reform. Finding an institutional commitment can mean dealing with the oft-held contention that students are primarily interested in gaining jobs, not moral profiles. This so-called realistic argument on the micro level says that students are essentially consumers purchasing occupational preparation. Even students who choose Christian schools are assumed to place career preparation over other priorities. Their spirituality and morality are considered to be their private business. As long as they learn the right competencies for doing a job properly, their moral formation is not the concern of the school. In short, schools do not count morality in their missions. Such arguments are cynical and shortsighted.

Our rebuttal to these arguments begins by recognizing the distinct nature of higher education in relation to other professional social practices. None of our social practices, including our schools, are in fact morally neutralized or value sanitized. We argue next that vocational preparation cannot be treated as an endeavor distinct from moral formation. In "real life," carrying out a vocation is quite a moral matter, particularly as it concerns professional ethical conduct. No serious stu-

---

67. See Gunst Heffner and DeVries Beversluis, *Commitment and Connection*.

dent returns from an internship to claim that "ethical neutrality" rules there. It is therefore fiction that higher education does without moral formation.

As we pointed out above in describing Bildung, the existing historical social practice of education already contains a certain remnant of moral formation. Avoiding these values out of the misplaced idea that moral formation is a private affair deprives students of the contribution a school could give them toward turning their occupations into callings and thereby becoming better professionals.

Hence, it is unthinkable that a social worker aiming for a moral profile displays a racist attitude towards foreign or immigrant clients (for instance, North African guest workers). The character that goes along with the racist behavior would not survive a moral assessment aimed at carrying out the standards of excellence our society expects of that social practice. If a student has not been sufficiently challenged during training to examine his or her leanings toward foreign citizens, the student has been failed—and mostly by educators. If a department does not have a stated policy on such reprehensible behavior (because, on a macro level, university management does not care), then higher education is obviously in trouble.

We conclude that our response to the question of whether moral formation is feasible requires a very keen assessment of the priorities of the entire institution of higher education.

3.5. Challenge 5: How Can We Handle the Weaknesses of Moral Formation in Higher Education?

The weaknesses of moral formation in higher education are evident. If we want to meet the needs of students—which are also quite evident—then we must address the problem by devising a strategy. The way forward is fraught with opposition, and there are certainly no easy answers. Clearly, the issue of moral formation requires a thorough understanding of the right preconditions for a revitalization of Bildung.

Our review of the effectiveness of moral formation thus far may create an impression that its feasibility is doubtful. We have good reason to consider this as a common perception in most of higher education. Garber writes:

> True education is always about learning to connect knowing with doing, belief with behavior; and yet that connection is incredibly difficult to make for students in the modern university.[68]

Yet, as we argue above, there is a distinct need for students to discover if they are morally suitable to function in a certain practice. This means that sources of normativity other than the educational must provide a basis for realizing our mission of proper moral education. How do we draw this normativity into the educational practice? This is clearly a challenge for higher education. We also recognize that not all educators share the desire to meet this challenge.

Despite its pervasive historical roots, Bildung as a practice in higher education remains troublesome. From our research for this book we have come to know that many good Christian educators still practice Bildung, to the effect that some young adults are properly formed for services in vocations and society. At the same time, knowledge of this formation practice may remain implicit or even hidden at Christian colleges and universities in Europe.

Perhaps formation practices are not as covert as we think if we take into account how leading opinion makers in higher education frown on the very idea of moral and civic training. Repeatedly, *Chronicle of Higher Education* and *New York Times* editorialist Stanley Fish argues that universities should stay out of the business of moral and civic formation altogether.[69] This popular neoliberal ideal flies in the face of the essential missions of Christian liberal arts schools.

Interestingly, this clash takes its form on campus as not strictly for and against virtue training or Bildung. A study of moral education at four top-tier religious research universities in the United States,[70] shows that a majority of faculty members at these schools support both the general goals of moral and civic education and specific suggestions for integrating moral and civic education in the curriculum.[71] Nonetheless, three major concerns emerge about the implementation of moral and civic virtues in the classroom. Many of the faculty members questioned

---

68. Garber, *Fabric of Faithfulness*, 57.
69. Fish, All in the Game; "Ivory Tower"; "Conspiracy Theories 101."
70. Boston College, University of Notre Dame, Baylor University, and Brigham Young University represent intentionally religious, academically successful schools in the USA.
71. Glanzer et al., "Moral Education."

had serious qualms on "how to do it," leading to positions such as: (a) virtue and good citizenship must be chosen and cannot be coerced; (b) no agreement exists on how to define virtue or good citizenship for students; or (c) being virtuous and living out good citizenship cannot be taught in courses.[72]

It appears, then, that the majority of the faculty at four universities gives us a double signal: "Yes, we must engage in moral formation"; as well as: "No, we can't do it properly, so desist—or at least be very cautious." These results bring to mind the pedagogical paradox (see above). They also call into question the sincerity of promises made to students regarding their moral and professional formation, generally referred to as good citizenship. This research underlines the importance of a strategy of moral formation that is effective in achieving moral formation and provides a full ethical context.

This study by the Baylor researchers raises the specter of schools strategizing moral formation with a double standard: preaching it on campus but not practicing it in the classroom. At the same time, the Baylor study also reflects the quandary of most Christian institutions of higher learning today: as good educators, we may love to do Bildung, but we do not know how (any longer). Sure, we desire moral integrity in our graduates, but we may leave them to their own devices to choose such a moral profile for themselves. This may be because we are unable to develop a good didactical strategy to help them in this difficult venture. If so, we should not be surprised if such a lapse in educational strategy becomes a factor in the general marginalization of moral education at Western universities.[73]

Must we conclude that Bildung is a wonderful idea but cannot be done? No. The current situation requires us to reinvigorate moral formation. We can handle the weaknesses of moral formation, if there is the proper will to do so. There is no reason to assume that the concept of Bildung that once had such wide use and great importance in nothing less than the founding of most Christian universities in the Western world would have no more relevance today. For reasons spelled out above, we believe that being morally formed is still the foremost practical understanding that students actually need in order to gain professional positions in society.

72. Ibid., 401.
73. Henry and Beaty, *Schooled Heart*.

3.6. Challenge 6: How Do New Educational Developments Aid Us?

Recent and vast changes in the didactics of learning provide new avenues for exploring how to make moral formation more effective. For unexpected reasons, new developments in professional learning and the onset of new learning, also known as learner-centered educational philosophies, aid us as educators to help students engage in moral formation. Here we discuss the latter developments.

The saying that an educator can no longer be a "sage on the stage" but must yearn to become "a guide by the side" encapsulates much of what is called the new learning. By this we mean the influence of social constructivism at all levels of education in the Netherlands and beyond.[74] The opposition to traditional instructivism (supposedly now in an *Index of Forbidden Pedagogies*) has been sold to educators by education managers who doubt the effectiveness of traditional higher education.[75] The changes brought about by the startling diversity of the current student body in age, ethnicity, social class, and preparation in secondary schools, along with stunning rises in information technology, make modern educators more than simple coaches. These trends have shifted educators' attention away from classroom-based pedagogy and didactics. Now the question is how the individual student is to be serviced in his or her learning as a client.

This reemphasis on what was derisively termed the "soft side" of education has nonetheless led recently to hard indictments that undergraduate teaching in higher education overall is didactically poor, embodying "a crust of inertia and complacency that keeps most colleges from challenging accustomed methods of teaching to become genuine learning organizations."[76] Interestingly, the core of this problem is a lack of competency among traditional educators in their ability to help students along in their development.[77]

Therefore, in order to ameliorate such weaknesses of education, this book will examine more deeply how knowledge of moral formation can support education. Notwithstanding social pressure by neoliberals to disinvest the ethical traditions from practices, we argue that good

---

74. De Muynck and Van der Walt, *Call to Know the World*.

75. Burgan, "Defense of Lecturing."

76. Bok, *Underachieving Colleges*, 330–31; see also Garber, *Fabric of Faithfulness*, 141.

77. Henry and Beaty, *Schooled Heart*.

educational strategy should be oriented in what good practice requires of students: being moral in that practice. This is a promising training ground, for reasons cited below.

3.7. Challenge 7: How Do We Understand the Rise of Practical Virtues in Competence-Based Learning?

The recent push for competence-based learning points out the legitimacy of virtue theory, ethics, and moral reasoning in curricula. Competence-based learning is of course necessary for professional schooling, but it also has great utility in academic learning.

Being oriented in the morality of practitioners in professions implies that educators as well as students must know which values and norms define a given practice. This principle is clearly demonstrated in new developments involving competence-based learning. For instance, for the social practices of care and social work, the required competencies are providing service on demand, being competitive, succeeding within a wide range of disciplines, and soliciting the input of various professionals. Even questioning the type of professional conduct required in learning competencies leads to another question: which standards of excellence are needed for good practice? Increasingly, these standards are portrayed as tendencies within moral profiles, for instance, displaying affinity in relations, showing empathy, being assertive, being properly evocative, and having integrity. These profile qualities are linked increasingly to virtues, the adoption of which gives clear direction to the practice of care. Professionals are expected to demonstrate these virtues.

It barely needs mentioning that teachers, even poor ones, are role models. Without doing injustice to the truth that traditional teachers are irreplaceable as models of knowledgeable adults and that their proficiency as thinkers is valuable for students to emulate, it is also an unmistakable fact that the new philosophy of education calls for teachers to care for the development of students and their learning. It calls for a new profile of the educator or learner as a knowledgeable, trained, and passionate professional in a new type of educational practice. In a way, the new learning is a return to Bildung but in a completely new setting of the Internet and consumerism.

SIDEBAR 3. AN EXAMPLE OF PROFESSIONAL PROFILES

Common wisdom often maintains that becoming socially successful has little to do with formal education, let alone moral formation. We examine the most successful profile in Western society, that of the entrepreneur, to determine the relevance of moral formation. Commonly considered a hard-nosed capitalist inspired by risk, the entrepreneur is a distinct profile. Surprisingly, an extensive study by University Nyenrode of the characteristics of successful entrepreneurs in the Netherlands brought out distinct moral and psychological qualities of successful entrepreneurs.[78] They studied 205 entrepreneurial ventures, as well as intrapreneural ventures (entrepreneurs inside companies). Irrespective of the life cycle of the venture, the following characteristics and qualities were related to the success of the entrepreneur: the entrepreneur must have courage and the willingness to take risks, the ability to reflect, the ability to strategize, and the capacity to lead and communicate.[79] Furthermore, certain virtues—often portrayed as competencies or psychological qualities—serve the profile of the entrepreneur in certain phases of their ventures. In the start-up phase of ventures, creativity, performance drive, empathy, and persistence were found to be critical ingredients. In the expansion and mature phases of ventures, decisiveness and reliability were among the desired normative characteristics of entrepreneurs. Interestingly enough—ordinary wisdom is not always wrong—the study also determined that an advanced level of formal education is not a determinant of entrepreneurial success. Their unmistakable conclusion is that being a successful entrepreneur can be viewed as a profile that emphasizes character (or virtuousness) above knowledge.

Given the increasing input of professional experience to the so-called new learner-centered education in recent years, we see new demands placed on educators to deal with moral formation. Precisely because character and attitude are less tangible characteristics than knowledge and skills, we observe that educators are looking for practical virtues that students may apply in learning tasks to gain further proficiencies. Yet, this description of the entrepreneur makes us wonder just how such virtues and dispositions can be learned.

78. Nandram and Samsom, *Succesvol Ondernemen*.
79. Ibid., 19.

Given the perceived weakness of virtue training as such,[80] there is cause for concern whether apprentices in their professional studies properly induct work-related dispositions and vocation-related virtues. Without substantive and clear knowledge on how virtues can be used in the new learning, we should not be surprised to see that the moral formation of students often takes a variety of forms, or disappears into fragmented forms of mentoring, because there is no explicit educational strategy involved. For professional studies, this outcome is a disaster, because professional education still implies a certain formation in becoming a professional, or gaining abilities and dispositions that are generally effective in professional practice.

3.8. Challenge 8: How Do We Appreciate the Rise of Reflection?

The need for improved professional performance requires better reflection practices. This need also reintroduces the need for the moral formation of the professional.

The rise of the significance of professional supervision and reflection within professional education was a response to the need to improve competencies. Reflection is the interpretation or reinterpretation of experience and knowledge. Reflection tools allow participants to think actively and consciously about their experiences, actions, behaviors, and choices. This kind of reflection places high demands on the self-image of graduates, by challenging their perceptions of being competent. More and more institutions of higher education ask their graduates to take on higher profiles in society, whether as entrepreneurs, professionals, or leaders. Much place is given all types of didactical novelties that stress greater autonomy in learning, to the extent that building the right portfolio may take precedence over grade point average. Admittedly, budding professionals must learn the required competencies and qualities before they start their careers. Their display of their qualities in a portfolio is certainly a good thing.

At the same time, we see too little concern for how students are to meet these expectations, given their greater autonomy in learning. On the one hand, there is an increase in all types of low-level formation exercises. On the other hand, this plethora of exercises does not flow from clear strategies for effective moral formation in education. As

---

80. In the Netherlands: Verbrugge, "De Vraag"; Wetenschappelijke Raad voor Regeringsbeleid. *Waarden en Normen*.

a direct result, pragmatic choices concerning profiles take the place of well-wrought design.

The wisdom students need to garner for carrying greater responsibilities is endangered through too much emphasis on limited views of their competencies.[81] Gifted students designing attractive portfolios may still run the risk of displaying a false image of their acumen in general and may end up failing in the practice itself. How prudently students learn what their proper profile is must not be left to the devices of their own natural development or to the devices of the market. It remains the duty of educators to help them—"if called for," as the new educational doctrine insists—but prepared educators still must be.

3.9. Challenge 9: Can Moral Formation Be Useful with Young Adult Learners?

The idea that choosing a moral profile is the exclusive privilege of dreamy teenage students attending traditional classes in brick buildings on parklike campuses isolated from the real world is outdated. The situation for most educators is quite different. Students entering college and university are increasingly adult learners. While more mature students are entering colleges, they come with their adult profiles formed to a large extent. They may include those returning to finish a degree but also working mothers preparing for careers after childrearing, and individuals temporarily out of full-time employment. Because these learners have formed their worldviews and their related moral profiles, they typically want an adult approach to their moral formation. Many mature students study part-time, which means that their presence in class and their study time may be too limited for working on a profile in deep reflection. This becomes a challenge for career mentoring with mature students.

Added to this is the consideration that competence may count more than having an integral character. The success of competence-based learning increases the expectations that graduates really do fit their occupations at the outset of their employment. For this reason, students focus on achieving high competency levels in order to gain jobs and please employers. Consequently, much effort goes to instilling technical acumen in adult learners. The result is often the lack of a comprehensive view of what it is to be a member of a certain profession. Many students

---

81. Burgan, "Defense of Lecturing"; Boele, *Overtuigend Anders*.

attending vocational schools, commonly called community colleges, gain only a fragmented image of what it is to be a professional in an occupation. Educators do thus not correct the bane of having a low profile. Reflection remains shallow.

These challenges, among many others introduced in this book, indicate that a quest for a moral profile in deep reflection becomes difficult to achieve. This is especially true if the managers of educational curricula and the educators involved—the increasing ranks of part-time faculty members in particular—do not have a solid grasp of the need to gain a moral profile. The argument of this book is that any student of any age seeking seriously to become a professional in an occupation must (despite the educational track followed at an academic university, professional school, corporate digital training, or vocational school) be given learning opportunities to gain the proper moral profile for an occupation. A key consequence of this argument is that Christian educators are to innovate the best ways to develop moral profiles. This is what this book is about.

We conclude this discussion of the challenges to moral formation with two positive signs. First, we established that various challenges to moral formation indicate that educators need substantial help from their institutions. Hence, an increase in institutional commitment to moral formation can work wonders in and of itself. Second, many new developments in teaching and learning can serve to support moral formation.

The list of challenges to an ethics of moral formation presented here is not exhaustive, but they are indicators of the multitude of issues influencing moral formation. A number of these are no more than modern versions of the old social sins that have always afflicted Western societies. We think here of the dominant neo- or social-liberal ethos, general exasperation with ineffective teaching, the burdensome complexity of moral formation in communities, the drawbacks of consumerism, the lack of academic guts, or higher demands by students. All of these can be perceived generally as peccadilloes of our societies that simply do not go away no matter how hard we try to do moral formation well.

Yet, all of the factors treated above provide very good grounds for the renewal of moral formation. We see distinctly new signs of hope and exciting opportunities arising. The most interesting is the phenomenal rise of reflection practices needed in competence-based learning. Because such factors remind us so strongly of the tradition of Bildung, as well as of deep reflection, we will present an outline of the ethics of moral formation in professional education that we believe is desirable and feasible. This ethics is one of responsibility, but it also takes the basic notion of deep reflection as indicative of what happens when this ethics is applied. We will first describe what it is. Then we will point out several conditions that hold for its ethics.

4. A RENEWED STRATEGY OF MORAL FORMATION

In this section, we point out the implications of our argument by dealing with the ethics of responsibility involved. In section 5, we spell out the conditions that hold for this strategy.

We propose a revitalization of the ethics that defines the issue of the involvement of teachers in the moral formation of their students as a shared responsibility. By this we mean that we hold educators as well as students accountable for the choice of moral profiles that students make. A major reason we do this lies in the unmistakable strength of vocational education that allows apprentices to become well-developed professionals by viewing all aspects of the master's professional's life when engaged in practice. This strength lies in the unique relationship between the master and the apprentice and the inherent possibilities for him or her to engage with the professional life of the master. We will describe this phenomenon in detail later in this chapter.

At this point, we argue that successful practices require an ethics of responsibility to bring the involvement of educators (masters) and students (apprentices) into focus. This ethic already fits the practice of formation as found in well-established societal institutions such as schools, churches, and sports. It is an ethic that allows us to look at the more recent involvement of other institutions, such as the media.[82] It requires us to have an understanding of our own history, tradition, and *telos* of formation within higher education. We need to find clear ethical conditions whereby pedagogues can learn to open their hearts to objective truth and to show compassionate involvement in the lives of students. Together, teacher and learner tackle the educational challenges found in Western culture, thereby allowing the student to make the right choice of a moral profile.

---

82. Nijhoff, *Identiteit Onder Invloed*.

We illustrate our proposed maxim requiring teachers to share with students a responsibility for gaining a moral profile by examining the vocation of being a good pedagogue, although it may be an old-fashioned profile for many readers.

Educators may rise again to the challenge of being good pedagogues. We refer here to the profile of the one who brings learners to the right learning place. We have good grounds to rediscover the central role of the teacher in gaining faithfulness: "teachers opening their lives to students, allowing an apprenticeship in what is supremely important."[83] The reason is that with the newer forms of learning, we see present-day novices going beyond first mastering knowledge then gaining skills. Early in their study careers, they need to learn (no longer to be taught) to make the right vocational choices that form and shape their professional identities. In all modern vocational schooling, this is of vital importance, as student mentors can relate. Increasingly, it belongs to the professional aim of each educational institution to deliver highly qualified starters in professional fields who can maintain a certain moral grade already established during the course of their studies. We may, therefore, expect a good many educational Bildung practices to buttress competency learning in curricula, simply because we feel that it is our job to help students along and to ensure that their personal development coincides with their competency learning.

We see no reason why we cannot emulate what was considered traditionally (and not only by Christians) as a source of honor. Self-respecting educators over the centuries engaged in teaching students the right virtues that support their choosing the right *Bild*. We call this moral formation using deep reflection. Rising to this ancient challenge these days is admittedly difficult. Explicit training in virtues is tough. Moral formation requires expertise. The newer educational developments have gradually repositioned the formation of students as the primary didactical challenge on our agenda. As of old, we are called upon as educators to be pedagogues—that is, trusted as guild members and guides in the moral and spiritual development of students, and not only young students. An erstwhile and noble calling is rising again on the horizon. In addition, because the pitfalls of the pedagogical paradox persist, we are called to develop an educational strategy to exercise leadership while al-

---

83. Garber, *Fabric of Faithfulness*, 151.

lowing for deep reflection or deep learning on the choices students make for their virtues and for their moral growth.

Common sense tells us that no student will be morally formed if there is not an explicit choice, an innate and intrinsic desire of that person, to do so. We term this the choice of a moral profile in the process of deep reflection. We see this choice as the result of Bildung but not in the superficial sense of a rising up defined by social conventions. We aim for Bildung that truly follows the Bild of having a calling or a vocation. For most students, that is deep.

Given such a need for deep reflection, educators together with students continue to examine their responsibilities as individuals for fleshing out the normativity in our lives. This is why we argue in this book for choosing a profile. A profile is essentially an innovation of what has been termed traditionally a vocation or a calling. Choosing a profile or calling requires a serious and committed choice to be a certain person in a profession.

Again, we believe that a student should choose a moral profile by taking into regard the normative conditions that hold in educational and professional practices. Because we follow the belief that all of reality falls under an existing normativity, we do not accept that choosing a profile is simply a random happening to which we must adjust out of sheer pragmatism. In our conceptualization, choosing a profile is always an explicit principled choice. It is an intentional choice to be a moral person in one's profession that meets the conditions of all of God's truth.

Rediscovering our calling as professionals is more than knowing our psychological identity. It is also more than knowing Christian worldviews. It is the ability to combine the right normativity with a determined focus to be moral. This is what we term having a moral profile. It is being moral in a concerted way because we access normative sources such as our worldview, our spirituality, and our ethics, and we apply these in our own individual lives. It is engaging a Bild that has distinct normative origins. It can only be done in deep reflection.

Our explicit focus on the role of choosing a profile also brings to the foreground new questions concerning how we learn about moral formation. Which moral profiles must students learn to adopt in order to become professionals? How can they adopt them? How does adoption relate to their spirituality? Given the created partial identities in professional roles, how do they relate to the real identities of students? How do the various profiles they aim for as professionals cohere in their performance? Such questions on integrity call for deep reflection or deep learning in relation to existing practices of supervision and reflection.

As we pointed out above, one particularly new challenge to studying moral profiles concerns the increasing role of practical virtues in relation to competency learning as found in professional studies. Of course, interest in all types of virtues is not new. Traditionally, when engaged in character development, learners have been expected to induct the required social virtues. Examples of these virtues are trustworthiness, mutual respect, open-mindedness, concern for the welfare of others, and active, thoughtful citizenship.[84] The ability to be professional and prudent at the same time is a very important moral proficiency. It may be obvious that deep contemplation is needed to foster virtues, but we will treat this in detail in chapter 3.

What is different and new is how students learn social virtues like these. They are detached from traditional training, yet quite affixed to the often very individualistic profiling practices in modern life. Modern students choose quite readily between profiles embodying a variety of virtues or vices. It is important to understand this development. For instance, at modern universities, the internet-based creation of profiles proliferates (in Facebook, Linked In, Myspace, and Hyves [Dutch]). These are superficial efforts at choosing moral profiles, simply because the digital world makes it so easy to create a profile.

The aim of our educational strategy is clear. Because we believe that only the actual practice of virtuousness in real-life social practices makes it possible for students to create an enduring self-identity incorporating moral, spiritual, and professional concerns, we need to rediscover moral formation as a major strategy for learning. We do this with the explicit aim of choosing a moral profile so that deep reflection cannot be done without recognizing how we carry out roles in the context of social practices that entail values and norms for this profile. The implication is that a quest for a moral profile requires knowledge of conditions holding in the practice of higher education as well as in the vocational practices students aim to enter.

---

84. Colby, "Whose Values," 169.

5. HOW DO WE STRATEGIZE MORAL FORMATION?

Based on our research, we contend that four views or windows hold for an educational strategy regarding moral formation in higher education, where we use worldview training, ethics, and deep reflection. We use the metaphor of windows to explain how these four conditions shed light on this type of moral formation. The acronym PISA (practice-minded, integral, spiritual, and answerable) outlines our strategy of moral formation. Below, we introduce the four elements of our PISA strategy as four complementary ways of looking at moral formation in higher education. These four perspectives are also useful for inquiring about the perspectives that hold for moral formation.

5.1. P: Being Practice Minded

The window P stands for knowing the characteristics of social practices and subsequently being able to position one's profile within the ethics of a professional practice. In line with our philosophical approach, we open this window first to see the normativity inherent in social practices. Next, we are interested in how professionals observe this normativity in an ethics of responsibility in their professional practices, and how they perceive themselves as professionals. This can mean, for instance, that a student chooses certain core qualities or virtues as touchstones for his or her professional profile, such as being present, empathetic, assertive, relational, representative, or having integrity. Being oriented in relation to P means that the student is able to understand how the practical virtues of his or her moral profile fit the demands made by the professional practice. This requires the student to think of him- or herself as having a certain moral profile within a normative practice.

Professional education curricula already set certain profiles that embody what it is to be a good journalist, church worker, physician, or lawyer. Some professions even have variations to choose between profiles. For instance, an educator could choose to become a teacher-servant or a teacher-mentor. There are other such idealized portrayals of being a good professional. Each practitioner is expected to arrive at a certain choice of what kind of professional he or she wants to be. This is a fully normative matter, as explained in chapter 2. Therefore, it must be taught explicitly.

5.2. I: Being Integral

The window I stands for knowing how moral formation takes place in all aspects of learning. Being integral is being in touch with all of the facets of one's life and being able to incorporate them into one's choice of a moral profile. It expands on what is often referred to as the relationships between "head, heart, and hands." Being integral brings to mind the holistic profile of the Renaissance man or woman, which we recall from traditional liberal arts education. In more recent years, we have the well-rounded and adapted social entrepreneur. In Christian circles, we admire those who seek public justice as shalom-seekers or agents of shalom. These profiles embody basic notions of being integral or holistic that are sought after increasingly thorough use of reflection exercises.

We realize how glib the use of the term "being whole" can sound. We therefore hark back to traditional conceptions of calling and integrity in Reformed evangelical education. The idea of calling has gained new prominence in a confrontation between Christian education and social constructivism, whereby students require social morality to engage in communal learning.[85] An even greater challenge comes from competence-based learning as a paradigm for higher education. Being integral in performance is a difficult goal pursued by many students at universities of applied sciences in the Netherlands. Inherent in these efforts are student mentoring and Bildung.

In line with the condition P, our approach is to place the development of becoming integral within the context of higher education. We show how students are motivated to adopt the integral moral profile of the teacher. We build on the master-apprentice model, as reinvigorated by the work of Alasdair MacIntyre.[86] He emphasizes that being integral is more than just knowing that faith and learning ought not to be separated. It is part of the growing practice of schools to apply rigorous student mentoring, various reflection exercises, and in-depth supervision toward developing practical virtues in the professional formation of students. Such educational practices coincide with a longing for authenticity found among young adults in Western societies. Thus, the demand for competence (via CBL) gives space to deep desires to discover the self. Its place in self-discovery makes the need for a better understanding of

---

85. Hegeman, "Stewardship and Integral Learning."
86. MacIntyre, *After Virtue*.

practical wisdom evident. Opening the window of being integral discloses possibilities to recognize how normativity in professional practices (as addressed in condition I of PISA) can help students become more whole.

5.3. S: Being Spiritual

S is a window open to understanding how spirituality feeds morality. It looks onto the basic motives that guide one's calling and reflection. We open the skylight of spirituality so that the student can realize which fundamental sources of meaning and quests for transcendence aid him or her in choosing a calling in life. We follow here a functional approach to spirituality, which emphasizes that all persons function in relation to spirituality. This brings us to consider the process whereby students and educators use religiously based virtues to guide their moral behaviors. We explore how this process can be integrated into moral formation.

The lens of spirituality allows for depth perception. It allows for deep reflection on the choices a student makes, in particular for being moral in his or her profession. Focusing on this condition allows us to see what students are actually doing when they try to relate their spirituality to their learning, particularly in practice. It gives new impetus for examining the actual practice of faith formation.[87]

Examples that can be drawn from the broad range of Christian practice are: being a steward, being a disciple, being a servant, and being a sojourner or pilgrim. Christians have followed these basic profiles in various areas of their lives. Christians adopt such profiles to express their basic spiritual goal: to do the will of God in their lives.

5.4. A: Being Answerable

The window A refers to our ability to be answerable, or responsive, to normativity—and in particular to be willing and able to answer for our choices concerning our moral identities. Through this lens, we see how students reflect on their own behavior while engaging in their education. We observe in particular how students partake in supervision, intervision, and reflection exercises to discover who they are within a professional practice. We also recognize that traditional ethics and Reformed philosophy require us to be answerable. We will provide a model of these

---

87. Edgell, "Preparing Business Students."

processes. Finally, we use the concept of answerability to sharpen our focus on the formation of moral identity in order to become responsible as a professional and also to sharpen our focus on how common approaches to moral formation are used to deal with this.

Examples of profiles that call for being answerable are commonly drawn from the general literature, and are often quite broad in their scope. Examples of modern profiles are being an author of oneself, being a moral communicator, being an honest and dependable person, or having integrity. In addition, social-psychological profiles, like "generation me" or "look at me," imply that choosing a certain moral profile makes one answerable in a certain way. If, for instance, a student fills him- or herself with cultural sayings like "believe in yourself and anything is possible" and "do what's right for you," it will not be easy for a moral coach to wean the student from such high levels of selfishness. At the same time, such a radical reorientation creates openings for talks on being answerable.

Answerability is disclosed through analyzing certain basic assumptions about identity. It is also revealed through examining how these assumptions are used in modern reflection practices at our universities, and via application of an ethics of responsibility.

5.5. What to Expect

PISA is a *working model of spiritual and moral formation* meant for:

- *Educating* students in vocational studies and professional studies.
- *Training* practitioners in ethics and/or practitioners receiving supervision.
- *Analyzing* educational systems of spiritual and moral formation.

Each of the coming four chapters opens one of the windows of PISA. In a final chapter, we provide a heuristic for applying PISA, where the perspectives discovered become part of a checklist for monitoring moral formation in professional education. This approach is also intended to reinvigorate other forms of learning, such as the liberal arts. We hope that it will also have the effect of boosting post-graduate training programs for practitioners.

2

P: Being Practice Minded

1. INTRODUCTION

THE LETTER P STANDS for practice and its ethics. Being practice minded is engaging with the morality of practice. We use the shorthand of the letter P to denote this. In chapter 1, we pointed out that this allows us to look at our performance in a special way. In what follows, we will also call this a condition to be met. For many educators, the understanding that we live, work, and learn in the context of social practices is not completely new. Students are often involved in field trips, internships, and cultural extracurricular programs at the urging of their colleges. What may be new is the idea that "real-life practices" are loaded with values, norms, and rules. Practitioners not only employ these norms; they also create their identities as professionals by working in ways guided by these norms.

Condition P relates to what happens when students step outside the campus to interact with practitioners and, in so doing, absorb the morality of their profession. Because practice is in essence social, those engaging with the morality of practice include students, teachers, and professionals. We stated in chapter 1 that formation is a shared ethical responsibility of both teacher and learner. In this chapter, we continue to explore how mentors apart from teachers, in many cases practicing professionals, also influence the morality of students. The key implication here is that moral training is not enacted solely by teachers.

Modeling is an obvious social aspect of the morality of practice. When teachers and students are involved with excellent practitioners in various arts, sports, professional fields and institutions, they are inspired by their models. It is quite natural for practitioners with attractive profiles to inspire students to seek to become like them. It is not uncommon for a student to report to their instructor after an internship with an admirable professional that they were thrilled to learn the ropes from such an excellent model. The student's enthusiasm is contagious. The instructor is often inspired as well.

Condition P as described here meshes well with competence-based learning (CBL). In our opinion, the interactions between morality of practice and CBL are dynamic in preparing students to become morally proficient in professional practices. This is because enacting P focuses on two foci: short-term experiential learning and the later profession itself (viewed through CBL). Condition P is thus a bifocal lens. The long field of vision inspects the professional fields and the required performance for which our students are to prepare themselves. The job situation may seem far in the future, but, through the bifocal lens of CBL, students and instructors can view the future utility of their training with clarity. Simultaneously, they experience present training via the short field of vision, which views their current moral formation via moral experiences in fieldtrips, internships, practical research, and jobs on site.

CBL, which is universal in the Netherlands, is basic to moral development in the professions. All universities of professional education in the Netherlands require their degree programs to have a clear and distinct curriculum following CBL.[1] We use the wider scope of higher education, which is grounded in CBL, to deal with the conduct of professionals in certain fields. The knowledge deriving from the CBL-based curriculum is basic for understanding the moral development of students entering a professional field.

The PISA model provides opportunities to test the utility of CBL in teaching professional norms and ethics. The authors do not argue for CBL—the preeminence of CBL is a fact for professional schools (and, increasingly, for research universities). Instead, we go further to develop a normative model that analyzes the value of this educational development for Christian higher education. The PISA model, because it is a normative model, allows us to evaluate various types of values, norms, rules, and virtues as they are encountered in professional practice. The result is a clearer understanding of professional ethics, as well as the sig-

---

1. Klarus, "Competentiegericht Opleiden," explains how the context of practice must be the starting point for the formulation of competences. This approach is now standard in the Netherlands.

nificance of professional practice as a normative structure. We describe this ethics in the context of the practice of education and care practices.

The model does not marginalize the tacit knowledge that professionals contribute to their ethical practices. A close reading of practices helps us to recognize the importance of the intuitions and tacit knowledge that professionals have of values, norms, and virtues. These are regarded as an integral part of what we consider to be a "competent practice." Such qualities are not incidental; rather, they are intrinsically connected to the professional practice.

This chapter will explain how moral profiles shape practice via deep reflection. Our discussion of deep learning associated with PISA will specify how condition P allows us to see how modern moral profiles for practitioners figure prominently in professional practices. Moral profiles embody a distinct notion of the desirable direction for practice. In this chapter, we will explain how practice and profile presuppose each other in deep reflection.

2. COMPETENCE-BASED LEARNING AND HIGHER EDUCATION

2.1. The World of Competence-Based Learning (CBL)

We begin by questioning the adequacy of a diploma to the exigencies of practice. After four years of a decent education at the bachelor's level, and the experience of many tests—and many perhaps self-inflicted trials and temptations—students at most colleges consider themselves strong enough to embark upon a career in society. Often after a final exam, a student receives a diploma as a social license to enter a line of work. The student can then depart from school to cross the threshold into "practice."

In direct contrast, professional degrees give students familiarity with practice before graduation. In the event the student followed a general, liberal arts, or even science education, a certain anxiety upon entering the working field is common. For those graduates missing the required competencies for gaining and sustaining performance in a desired vocation, a feeling of haplessness or dependency on luck often arises. Such students are only vaguely aware of their future job situations, whereas those graduates completing a professional education have had the distinct advantage of being familiar with the field they hope to enter.

CBL in Europe requires students to learn entry-level competencies before graduation. Education by CBL acknowledges the possibility that a learner can acquire competencies outside a formal learning setting. In the case of Dutch students in professional studies, their step from the educational practice into their future professional practice is guided through curricula that allow for carefully constructed internships and field exercises. By being in contact with mentors from certain communities of practice outside the school, they learn the rules, habits, and skills that belong to the new practice they seek to enter as novices. Moreover, before graduation, they have mastered the required entry-level competencies, as taught by skilled practitioners. For most graduates, this is a highly successful model. CBL is the result of efforts by European education ministers to standardize outcome-based learning.

As such, CBL is a response to outcome-based European quality control reforms in higher education. CBL is a direct response to the quality demands made by educational ministers from the European Union. The so-called Dublin Descriptors, which are shared expectations of a student's achievements and abilities at the end of the bachelor's and master's cycles of learning, have been adopted by higher education throughout Europe. Drawing upon widespread experience and expectations, the "joint quality initiative" developed shared criteria that could be used as reference points for the bachelor (end of first cycle) and the master (end of second cycle) qualifications. These qualifications in the areas of attaining knowledge and understanding, making judgments, engaging in communication, and having learning skills, are the backbone of both quality control and accreditation of institutions of higher learning in the Netherlands.[2] Accreditation relates to the assessment of the quality of the professional programs and focuses on learning outcomes achieved by the learner.[3] As a result, the degrees awarded in higher education are no longer seen as proof of participation and successful completion of a program, but as recognition of having achieved certain predefined learning outcomes.

---

2. See http://www.nvao.net for accreditation in the Netherlands and Flanders, Belgium.

3. Learning outcomes are the crux of the accreditation system of the Netherlands. Retrieved from http://www.nvao.net/learning-outcomes.

CBL is finely tuned to each vocational field. In this respect, each professional training program can be expected to have end-level, competence-based formulations that a certain vocational field has accepted as entry-level performance by aspiring professionals.

CBL requires the specific competencies that are necessary to perform in each specific profession. Competency as a criterion corresponds with its synonym of being capable. This goes beyond the older performance-based education that focused too much on tasks. Someone who is capable in terms of CBL possesses all the competencies required for performing adequately in a certain vocation or professionally related situation. A competency is then a unit of partial qualification that serves as a standard of excellence in a certain practice. But the educational philosophy behind CBL is that the end outcome of being a professional is what counts. Seen in this way, competencies can be defined as "the abilities of a professional practitioner required for adequate performance."[4] CBL is then best characterized as education that focuses on the acquisition of the requirements necessary to be able to perform professional roles. In this respect, competencies refer to the structure of professional practice (a feature we will return to in section 3).

CBL will only be truly useful if it adapts its focus to requiring professional competencies as holistically embodied in the individual. In our view, CBL must go beyond learning competencies as a set of standardized requirements for an individual to perform properly in a specific vocation. CBL ought to point toward an integral profile of all competencies in one person. Only if CBL encompasses a combination of the knowledge, skills, personal traits, and behavior utilized to improve performance will there be learning. Without this holistic aspect, it remains questionable whether a student can come to know if he or she is sufficiently qualified. More than the ability to perform a specific role, CBL means that a person knows authentically whether his or her personal profile fits the competency profile of that particular practice. And, as we will point out in more detail below, that means CBL requires a strong notion of what it is to be morally formed.

---

4. De Muynck and Roeleveld, *Competentiegericht*, 21.

2.2. Competence and Bildung

The skills required by CBL could be inadequate to the formation of professionals. Despite the emphasis on quality education for learning entry-level skills in the job market, not all is bliss in professional studies. The vocational success of a graduate of professional studies is not only due to the mastery of competencies as required by future employers and legislated by European government. Adopting certain learning outcomes for a curriculum does not yet make a successful practitioner out of any student. Piling on more technical skills does not alleviate the deficiency of a student lacking the required social dexterity for being a qualified practitioner. More than just know-how is needed. There is more to professional performance than just performance.

To develop this perspective, we return to certain basic facts concerning CBL. (See sidebar 4 for highlights.)

> **SIDEBAR 4. COMPETENCE-BASED LEARNING IN EUROPE**
>
> CBL in European higher education follows the so-called Dublin Descriptors—the criteria holding for education within the European framework. The criteria displayed here pertain to the first cycle (bachelor) and second cycle (master) qualifications.
>
> Qualifications that signify completion of the first cycle are awarded to students who:
>
> 1. have demonstrated knowledge and understanding in a field of study that builds upon and extends their general secondary education, and is typically at a level that, whilst supported by advanced textbooks, includes some aspects that will be informed by knowledge of the forefront of their field of study;
> 2. can apply their knowledge and understanding in a manner that indicates a professional[5] approach to their work or vocation, and have competencies[6] typically demonstrated through devising and sustaining arguments and solving problems within their field of study;

---

[5] The word *professional* is used in the descriptors in its broadest sense, relating to those attributes relevant to undertaking work or a vocation, and such undertaking involves the application of some aspects of advanced learning. It is not used with regard to those specific requirements relating to regulated professions. The latter may be identified with the profile or specification.

[6] The term *competence* used here is to be taken in its broadest sense as the ability to do something successfully or efficiently. See also note 3.

3. have the ability to gather and interpret relevant data (usually within their field of study) to inform judgments that include reflection on relevant social, scientific or ethical issues;
4. can communicate information, ideas, problems and solutions to both specialist and non-specialist audiences; and
5. have developed those learning skills that are necessary for them to continue to undertake further study with a high degree of autonomy.

Qualifications that signify completion of the second cycle are awarded to students who:

6. have demonstrated knowledge and understanding that is founded upon and extends and/or enhances that typically associated with the Bachelor's level, and that provides a basis or opportunity for originality in developing and/or applying ideas, often within a research context;
7. can apply their knowledge and understanding, and problem-solving abilities in new or unfamiliar environments within broader (or multidisciplinary) contexts related to their field of study;
8. have the ability to integrate knowledge and handle complexity, and formulate judgments with incomplete or limited information, but that include reflecting on social and ethical responsibilities linked to the application of their knowledge and judgments; can communicate their conclusions, and the knowledge and rationale underpinning these, to specialist and non-specialist audiences clearly and unambiguously; and
9. have the learning skills to allow them to continue to study in a manner that may be largely self-directed or autonomous.[7]

The Dublin Descriptors specify competencies such as problem solving, judgment, and communication, which are more abstract competencies than the professions themselves require. The qualifications in

---

7. Joint Quality Initiative, "Shared 'Dublin' descriptors for Short Cycle, First Cycle, Second Cycle and Third Cycle Awards," October 18, 2004, 2–3. See http://www.jointquality.org, and click on Descriptors, then General Descriptors to download the Word document.

sidebar 4 regarding problem solving (number 2), judgment (number 3), and communication (number 4) in both cycles clearly call for personal qualities of the student. These qualities are addressed by Bildung (see chapter 1, section 2). Yet, the realization of these formulated qualifications is still too generalized to determine how students can be assessed according to them. These high-level competencies require more operational indicators that involve basic knowledge of the professional practices themselves.

Most CBL requirements lack concrete specification of the personal qualities of a professional. Therefore, more concrete formulations of personal qualities are needed. However, we see little demonstration of that on generic levels. The emphases of CBL are rather on instructional design and quality control.[8] Much attention also goes to the utility to employers of partakers of professional education. Hence, it is not surprising that several European authorities on professional education have developed criteria primarily related to the labor situation.[9] Concerning the first cycle (bachelor in professionally oriented higher education and applied sciences), each European graduate of a professional school can be expected to have the competencies portrayed in sidebar 5.

> SIDEBAR 5. INDICATORS FOR PROFESSIONAL PERFORMANCE IN LABOR SITUATIONS
>
> *Professional Knowledge and Understanding*
>
> Use broad and integrated knowledge of the scientific basics of a professional field of learning. Combine theoretical and practical knowledge of current problems, applications and new insights in the world of work, which sometimes are at the forefront of the professional field. Able to use international sources of information and understand the effects and opportunities of internationalisation.

---

8. The literature regarding CBL is vast, in particular for professional schools in the first cycle. Representative of the educational scene in the Netherlands is the report published by Netherlands Association of Universities of Applied Sciences (NUFFIC) and Hanzehogeschool Groningen entitled *Competency-Based: A New Approach to Learning in Dutch Higher Education*. For a standard approach to instructional design and quality control in CBL, see Van Merriënboer et al., "Blueprints."

9. The European Network for Universities of Applied Sciences (UASNET), *Eight In-depth Country Surveys*.

Innovative Competencies

Demonstrate a critical understanding of the most important theories, principles, methods and tools in a complex and specialised professional field. Show profound knowledge of the basic principles of applied research and of the current applications and developments in this specialised field. Conduct small-scale research and project work applying existing knowledge of the field. Develop an initiating and proactive method of working in the associated profession sustained by legitimate arguments. Understand demand-driven operations and possess entrepreneurial skills.

Organizational Competencies

Dispose of knowledge of the basic principles of organisational management, leadership, and supervision tasks. Demonstrate knowledge of the methods of working life and operate in complex working communities and changing environments. Recognise and utilise available learning opportunities and scopes for action. Possess capability to take over responsibility in a team.

Learning Competencies

Capable of self-evaluating own competencies and define development and learning needs.

Communicative Competencies

Able to function in the communicative and interactive situations typical of the professional field. Adapt communication to innovation requests from society. Formulate subject-related positions and solutions and sustain them with reasonable arguments. Compare information, ideas, problems, and solutions with specialists and non-specialists.

Social and Ethical Competencies

Dispose of knowledge of the socio-economic interdependence and influence of the organisations in the professional subject field and able to put this in the regional, national and international contexts. Demonstrate operational experience in multidisciplinary teams.

Able to apply the value systems of the subject field and to develop sensitivity for innovation demands from society. Use knowledge of language and culture to operate in an international context.[10]

CBL, as currently constructed to fit labor needs, favors skill development over human development. The competencies described in sidebar 5 clearly focus on adequate performance in the labor market; they are designed for carrying out tasks effectively. The more generic personal qualities found in sidebar 4 are presupposed or taken for granted. This reveals a strong tendency to emphasize the immediate employability of the graduates above their psychological, social, moral, and even spiritual development. It is too quick to conclude that institutions applying the qualifications in sidebar 5 would *not* allow for Bildung. However, it is not obvious either that they *do* succeed in producing well-formed practitioners. In our view, pursuing employability without regard to being able to maintain a job and continue to grow in following one's *vocatio* (calling) does not count as good CBL. The question then is, what does it mean to realize Bildung in the context of CBL?

The current requirements are based on the assumption that CBL fits well with professional practice. We have seen that the competencies displayed in sidebars 4 and 5 assume that knowledge-related abilities, problem-solving acumen, and agogical talents can flow together in the stated criteria for professional performance. Therefore, we can state that the competence profiles that govern curricula in higher education, along with the professional profiles that are required in the world of work, somehow are assumed to be part of existing practices. Both systems—the world of higher education and the world of work—somehow are

---

10. Ibid. See Netherlands Association of Universities of Applied Sciences [HBO-raad], *Eight in-depth country surveys and general report BaLaMa project 2007*, http://werkeninhethbo.nl/?i=1515&t=doc. (Emphasis removed.) This report has been written by a group of representatives of associations of professionally oriented higher education and applied sciences (rectors' conferences) in seven member states of the European Union (Austria, Denmark, Estonia, Finland, Germany, Ireland, and the Netherlands) in cooperation with Switzerland. Within the European Socrates program of the European Commission, the members of the network have agreed to share and discuss their work in the field of professionally oriented higher education and applied sciences by collaborating in a European project. A main target of this project, labeled the Bachelor for the Labour Market (BaLaMa), has been the clarification of a European profile of professionally oriented higher education. For this purpose, the network has made an analysis of similarities in higher education in the eight participating countries. From these similarities, a common profile and common objectives have been formulated. Also a set of general descriptors has been devised, which could fit the European Qualification Framework.

based on the basic notion that within higher education, both worlds not only meet but even can meet favorably—for the student, that is. This brings us to examine the institution of higher education more closely to confirm or reject this assumption.

2.3. Higher Education and Bildung

The assumption that the worlds of higher education and employment can meet favorably is correct, thanks to the tradition of Bildung. Bildung is carried out in three distinct learning tracks. Indeed, it can be said that modern European higher education embeds Bildung practices along with CBL. Remarkably, the situation is no longer either-or but both-and. A quick look at learning systems in higher education reveals the three practices or tracks of learning found in higher education that allow for this.[11]

Instructivist Track
Bildung traditionally has been accomplished in the instructivist track via extracurricular activities. The oldest track of education is the paradigm of learning using formal teaching methods, such as instructivist methods (often in classroom-based teaching, more recently in e-learning). Previously, Bildung was clearly associated with facets of this first track, commonly termed extracurricular activities.

Constructivist Track
Bildung nowadays is accomplished in the constructivist track via group processes. The second track of higher education is called "new learning" in the Netherlands. It applies constructivist learning methods achieved through project learning, problem-solving methods, learning agogical skills in dealing with peers and professionals, and learning management skills. The second track has become utilitarian and instrumentalist in nature, hence Bildung tends to be subsumed in group processes.

Reflectivist Track
Bildung is undertaken in the new reflectivist track via supervised reflection. The third track is the newest, whereby supervision and reflective methods contribute to the improved academic and vocational performance of the student. The reflectivist track focuses mainly on having the required traits for doing the job, such that we see a recurrence of what originally was termed Bildung in the focus on the individual.

---

11. Jochemsen and Hegeman, "Ethiek van de Zorg," 91–93.

Although CBL occurs mainly on the second track, its group processes raise the need for further thought and mentoring along the third track. CBL builds foremost on the second, constructivist track, whereby proficiencies as needed in the workplace or academic research practice figure as utilities. Yet, the empirical learning practices of this second track tell us that these skills are not achieved without much discussion, feedback, and appraisal. Therefore, most CBL profiles in professional training include lists of practical virtues for students to realize in order to make them socially proficient while solving problems. The implication is that students are to be coached, encouraged, and stimulated to take on more responsibility for developing these practical virtues in themselves. This in turn calls for the third, reflectivist track. It is on this third track of learning that student mentors working with CBL come to use Bildung, which may come as a surprise to many who consider it more amendable to instructivist learning.

Christian professional universities in the Netherlands tend to use competencies set in the context of the development of the individual professional. By taking a formation-directed approach to CBL, we are following a trend established at Christian professional universities in the Netherlands to emphasize the personal competencies of the learning professional.[12] This can best be illustrated with an easy-to-understand example from the competency profile of the church worker, as displayed in sidebar 6.

> SIDEBAR 6. EXAMPLE OF A REFLECTION ON PERSONAL CAPABILITY IN THE COMPETENCY PROFILE OF THE CHURCH WORKER OR PASTORAL WORKER
>
> The published domain competency profile for the (first cycle) bachelor of theology professional education contains nine competencies holding for a church worker or pastoral worker: (1) hermeneutic competency, (2) pastoral competency, (3) liturgical competency, (4) missionary-diaconal competency, (5) educative competency, (6) social-agogical competency, (7) leadership competency, (8) communication competency, and (9) reflection on personal capability. If we take the final competency as an illustration, we see formulations of capacities that require the adoption of certain practical

---

12. De Muynck and Roeleveld, *Competentiegericht*, 80–85.

virtues. In these virtues the reflection on the person, the conduct, and the setting for professional action come together.

Competence (9) the "reflection on personal capability" is defined as the capacity to reflect on one's ethos, identity, and performance in professional practice and to engage in personal and professional development by drawing upon one's own spirituality or the spirituality belonging to the religious community or organization one represents.

The indicators that hold for the reflection on personal capability are that one:

- Analyzes one's own conduct from an understanding of one's competency profile and thereby continues to advance one's personal development.
- Develops a perspective on professional practice based on theological insights, one's worldviews, and one's experiences in conduct of practice, as fitting within the religious tradition or organization one represents.
- Reflects on the religious tradition of the movement or organization one represents, the related documents, sources, customs, and symbols, and recognizes their value.
- Defines one's identity in a balanced way and conducts oneself in an authentic, honest, and ethically responsible manner.
- Reflects on one's own religious and spiritual development.
- Demonstrates abilities to weigh the relative value of one's perspective and to acknowledge one's own limits.
- Demonstrates accountability for personal choices.[13]

Such use of CBL amounts to Bildung in several ways. Obviously, the references found in the indicators of the reflection on personal performance competency to theology, religious and spiritual development, and religious traditions hold for the church worker. At the same time, the presentation of these indicators also includes the practical virtues required, for instance, self-analysis and self-understanding, reflection,

13. Landelijk Overleg Opleidingen Theologie, *Professional met Diepgang*. Translation by Johan Hegeman.

the definition of one's identity, prudence, and accountability. Becoming oriented in these personal qualities, as well as in other practical virtues in the other eight competencies of the church worker allows for and calls for Bildung. In addition, the ability to integrate these nine competencies belongs to Bildung.

2.4. Learning Competencies Require Authentic Learning Environments

CBL requires learning environments that reflect professional life and assess performance in ways authentic to that life by including professional norms. Many colleagues at professional schools using CBL have become aware of the need for authentic learning environments. By this we mean environments that do justice to the complexity of the real-life situations of professionals. Hence, in order to prepare students for the workplace of today, authentic assessments are relevant. Such assessments not only need to take into account the complexity of real-life situations but also the various types of norms that professionals have to observe in such situations, viz. norms regarding professional knowledge, skills, and attitudes (virtues). Presenting an authentic learning environment requires knowing which particular values, norms, and rules hold for that situation.

CBL and the assessment of CBL must allow for the complexity and variety of professional life. On the one hand, students in professional programs must graduate according to strict views on the learning outcomes, as indicated in competency profiles. At the same time, one knows that each situation they encounter is unique in a sense, and requires a unique application of knowledge, skills, and attitudes to attain authenticity. Students must learn to adjust CBL to that specific learning environment, which again calls for their sufficient formation.

Authentic learning, or learning that includes the social practice of the professions, is offered in some professional programs, such as nursing. In North America, social practices are often learned in sports, music, and other extracurricular activities. Already, many schools expose students to authentic learning environments embodying many types of norms. A common requirement in all types of professional schools is that students not only must excel in the educational practice while at school but also in the new social practice (for instance, nursing) that they intend to enter. Thus, they must learn to become proficient in more than one practice, in that they must understand the basic norms and values of these practices. This is analogous to the way students in North

America are given ample opportunity during their college years to become proficient in other practices, such as sports, music, or military arts. Granted, professional training is not nearly as spectacular as the fancy extracurricular activities found in liberal arts education, but in both, a basic social custom of seeking authentic learning figures strongly.

Employers value activities that promote Bildung. A primary example is the rather mundane questioning that employers conduct with prospective employees on their authentic experiences. Many future employers want to know whether prospective employees have engaged in extracurricular activities during their schooling. In this way, employers assess applicants' abilities to adopt the rules, virtues, and customs of other practices, while also maintaining those of the educational practice. Such adaptive learning on the fault line between differing social practices allows the pursuit of Bildung. We infer that authentic learning of the norms and values of various practices is valued, rather than discounted.

The new learning philosophy that requires students to be co-responsible for their learning allows them to incorporate Bildung purposively. Seeking authentic learning is warranted by the new learning philosophy, which calls for students to become co-responsible for their own learning process. This means students become accountable for taking the step of moving from the practice of education to the practice they hope to enter. Such responsibility heightens their ability to perform self-analysis with a view to determining their potential. Students acquire social proficiency by engaging in various social roles at school as well in the vocational area. As they do so, we see students and educators lean on or borrow the first educational practice to cultivate proficiencies in a second social practice, and vice versa. This allows them to become sensitive to the various values and norms holding for learning (we return to this matter in chapter 3).

The formation of students must allow the norms of education to mesh with professional norms. The values and norms of the educational practice must somehow intermesh with those of other practices, especially vocational practices. Professional training aims primarily to form students to be competent in the new practice of their vocation. This means that, during their formation, students should learn explicitly the normative structure of their practice of vocation and its related ethics. In the following section, we will explain what we mean by the normative structure of a social practice, as well as its implications for an ethical performance of the practice. We call this condition P.

3. THE NORMATIVE STRUCTURE OF PROFESSIONAL PRACTICE AND ITS ETHICAL IMPLICATIONS

3.1. Introduction

Our concern is how to merge morality with professional practice, despite the drawbacks of CBL. In the first chapter, we identified several perils of modern professional education. In the above section, we argued that professional education is positively influenced by the rise of CBL. At the same time, the fear prevails that CBL overemphasizes attention to skills and gives too little attention to the proper dispositions of a well-rounded professional. Such concerns are certainly not without ground. If too little emphasis is put on the moral character and behavior of future professionals, moral weakness in vocational performance may be the result. Given our belief that education is about connecting knowing with doing and skills with virtues, just how does a young professional in training overcome the drawbacks of CBL as it is often practiced? In the following section, we introduce a model that calls for the professional to willingly accept morality while engaging in excellent performance in a certain practice. We call this the ethics of professional practice.

In this section, we argue that the performance of professional practices not only requires skills but standards and virtues as well. Such practices embody sets of values and norms that should be taught and learned effectively. Hence, an important goal in professional moral education is making students aware of the inherent normativity of their future practice.[14]

The following metamodel provides a philosophical foundation for CBL and Bildung. We introduce here a model that depicts the normativity of professional practices that we deem necessary for students to achieve morally competent performance of their practice. This model is a metamodel, meaning it provides the philosophical foundation for

---

14. It can be argued that it would be better to speak of "normed practice" instead of "normative practice." It is true that the practice is normed by what will be called its constitutive rules. At the same time, the normed practice is normative, in the sense that it prescribes norms for the practitioner performing that practice. So both formulations are valid, and they refer to the same phenomenon.

CBL as well as Bildung. Using this model as a foundation, the teaching of ethics can also become instrumental to the moral formation of professionals.

3.2. Professional Practice as a Normative Practice

3.2.1. A View of Professional Practices

An important presupposition of our approach to practices is that morality is an essential human feature that manifests itself very clearly in social life. In human communities, ideals, motives, and beliefs always define good and bad, the good life versus what is not the good life, and what ought or ought not be done. People always respond in certain ways to the challenges presented to them by simply living in this world. In doing so, they always give expression to such ideals, motives, and beliefs.

Tacit moral knowledge has a strong function in professional communities. These expressions often are not clearly apparent to us, yet they function strongly in the form of unwritten, sometimes even unspoken codes of conduct and customs, or convictions on what is decent or indecent. It is this tacit moral knowledge that forms the fabric of human community. The rules governing the life and behavior of communities often are not made fully explicit. This certainly holds for professional practices. Nevertheless, this shared moral knowledge embodies core beliefs that may be very indicative of the existence of the community, or of the existence of a specific profession.

The morality of a community involves worldview and ethics. The morality of a group of people gives expression to the normativity that those people have encountered in reality, whether it is made explicit or not. The morality of a community is not just a historical construction of what the community decides to call good. It reflects the community's moral experience of what kinds of behavior turn out to work well or not, evaluated from the specific worldview held by the community. For example, no community can survive if there is not some understanding of truthfulness that functions in the community. Ethics, in its turn, is the study of and reflection on morality in the light of two questions, which kind of life is desirable? and, which conduct allows such a desirable life to flourish?

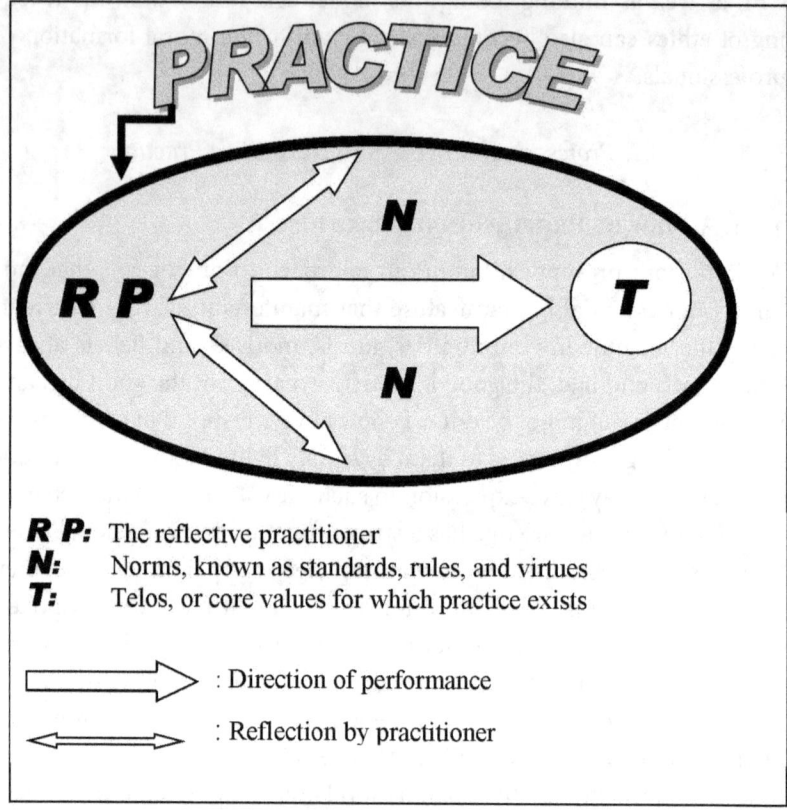

Figure 1. The normative reflective practitioner model

We present the normative reflective practitioner (NRP) model, explicated in figure 1. This approach to professional ethics and reality holds that normative ethics entails an analysis of the situations in which people find themselves. Such situations involve a variety of social relations and structures. In our view, a fruitful start for such an analysis is Alasdair MacIntyre's definition of a practice. This famous definition is as follows:

> By a "practice" I am going to mean any coherent and complex form of socially established cooperative human activity through which goods internal to that form of activity are realized in the course of trying to achieve those standards of excellence which are appropriate to, and partially definitive of, that form of activity, with the result that human powers to achieve excellence, and human conceptions of the ends and goods involved, are systematically extended.[15]

---

15. MacIntyre, *After Virtue*, 187.

Starting from this definition and using insights drawn from Dooyeweerdian philosophy,[16] we present a view on professional practice that we call the normative reflective practitioner (NRP) model.[17] As the term *practitioner* suggests, we take the concept of a professional practice as the primary focus for our model, stressing at the same time that the model is applicable to other social entities as well (e.g., to associations). We start our analysis of a professional practice by distinguishing between the constitutive side and the regulative side of the practice, analogous to the distinction between structure and direction found in Reformational philosophy.[18] We present an analysis of practices using this distinction, which we will explain below, and start with a description of the constitutive side of normative professional practices (see figure 1).

3.2.2. Norms Constituting Normative Practices

In this subsection, we introduce the concepts that define the constitutive side of the NRP model. We will show that certain norms function as a charter for practices and for professional practices in particular. The practitioner (in the NRP model) is subject to these norms. The following features are characteristic of the NRP model:

1. Practice as socially established human activity
2. *Telos* as core value for which a practice exists
3. Standards of excellence in a practice
4. Constitutive rules qualifying practice
5. Constitutive rules founding and conditioning practice
6. Rules and virtues

---

16. For an introduction in English, see Clouser, *Myth of Religious Neutrality*. For an introduction in Dutch, see Van Woudenberg, *Gelovend Denken*.

17. The normative reflective practitioner model was philosophically introduced as a model in Christian philosophy by Henk Jochemsen in his "Normative Practices," formally presented as a keynote adddress at the Association for Reformational Philosophy International Symposium, Hoeven, the Netherlands, August 2005. The model received its first application in practices in Jochemsen and Glas, *Verantwoord Medisch Handelen*. See for later application, see Jochemsen et al., *Theorie over Praktijken* and for application in higher education, Jochemsen and Hegeman, "Connecting Christian Faith."

18. Wolters, *Creation Regained*.

3.2.2.1. Practice as Socially Established Human Activity

First, a professional practice is a form of socially established human activity. This statement entails that the practice exists before the individual practitioner enters the practice. For instance, the practice of medicine has developed by a long historical process as the result of many decisions and processes that embody normative choices. In this sense, medicine and other caring practices are in themselves already normative practices. The practitioner is subject to that normativity. To be sure, this is also true for newer practices, such as accountancy, business management, and education.

The individual practitioner is initiated into the practice by learning a certain way of doing things. The practice shapes the behavior of individual practitioners before they can begin to reshape the practice.[19] The practice influences the way practitioners interrelate as well. Hence, the relationship between, for instance, a patient or client and a professional is not just a voluntary relation between two free rational agents on the basis of mutual consent and interests, as the social-liberal model of social relations wants us to believe.

3.2.2.2. Telos

Secondly, a practice has a certain finality, a reason, or a core value for which the practice exists. The Aristotelian term *telos* probably suits best here. The activities making up a practice are directed at the realization of this finality, this telos of that actual practice. It is important to distinguish this finality from goals that individual practitioners may have. Goals set by individual or collective actors, for example, in medical practice, do not necessarily contribute to the realization of the telos of medical practice simply because one is a practitioner.[20] A physician may want to be an entrepreneur and make money, but trying to realize this goal does not necessarily serve the optimal realization of medicine or of

---

19. See Benner, "Using the Dreyfus Model."

20. This is pointed out by Miller, "Virtues, Practices and Justice." He argues that the internal good of medicine according to MacIntyre would be the good of being an excellent doctor. If this means "being an exemplar of those standards of excellence which have evolved in the medical community," it should be noted that the two may diverge. In a medical community sometimes, the one with the highest technical ability is considered the exemplar of the standards of excellence whereas that person may not be the best healer of the sick. So the concept of the internal good can become too "internal" and lose its power to characterize the reason of existence of a practice in society. The concept of *telos* is defined in this way and therefore serves better in describing the normative structure of a social practice.

the enterprise. The telos of a practice belongs to the very nature of the practice and is not founded in the intention of the practitioner or the client, patient, or user.

3.2.2.3. Standards of Excellence

The third essential element of a practice is that human activities in a practice are seen as rule-guided behavior in which the rules of play are understood as the standards of excellence for that practice. These standards or rules constitute the practice and at the same time define excellent practice.[21] They provide criteria to evaluate the activities of individual practitioners. In this context, the concept of rule does not so much refer to rules in the sense of *knowing what*, which implies the ability to explicitly formulate the applied rules. Rather, it includes knowing rules in the sense of *knowing how*, in which the rules are embodied in professional conduct consisting in the ability to act according to a rule and to assess the correctness of this application even without making the rule explicit.[22] One can easily see that performing a practice, e.g., playing the violin, practicing medicine, or managing a company, cannot be learned just by theoretical instruction about the practice even to the point of demonstrating (showing how). Actually engaging in the rule-governed forms of activity of that practice is indispensable.

When the rules of the practice are observed well by carrying out those forms of activity, the telos of the practice is being realized. A practitioner who is able to practice in accordance with the rules in compliance with the telos is a competent practitioner. In other words, competence reflects the ability to act according to the (largely implicit) rules of the particular practice. These rules have an intrinsic normative nature in the sense that they reflect competent practice.[23] Knowledge of these rules enables the assessment of the actions performed within practices. This is a second way in which a social practice, as meant here, is a normative practice (see the first characteristic).

---

21. Gremmen, *Practical Use of Scientific Knowledge*.

22. From this description, it will be clear that we use the word *rule* here in a broader sense than a strict directive for action that has the structure of "If *a*, then do *b*." Our use of the word composes directives for action but also norms at a higher abstraction level. Roughly stated, we mean context-dependent norms and directives that can be derived from context-independent normative principles.

23. Unen, *Professionals*.

3.2.2.4. Constitutive Rules Qualifying Practice

The constitutive rules of a practice are found in its normative rule, according to Dooyeweerdian philosophy. An important question that arises from this description of practices is, how do we find the constitutive rules of a practice? To answer this question, we draw more deeply from Dooyeweerdian philosophy. As a social entity, the practice functions in all the modal aspects described in Dooyeweerdian philosophy. Modal aspects in this philosophy are irreducible ways of experiencing reality that at the same time are perspectives on reality from which things and events can be evaluated. Each modal aspect has a core value, also called its meaning-kernel. That a practice functions in all aspects means that all the meaning-kernels of the modal aspects can be understood as normative principles for the performance of the practice. These normative principles are still context independent. By making the principles operative in a specific context, we can formulate more context-dependent rules. In the NRP model, such rules are the constitutive rules that constitute the professional practice.

We offer two examples of how rules are drawn from a moral principle. An example of a moral principle is the principle of respect for a patient's responsibility and freedom of choice. In caring practices, this principle is made operative in the rule of informed consent. This can be elaborated further into a number of rules, such as providing relevant information, checking whether this information and its consequences have been understood, and obtaining consent. These rules come to constitute practice. Another example is the medical-technical normative principle of effective or meaningful intervention.[24] This is elaborated for the medical profession in the manifold rules and standards that constitute the medical-technical professional standard, to which courts hold professionals accountable. The same can be said, mutatis mutandis, for other practices.

Several principles apply to any given practice, but only one is the qualifying principle of that practice. Of immediate importance for most professional practices are principles pertaining to aspects of reality such as the scientific-logical aspect, the technical-formative-historical aspect, the psychic aspect, the lingual aspect, the social aspect, the economic aspect, the juridical aspect, the aesthetic aspect, and the ethical aspect. However, it is important to point out that the normative principles related to all these aspects do not function in the same way in all practices. One of these

---

24. Widdershoven, "Technology and Care."

will function as the qualifying principle of a certain practice. A qualifying principle can be identified in our model as the telos of that practice.

Here is how the telos operates as a qualifying principle of a practice: knowledge of what figures as central "motif" of professional performance flows forth from a clear understanding of the telos of a practice. For example, we can take the practice of nursing and ask what the qualifying principle of that practice is. We may answer that the principle of care, which we hold to be the normative principle of the ethical aspect,[25] is the telos of all caring practices and therefore qualifies the practice of nursing. This means that the other normative principles should be observed under the guidance of the qualifying principle. Extrinsic motivations such as becoming a famous nurse are subservient to the telos or qualifying principle of care. Other examples are the practice of a musician that is aesthetically qualified and the practice of an entrepreneur that is economically qualified.

3.2.2.5. Constitutive Rules Founding and Conditioning Practice

Our educational effort to bring the learning professional to a better understanding of what constitutes vocational practice does not stop with simply knowing the telos of a practice. Practices not only function in the qualifying aspect that is related to the telos of a specific practice; they also function in all other modal aspects of which those mentioned above are most important for our purposes. These aspects also provide normative perspectives in which the meaning-kernels of those aspects function as normative principles from which rules can be derived. Among these other modal aspects, we can distinguish between the founding aspect and the conditioning aspects that, in addition to the qualifying aspect are all constitutive for the practice. From the founding aspect and its normative principle, the founding rules can be derived. The founding constitutive rules are those rules that prescribe the activities that give a particular practice its characteristic content. As we pointed out above, when these aspects are recognized in practice, it brings a certain understanding of what makes this practice, say, in the Netherlands, similar to a practice, say, in Canada.

We offer an example and description of how a foundational aspect operates. For caring practices, it has been argued that the historical as-

---

25. Tapio Puolimatka in *Moral Realism and Justification* defines the core value of the ethical aspect as a normative attitude that regards the well-being of others as intrinsically valuable. We use the word *care*, which can also be understood as the combination of benevolence and beneficence, to refer to this attitude.

pect is foundational, which in the context of this analysis of practices can best be understood as the formative or technical aspect. The state of the art of methods and techniques in a practice reflects a moment in their historical development. At the same time, it refers in particular to the formative power manifest in the possibilities to intervene technically or methodically.

Aspects other than the qualifying and founding aspects—as in the case of a caring practice, the psychic, the social, the economic, and the juridical aspects—are conditioning aspects from which the conditioning constitutive rules are derived. These rules formulate conditions that should be observed in performing a practice, but they neither define the technicalities of the practice (as the founding aspect does) nor its finality (as the qualifying aspect does). They are conditions that should be fulfilled in a competent performance of the practice.[26] In performing a practice, compliance with the founding and conditioning rules should be guided by the normative principle of the qualifying aspect. For example, in a practice of education the economic aspect requires efficient organization and use of means. However, the question of what should be realized efficiently cannot be answered by referring to the economic aspect, but only by referring to the telos, the qualifying aspect of education.

Field experience is essential to internalizing the conditioning aspects of a practice. The social, economic, and juridical rules relate to the professional practice at the micro level (e.g., individual caring relations). But these rules relate the practice to the broader institutional context of, for example, economic constraints and legislation that must also be observed in the practice. It is precisely for this reason that professionals in training cannot do without extensive internship and field experiences where they holistically and experientially come to adopt values for rating their performance. They must come to internalize these standards.

Assessment of professional performance relies on all the constitutive norms. An adequate, competent performance of a practice requires the simultaneous realization of all the constitutive rules, thereby complying with an integral normativity. In an assessment of the way in which a certain practitioner performs his or her practice, those constitutive rules function as norms. We see this illustrated in competencies, as in sidebar 7.

---

26. This is elaborated to some extent for the (founding) technical rules and the (conditioning) economic rules in work by Jan Hoogland and Henk Jochemsen titled "Professional Autonomy and the Normative Structure of Medical Practice."

SIDEBAR 7. THE CONSTITUTIVE SIDE TO COMPETENCIES

Competence-based learning utilizes sets of competencies called competency profiles. In sidebar 6, we listed the nine generic competencies holding for the profession of church worker in the Netherlands. The collection of competencies describes what performance in a certain vocation is all about. Altogether, these nine competencies reflect most rules that form the constitutive side of the practice of church worker.[27] We take as illustration the second competency of the church worker, the pastoral competency:

The pastoral competency can be defined as the capacity to support people, as individuals and groups, from a contextual point of view and when dealing with their religious and worldview issues in very diverging situations, doing so in a hermeneutically proper manner. Indicators:

- Applies the distinction between holding a regular conversation, care giving, and the pastoral performance
- Initiates pastoral care from the perspective of what is needed and required
- Applies different techniques for conversation and discussion and thereby formulates adequate pastoral diagnoses
- Recognizes and maintains the boundaries of one's own professional authority and conduct and can, by way of one's own analysis, determine possible further referrals to third parties
- Understands human behavior and the psychological and spiritual processes of such and thereby heeds pastoral care seekers in their context
- Relates to pastoral care seekers in their situations with integrity and in an ethical manner, demonstrates presence and sympathy, while taking into account a proper professional distance
- Refers to religious sources and traditions, appeals to the self-help abilities of pastoral care seekers and thereby makes them aware of their situation

---

27. By this, we do not mean competency profiles exhaust all rules that constitute a practice but rather represent authoritatively established rules designed for learning the structure of a practice.

We offer as an example the constitutive norms for a pastor. The indicators for the pastoral competency illustrate the core constitutive rules of the competency. We see here a reference to the founding and conditioning functions, which answers the question, what principles and rules is performance as a pastor based on? In other words, what is a high-performance pastor meant to do? In terms of the competency, what is a hermeneutically proper manner? The pastoral competency also refers to the qualifying function of supporting others, which answers the question, what is pastoral work for; what is its telos? In this respect, we recognize the strong social agogic component of this professional profile in the Netherlands.

We can also go on to recognize the standards that are conditional for delivery of quality in this particular form of care, such as dealing with religious context, spirituality, and worldviews. We could acknowledge in the list of indicators the conditioning factors that the pastoral worker is guided by professional requirements, applies vocational ethics, and cooperates with others. If we read between the lines, we can assume the interrelationship with the other eight competencies of a church worker. The result of such analysis of the constitutive side is that we only come to know what this particular competency is all about—its structure. We do not fully know what the competency is meant to do—its function—other than to be pastorally competent agogically.

3.2.2.6. Rules and Virtues

The rules of a profession are often followed tacitly. Competent performance of a practice requires the observation of the principles and rules of the practice. Such observation realizes its finality—its telos. As became apparent, the rules governing behavior have an implicit, tacit character. This means that rules can be followed even without a conscious decision of the practitioner at each moment they are applied.

Our understanding of virtues allows us to establish a link to the role, which MacIntyre defines for virtues in the performance of practices. Practitioners need to have certain virtues in order to competently perform a practice. In our terminology, we would say that practitioners need to have certain virtues in order to competently observe the constitutive principles and rules. In our view, virtues can be considered as the embodiments of the normative principles in stable normative attitudes of the practitioner. Hence, we agree with MacIntyre that indeed virtues are essential for a competent performance of practices.

So far, we have gained a clear insight into the architecture of a practice. We can say that the structure of a practice, or its constitutive side, can be adequately described with the aid of a Dooyeweerdian view of reality, in particular his theory of the modal aspects. However, our analysis is not yet complete. We have only dealt with the *structural* side of practices. We do not yet know why someone would want to perform professionally in a practice, nor do we yet know which standards they apply to themselves for doing so. These concern their direction, which pertains to its regulative side.

3.2.3. Regulative Side

To fully understand a practice, we have to consider not only its structural side, but also its regulative side, that of providing direction to practitioners in the concrete performance of their practice.[28] What we mean by the regulative side can be described in the following three observations:

1. Practitioners use and are influenced by their worldviews.
2. Practitioners perform according to their fundamental attitudes, beliefs, and motivations.
3. Practitioners must reflect critically on what regulates them.

We will explain below how practitioners cannot escape being regulated in these ways.

3.2.3.1. Practitioners Use Their Worldviews

Because individuals must interpret the rules of their practice, individual performance flows from the individual's worldview. To start with, the constitutive side of a practice described above embodies the normative

---

28. We realize that the regulative side (the direction) of a practice in actual performance can influence the structure to such a degree that the structure is blurred. In other words, the distinction is in practice not as sharp as the theory suggests. We acknowledge that this can be the case, but in our view this does not deny that this theoretical distinction is a useful tool to analyze practices. We even think it can help in sorting out when certain regulative beliefs are distorting the normative structure in practice. As examples, we think of the practice of medicine that accepts euthanasia as an option and the practice of the economic entrepreneur that sees the economic company as a means to increase shareholders' value instead of a social practice that is aiming at a variety of values for the different stakeholders.

constitutive principles and rules that should guide the performance of the practice. It should also provide the norms required to assess that performance. However, any performance and assessment involves a specific interpretation of the rules (e.g., the interpretation of a piece of music in a particular performance). Each practitioner carries out these rules in his or her own fashion. Such an interpretation departs from a wider interpretative framework concerning the meaning of that practice for human life and for society and, hence, on the direction that the performances of that practice should have. In addition, one's understanding of the virtues required to competently perform practices depends on a wider view of the telos of human life.[29] This wider interpretative framework is the worldview held by the practitioner. Although we do not discount the possibility that practitioners have fragmented beliefs that make up their worldviews, either consciously and explicitly or implicitly, nonetheless, their interpretations of what it is to perform as a professional have their foundations in their worldviews.

3.2.3.2. Practitioners Perform according to Their Fundamental Attitudes, Beliefs, and Motivations

The regulative side of practices pertains to motivations and beliefs about human life in the world. Such motivations and beliefs include our past, our future, our reason for existence, and the role and meaning of the practice for human life. These fundamental attitudes, beliefs, and motivations reflect a worldview. If they are religious, they also reflect the religious beliefs of the people involved. These attitudes, beliefs, and motivations are core elements in the reflection by practitioners on their own performance and their motivation to practice that specific practice.[30]

Furthermore, any performance of a practice is regulated by those worldview beliefs and religious beliefs—in other words, by the practitioner's spirituality. There is no neutral performance of a practice, even though the secular liberal understanding of society tends to claim a neutral point of view that should govern the public discourse. Particularly in our pluralist society, the beliefs and ideas that regulate the performance of practices should be open to debate.

---

29. MacIntyre, *After Virtue*, 185–87.

30. Excellent illustrations on how the practitioner's moral and spiritual frameworks influence the practice, in this case language education, can be found in D. Smith, "Moral Agency."

3.2.3.3. Practitioners Must Reflect Critically on What Regulates Them

Finally, these beliefs pertaining to the regulative side also form the reference points for a critical assessment of existing ways of performing practices by practitioners, as well as for the innovation and improvement of practices. This is a very important point. Without this explicitly critical function of the regulative side being an integral part of a full description of a practice, the concept of normative practices easily achieves a conservative and self-referential character. The fact that a certain community of practitioners accepts certain standards of excellence does not mean that those standards are the best possible. In the light of other regulative ideas, standards may need revision.

In summary, we see the regulative side of social practices as essential for a fully normative understanding of the reality of practices and of the behavior of practitioners.

3.2.4. CONSEQUENCES OF THE NRP MODEL FOR PROFESSIONAL PRACTICES AND ETHICS

Having presented the results of our analysis of social practices, the question that should be addressed now is, what are the important consequences of the NRP for the ethics of professional practices? We suggest eight that together form a coherent pattern.[31]

3.2.4.1. Professionalism Related to Telos

To start with, we hold that the professional quality of a professional does not primarily reside in his or her specialized knowledge and technical skills, but instead in the competent realization of the telos of the practice. This has two implications.

Our first inference is that the meaning of the practice does not reside primarily in measurable goals or effects of the practice but also in the *good* performance of the practice itself. For example, the meaning of giving care resides first in the good care giving itself and is not determined solely by its measurable effects on health.[32] To mention another example, the ethical quality of farming is not just directly dependent on the production volume of a hectare of land or of cattle. The way this production is achieved also counts.

---

31. See Koehn, *Ground of Professional Ethics*.
32. See Olthuis et al., "Caring Relationship in Hospice Care."

Our second inference is that ethics is not just a special kind of decision-making skill to solve ethical dilemmas that confront the practitioner. Professional ethics should not just deal with the big issues in a field, e.g., weighing the interests of shareholders versus the employees of a company. Ethical issues should be placed in the context of the integral normativity of the practice. The normativity of a practice can be formulated in its constitutive principles and rules, of which the ethical are one type, the realization of which requires the related virtues of the practitioner. The adoption of an ethical code by a business enterprise is one thing. More important is the realization of a well-understood normative structure of the business enterprise in which all the constitutive rules are observed under the guidance of the normative principle of the qualifying economic aspect.[33]

3.2.4.2. Constellation of Rules

We hold that different professional practices are to be characterized and distinguished from each other in terms of the typical constellations of the founding, conditioning, and qualifying rules, as well as by the historical state of the art with respect to the specific skills that belong to the founding aspect of that practice. The insight that, for a certain practice, the skills (or methods and techniques) used by the professionals to realize the telos of that practice are foundational and not qualifying, is crucial. It implies that practicing should not be characterized by the goal rationality (fixed ends) of technical intervention but by the normative principle of the qualifying aspect. Examples are care for caring practices, justice for juridical practices, efficiency for economically qualified practices, etc. Because the practice develops and society changes, formulation and interpretation of the principles and rules require a constant process of reflection and debate.

3.2.4.3. Output Not Morally Decisive

A similar reasoning applies to the conditioning constitutive aspects of practices. For example, economic efficiency is a principle that should be observed in caring practices as well as in education practices, to mention a few. However, if those practices are organized primarily as economic activities that are evaluated on the basis of measurable output in terms of financial return, or even of satisfaction of their users or clients, those

---

33. Verkerk and Zijlstra, "Philosophical Analysis."

practices are bound to become perverted. Patient satisfaction is not a sufficient criterion for the quality of medical care. Neither is student satisfaction for the quality of education. In our opinion, the present tendency in the Netherlands and other Western countries toward such thinking endangers the wholesome functioning of those practices and the related institutions.[34]

3.2.4.4. Clients', Patients', Employees', and Users' Voice

This means that the opinion and experience of patients, clients, employees, and other users of practices should be properly understood within practice. The integral ethical responsibility not only applies to professionals but certainly also to those they serve. Taking the practice as a focal point of our ethics does not mean that we want to lose sight of the importance of the involvement and voice of stakeholders in the decision making processes, i.e., the patient or client in caring practices, the client and employee in an economic enterprise, the citizen in public policy, etc. They should be heard in the debate on what is a desirable understanding of the telos of the specific practices. Such respect and participation are vital elements of our model, because the professional also ought to observe the psychological, social, and juridical rules of the practice. In addition, the professional ought to demonstrate the corresponding virtues of empathy, openness, and respect for freedom of choice (among others).

In the final analysis, professional practices do not exist primarily to make virtuous people out of practitioners (see point 6 below) but to render help, care, or service to people who need them. In fact, the virtues of helpfulness and readiness are indispensable for all professional practices.

3.2.4.5. Cultivation of Virtues

We have seen above that the virtues holding for the professional can be understood as the embodiment of normative principles in the professional. Hence, competent performance requires certain virtues in the professional. Therefore, professional education striving for excellence requires the cultivation of such virtues as care, respectfulness, justice, integrity, courage, truthfulness, and confidentiality.

---

34. Polder et al., "Profession, Practice, and Profits"; Reinders, *Future of the Disabled*.

Virtues and worldview interact. The valuation and cultivation of professional virtues is necessary to have professionals observe the rules of their practice as their second nature, or as their professional habitus. But the motivation to do so and the content of those virtues needs to be nourished by a broader framework of an understanding of reality, from which the professional interprets his or her practice and forms an understanding of the meaning it is supposed to have for those who need the practice. These are convictions and motivations that belong to the regulative side (see section 3.2.3).

Here is an example of convictions and motivations that belong to the regulative side: In the case of nursing, for instance, the formation of a good, virtuous, caring professional needs the mobilization and disclosure of certain beliefs and motives pertaining to the practice's regulative side.[35] In the practice of an entrepreneur, the virtues may be risk taking, inventiveness, or decisional power, among others.

3.2.4.6. Life Narrative and Moral Traditions

Ethical reflection is not limited to practices. Again, we draw upon MacIntyre for explanation. He has argued that outside social practices, people do strive for the moral good in individual life narratives and moral traditions.[36] People normally participate in a variety of practices, but their moral behavior does not coincide with these practices. In addition to a professional caring practice or managment practice, one can think of the practice of raising children, of singing in a choir, and of participating as a board member of a local political party. Each practice requires certain virtues for excellent performance in that practice.

Significantly, for the moral development of the person, each practice itself gives the practitioner opportunities to develop certain virtues as part of a virtuous life. Ideas about how a virtuous life as a whole ought to be lived relate to the regulative side of practices. Therefore, it is paramount to link professional ethics with one's individual life narrative through ideals, motives, and beliefs. Beliefs include those regarding the purpose of life, what a good life looks like, and what contribution practices should make to a good life. So, the relation between moral traditions and professional ethics largely runs via the individual's life narrative.

35. Cusveller, *Zorg Dragen*.
36. See also Higgins, "MacIntyre's Moral Theory."

Furthermore, the ideals, motives, and beliefs of the individual with respect to the good life will mostly be derived from and nourished by the moral tradition and community to which the individual confesses him- or herself. A consequence of this insight is that moral education of future professionals will only be effective if the beliefs, ideals, and motives of the individual are challenged as a resource for giving shape to the concept of a virtuous life. If we refer to this functioning of fundamental beliefs, ideals, and motives in a person with the term *spirituality*, then it is clear that we touch here on the relation between spirituality and moral formation (see chapter 4).

3.2.4.7. Practice and Normative Ethics

The concept of professional practices as presented above also provides a useful starting point for ethical evaluation of professional performance from different normative ethical perspectives. At this point, there is a direct link between our way of doing normative ethics and metaethics. The focus on the virtuous practitioner links the ethical reflection on professional performance to the virtue approach in ethics. The idea of principles and rules of a practice to be followed in competent performance provides an opening for deontological reflection. In addition, the notion of the telos, the finality of the practice, implies that also the teleological and consequentialist approaches must contribute to the ethical analysis and assessment of moral conduct in practices. By combining the different perspectives in what we call a responsibility ethics, we want to refer to our understanding of the human being as *homo respondent* and stress the integrality of the individual's responsibility.[37]

3.2.4.8. Common Ground

The interaction of worldview with the norms of a practice creates a common ground of norms of practice from which a plurality of worldviews can be discussed. The practice-based ethics of professional practices recognizably does justice to the importance of worldview and religious beliefs. At the same time, the insight that professional practices have a finality of their own and a certain normative structure that should be followed in order to achieve that finality does not directly depend on an

---

37. Jochemsen and Glas, *Verantwoord Medisch Handelen*, 174–218; Jochemsen, *Ethiek van de Zorg*, 49–71; Jochemsen, "Christian Medical Ethics."

individual's beliefs.[38] Hence, this view on professional activities can, on the one hand, help Christians to express their faith in their professional performance. On the other hand, it can provide a common ground for moral reflection and debate in a pluralist society and also create opportunities to show the relevance of the Christian faith to realizing the finality of social practices in our fragmented society.

3.3. Conclusion

In this section, we introduced a model that calls for the professional to willingly accept morality while engaging in excellent performance in a certain practice. We called this the adoption of the ethics of professional practice, and we provided a philosophical support for this ethics in the NRP model.

The NRP model holds that professional practices can be understood as normative practices that possess an intrinsic normativity. This intrinsic normativity can be described as a constellation of principles and norms. This is an ethics that can be applied by practitioners and learned by students.

We have pointed out that CBL, as devised for professional curricula, must take the constitutive and regulative sides of vocational practices into account. The assessment of whether a student is fully competent thus involves their ability to deal with various types of normativity belonging to that particular vocation. The student is called upon to differentiate and acknowledge those factors that determine the moral quality of a practice. Knowing the difference between constitutive and regulative norms and values is essential for engaging in CBL.

The NRP model also provides a useful concept that can help bridge the gap between normative ethical theories and everyday practice of the profession that is often experienced by professionals. Morally sound practice involves the observance of all the principles and norms of the practice. This not only implies certain normative constraints for the practitioner but also certain virtues, as well as a degree of freedom, a professional discretionary power.

For realizing the full range of normativity of the practice, the normative reflective practitioner needs to be able to reflect on his or her

---

38. Of course, our analysis of practices itself has ultimately a worldview background. But being an analysis in general philosophical terms, in our view it has sufficient distance to a specific worldview for being acceptable across worldviews.

professional performance, both with respect to the constitutive side and the regulative side. This means that practitioners must be able to reflect and communicate on their regulative ideas with respect to their practice and the values it is supposed to realize, as well as on their motives to work in their specific practice.

4. PROFILES AND THE REGULATIVE SIDE OF PROFESSIONAL PRACTICES

4.1. Having a Moral Profile

In this section, we examine the profiles that regulate practice. In chapter 1, we introduced the notion of profile. We are interested how we choose a profile, because professional vocational training requires candidates to have a certain successful shape or appearance before entering a licensed practice. Students are increasingly being asked whether their identity fits a certain competency profile, a vocational profile, or a practice profile. They are put under pressure to shape themselves to a certain professional mold. That shape is their profile.

We have also determined that the *Bild* (or image of oneself) is crucial for Bildung, the moral formation practices found in Western civilizations. We have held that the core of this Bild is the individual's spirituality. However, the way we choose a professional profile using spirituality is by way of morality. We call that the choice of moral profile because we do this from our understanding of who we are as moral persons and what the professional practice we want to belong to requires of us in terms of professional ethics. Why we choose a moral profile is inherent in how we see ourselves as moral persons. We are saying here that any student seriously intending to be a "good" professional aims to be a moral person in that profession, and that is a matter of choosing a moral profile.

We illustrate this from the work by Patricia Benner et al. in professional education. Based on their research, which included surveys and site visits, they studied students' and educators' experiences in nursing education. One of their major findings was that American nursing programs are very effective in forming professional identity and ethical comportment.[39] Along the lines treated above, they emphasized that the

---

39. Benner et al., *Educating Nurses*, 11.

nursing practice requires a flexible and nuanced ability to interpret a not-yet-defined situation as an instance of something *salient* that should call forth an appropriate practitioner response. They posed the question: "How does the student nurse learn to recognize possible good and less-than-optimal ends in an actual clinical situation?"[40] In PISA, we say with conviction that this is best done by moral formation of the student in the context of the practice. Benner et al. point out convincingly that today's practitioners must be able to draw upon all they learn (including cognitive knowledge, skills, and affective learning) in each of the professional apprenticeships, and they must be able to integrate these in practice. This is accomplished in the context of a high degree of normativity. It also requires that students as well as educators are confident that they can do so. In other words, their command of their own moral profile must be accurate.

In this section, we examine how this takes place within the context of normative practices. To introduce this approach, we turn to Timothy Wineberg's contemporary and thorough study of ethical narratives and profiles in vocations.[41] The fact that Wineberg writes from the locus of the care practices (teaching in particular) does not diminish the value of his model for all professions. What follows is a discussion of the highlights of this model, as well as important requirements for deep reflection.

Wineberg conceptualizes the notion of professional profiles through metaphorical images that serve as directive moral categories in education. For the profession of teaching, he delineates the ethical profiles of teacher-servant, teacher–moral friend, teacher-mentor, teacher-covenanter, and teacher–moral companion. Each of these profiles has an ethics to support it. Wineberg discusses each in detail. Each of these metaphors also presupposes certain practices that support adopting the profiles. The first standard in his ethics is that becoming someone in a profession requires having an ethical image, or a profile of what it is like to be a person laboring in that profession.

We see this, for instance, in how Wineberg treats the profile of the teacher as "servant." This is a moral profile that many committed Christians may adopt in their teaching, only to encounter the many hazards of taking a stance of sacrificial help vis-à-vis students. Hence,

---

40. Ibid., 15. See Commissie Kwalificatiestructuur, *Gekwalificeerd Voor de Toekomst*, for Dutch framework.

41. Wineberg, *Professional Care*.

the question arises, how can a teacher negotiate the desirability of servanthood with its feasibility? Wineberg's answer is to adopt a proper ethics of sacrifice, which is a moral stance enabling an attentiveness and responsiveness to the particularities of the persons and tasks around us, and allowing us "to respond to students with care and love." Yet, seriously adopting this stance in deep reflection needs explicit recognition, for instance, of the truth that "loving service cannot be compelled; it can only be given freely."[42]

The key point here is that, to realize such a high ethical stance in a feasible way, significant *contemplation* is needed, thereby achieving a core quality that we term deep reflection. "Contemplation involves a disciplined detachment from the willful machinations of the self, as it opens our hearts in attentiveness to the particularities of the persons and tasks around us."[43] This implies that aiming for the moral profile of servant requires exercising central focal practices in a serious effort to not only achieve one's moral choice to be such but also to avoid the pitfalls of the desired moral profile—no small feat.

In the ethics of professional practice we have put forward above, knowledge of the constellation of principles and norms that make up professional practices are indispensable for the choice of a moral profile. In the following, we point out how certain moral profiles serve a *regulative* function for a professional who wants to follow the NRP approach. We will determine that this particular choice, in turn, may influence how one performs within the practice.

In their turn, these profiles color the practices involved. They provide normative direction for professional conduct. We illustrate this by pointing out that current modern moral profiles in care and social work display a responsiveness to certain ethical aspects of the practice. In other words, moral profiles reflect the normative character of the practice to a certain extent. At the same time, they depend on a very high degree of competency in those practices with respect to the institutional rules.

We described two profiles found in modern nursing: the patient advocate and the skilled companion. We continue with two profiles used in modern social work in the Netherlands: the creative professional and the presence worker. In all four profiles, morality is carried out in explicit and sometimes implicit ways. Each of these profiles can be taught

42. Ibid., 37.
43. Ibid.

to students in their respective professional practices. Their adoption of a certain profile makes a moral statement, thereby to a certain extent also characterizing them as persons, at least as far as the practitioner wants to be recognized as such, but not without cognizance of the professional practice involved.

Hence, in the following section, we show with four examples how the normativity of the practice and the moral profile of the practitioner mutually reinforce each other.

4.2. Profile of the Patient Advocate

The moral profile of the patient advocate is defined and described as follows. A patient advocate can be typified as an active representative of the patient.[44] A care provider using this profile serves as a promoter and as a voice for patients, in particular when they are insufficiently able to protect their own interests. We commonly see this profile used by nurses who want to act as go-betweens for vulnerable patients in dealing with medics and other professionals. The conduct belonging to this profile can be qualified in terms of normativity of practical conduct reflecting constitutive principles of the practice of nursing: informing the patient of the situation and advancing informed consent; empowering the patient and defending the autonomy of the patient; defending the rights and the interests of patients in situations where they are unable to do so themselves; ensuring that patients gain full access and disclosure of available sources; supporting the patient, despite costs involved; and supporting the views and feelings of the patient and not just his or her needs.[45] These principles reflect aspects of good practice and demonstrate the excellence of nursing. The ethics of the profile strongly comply with human rights ethics, and also with deontological morality.

The negative side of this moral profile should be moderated by regulative principles. The shadow side to pursuing the profile of patient advocate is that a nurse risks becoming paternalistic. Paternalism is a disposition not infrequently reflected among nurses. Or, even worse, it may involve dissonances in the event that the nurse is prompted by the patient to engage in bizarre and dangerous matters or in the event that the nurse through representation of the patient runs into a conflict of

---

44. See Van der Arend, "De Verpleegkundige"; Benner et al., *Educating Nurses*.
45. Schwartz, "Is There an Advocate?"

conscience.[46] Clearly, adopting such a moral profile is not without risks to the practitioner. It places the need for certain balancing virtues (i.e., prudence) in the foreground. Therefore, according to the Dutch nursing scientist Arie van der Arend, the profile of patient advocate is not always positively appreciated.[47] Whether professionals will be able to follow this profile well depends on certain factors. These can be: their working attitude and relations with patients, their internalization of the values and interests of the organization, their perception of their tasks, their rewards (pay), their ability to work within the limits of the profession, and their experience of multiple loyalties (to their profession, colleagues, and organization). Together, these factors require strong regulative principles because one's morality is integrally related to the context in which one has to perform as an advocate.

This profile requires the balance of considerations to tip toward patient advocacy. The regulative side of this profile requires that a nurse adopting it has the disposition to ensure that, all things considered, the advocacy interests of the patient prevail.[48] This profile thus requires that a nurse have a strong character. The related virtues in this profile allow a nurse to demonstrate being morally involved. Nevertheless, this cannot take place without strict cognizance of the best practices, as well as a competent performance.

4.3. Profile of the Skilled Companion

A prominent development in the ethics of nursing concerns the conceptual framework of skilled companionship designed by Angie Tichen and introduced by the Belgian nursing scientists Patricia Claessens and Bernadette Dierckx de Casterlé.[49] In this model, the profile of skilled companion is advanced as the image of an expert who demonstrates a certain type of companionship or friendship toward patients. This could also be the profile of a physician practicing in long-term care.

Skilled companionship clearly builds on various constitutive conditions holding for good nursing care. It can be visualized metaphorically as an onion with many layers. The core of the onion is the relationship

46. Ibid.
47. Van der Arend, "De Verpleegkundige," 24.
48. See Van der Arend, "De Verpleegkundige"; Schwartz, "Is There an Advocate?"
49. See Claessens and Dierckx de Casterlé, "Skilled Companionship"; Dierckx de Casterlé et al., *Verpleegkundig Beroep*.

between the caregiver and the care receiver (the nurse and the patient). Moving outward from this inner core, four processes appear that together form the relational domain of skilled companionship (graceful care, particularity, reciprocity, and mutuality). Embodied in professional behavior, they refer to virtues that are integrated into strategies (intentionality, temporality, and saliency), which in turn influence nursing conduct, such as knowing, sensing, perceiving, intuiting, being, becoming, feeling, engaging, and doing. When we move toward the outside ring of the onion, we meet the regulative principles in this moral profile.

In analyzing the outer regulative layer, we encounter a mix of deontological and teleological morality. The profile of skilled companion is very complex. It requires a structure in practice, which is provided by the telos of beneficence or humane care. In addition, this profile—sometimes called critical companionship—is a reflection of how the skilled companion assists others in developing expertise by sharing in the experiential relations of being ill. In this way, skilled companions behave as partners to those involved in a quest for meaning. A skilled companion is presented as someone who can be trusted in this quest, or as a supporter who truly is interested in the growth, development, and improvement of the client or patient. In this respect, they follow a morality of virtue ethics.

Maintaining this moral profile is not possible without a very good command of the rules of practice, which is the constitutive side to nursing. Similar to the profile of the patient advocate, only the most proficient nurses are normally in a position to follow this profile, which demonstrates that a sound moral profile cannot be achieved without the necessary competencies.

4.4. Profile of the Creative Professional

The Dutch National Curricular Council Social Pedagogical Care published an extensive document in 1999 outlining the profiles and qualifications for social workers working in long-term institutional care situations.[50] The most generic profile for the social pedagogical profes-

---

50. Landelijk Opleidingsoverleg SPH, *Creatieve Professional*. In the Netherlands, social pedagogical care (*Sociaal Pedagogische Hulpverlening*) traditionally has been distinguished from social work (*Maatschappelijk Werk en Dienstverlening*); the former mainly oriented on group work and institutional care and the latter on case management and prevention. Both varieties are now in the process of merging into one discipline of social work.

sional was then called the creative professional. The image of this professional on the bachelor level is that of a resourceful and proficient person able to design standard solutions to problems yet also able to let go of rule-governed practices to seek new and often unorthodox solutions to difficult problems that may arise. A combination of the right dispositions form the core of this moral profile. Like other nursing profiles, this profile also demands a high standard of performance.

Being creative is the key aspect of this moral profile. The profile of the creative professional is of a person who is able to proceed with discretion based on theoretical insight. A creative professional is able to warrant choices made in the company of social workers and other professional colleagues, which requires reticulate skills. Even more so, this profile calls for persons having a certain artistic-agogical [Dutch: *muzisch-agogisch*] character. Another way of putting it is that they are not limited by an unimaginative character. The foremost dispositions in this profile are being articulate, resourceful, and ingenious, including being able to design unorthodox solutions to new problems and situations that are accepted by colleagues.[51] This profile typifies the central role that a social pedagogical professional occupies in the daily lives of people who, due to special circumstances, impairments, and obstacles, are dependent on specific types of care to function socially in meaningful ways.

We cannot understand its quality without recognizing the strong regulative function of the moral disposition involved. A creative disposition is necessary to take the context of the client continually into account and to actively ensure the daily common life of clients in their living context. The expertise of the creative professional goes beyond the programs (oft ad hoc) geared toward the ability of clients to live meaningful and acceptable lives, by supporting their social integration and their autonomy within social competence–based structures.

Being creative presupposes a mastering of the constitutive rules of the practice. It also presupposes an orientation to the best possible help for the client. Here it is evident that the constitutive and the regulative principles of social pedagogical care interrelate in the profile of the creative professional.

The weakness of the creative professional moral profile is that it must be balanced by a strong virtue of accountability. This moral profile

51. Ibid., 3.

requires a very strong ethic of responsibility on the part of the practitioner. This is not so much having a proper psychological disposition but having the right habitus (basic attitude) of accountability. When positive outcomes in large part depend on creativity and on a teleological morality, the call for accountability, trust, and concern for justice increases.

4.5. Profile of the Presence Practitioner

The profile of the presence practitioner was developed by Andries Baart primarily for pastoral workers. Later this view was developed for the agogical disciplines, including social work and pedagogy.[52] This profile describes the type of practitioner characterized by being there for others without focusing directly on problem solving. Baart does not dissociate problem solving from the presence practitioners' performance; it can indeed emerge from their efforts, but that is not their overt intention.[53] This marks the profile as strongly bound to virtuousness.

The main characteristics of the presence practitioner are distinctive. First, presence practitioners tend to follow others rather than expect others to come to them (e.g., for an office appointment). This tendency applies to time as well as place: they follow the life rhythm of those they seek to serve, on a daily and long-term basis. Second, presence practitioners also, according to the theory, work in an integrated fashion, seeking to immerse themselves in an unfragmented and unconditional way into the whole life systems of others. A third characteristic of presence practitioners Baart identifies is the tendency to involve themselves in life as it is actually lived. That is, they seek connections with others not only in the problematic areas of their lives but also in the mundane and joyous aspects of their daily lives. Fourthly, presence practitioners tend to prioritize the good of the other, keeping a low profile for themselves and opening themselves (attuning themselves) to the agenda and life world of the other. Finally, presence practitioners, according to Baart, find meaning in the experience of encountering one another. That is, they value making a difference in the lives of others, but they also value that the reverse is true as well: those encountered are allowed to make a difference in the life of the presence practitioners. In table 1, we find a table drawn up by Schilling to explain how this profile coheres.

---

52. See for general treatment: Baart, *Theorie van de Presentie*; Baart and Steketee, *Wat Aandachtige*; Schilling, "Presence Approach"; for an application in teaching, de Muynck, *Christelijk Leraarschap*.

53. Baart and Van Heijst, "Inleiding."

TABLE 1. PRESENCE PROFILE[54]

CHARACTERISTIC	ASSOCIATED TENDENCY
1. Mobility, in place and time	1. Following the other
2. Space and boundaries	2. Working in an integrated fashion
3. Seeking connection	3. Being involved in lived life
4. Attuning oneself	4. Prioritizing the good of the other
5. Meaningfulness	5. Counting for one another

The moral profile of the presence practitioner describes its telos rather than its constitutive principles. The profile of the presence practitioner is especially laden with social moral values and as such is highly virtuous in its nature. The constitutive principles of regular social work are substituted by a focus on the telos of the care for people within or without standard procedures. In this respect, Baart avoids the technicistic, interventionist, goal-oriented approach to care (goal rationality) he ascribes to regular social work. Instead, he chooses the personal approach, emphasizing humane values (value rationality). Criticism has focused on Baart's dissociation of the two; there is no clear view of integral professional performance. The practice of the presence practitioner is seen as a complement to the agogical conduct of professionals.[55] The emphasis is on the maintenance of the moral profile of demonstrating presence, which calls upon a strong sense of morality, which regulates the conduct of the practitioner.

4.6. Profiles Regulate Practice

The above analysis of four moral profiles demonstrates how they reinforce moral practices in two professions. Our analysis of four modern moral profiles for practitioners, with examples drawn from two different care practices, clearly demonstrates how the normativity of these practices and certain moral profiles mutually reinforce each other for the practitioner. We have shown that each profile contains a distinct notion of the direction in which the care is to go. In this way, the profiles regulate the practice. At the same time, we note that such regulation of practice is not possible without very clear evidence of competency of practitioners in the practices themselves.

---

54. Schilling, "Presence Approach in New York."
55. De Muynck, *Christelijk Leraarschap*.

We draw three conclusions from this analysis. First, the role of virtues in a moral profile varies in intensity. The way in which morality colors a profile varies by profile. Even though virtuousness is apparent in all profiles, the degree to which a person must and can demonstrate virtue varies by profile. This last point is illustrated, for instance, by the great need for caution and prudence in sustaining the profile of the patient advocate.

Second, each moral profile captures the most relevant aspects of its practice. The internal coherence in all of the profiles examined is great enough to capture the most relevant properties of the professional practice itself. An exception could be the profile of the presence practitioner. It was devised originally as an alternative to another interventionist profile in social work.

Finally, we see how each of the moral profiles discussed contains basic ethical notions of wellness of patient or client that clearly impinge on the conduct of the practitioner. Clearly, these profiles are integrally connected with philosophies of care, and in particular the ethics of care, taken broadly. Some profiles may have indistinct expectations of the morality involved, as, for instance, the creative professional. Nonetheless, each profile discussed represents core values belonging to the social practice.

These three conclusions affirm our conviction that professional practices are demonstrably normative. The direction that is chosen by adopting a moral profile regulates the interpretation and discretionary choices of practitioners. It appears to us that this is precisely one of the most important functions of a moral profile: its cohesive self-image provides a sense of direction for the practitioner.

5. CONCLUSION: BEING PRACTICE MINDED

Viewing moral formation from the window of condition P generates several perspectives that we summarize here:

- In PISA, the practice for professionals is normative and guided by ethics.
- The focus on practitioners in PISA qualifies a choice of a moral profile.
- PISA provides a normative framework for outcome-based education.

In this chapter, the condition P was outlined both as a view and as an ethics of practice. We began by examining how competence-based learning (CBL) in higher education must be buttressed by Bildung and moral formation. We argued that employing CBL in curricula creates the need for knowledge of the normativity of practices. We have explained how the model of normative practices serves as an educational instrument in learning the normativity of practice. The normative practices model describes what a vocational practice possesses in terms of values and norms. It delineates the framework in which the professional operates and places the competencies that professionals use within the proper context. Any curriculum using CBL must use this constellation of norms for teaching competencies.

We do not underrate the difficulties in applying the ethical demands of this model. We saw in our examination of modern moral profiles in nursing and social work that the demands for morality of the practitioner are as high as the demands for their competence proficiency. In this respect, CBL can enhance or upgrade a learning outcome but, we argue, not without including strategies for the moral formation of students.

We conclude that moral formation using the PISA model must involve a solid didactical approach in order to achieve moral formation outcomes. This conclusion leads us in the next chapter to the condition I, where we examine how becoming integral in learning aids us in achieving the standards of condition P, being practice minded.

3

I: Being Integral

1. INTRODUCTION

IN THIS CHAPTER, WE will define and describe the second condition for moral professional practice—being integral. We use the shorthand of the letter I to denote this. As the second of condition of PISA, being integral is essentially an educational strategy of deep reflection. In common language, integral means "necessary to make a whole complete."[1] Being integral is a prominent feature of moral formation, which requires a hanging together, a cohesiveness of sorts, or a wholeness. Such an integrative quality has an attractive, almost golden ring to it.

Yet, we must ask, what precisely is being holistic, or becoming integrated, or having integrity? Our response calls upon lofty ideals. Being integral stands for a life in harmony. A harmonious life is in touch with reality, particularly realities about ourselves and our environment. Often such rootedness in reality is the wellspring of practical wisdom. To put it succinctly, being integral entails a certain kind of good character. Consider the commonly held belief that a good professional is one who can perform in an all-inclusive way. A good professional performs with integrity because he or she is a person *uit één stuk*, the Dutch phrase for a person of character, literally "out of one piece." Many educators of professionals believe that being solid in this way will enhance the exercise of good judgment.

Consequently, a graduating business student is trained not only in various capabilities. More importantly, we argue, the student should be coached to develop an overall personal accountability for high per-

---

1. *New Oxford Dictionary*, s.v. "integral."

formance within the work situation. While students perform, they integrate various qualities and competencies that come to form a whole within them, thereby helping them to gain and maintain their integrity. These statements lead to the question, can such almost-heroic values be learned in an academic setting? This issue occupies the current chapter.

The usage of the term *integral* refers to "what is necessary to make a whole complete." The term *integrative* or *integrated* refers to "combining things to make a whole." *Integrity* refers to "the state of being whole and undivided." We see these definitions as distinctions between the principle, the process, and the effect of the function of being whole. In this chapter, we focus on the principle and process. In chapter 5, we return to the virtue and psychology of having integrity and thereby its effect.

Traditionally, being whole has been a core goal of education. Being whole is an age-old quest that coincides with Bildung to form orderly and well-adjusted citizens. It is the call to live in touch with reality, which the previous chapter encapsulated in the intrinsic normativity of practices. The key implication for professional education is that norms of practices can be taught.

In this chapter, we go on to explore how the learner fits the whole by being able to be responsive in a harmonious way in various roles and practices of education. We therefore follow up on the P in PISA by regarding the student in context. That is, we acknowledge the student as a learning person living *coram Deo* (before the face of God) in social contexts, in particular the social context of education.

We use the practice of higher education to demonstrate what it means to be integral. We describe how a student adopts a moral profile and follows basic notions of harmony to become a good professional. Our central claim is that the student cannot become integral without knowing thoroughly what the intrinsic normativity of practice means for him or her. The student must be able to understand the normativity of practice from the understanding of education as practice. For deep reflection to be meaningful in professional training, the student and his or her teacher (mentor, trainer, and coach) must have a thorough understanding of the guiding function of education.

In our treatment of wholeness, we see the condition I embodied in the new learning, in particular in the current vogues of competency-based learning and social constructivism. According to these perspectives on learning, full competence is the aptitude to bring knowledge, attitude, and skills together in a professional performance. We see here an implication of what we term virtuousness. We will deal in this chapter with two prominent virtues found in new learning: authenticity and practical wisdom. We will seek a balance between the two in deep reflection on being integral.

We do not underestimate the requirement to be integral. Applying it means that the student must be aware of the direction of his or her own formation by choosing a personal profile that embodies wholeness. Because wholeness is a very high standard to achieve, students can encounter it as an obstacle rather than a competency, because it can seem so hard to achieve. The danger here is that students adopt a negative and inaccurate view of themselves as unable to achieve wholeness. It is easy to question who can meet such a high standard. For these reasons, we will have to select with care and pragmatism the expectations that figure in the Bildung of the student.

As a result of these important considerations, we endeavor to provide a practical ethics based on the notion of being integral, which we describe as an ethics of responsibility. All parties involved in the development of moral profiles in CBL must follow this complex web of responsibilities. The fact of this necessity also reveals much about being integral in the practice of higher education.

2. THE IDEAL OF BEING INTEGRAL

2.1. Being Integral or Dual

Dualistic approaches to learning conflict with integral (constructivist and Christian) approaches. In chapter 1, we encountered the idea found in Western circles that universities have no business requiring a certain morality of their students. This we now characterize as a clear case of dualism, whereby the moral (together with the spiritual) is divorced from other aspects of learning; the personal sphere is isolated from the public or scientific sphere. This portrayal complies with the liberal idea that higher education has no business addressing personal values and so may ignore a student's religious and spiritual ideas. Such dualism not only conflicts with our model of normative practices put forward in chapter 2; it also conflicts strongly with the modern idea that students need to learn integrally, as found in constructivist philosophies of education. It may even conflict with Christian practices.

A somewhat unusual example of the clash between integral and dual learning is given in sidebar 8. This case received much attention in the early months of 2007 and is quite interesting for Christians adhering to the normativity of integral learning. It addresses a nonintegral approach—actually, a type of dualism found in Christian circles.

> **SIDEBAR 8.**
> **BELIEVING SCRIPTURE BUT PLAYING BY SCIENCE'S RULES[2]**
>
> There is nothing much unusual about the 197-page dissertation Marcus R. Ross submitted in December to complete his doctoral degree in geosciences here at the University of Rhode Island.
>
> His subject was the abundance and spread of mosasaurs, marine reptiles that, as he wrote, vanished at the end of the Cretaceous era about 65 million years ago. The work is "impeccable," said David E. Fastovsky, a paleontologist and professor of geosciences at the university who was Dr. Ross's dissertation adviser. "He was working within a strictly scientific framework, a conventional scientific framework."
>
> But Dr. Ross is hardly a conventional paleontologist. He is a "young earth creationist"—he believes that the Bible is a literally true account of the creation of the universe, and that the earth is at most 10,000 years old.
>
> For him, Dr. Ross said, the methods and theories of paleontology are one "paradigm" for studying the past, and Scripture is another. In the paleontological paradigm, he said, the dates in his dissertation are entirely appropriate. The fact that as a young earth creationist he has a different view just means, he said, "that I am separating the different paradigms."
>
> He likened his situation to that of a socialist studying economics in a department with a supply-side bent. "People hold all sorts of opinions different from the department in which they graduate," he said. "What's that to anybody else?"

The *New York Times* article concerned thorny philosophical and practical questions and raised the question of "whether it was intellectually honest to write a dissertation so at odds with his religious views."[3] The issue

---

2. Dean, "Believing Scripture."
3. Ibid.

in the article concerned mainly the morality of the dualism of profiles attributed to Dr. Ross. This question about having more than one profile in a professional practice concerns the condition of being integral. Is it virtuous—according to virtues of honesty and integrity—to work within one paradigm according to the profile of the paleontologist (the supposed secular paradigm) and simultaneously to hold on to the profile of being a young earth creationist? The question goes even deeper: is it bad not to be integral? Must we always be integral?

We cannot give a good answer to the question of whether Dr. Ross is virtuous or not, but we can say that being integral may depend on where we draw the line. If Dr. Ross holds that his practice of paleontology is completely separate from his practice of faith, then his personal stance of "what is that to anybody else" holds. However, if we take the practice of paleontology to be broader than the narrow practice of paleontology and see it as part of the profession of secular science, then faith matters cannot be avoided, and his dualism should be a focal point for scrutiny. The issue of being integral and virtuous is then unavoidable. So, being integral also depends on how one defines the range and normativity of one's practice. It depends on what we believe must be connected.

2.2. The Call to Be Integral

The call to be integral is not solely a Christian crusade. Many in the secular realm of teaching are bothered that even well-designed curricula do not always harvest good integral qualities in their graduates. This void impacts business studies, which is the most popular major in American colleges. The risk for business studies is that its graduates may not possess the required moral competencies to become good citizens. Studies show that the more courses they take in business, the less students are active in citizenship. Citizenship is a desired social moral profile for a professional.[4] Derek Bok even points to a lack of being integral in the way certain curricula in business studies are not assimilated with moral formation:

> Management studies seem to have an adverse effect on some important aims of a college education. After surveying many thousands of undergraduates, Alexander Astin found that majoring in business is negatively correlated with appreciation of

---

4. Bok, *Underachieving Colleges*, 182.

other cultures and interest in promoting racial understanding. Norman Nie and Sunshine Hillygus report that taking business courses leads to lower voting rates and lower political and civic involvement.[5]

Bok concludes that, whatever the cause, the findings are distressing, since they not only run counter to the aims of undergraduate education but also contradict what most companies claim to want in the students they hire. This is not just an anomaly of business schools, since similar findings hold for engineering studies.[6] This lack of integrity becomes understandable when we realize that students may not regard their education as building a public good, but rather as a private investment in future earning capacity. This is one of the reasons why many American colleges have engaged in extracurricular efforts to improve on the quality of moral formation, in forms of community service, including service learning.[7]

The next question to address is, do Christian schools fare any better?

2.3. Head, Heart, and Hands

We expect Christians to follow the call to be integral. The high moral standards of the Bible set a Christian standard of becoming whole in the coveted sacred realm. Even dualists can agree with this standard. The implication is that education and learning must involve what the Bible calls our "heart" so that our lives may become meaningful wholes. This type of coherence harks back to basic notions, which we now explore.

Being integral in education means learning with "everything that you have." An older and attractive metaphor used here is *head, heart, and hands*.[8] This image requires more than just emphasizing the profile of using one's "hands" in education; it involves three main dimensions of being human. The "heart" stands for our soul, spirit, or innermost commitment; the "head" for all our intelligences, cognitive as well as affective; and the "hands" for our ability to perform. We discover in this metaphor a maxim that the person is a whole composed of integral parts. Yet, the metaphor is more than just a charming reference to the nature of humans.

---

5. Ibid., 303.
6. Bok, *Underachieving Colleges*.
7. Gunst Heffner and DeVries Beversluis, *Commitment and Connection*.
8. Hegeman, Kole, and Jochemsen, *Hoofd, Hart, en Handen*; Hollinger, *Head, Heart, and Hands*.

Head, heart, and hands refers as metaphor to more than three main motivational systems that affect people. In our approach, we follow the guidelines set out by Hollinger to avoid our natural tendency to adopt one system only. We share with Hollinger the vision to bring head, heart, and hands together in mutual reinforcement.[9] What holds for the faith practice, as pointed out by Hollinger, holds also for the moral formation practice in higher education.

Being integral is not to be limited to our view of humanity. Head, heart, and hands is not a simplistic human-model. It supposes that a person with his or her entire being is part of a tradition, a way of life, and a context that calls for being connected. Using this metaphor is also more than merely acknowledging the parts involved. It is more the differentiation of skills (hands) from what we know (head) and believe (heart) and then the recombinination of the three components. The core of the metaphor is acknowledging how one's performance flows from one's belief system, lifestyle, biography, and community. It focuses our attention on our ability to live meaningful lives in a holistic way.

The metaphor of head, heart, and hands calls for the cohesion between significant elements in one's life. The ideal involved harks back to an ancient version of CBL—the medieval guild. The guild was made up of experienced and confirmed experts in their field of handicraft. They were called master craftsmen. Before a new employee could rise to the level of master craftsman, he had to learn the basics of the craft as an apprentice. After this period he could rise to the level of journeyman (Dutch: *ambachtsgezel, knecht*; German: *Geselle*). After being employed by a master for several years, and after producing a qualifying piece of work, the apprentice was granted the rank of journeyman. He was commonly given documents (letters or certificates from his master or the guild itself) that certified him as a journeyman and entitled him to travel to other towns and countries to learn the art from other masters. These journeys were an unofficial way of communicating new methods and techniques. After this journey and several years of experience, a journeyman could be received as a master craftsman.

While guilds as described no longer exist, many practices continue the apprentice-journeyman-master model. Even in academia, the tradition survives, with PhD students as apprentices, post-docs as journeymen, and professors as masters.

9. Hollinger, *Head, Heart, and Hands*, 33.

In the apprenticeship situation, the novice learns knowledge, skills, and attitudes as part of a community where head, heart, and hands are joined together. Becoming a journeyman was a choice of a particular life involving journeys as forays into new knowledge and experience. One's entire being became involved in the quest for becoming a master craftsman. This sense of being integral or having wholeness in one's craft implies having a coherent sense of whom one is (*Bild*) and where one is going and performing accordingly in a certain practice. Being integral was needed to become a master craftsman. In this example, the bond between head, heart, and hands allowed the journeyman to achieve excellence.

We should therefore not assume that head, heart, and hands is an exclusively Christian mantra for learning. The maxim that our heart really matters for our job is found in many situations. An unattractive but realistic case in point would be the suspicion held by the director of a hospital concerning the integrity of the orthodox Christian woman applying for a position as nurse on the gynecology ward. Considering that the hospital engages in practices of abortion, the director is concerned whether the nurse will be able to demonstrate empathy for women seeking abortions who in the nurse's view are living lives contrary to biblical morality. If she believes abortion to be wrong, can she be authentic in this position? Or, could it be that she would be faking her loyalty in order to do undercover exposés (a serious possibility if it would concern a private abortion clinic)? In essence, is she trustworthy? These are questions about how our innermost feelings affect our performances—whether or not our hearts are in it. These questions may be daily fare for orthodox Christians in such practices, but they certainly belong to a nonsecular expectation of congruency in "head, heart, and hands." We are facing here the demand to position ourselves as persons seeking integrity in a social practice.

The metaphor of head, heart, and hands in principle assumes the broader sense of a practice in which practitioners have roles and do not simply carry out tasks in a narrow sense. This implies that it is not simply doing things but being somebody in a role that counts. Christians may rightfully complain about being discriminated against when a suspicion that they do not fit a role disqualifies them, but most of us would not want to have it otherwise, because, on some level, most of us sense that being integral is good. The notion of being integral is basic, even when our job prospects are affected.

As we mentioned in chapter 2, professional practices are unmistakably connected to tradition and community. Here practices involving head, heart, and hands are carried over within communities. Implicitly, we assume that character education takes place in these situations—that head, heart, and hands are bound together in community. Each student entering a curriculum brings with him or her a background and legacy. Students enter into the new communities—educational and vocational—as they learn new aptitudes. In organizational terms, we call these communities of practice (often abbreviated as CoP).

2.4. The Importance of Communities in Being Integral

Support for being integral comes from the sociology of learning, but not solely for the sake of being integral. Bok's indictment, treated above, calls upon our understanding that vocational people are successful in gaining certain working identities. We assume that high-quality professional schools similarly aim at delivering qualified apprentices for a highly complex professional environment. If so, then support for Bok's call for developing the proper character comes from the social scientist Etienne Wenger.[10] A primary focus of Wenger's work is on learning as social participation. He views the individual as an active participant in the practices of social communities and in the construction of his or her identity through these communities. In Wenger's approach, the character formation of a person in terms of a social identity requires acknowledgement of the environment of social practices. His work implies that higher education ought to provide environments for learning the required identities through participation in communities.

The point here is to recognize that social participation and learning (Wenger calls this reification) presuppose each other. Participation is the social experience of living in the world in terms of membership in social communities and active involvement in social enterprises.[11] Reification, i.e., learning, refers to engagement with the world as productive of meaning. The latter consists of projecting meanings (images and metaphors) on the world and perceiving them as existing in the world with a reality of their own.[12] Reification is an essential part of gaining knowledge.

---

10. Wenger, *Communities of Practice*.
11. Ibid., 55.
12. Ibid., 57–58.

Now, it may not be the case that all learning requires social participation, but it certainly is the case that moral learning without social participation is doomed to fail. The clue here is that morality, or knowing good and evil, requires knowledge of oneself. Self-knowledge is preeminently a matter of gaining an identity of self through social participation. This premise is an important part of the moral philosophy of social constructivism.[13]

The negotiation of identity, which is the basic function of apprenticeship and education, occurs in community. Wenger makes the related point that apprenticeship in a practical community is not instantaneous, but rather it is a broad experience of coming into that community. We see this in the characteristics of social identity.[14] In this respect, identity is not the same as having a self-image; it is produced by undergoing a lived experience of participation in a specific community. This can be learned. Wenger's theory of education fits as follows:

> Education, in its deepest sense and at whatever age it takes place, concerns the opening of identities—exploring new ways of being that lie beyond our current state. . . . Education must strive to open dimensions for the negotiation of the self. It places students on an outward trajectory toward a broad field of possible identities.[15]

The concept of a community of practice refers to the process of social learning that occurs alongside shared sociocultural practices that emerge and evolve when people who have common goals interact as they strive toward those goals. Highly developed CoPs remind us of the medieval guilds. They encapsulate the knowledge management of head, heart, and hands in social participation. Students entering professional training become proficient in these new communities of practice by combining various intelligences, cognitive as well as emotional. Because these adhere together in practice, we see a remarkable rise in positive appreciation of the value of work experience in situations where a good balance of head, heart, and hands is achieved.

Moral education requires the presence of moral communities of practice, meaning that no serious moral identity can be developed (we

---

13. Hegeman, "Stewardship and Integral Learning." See also Noddings, *Educating Moral People*.

14. Wenger, *Communities of Practice*, 149.

15. Ibid., 263.

say in line with Wenger) without discovering one's self within the social identities that participation in communities brings about. Moral identity develops while coming to terms with oneself within the job situation. Such coming to terms involves deciding whether or not to adopt the profiles required for doing the job well.

The sociology of learning brings to the foreground the requirement that curricula provide authentic learning environments emulating social practices. Our claim is that any professional curriculum—even those without a clear call for moral formation—embodies a concern for ethical and social responsibility in occupational practices. In our opinion, a nursing curriculum that does not teach "good" nursing in the proper environment does not deserve students.[16] If it does not provide a social environment that allows for moral development, students cannot engage in deep reflection. In our view, such learning requires the explicit recognition that students must learn what their proper social identity is to be in that profession.[17]

3. THE PRACTICE OF BEING INTEGRAL IN HIGHER EDUCATION

3.1. Introduction

In order to understand how gaining wholeness is possible in education, we need to retrace the route set out in chapter 2. In the current chapter, we build on the philosophy of normative practice to inquire deeper into the structure and direction of higher education. This exploration leads us toward the telos and the roles of teacher and student in social practice. We take as point of departure not only the traditional instructivist relationship between teacher and learner, but also the newer constructivist model, where the teacher often takes the role of coach. We will then return to discuss the moral basis of mentoring. The result of our analysis is the recognition that learning to become integral in higher education is quite attractive because it involves more than just mentoring. It deepens the mentoring relationship to make it similar to that between apprentices and masters, wherein the narrative unity of life is shared.

---

16. Our argument is that being integral requires moral integrity. See for an example from nursing, Kelly, "Preserving Moral Integrity."

17. See Noddings's emphasis on relations in "Is Teaching a Practice?"

3.2. The Double Goods in Higher Education

This section addresses new learning approaches. Christians working in all levels of education in the Netherlands face the challenge of the new learning as supported by the philosophy of social constructivism. One issue is the new emphasis on the acknowledged learning dependency between teacher and learner.[18] In the following, we explore this phenomenon from the perspective of the changes in responsibility for learning. We include the level of higher learning, particularly that of professional education, where the interrelationships between masters and apprentices are part of the professional development of competencies.

The first new learning approach, termed *learning dependency*, is defined and described as follows. We build on what has been previously asserted about the guiding function of education practice and the acknowledged learning dependency between a teacher and a student.[19] The guiding function is that a learner aims for the good of achieving knowledge as well as for the good of personal formation that is congruent with the gain in knowledge.[20] The guiding function translates into the teacher leading the student in his or her self-formation. The dialectic between these two complementary goods forms the constitutive structure of education. In practice, it is better known as the acknowledged learning dependency between the teacher and the learner.[21] The dependency is acknowledged, that is, legitimized socially and morally.[22] We see this illustrated in a description of the mentoring required for CBL, as depicted in sidebar 9.

> **SIDEBAR 9. DOUBLE GOODS IN CBL**
>
> One of the most highly regarded capabilities for business students is entrepreneurial competence. Entrepreneurship requires the ability to guide others. The requirement is described as follows: you observe opportunities within the business environment and are not afraid to take risks by bringing ideas to reality. On the bachelor level, it means at least that you see opportunities for the organi-

---

18. Hegeman, "Stewardship and Integral Learning"; De Muynck, *Goddelijk Beroep*.
19. Hegeman, "Stewardship and Integral Learning."
20. MacIntyre and Dunne, "MacIntyre on Education," 7–8; Dunne, "Arguing for Teaching as Practice," 356.
21. Dunne, " Arguing for Teaching as Practice," 354, 358.
22. Hegeman, "Stewardship and Integral Learning."

zation that are related to company objectives and preferably you explore windows of opportunity, unafraid of taking risks by bringing ideas to reality. On the professional master level, entrepreneurs make investments and start off important projects on the bases of vision, intuition, and professional business knowledge. Formulated in this way, this competence requires distinct knowledge as well as certain basic character qualities. The latter are developed over the years. An entrepreneur not having core business knowledge may not get far, but with poor people skills, progress is minimal.

A core competency in business is therefore the ability to guide others. This capability is part of the whole of CBL for business professionals of the Christelijke Hogeschool Ede (CHE). The characterization of the guiding capability is that you help people to find or regain self-regulation in a transitional phase of professional functioning. On the bachelor or major level, this is specified as methodically guiding HR conversations within the organization.

The ability to guide others requires the ability to self-regulate. Aiming for this specific type of knowledge requires a compatible good regarding the character of the business student: the capability of self-regulation, which is one of the nine competences. Self-regulation is shown in a student's character as the ability to reflect on professional behavior critically and the ability to adjust it to create a good result based on one's functioning. On the bachelor level it is described as the ability to develop oneself, with self-reflection, step by step in the right direction.

We place these two competences—self-regulation and guiding others—at the core of being integral in business. The good of having sufficient knowledge in order to be a good entrepreneur is complemented by the good of having been sufficiently formed to guide others and to reflect critically on one's performance. These two goods form the core of being integral in the education of business students.

Here we explain how to teach being integral because these core competencies must be taught at some point. We see the basic need for being integral in what educational philosophers MacIntyre and Dunne tell us about the pedagogical duty of the teacher.[23] MacIntyre formulates

---

23. MacIntyre and Dunne, "MacIntyre on Education."

it as a specific calling of the teacher to make students more conscious of the fact that their lives need integration, or wholeness. Above, we have termed this as the condition of being integral in learning. MacIntyre places this disposition in a broader perspective as the characteristic wholeness of our lives.

MacIntyre points out how this pedagogical duty of the teacher, involved in relating the role, the narrative, and the tradition, fits as follows:

> What is important is to recognize that each life is a single, if complex, narrative of a particular subject, someone whose life is a whole into which the different parts have to be integrated, so that the pursuit of the goods of home and family reinforces the pursuit of the goods of the workplace and vice versa, and so too with the other diverse goods of the particular life. To integrate them is a task, a task rarely, if ever, completed. That task is to understand those diverse goods as contributing to a single overall good, the ultimate good of this or that particular individual. This important type of understanding is of course primarily practical rather than theoretical—it is not that theoretical understanding is unimportant—and to acquire it is to see each individual human life as an answer to the question: "What is the ultimate human good?" The educator's problem then is to take students from a grasp of narratives and of narrative forms to the point at which they, having recognized their own lives as narratives, begin to ask: "*What would it be to complete the narrative of my life successfully? What good would I have had to achieve, if I had achieved that?*" The student who becomes able in later life to ask such questions seriously is in the best position to resist those tendencies to fragment the self that arise from the compartmentalisation of social life.[24]

We read in this citation three elements that fit our own perspective on integral learning. To start with, we agree with MacIntyre and Dunne in placing the ultimate human good or telos as the foundation for integrating the other goods of life. They point to the role of the telos, or the ultimate human good of our lives, to achieve this integration. Being integral is in the first place knowing how we aim to achieve this good as part of moral and spiritual formation (we discuss this further in chapter 4).

Furthermore, we note that MacIntyre and Dunne's discussion of integration presupposes that we have a moral profile into which we fit

---

24. Ibid., 10. (Emphasis added.)

questions and answers on how one's life is a single narrative (or not). It means having tried to give answers to the questions, what is the ultimate human good? and, what would it be to complete the narrative of my life successfully? These are questions of how the individual perceives the self as narrator of his or her life. These questions also concern choices that require answers having meaning for the individual's perception of self. Without answers to these questions, it may be quite difficult for an individual to feel wholeness in his or her life.

Their discussion of integration also connects with our conceptualization of the role of calling. It is characteristic of the narrative unity of life that the individual has an understanding of it. What kind of an understanding is this? MacIntyre and Dunne do not tell us, aside from stating that it creates an accord between all of the goals I may have in various compartments of my life: "Each life . . . is a whole into which the different parts have to be integrated."[25] Whether we call this a mission or a calling, it is an achievement we must attempt to realize even though we may not always accomplish it in our lifetimes.

At this point in our analysis, we can conclude that seeking to become integral in the practice of education requires knowledge of a telos, as well as profiles, narratives, and a tradition that influences narratives and roles in practice. These factors form a type of fabric that finds its coherence in the normative practice of education characterized by the acknowledged learning dependency between teacher and student, as we will explain below. With this framework, we can go on to examine the role of I in PISA as a central element in this fabric of meaning.

3.3. The Normativity of Higher Education and Being Integral

3.3.1. INTRODUCTION

Education as a process is like a tapestry. The acknowledged dependency relationship between teacher and student strives for the double goods of gaining knowledge and of contributing to the narrative unity of life. This normativity has an abstract quality that needs some explaining. Perhaps the metaphor of a hanging tapestry is appropriate to picture the process of education. The front side of it demonstrates the beauty of the design, whereas the back side with all the crossed needlework may look chaotic to an uninformed observer. Similarly, when a well-designed webpage

25. Ibid.

on the Internet is opened in the software language window, showing the codes in which it was written, most of us do not grasp at all this different representation. Similarly, the attractive frontage dealt with in section 3.2 shows the integral nature of education, which displays the guiding function and the double goods. In contrast, the back side shows the very intricate latticework of norms and codes too complex to decipher. The nature of a tapestry calls to mind the artistic, yet also realistic, image of what happens in education.

In this section, we look at the back side. We examine how certain roles, traditions, narratives, virtues, and practical rationality come together in a practice. We add to our focus the phenomenology of how values, norms, and rules cohere in a practice and thereby provide guidance for a practitioner. We will apply the term *integral* to those principles in the social context that guide professionals in their performance.

To proceed, we hark back to the basic theory of Alasdair MacIntyre.[26] We revisit certain elements of the NRP model touched on in chapter 2 regarding the manner in which practices regulate performance. We continue by using MacIntyre's theory of the three ways or levels to describe how persons aim for goods in life. They also depict for us the nature of higher education. These levels are: (1) the level of carrying out roles in social practices by practitioners, (2) the level of the narrative unity in the life of a practitioner, and (3) the level of the traditions that carry the practices and the practitioners. We draw examples from the daily practice of education in professional schooling. The discussion leads us to emphasize the importance of understanding social practices as being integral in the moral formation of students.

3.3.2. Level 1: The Exercise of Practice and the Role of the Professional

The first level—carrying out roles in social practices by practitioners—incorporates the educational practice and the role of teachers in it, as we explained above in terms of the guiding function of education. The normative practices model claims that, while doing their practice, all practitioners exhibit certain continuous complex human endeavors having an explicit moral aim. During their performance, practitioners aim at fulfilling the guiding function of the practice. They do more than just carry out tasks. They do so by taking on specific roles, which are suffused with morality.

26. MacIntyre, *After Virtue*.

3.3.2.1. Existential Element

Simply being a professional is not enough; there is an existential element involved.[27] This existential element refers to the personal choice of virtues, values, and norms for carrying out a practice in a professional manner. In chapter 2, we termed this the regulative side of our practice, because it decisively directs and governs the work of the practitioner. In this section, we explain that following roles leads to integral performance, because of the existential element involved.

We find in education practices salient examples of how existential elements are involved in social practices. The role of the Christian teacher cannot be understood without accepting that the teacher continuously performs with an explicit moral aim for that practice.[28] The school exists through the benefit of the way the teacher incorporates into performance his or her beliefs and morality, which are founded in religiosity. The teacher's responsibility is not only to be proficient. It is also do the work of a teacher with the aim of serving God, because serving God is a core aspect of the identity of a teacher's working practice. We may expect that the teacher knows how to integrate spirituality with professional performance so that the direction he or she takes in teaching complies with that of the school.

In order to ensure that the Christian teacher takes the right direction in accordance with the religious identity of the school, the school management may monitor how a teacher actually carries this out. Aside from screening the lessons, they may look for congruence in the way the teacher performs his or her religious duties in church with the way that the teacher aims at realizing the identity of the school. They thereby seek evidence of integration between the teacher's faith and professional performance.

To assess only the religious qualities of a teacher would not be wise; teachers certainly must teach well. It is obvious that teachers in religious schools do not perform the same function as pastors. This is because the guiding function of education is different from that of religious work. For this reason, one could dismiss the teacher for the incompetence demonstrated in teaching but not necessarily for a lack of competency in other social practices.

27. Cusveller, *Met Zorg Verbonden*.
28. De Muynck, *Goddelijk Beroep*.

To assess only the technical performance of a teacher at a religious school would not be wise either. Our theory makes clear that, in special situations such as religious schooling, merely doing a job is not enough. It illustrates that we hold practitioners accountable for having moral aims that lead to the excellent performance of roles that comply with the specific nature of that particular social practice.

Another normatively thick example is serving in the military. A good soldier is one who excels in the judicious use of controlled violence for legitimate aims. Without such a morality, the soldier would become an amoral machine and run the risk of becoming an immoral one, because using one's existential discretion is always needed when violence is at play. Like teaching, such social practices emphasize that the entire person is involved. This is an element of being integral.

3.3.2.2. Carrying Out Roles

A second crucial aspect of being integral can be seen in how roles are carried out. Secondary roles support the basic or primary role of the teacher, yet all fall under the same guiding function of the practice. Next to the primary role of teacher, we recognize, for instance, the secondary roles of the supervisor, the mentor, the manager, and the supporting educator, such as librarians and custodians. These secondary roles support the basic or primary role of the teacher, yet all fall under the same guiding function of the practice. This emphasizes that the role of teacher has specific properties that are directly related to the telos of education, giving the teacher's primary role a special sense of responsibility. Of course, the work of an administrative assistant is crucial for operation of a school. However, everything that the administrator does falls under the condition of maintaining the quality of the dependency relationship between a teacher and a student and thereby fulfilling the guiding function of education. In this way, the guiding function must also strongly influence what the specific roles are. We reiterate briefly what was introduced at length in chapter 2.

Our point is that the practitioner is beholden to certain standards that steer practice. Such standards concentrate themselves in the role. This is not far different from the dependency relationship between a nurse and a patient, which is governed by standards of excellence in nursing practice. At the same time, the nurse must support the dependency relationship that a physician has with a patient. Being able to recognize the special qualities of roles in other practices and adjusting to them is among highest competencies in a practice. All roles of practitioners involved in professional practice are to be guided normatively by the guiding function of that practice.

Examining the educational role more deeply, we realize that, within higher education, and in vocational education in particular, teaching has a special quality in the way that teachers carry out their roles. As we saw before, most educators, particularly those in professional schools, have a double role. They have the first role of being a good professional teacher, and often they have a second role of being a good professional in a second practice, for instance, social work.

Knowing when to engage in the one practice and not the other is the work of an expert. We see the lines blur between these practices when, for instance, students studying psychology and therapeutic methods start practicing on each other. This activity will prompt their instructor to demonstrate the required prudence and sensitivity for performing therapy. It remains important to acknowledge the integrity and virtuous performance of each practice. Excellence in professional schooling is demonstrated by an understanding of the nuances of each practice.

We take the example of a student called to competently express empathy regarding clients, guided in this effort by a teacher–social worker. When the teacher–social worker demonstrates certain empathetic skills, the individual can perform as a teacher but also as a social worker. It is precisely his or her professional choice how it is done. In this way, we see that, in the same person, a certain latticing of roles of the teacher comes about. The crucial matter for the student is that he or she leans, as it were, on the good performance of the first role of the teacher (as teacher) in order to be able to learn the qualities of the second role of the teacher (as social worker). This double quality of the acknowledged learning dependency marks the core of learning competencies as displayed, but in particular, the expertise of the teacher in combining roles.

We see how important this is when a student makes a serious mistake, say, in a practical situation, having a marked effect on the client. Because of the student's dependency relationship, the student can fall back on the help of the teacher and thereby on the guiding function of education. This dependency actuates the care and related reliance that exists between the student and the teacher-practitioner. The student may trust that the teacher will coach him or her in areas of weakness so that the student can learn.

3.3.2.3. Condition of Trust

We belabor what may seem evident because we have approached the essential condition of trust in the relationship between teacher and student. Suppose the student lacks the protection of the guiding function while still being required to undertake perilous practical duties without such protection. The student would not have the confidence that he or she is guided and may not be willing in such circumstances to run the risk of making errors. When the teacher is negligent on this point, the student runs greater risk, responds negatively to that risk, and becomes learning disadvantaged. Worse, a student willing to take risk could conceivably damage the interests of the client and the reputation of the practice. The student's prerogative to lean on the teacher is the buffer the student needs in order to receive a second chance and to continue to grow from novice to expert.

The dual role of many teachers in professional higher education points us toward possibilities of moral learning. Both roles are conditioned by strong virtues (for instance, prudence for a teacher and trustworthiness for a social worker). Also, the integral relation between the roles is normed. We see that, for instance, when a social worker in a correctional institute allows an intern to guide young delinquents, the social worker thereby relinquishes certain authority to the intern. The social worker's shift to the role of a coach relinquishes a degree of status and respect. In doing so, the social worker accepts a higher degree of vulnerability toward the incarcerated delinquents as well as the intern. It is precisely because the teacher sublimates his or her interests for the learning advantage of the student that the student gains the opportunity to learn.

One of the most valuable rewards for the student within the safety of the acknowledged learning dependency is that the student can see how the moral conduct of the teacher works. Embedded in the structure of professions, roles are continuous; complex human performances cohere meaningfully with the pertaining practice. Within the latticed structure of these roles and their embedded place in a social system, both teacher and student are continuously guided by normative conditions holding for that practice.

We therefore contend that students can best learn moral formation when teachers demonstrate the integrity and ethics of character within the safe margins of a social practice.[29] In this respect, students in vocational studies have a distinct advantage over those doing academic studies. As we point out below, this is not merely a matter of learning a role as such but of being able to connect integrally to what is called the second layer (or level of normative practices) of that role.

3.3.2. Level 2: The Narrative Unity of Life of the Person of the Practitioner

The second level is that of the narrative unity of life. This is the narrative or life story of the practitioner, which is the practitioner's own story of coherence in his or her life, which may have strong moral and spiritual overtones.[30] Narratives help us to verbalize the shape or form of that life. The practitioner's contribution to professional performance is shaped by his or her personal motives, goals, expectations, and experiences. In this respect, the practitioner shows his or her heart, so to speak, but in relation to head and hands.

Our focus here is on the unity of life that must become apparent in the narrative of the practitioner. Often a person fulfills different roles. A woman can be a nurse (or another practitioner), but also a mother, a sportswoman, and an active participant in church activities. We assume that all of these practices and roles differ considerably, but we do not assume that the person of the teacher is neatly divided into different identities. The separate roles of nurse, teacher, mother, etc. differ, but the person is the same. The connection between the various roles we call her narrative, or the story of herself. We expect that the person portrays herself as a unity in her narrative. Her narrative tells others how her life achieves unity. The telling of the narrative creates integrality. At the same time, the telling is an important demonstration of being integral. The narrative includes a moral profile, or a demonstration of how one is moral.

In Christian higher education, we could say that teachers are hired to tell their narratives. We expect that teachers tell their narratives to students because they want the student to learn how various, fragmented parts of themselves can cohere meaningfully in one solid profile as practitioner and as Christian. Students seeking unity in their lives need to reflect what they

---

29. We agree with Garber, *Fabric of Faithfulness*, on this, but we locate the quest within a certain established social practice more than he does.
30. Mouw, *God Who Commands*.

experience in regard to what they see demonstrated in the life and narrative of their teacher and mentor. In this respect, they are moral apprentices of the teacher, who serves as an ethical guide and master. Commonly we call this being a role model, but it is the unity and authority of the living narrative that counts in this regard.

Why is the unity of a narrative so important? Coherence in the way the master performs in a practice must be learned by the apprentice, at best by being inspired to imitate this harmony in thought and behavior. We have shown above that competency learning requires certain coherence in knowledge, aptitudes, and skills. A master demonstrates an excellence in this coherence. Of great importance is that the moral aspect also coincides with the demonstrated behavior. The moral profile of the teacher is thus the narrative that the student reads. This reading can vary from explicit talks about what motivates us to implicit demonstrations of certain stances. Because this narrative is an integral part of practice, it becomes one of the best ways students are morally formed. This is because the student hears more than just words. The student sees how the stated words become incarnated.[31] It is more than walking the talk; it is fleshing the walk.

Fleshing the walk is not mere idealism. It embodies exactly how being integral works out in the master-apprentice relationship. Certainly, such a living example is very different from applying methods and techniques of learning. Meeting a personification of being integral is often catalyst for the golden moments or pedagogical moments that serendipitously appear, which may be deeply influential in the lives of students.[32] In such instances, the practitioner has the opportunity to demonstrate to students how spirituality figures in the practitioner's narrative and thereby in his or her performance as a practitioner. In the practitioner's narrative, he or she deals with certain virtues that demonstrate the harmony that the practitioner's life. We call that the narrative unity of the practitioner's life.

Narrative unity, as we said before, portrays the practitioner's moral profile. Narrative unity demonstrates how human relationships, which are the basis of morality, have meaning in terms of people, values, and norms. Keeping these narratives away from students jeopardizes their learning processes. Narratives create for students opportunities to compare their lives to those of their teachers.

31. Garber, *Fabric of Faithfulness*.
32. An issue well argued by Plantinga, *Engaging God's World*.

We conclude that choosing not to confront students with one's narrative amounts to not giving enough warrant to the acknowledged learning dependency between teacher and student. We believe that the narrative is crucial for showing the novice how the heart of the master beats in the excellent performance of competencies. It is a source of unity and integral learning that, properly disclosed, may provide excellent direction on an individual level.

3.3.3. LEVEL 3: THE TRADITIONS THAT MANIFEST THEMSELVES IN EDUCATION

The third level is that of traditions. Here we refer to the traditions that support the practices of education, as well as the traditions of the practices studied—for instance, the traditions of business practice. MacIntyre tells us that practices have the coherent and complex form of socially established cooperative human activity, through which goods internal to that form of activity are realized. The NRP model introduced in chapter 2 characterizes the values and norms of that practice. The focal point here is that each practice has a tradition. By coming to know the tradition, we learn how the telos of human flourishing has been realized in that practice.

The traditions behind practices embody social artifacts. Such social artifacts have served us in the past by providing policies for realizing the good—the telos of human flourishing.[33] These social artifacts are the touchstones we use to determine in which respect a practice is on course or off course. In this sense, tradition means the transmission of customs or beliefs from generation to generation, as well as what educators do concretely with the contents of these beliefs.

For some practices, such as medicine, this seems evident, for others, like business, less so. The reason is that a tradition does not always speak for itself—it must be disclosed. We focus here mainly on the manner in which a tradition is passed on. On this third level, we do well to consider the choices made by institutions that reflect their various traditions. These can be systematized into one tradition or strategy. A good example is the tradition of Christian education at the Christelijke Hogeschool Ede (CHE). We find here a statement of tradition in terms of three value statements that together also form a strategic vision for the institution:[34]

---

33. MacIntyre, *After Virtue*; MacIntyre and Dunne, "MacIntyre on Education."
34. For the historical background of this strategic vision, see Burggraaf, *Christelijk*

Relation [Dutch: *relatie*] to God and with each other
Content and quality [Dutch: *inhoud*] of the curriculum
Responsibility [Dutch: *verantwoordelijkheid*] for the formation of the student

The substance of each statement is colored by the school's Protestant Reformed tradition, which clearly favors mentoring of students.[35] These statements serve as benchmarks for determining whether institutional practices are on course.

Teachers, supervisors, and coaches in particular need to incarnate this traditional vision in their roles and to display it in their narratives. In these ways, they build on the explicit Christian culture of the institution. As of old, all professions at CHE must determine how the guiding function of that practice is in turn governed by this tradition. At the same time, we see that this tradition pertains to not necessarily just a certain practice, or only to teaching, but to the entire institution of CHE.

3.3.4. The Integral Master and Narrative Unity of Life

In varying ways, roles, narratives, and traditions create a normative basis for understanding how direction in and of a social practice takes place. Much of this understanding remains tacit knowledge for the simple reason that what commonly transpires in the acknowledged learning relationship between a teacher, coach, or trainer and a student is relatively unknown. The process is on the hidden side of the beautiful tapestry.

In inquiring what transpires in the moral formation of students, we assume that the practices we are familiar with give us the best indications. In terms of our earlier discussion, we find clues by observing how virtuous roles are carried out, by listening to the incarnation of narratives (that is, fleshing the walk), and by relating what we hear and observe to a tradition of a practitioner. To be sure, what we describe here is the very substance of what takes place in reflection practices in professional education.[36] In chapter 4, we deal with the spirituality involved. In chapter 5, we discuss the accountability practices involved. For now, we can affirm what we presented in chapter 2 as the model that calls for the professional to will-

---

Onderwijs Vandaag; and Vermaat et al., *Vieren en Vasthouden*.

35. Van Hoorn, *Onderwijsportaal*.

36. Our position here is partly normative, partly practical experience and recognizes that such ideals do not always come about. Cf. Van Leeuwen et al., "Thematic Peer Review."

ingly accept morality while engaging in excellent performance in a certain practice. We have demonstrated in this section how roles, narratives, and traditions together form an integral lattice of normativity that guides the novice in seeking direction. We also demonstrated that being integral is a good that can be known, taught, and learned.

We do well here to acknowledge the very uniqueness of how masters demonstrate to apprentices what it is to be formed as a professional. The concept of formation may be applicable not only to students but also to teachers, who also must be reformed in the sense of engaging in continual reformation of the moral self. As professionals, they are to be held accountable for their failures. The accountability process may bring them to engage in intervision or supervision. There is no reason to assume that professionals in any practice are not being continually formed. Even the choice of not wanting to form oneself is an exercise to engage in certain self-formation. In this way, the choice to form oneself is part of the desire to be integral.

There is great beauty in the thought that both master and apprentice are formed in and by the same practice. It is one of the most splendid demonstrations of artistry in our field of work. The condition involved is that both must orient themselves to the direction taken by the practice (condition P) and adjust themselves accordingly to being integral in their orientation (condition I). The profile adopted by each of them reflects the roles, narratives, and tradition in a cohesive way. To be sure, they each have their own ethos, their own spirituality and morality, and their own worldviews. All these figure in the way they carry out their practice.[37] The way that they share this search for wholeness in that practice is the demonstration of the unity of life. It is now opportune to delve into this on a deep level to observe which basic tensions exist in being integral.

4. DEEP REFLECTION ON VIRTUES AND BEING INTEGRAL

4.1. Introduction

One of the foremost virtues sought after in reflective practices is that of authenticity. Students in all of Western society are called upon to bare their souls. The narcissistic among them may come to choose the moral

---

37. De Muynck, *Goddelijk Beroep*.

profile embodied in "generation me" simply because their personalities readily fit their generation. At the same time, most of the proficiencies required for professional performance in CBL hark back to the ancient ideal of practical wisdom or *phronesis*. How do authenticity and practical wisdom mix in learning? In this section, we discuss how the relation between authenticity and practical wisdom influences our expectations of being integral. Changes in basic conceptions of the self in Western society complicate the way practitioners see themselves as being integral in practice. Background studies by the philosophers Charles Taylor and Alasdair MacIntyre will explain how these virtues come into conflict with each other. We will posit that dealing with these two virtues influences how deep reflection on being integral takes place.

4.2. The Call for Authenticity in the Secular Age

Charles Taylor is well known for his coverage of how radical changes have occurred in Western culture over the last five hundred years.[38] In the medieval era, people lived in an enchanted world (as do scores of people today outside of the North Atlantic cultures). Individuals in an enchanted world live as porous selves. In effect, they are continually in contact with powers outside of themselves. These powers include spirits, demons, and gods, but also religiously determined forces, such as the wrath of God, or occult magic. Porous selves are vulnerable to factors that bring about the enchantment, as reinforced by cult religion, family, lord, and sect. The organic or porous conception of the self prevailed in the West into the Middle Ages, whereby one saw the self as part of the natural order, as well as vulnerable to mysterious forces.

In the late Middle Ages, a new view of the self appeared, of which Taylor sees the Protestant Puritan as a prototype.[39] The new self is the buffered self, an independent being who views the world from a distance. To be a buffered subject is to have closed the porous boundary between inside (thought) and outside (nature, or the physical). No longer does the natural environment influence the self; now it is inner conviction that rules. In the form of the Protestant Puritan who seeks the right inner spirituality along with an inner rationality (Descartes), the buffered self strives to create a new moral order in his or her im-

---

38. Taylor, *Secular Age*.
39. Taylor, *Secular Age*.

mediate surroundings. The medieval order of life became increasingly disenchanted, so that people centuries ago no longer felt influenced by the ghosts and gods.

The modern buffered self understands his or her position in a moral order by creating the "social imaginary." The "social imaginary" is the way that we collectively imagine, even pre-theoretically, our social life in the contemporary Western world.[40] The social imaginary of the buffered self offers people the freedom to create a social world and their positions in it. This new self was affirmed by the Reformation, and, later, the Enlightenment. In the nineteenth century, it became an ideology to see the self as a free rational being with the capacity to lead a fulfilled life here and now. The buffered self, freed from the shackles of the enchanted world, was viewed as able to act universally, dispassionately, and reasonably. This change marked the rise of the mechanistic conception of the self, whereby the individual feels part of the modern moral order that the individual helped to create.

In the last half century, a "new understanding of human life, agency, and the good" came about as an expressivist protest against the domination of rationality in the self. Taylor calls this the Age of Authenticity.[41] In this period, reactions against the social imaginary of the buffered self were found in the various romantic movements. In contrast to the idea of the disciplined self—concerned above all with instrumental rational control—it became important to allow each one of us his or her own way of realizing humanity. It also became important to find and live out one's own way, as against surrendering to conformity with a model imposed on us from outside by society, the previous generation, or religious and political authority.[42] Self-cultivation became the moral imperative, and self-authorization became the social narrative necessary to the new secular humanism of the Age of Authenticity.

The present culture is one informed by an ethic of authenticity. "I am called" in this new morality, Taylor explains, "to discover my route to wholeness and spiritual depth. The focus is on the individual, and on his/her experience. Spirituality must speak to this experience."[43] The basic mode of spiritual life is thus the quest for spirituality as opposed

---

40. Taylor, *Secular Age*, 146; J. Smith, *Desiring the Kingdom*, 68.
41. Taylor, *Secular Age*, 473.
42. Ibid., 475.
43. Ibid., 508.

to religion. This spirituality, its subjectivism, its focus on the self and its wholeness, and its emphasis on feeling led to new forms of spiritual quest (in chapter 4, we delve into this phenomenon). It also ties in with contemporary notions of human flourishing (in chapter 5, we return to this). This ethic is not so much nostalgia for the return of the porous self as much as a protest against the limitations of the rationality, disengagement, and discipline of the buffered self.

The buffered, rational self interacts with the authentic self, sometimes in conjunction, sometimes in direct tension. Nonetheless, the modern version of the buffered self is one that can tap into sources of personal creativity as well as be moved by elements of secular humanist worldviews, such as human rights. The tightly bound notion of selfhood, with boundaries between self and world, inner and outer, are more porous than often realized. Even though there is no longer an enchanted world—where there was a strong sense that things beyond the mind influenced the self emotionally and spiritually—some room is left for spirituality having a nonreligious source in the modern idea of a moral order. The modern self displays a powerful nostalgia for a kind of porous self but not one as vulnerable to magic as the self's medieval ancestors. At the same time, the modern self wants to be authentic, yet maintain the purposiveness and rationality of the buffered self. These tendencies are prominent in secular humanist morality. There exists a tension between a longing for being authentic (in the postmodern sense) and a drive to be purposive.

Exactly this tension has created a renewed interest in the virtue of practical wisdom.

4.3. The Return of Practical Wisdom in the Secular Age

The role of virtues is directive in moral formation. MacIntyre tells us that, in a pedagogical practice such as teaching, students are enabled to become reflective and independent members of communities but even more so by "the inculcation of those virtues that are needed to direct us towards the achievement of our common and individual goods."[44] The virtues are inculcated to give practitioners the required sense of direction. Without this direction, they would not be able to choose the right internal and external goods of a practice. They also could choose the

---

44. MacIntyre and Dunne, "MacIntyre on Education," 2.

wrong means and ends, or the wrong policies in a practice. In the following, we explore the role of virtues, in particular that of phronesis, in the way students can be formed.

Phronesis is an important condition for becoming integral in carrying out social practices in our Western culture. The word *phronesis* is the Latin term for prudence (*prudentia*), one of the four classic cardinal virtues. In ancient times, the philosopher Aristotle developed this concept, which has come to figure prominently in Western moral philosophy of virtues. Phronesis is indispensable for ethically correct professional conduct. Therefore, it serves as a description of what a good practitioner ought to be like or of a moral profile. Strictly speaking, phronesis is not a moral virtue, but a virtue of the intellect, referring to the moral quality of our thinking. It is not the same as prudence in our common language, which refers to acting with or showing care and thought for the future, however its meaning is related. The best equivalent in English as well as Dutch is the meaning of practical wisdom, practical reasoning, or even good common sense.[45] As such, it is a highly desirable quality for a professional.

Phronesis is contrasted with *sophia*. The use of the term *wisdom* is often confused with what Aristotle called the virtue of sophia (translated as wisdom), being the ability to think correctly about the nature of the world and to discern why the world is the way it is. Sophia is more the deliberation about universal truths, whereas phronesis is the capability to deliberate with a view to the good life as a whole by applying one's intellect. The person having the quality of phronesis will use his or her cognitive faculties to consider the type of action needed for bringing about a certain change. Following Aristotle, this is a change to improve the quality of life, yet there is more to it than calculating costs and benefits. Phronesis involves the ability to determine through reflection how to achieve a goal, with a view to making it more adaptable to the professions of care and the social sciences.

Phronesis regulates the other virtues by balancing them appropriately. Aristotle describes practical wisdom as the virtue that allows us to determine the right mean or measure of following other virtues. For instance, the right use of the virtue of being courageous avoids the extremes of being either overly confident or cowardly. In a professional

---

45. Pannier and Verhaeghe, *Aristoteles*, 340; Jochemsen and Glas, *Verantwoord Medisch Handelen*, 136–38.

setting, phronesis aids decisions, such as choosing the right balance between high excessive involvement and detachment in a relationship with a patient or client.

Our Dooyeweerdian interpretation of phronesis follows. Practical wisdom goes beyond theoretical knowledge or the logical side of the mind—these are understood. Practical wisdom entails the right practical sense of how to act well. It is a capacity to exercise right judgment, which is developed in practice. A more general definition of phronesis is the ability to discern the existing normativity in concrete situations and to disclose normativity in the right way.[46] Such proficiency requires both an awareness of the structure and direction of practices, as described in chapter 2, as well as action on that knowledge.

Phronesis, when applied, looks like the following. A professional who places phronesis centrally in his or her profile is able to discern the right virtues for a certain situation. The individual is also able to go on to determine which of the values, norms, and rules of a practice to follow in a situation. The professional thereby determines the desired and undesired effects of certain decisions. In this respect, it is the judgment we expect of a scientist who knows what knowledge to gain and to apply. A professional with practical wisdom determines which techniques are best utilized or avoided.

The modern literature on phronesis (understood as practical wisdom) refers to being integral. Modern literature points to other highly desirable qualities of phronesis as well when it is defined as the ability of a person to aim at harmony, balance, and moderation in their manner of thinking and performance. The literature refers to being integral as defined in this chapter—the connection between roles, narratives, and traditions (see section 3).

The Western ethic of authenticity has come to depend on oral expressions of phronesis. Particularly, the emphasis has settled on giving oral expression and justification of one's practical wisdom. In this way, the emphasis on voicing phronesis is a response to the question, how can I *verbalize* that I know how to qualify as a person who can be relied on to do the right thing? We see this as a modern addition to the notion of phronesis. It can be described as a change in the concept of the self, influenced by the Western ethic of authenticity (see Taylor above in section 4.1). We offer two examples of this change in philosophies of moral formation: one secular and the other nonsecular.

---

46. Jochemsen, *Ethiek van de Zorg*.

The philosopher Sabine Lovibond is the author of a secular work on the philosophy of moral formation.[47] Phronesis as depicted by Lovibond is a modern crossing of the older ideals of practical wisdom with the ethic of authenticity as described by Charles Taylor (see section 4.2 above). Lovibond pointed out that the naturalistic (or natural history) approach to practical wisdom has become an attractive ideal in modern character development. If our first nature is biological, we need phronesis in our second, or social, nature in order to become properly civilized. This second nature is manifested in behavior that, though learned, is largely unreflective. Through ongoing socialization, a person becomes aware that a particular act is morally required of him or her in a given situation. A person becomes aware that there is a compelling moral reason to perform that act. Phronesis in this conceptualization is the ability of a person to function in a socialized way by following existing rules. It also entails the ability to give a narrative of this process. The practically wise use their moral thinking to register correctly or evaluatively both the significant features of their surroundings and the practical demands that those features exert. The practitioner high in phronesis has an "exemplary state of character such that those in whom it is present can be credited with certain 'uncodifiable' reserves of knowledge."[48] The uncodifiable knowledge is knowledge about values and reasons for action, which arise naturally in certain situations. The practitioner is hence able to narrate the position he or she takes as well as the authorship in coming to this position. Through the practitioner's authorship of practical wisdom, others come to view phronesis as part of natural development.

We encounter a similar modern development of phronesis in a non-secular study on moral formation by the Dutch philosopher-theologian Johannes van der Ven.[49] Following the philosopher Paul Ricoeur, he claims that phronesis is more than an intellectual bridge between projects in life and ideals of the good life. That is because phronesis is embedded in hermeneutics, as the "explanation" of the self.[50] Much like Lovibond's position, his focus is on the ability of the self to "write one's own narrative of one's own life." In this self-interpreting activity, there is a continuous dialogue with other selves outside and inside the individual. To the de-

---

47. Lovibond, *Ethical Formation*.
48. Ibid., 31.
49. Van der Ven, *Formation*; Van der Ven, *Morele Zelf*.
50. Van der Ven, *Morele Zelf*, 144.

gree that the self invests in activities or life projects and finds contentment there, the self experiences feelings of meaningful self-appreciation. This positive moral attitude about him- or herself is of great importance for aiming at the good life. Through feelings of self-appreciation, one comes to value oneself as the author of one's text, qualities, or self. Without such a basic moral attitude, phronesis does not come about.

Van der Ven's view of phronesis agrees with that of Lovibond in the attention given to the narrative aspect of phronesis. Authorship, or the ability to present oneself, concerns the capability to present one's phronesis as a personal exercise. Similar to Lovibond, Van der Ven emphasizes the self-representation, as well as the reflection on the inner side of the person, involved in phronesis. Here we see how the emphasis shifts from a rational approach to proper cognitive functioning in phronesis, whereby phronesis activates the ability to reflect on and portray one's inner being. Such modern conceptions of phronesis affirm the notion of practical reason as moral rationality grounded in the process of socialization. In doing so, they also comply with the ethic of authenticity.

Both conceptions call for modern people to invest in reflective activities in order to combine cognition with affect.[51] Such combinations are currently common in student mentoring and supervision. Reflection is necessary in order to arrive at practical wisdom in both one's own personal living situation and in one's in professional practice. The modern shift in views on practical reason from emphasizing cognition to emphasizing affect (aided by linguistics) agrees strongly with the phenomenal rise of reflection practices in higher education and in professional schools in particular. One reason we can pinpoint for this shift is the call to the ethic of authenticity, as described by Taylor.[52] In other words, being a true author of one's moral formation ties in very well with achieving the right habitus of being authentic in reflection practices. An example is provided by theologian Robert Doornenbal, who regards phronesis in practice as requiring knowledge of the self and reflection on the self.[53] For these reasons, we state that the modern demand for being integral involves combining cognition and affection.

But self-reflection without normativity is insufficient for professional practice. Although Doornenbal's perspective agrees with modern

---

51. Van der Ven *Formation*; Lovibond, *Ethical Formation*.

52. Taylor, *Secular Age*.

53. Doornenbal, "Klassieke oudheid."

conceptions, we believe that limiting phronesis to the ability to perform self-reflection has mixed blessings. On the one hand, it fits in very well with the popularity of authenticity, or being true to oneself, as well as the desire to understand oneself in one's reactions to varying situations. An understanding of one's affections in professional practices is important in order to be able to handle these affections in a constructive way. In this way, reflection practices can play an important role in striving for integrality (see further in chapter 5). However, the strong emphases on the psychological processes and the affections in modern conceptions of reflection entail the risk of taking one's own moral experience as the basis for the ethical evaluation of one's practice.

In chapter 2, we concluded that professional practices have an intrinsic normativity that should be brought to bear on conduct. Reflection on one's professional performance is meant to help improve that performance, not only in a technical sense but also in a moral sense. The implication is that, in reflection, the virtue of phronesis as a virtue of the mind should be practiced and strengthened. This virtue enables the practitioner to distinguish between the various types of normativity (the practice; concrete circumstances; convictions of the client, student, or patient; the professional's own beliefs; etc.). The virtue of phronesis also helps the practitioner decide which actions the norms require.

Precisely in today's situation, with its emphasis on authenticity and emotional balance, professional practices require a degree of self-control of practitioners. In supervision, the professional *in spe* learns not to be carried away by affections and beliefs. In reflection on the practice, the professional's affections, valuable as it is to identify and deal with them, are not to be determinative for evaluating a certain course of action. Yet, they are still part of being integral.

To deal with the risks of overdependence on the virtue of authenticity, we introduce the virtue of *sophrosyne* (pronounced as "soh-froh-soo'-neh"). It is here that we run into another one of the four classical Greek virtues, namely, sophrosyne (Greek: *sophrosyne*; Latin: *temperatia*), which is best understood as moderation, self-control, good common sense, or the ability to live a virtuous life.[54] The etymology of sophrosyne includes a root meaning of moral sanity. It was considered indispensable by the ancient Greeks for gaining life-long happiness. This corresponds

---

54. The *Westminster Dictionary of Christian Ethics*; *New Dictionary of Christian Ethics and Pastoral Theology*, s.v. "sophrosyne."

closely to the emphasis on persons living in the right balance of reason, affections, and good judgment (phronesis), as pursued in reflection practices. In addition, the ancients regarded sophrosyne as a required virtue for gaining wisdom and justice. Plato regarded sophrosyne as the ability to discipline one's excessive desires for food, drink, and passions through the instruction of reason and will. Perhaps this complex virtue finds its best expression in the two well-known sayings by the Oracle of Delphi: "nothing in excess" and "know thyself." This is a classic ideal of lives characterized by harmony and right proportionality.

The Christian use of sophrosyne as found in the New Testament differs from that advanced by Plato and Aristotle. It certainly is recommended[55] together with the term *egkrateia*[56] (a word that also means self-control), as the virtue of one who masters desires and passions, especially the sensual appetites. The Apostle Paul emphasizes that this virtue is not only a result of one's own efforts but a fruit of the Holy Spirit.[57] During the Protestant Reformation, sophrosyne was particularly emphasized in biblical prescriptions as the rule of temperance and the rule of moderation. In a Calvinist worldview, sophrosyne requires the corollary virtues of temperance, humility, chastity, resignation, patience, and prudence.

Sophrosyne contrasts with phronesis in that it gives greater place to affect. This discussion of the virtue sophrosyne in comparison with phronesis reveals that both require much reflection on the inner moral qualities of the person, in particular, the psyche. We hold that the increase in reflection required by sophrosyne almost naturally involves a focus on what has been described as the call for authenticity in the secular age. That sophrosyne, in addition, gives explicit attention to the affections in reflection practices may be a distinct advantage compared to phronesis. At the same time, we see a distinct disadvantage in the focus on the affections and psychic qualities of people in reflection practices if they downgrade or overly deemphasize the cognitive and judgmental facets of both practical wisdom and the normativity in the professional practices. The use of one's rational *and* volitional gifts as called for in phronesis becomes threatened by an overemphasis on the moral psychology of the person. We deal with this difficulty in chapter 5.

---

55. See Titus 2:2, 6; 1 Tim 2:9.
56. Gal 5:23; 1 Pet 1:6.
57. Matt 11:18–19; Gal 5:22–25; Eph 3:14–21; 1 Pet 1:13–16.

4.4. A Balance between Authenticity and Phronesis

As our analysis of phronesis indicates, the modern self is porous as well as buffered; it is open to transcendental truths as well as integrally bound to practicing phronesis. We have covered several prominent virtues found in professional schooling practices that clearly reflect our times and our Western culture. Authenticity as a virtue aids the discovery of personal routes to wholeness and spiritual depth. The focus of authenticity is on the individual and on the individual's experience. Spirituality must speak to this experience. At the same time, the overly dominant role of authenticity can lead to downgrading the cognitive faculties. Such tendency to downgrade is mainly due to a common preference, even in profession supervision, for facile, emotional, existential learning styles. Existential learning fits the times (we provide an example of this in the next section), but it is also quite detrimental to the pursuit of practical wisdom, because the modern self needs to be integral.

Education without phronesis leads to professional deformation. Phronesis is a major quality of the philosophical and ethical development of the professional practitioner. At the onset of training in professional schools, there ought to be a focus on practical wisdom. A subjectivist approach to phronesis, where the cognitive aspects of it are not balanced integrally with the affections and with related virtues, such as sophrosyne, entails a risk. This is the risk that students do no more than gain highly developed proficiencies in legitimizing their own preferences and beliefs. Legitimization renders the countless and expensive hours of reflective practice an exercise in moral deformation—at least for the profession. Legitimization does not satisfy condition I. Instead, it curtails the wholesomeness of harmony of spirit and good judgment, which is highly necessary to CBL.

At the same time, our realization that there must be an integral balance between the virtue of authenticity and that of phronesis raises our consciousness of an important source of meaning involved in the ethic of authenticity. Taylor tells us that this ethic is not so much nostalgia for the return of the porous self as much as a protest against the limitations of the rational, disengaged, and disciplined buffered self. Because we will go into spirituality in depth in the next chapter, we only state here that the ethic of authenticity has an important side effect, that of creating sensitivity to spirituality and its relation to being integral. This we study in more detail in chapter 4.

At this point, we turn to examine the means of deep reflection.

5. APPLYING DEEP REFLECTION IN MENTORING

5.1. Introduction

We understand several aspects of deep reflection from the view of using condition I. We treated the ideal of being integral in terms of head, heart, and hands. We next considered the practice of being integral as demonstrated by a master practitioner in terms of a narrative unity of life and of following the telos of practice. Next, we saw how the basic tension between the virtues of authenticity and phronesis figure strongly in how one aims to be whole. Such ethics assume that we can achieve these moral ideals.

Just how do educators go about fostering deep reflection by students? This is the concern of the current section. One of the primary ways colleges monitor the development of becoming integral is through student mentoring services. In the context of such practices we encounter challenges that impact the potential scope of deep reflection, as described above.

In the following section, we revisit the theory of deep reflection that we have developed—this time in relation to mentoring. We then deal with several factors that we have determined may influence its practice. The first factor is the tension between mentoring and CBL. The second is a compilation of factors that have to do with reductionism. Dealing with these factors allows us to interpret the feasibility of deep reflection in being integral in mentoring. We conclude that achieving the condition I in education remains a great challenge.

5.2. Deep Reflection and Its Organization in Practice

Is deep reflection with its required virtues feasible in a professional context? Deep reflection is portrayed above as a special type of learning that needs to be placed within the normative framework of practice and ethics. As we argued above, it requires great attention to virtues (such as responsibility, prudence, authenticity, or phronesis). It also requires an incarnation of these virtues in a master who serves apprentices. Is it feasible to meet all of these requirements in professional training?

Deep reflection is by nature highly subjective, hence its use in professional training is difficult to pin down. Because it relies strongly on the personal framework of reflection of the practitioner, deep reflection is quite difficult to characterize. In its performance, it is often elusive and difficult to organize. This problem has been recognized in actual reflection practice.[58] Because deep reflection is a manner of reflection or contemplation on the individual's core being, core beliefs, spirituality, and narratives on unity in life, it requires distinct structures for it to come to fruition. At the same time, we acknowledge that deep reflection does not always take place, even when organized properly. Sometimes this cannot be avoided. It often follows the serendipity of learning that arises as needed.

This section discusses the role of deep reflection in education. Because deep reflection is difficult to grasp, we differentiate the organization of deep reflection from the personal use of deep reflection. The latter will be treated in two coming chapters on spirituality and on answerability, so that we can concentrate here on the organization—that is, the nature and position—of deep reflection in education, as such.

Our treatment of mentoring begins with acknowledging its basic aim: achieving a narrative of self. Deep reflection by its nature assumes a preliminary process of getting to know the self in some deep way by of necessity approaching the core of one's being. We do well, then, to view the organization of deep reflection against the background of the normative side of practice, as treated above. We also introduce specific tools that we consider useful for deep reflection. Our discussion gives us a hold on what deep reflection is and also affirms its utility.

To start with, when engaging in deep reflection, the student must have sufficient knowledge of the normativity of practice. A second prerequisite to deep reflection is knowledge of being holistic or integral in that practice. As a result, when the practitioner draws up a narrative of his or her self-image (addressing the question, how do I see myself as a practitioner?), the practitioner does this best within the normative context of the practice.

Several benefits accrue immediately from deep reflection, as normed by the standards of a profession. It has self-esteem benefits by answering the question, am I a good practitioner? and thereby affirming what is expected, normatively, within the defining situation. It also produces job motivation by forming a response to the question, why do I want to be this particular type of practitioner or professional? This question re-

---

58. Vandamme, *Vork*.

quires knowledge of spirituality and identity (we cover these two aspects in the next chapter on spirituality). Deep reflection also engages basic, worldview-related beliefs (by responding to the question, what do I want to accomplish as a practitioner, and why is this a good?). Consideration of these three questions may ultimately lead to deep reflection on the prospects of becoming a practitioner (how do I see my future as a practitioner in this field?). Deep reflection can generate a working knowledge of what it is to be accountable or answerable for wanting a certain profile in a profession (we deal with answerability in chapter 5).

These questions begin to cohere as appropriate methods and tools are applied. Their coherence lies in the recognition of the normativity of practice and how it is interpreted in roles, narratives, and tradition (see above). Coherence also derives from an understanding that head, heart, and hands go together. It is certainly more than simply determining personal preference from being authentic. Deep reflection as part of moral formation must especially provide moral grounds for personal choices. Moral grounds include their understanding of how they can be moral in their chosen career or their understanding of their moral profile in the new practice they hope to enter. These are very specific ways of knowing oneself. They are developed along with their personal narrative of being authentic within the realm of achieving practical wisdom. In addition, the normativity of practice guides all of this development.

Deep reflection can be understood in comparison to alternative practices, such as single-loop learning. We keep in mind that deep reflection is different from the alternative reflection practices, but it often is combined with them. In common reflection in education, the student must first answer the question, do I perform properly in professional practice? *Properly* is meant here in the sense of meeting required proficiencies. Much of common reflection is on rule-governed behavior or on how one performs according to standards. This we call stage one reflection. It leads to the mentality of "I can do it." Its best result is a belief that the firm grasp of certain rules leads to proper conduct. This is essentially single-loop learning.[59]

The second stage of reflection is double-loop learning.[60] In double-loop learning, the student must go on to a second stage by the dealing with the question, do I engage the proper values with which to perform

---

59. Argyris, Putnam, and McClain, *Action Science*, 85–86.
60. Ibid., 85–86.

properly? Answers are now sought in the context of the professional practice. Toward this end, CBL brings to light what does or does not belong to the required competence of the professional involved. The student now must understand the practice sufficiently to know the goals, means, and standards of excellent performance. Double-loop learning leads to the mentality that "I know what this is good for." It emphasizes a belief that one's conduct meets the governing standards.

Deep reflection assumes that one follows both loops of reflection and that one goes on to enquire whether one reflects properly. It is not meant to be confused with triple-loop learning, deutero-learning, or meta-learning. In triple-loop learning, learning to relearn is the focus, leading a transformation of the learning process itself. A related concept, often confused with triple-loop learning, is deutero-learning. As originally used in the literature, it refers to behavioral adaptation to patterns of conditioning at the level of relationships in organizational contexts. This form of learning is continuous, behavioral, communicative, and largely unreflective, even largely unconscious.[61] Another related concept is meta-learning. This concept refers to reflection on and inquiry into the process of (single-loop and double-loop) learning on the individual and group levels in organizations. This form of learning is discontinuous, cognitive, and conscious. It is, to a large extent, amenable to steering and organizing. It is directed at organizational and individual improvement.[62] Precisely due to its limited focus on organizational benefits, we avoid referring to meta-learning in our analysis.

Deep reflection is distinguished from other forms of learning in that it draws explicitly from spiritual and moral sources. As a manner of normative reflection or contemplation on the core of one's being, one's core beliefs, spirituality, and worldviews, deep reflection requires knowledge of what is right—in the sense of being morally right. Deep reflection is a type of meta-reflection on the appropriateness of how one does reflection from moral and spiritual sources. It deals with the questions of how students see their own reflection, and of how they involve their worldviews, spirituality, and the moral demands of a profession in their reflection.

In order to reflect deeply, students must reflect on who they are as moral persons and how they regard themselves as performing in a

61. Visser, *Deutero-Learning*.
62. Ibid.

certain profession.⁶³ Deep reflection reaches the levels of understanding that require students to know and choose their vocation or calling. In line with our explanation above, we ask, why, and with what profile of myself, do I reflect properly? This same question, put in the vernacular, is, am I right in believing that I am right in doing it? Reflection on these questions leads to an integral belief that one's motivation is right.

Most mentoring practices suppose these questions and levels. They do not always take the need for deep reflection into account, primarily because the last question is difficult to answer. It can be addressed, however, by employing certain reflection tools, which we introduce below. They are reflection exercises used by college mentors in tutoring exercises in higher education in the Netherlands.⁶⁴ Also, the use of reflection in professional training is required.⁶⁵

Organizationally speaking, there is a basic tension between mentoring (getting the most out of reflection) and the demand for being integral in CBL. We discuss this below. Before dealing with this issue, we introduce in sidebar 10 a broad range of reflections that can be used in deep reflection.

---

63. The role of internships is crucial—see Geudens, "Via Reflectie Naar Expertise"—yet we limit our focus to what transpires in the interaction between instructor and mentor and student than on relationships in practice itself. This area needs additional study in relation to supervision, a topic we cover in chapter 5.

64. In higher education in the Netherlands, we find various forms of required tutoring involving reflection. In the event of a hierarchical relationship between student and teacher (superior and subordinate), "mentoring" and "supervision" are practiced. Mentoring has as goal that the student makes the right choices in scholastic development and career development. The student is tutored by a mentor, an experienced person, commonly a faculty member, who counsels and trains students in the learning environment. In this book, the term *mentoring* pertains only to student career mentoring (SCM). Supervision has as its goal one's learning to function optimally in a specific working situation, which includes internship situations for students. These two forms of required tutoring are studied in chapter 5 of this book for their value in achieving accountability for professional performances. Nonhierarchical tutoring forms are coaching, intervision, and collegial consultation, which also may use reflection. Coaching has as its goal the tackling of the developmental goals that the coached person formulates for a certain development; intervision has as its goal a change in behavior or growth in professional expertise, mainly with the help of peers outside the working situation; collegiate consultation has as its goal the exchange of expertise between peers within the working situation.

65. Supervision requires extensive reflection in order to learn from working experiences. In chapter 5, we examine the practical science of supervision more closely.

SIDEBAR 10. REFLECTION TOOLS IN THE PRACTICE OF PROFESSIONAL EDUCATION[66]

Reflection is the interpretation or reinterpretation of experience and knowledge. Using reflection tools allows participants to think actively and consciously about their experiences, actions, behavior, and choices. A prominent research group in the Netherlands distinguishes between three forms of reflection: (1) self-reflection, (2) reflection on method, and (3) reflection on society.

1. Self-reflection is formulating learning aims, making a plan for studying, and understanding and being able to describe one's own learning process. It has the following forms:

- Point Reflection: Learning to look at one's own situation from a different perspective
- Brainstorm Reflection: Collecting and ordering ideas and keywords in order to arrive at a new approach
- Metaphor Reflection: Using images to find new approaches
- Scenario Reflection: Making conscious choices by choosing from possible future scenarios
- Spiral Reflection: Systematic reflection by working though a number of phases
- Appreciative Reflection: Picturing an ideal future on the basis of participants' peak experiences

2. Reflection on method involves linking practical experience to theory, learning to judge the value of information, and acquiring knowledge of research methods (theory of knowledge and philosophy of science). It has the following forms:

- Line Reflection: Testing a product or (group) assignment against ideal quality standards
- Success Reflection: Group Reflection based on positive experiences, linked to theory

---

66. The most successful models in the Netherlands are put forward by the research group Reflection on Action in Amsterdam (http://www.reflectiontools.nl/). An overview of their model is presented in sidebar 10. These models are also available in hard copy in the publication by Bennamar, *Reflectietools*.

> 3. Reflection on society is being aware of the responsibility for one's professional behavior in the social context (professional ethics or cultural philosophy). It has the following forms:
>
> - Dilemma Reflection: Analyzing the answers to an imagined dilemma, which reveals the structure of ethical argumentation.
> - Socratic Dialogue: A group conversation about a fundamental, preferably philosophical, issue
> - Virtue Reflection: A narrative technique for gaining insight into the ethical motives underlying one's own behavior

These types of reflection can be applied by mentors in ways that promote heart learning. Most of the reflection forms displayed in sidebar 10 are adjusted by mentors to practices found in various vocational settings, such as supervision in work situations, methodical practice intervision (that is, cooperative supervision among colleagues) in social work, regular mentoring of learning programs (or study career mentoring), and regular reflection exercises in courses. In all these forms, students are invited to share many facets of their humanity in order to learn. We commonly refer to this ideal as learning of the heart.[67]

Related to the conviction that the core of one's behavior lies in the commitment to one's spirituality, the deeper we delve into the core of one's being, the more effective mentoring is thought to be. This notion fits squarely with the conviction of many mentors that such reflection forms advance the moral formation of their students. The aim of mentoring is to realize a particular integrity in a student, which is expected to improve the student's ability to become suited for the professional world.

Mentoring banks on the abilities and willingness of students to reflect on how head, heart, and hands cohere in narratives of their lives, but it is also the Achilles' heel of mentoring. If students become tired of reflection, a condition quickly achieved, what can we do as educators? It means that reflection is vulnerable on the precise object of reflection: the willingness to reflect. We return to this problem in chapter 5.

5.3. The Tension between Deep Reflection, Mentoring, and CBL

Student mentoring includes a responsibility to assess whether the student increases in proficiency. Mentors must determine whether a stu-

---

67. De Muynck and Roeleveld, *Competentiegericht*, 68.

dent advances from a foundational level (Dutch: *propedeuse*) to that of bachelor and from there to professional master. This applies for not only one particular capability but integrally in all capabilities belonging to the competences profile. The demonstration of these proficiencies is a significant contribution to growing student portfolios. The assessment that a student—sometimes despite unique cognitive or affective proficiencies—still may not be suitable to enter a certain profession is often a feared specter among up-and-coming students. It is one goal of mentoring that students themselves will arrive at such a conclusion.

Because moral qualities are required of professionals, and they are achieved only through complex and personal processes, the close observation inherent in the mentoring relationship is an effective way to monitor student progress. Typically, mentoring takes place within the context of CBL and adjusts to its demands. Mentoring is the best way to measure progress toward a complex set of professional competencies, which explains the ready fusion between CBL and mentoring. Mentoring is necessary to CBL: if student progress cannot be observed, it is impossible to meet the increasing demands of proficiency performance. For this reason, the requirements of CBL enhance the legitimacy of student mentoring. It is the nature of mentoring to call for students to both adjust their personal qualities to new competences and to reflect on their abilities to do so. For an example of the personal qualities inherent in CBL, see sidebar 11.

SIDEBAR 11. PERSONAL PROFICIENCIES IN CBL: THE CASE OF A BUSINESS SCHOOL[68]

The School of Business of the CHE has nine competences that flow together integrally in a competence profile for students. These are: (1) personal responsibility, (2) self-regulation, (3) methodical approach to business cases, (4) consulting capability, (5) entrepreneurial capability, (6) managerial capability, (7) formal review capability, (8) financial-quantitative perspective, and (9) guiding capability. Each of these qualities have their levels of proficiency for the propedeuse (foundation course in first year cycle), the bachelor level (end of first cycle), and the professional master (end of second cycle).

68. Drawn from the Department of Business, Christelijke Hogeschool Ede. We thank our colleagues for allowing us to use this example.

The first two competences are narrowly associated with the personal qualities of the student and have the following indicators for each level of proficiency.

1. Personal Responsibility

- Requirement: You are able to take personal responsibility at work and within society. You are accountable for your actions, you reflect critically on your own actions, and you take care of the consequences.
- *Propedeuse (foundation course):* You are accountable for the choices you make, based on your personal view.
- *Bachelor Major:* In situations of opposing interests, you keep on your own track, based on well-considered choices.
- *Professional Master:* You are prepared to make sacrifices if high-pressure situations require you to repudiate your personal convictions.

2. Self-regulation

- Requirement: You are able to reflect critically on your professional behavior. You are able to adjust your behavior toward positive results.
- *Propedeuse (foundation course):* You are able to use feedback to formulate specific learning objectives and are able to improve yourself by reflecting on feedback.
- *Bachelor Major:* With self-reflection, you are able to develop yourself step by step in the right direction.
- *Professional Master:* By employing anticipatory reflection, you avoid personal pitfalls. When crises inevitably occur, you are able to turn them into learning moments.

In business schooling, the mentor works with the student to ensure that these two personal capabilities become integral to carrying out the other seven capabilities and qualities on each proficiency level. When successful, the full process is no small feat.

Sidebar 11 points out good examples of how reflection aids in learning professional capabilities. These examples highlight the need for integral learning in CBL. They also give us a clear idea of what can be done, but they do not provide empirical proof that deep reflection works. Therefore, we focus below on the factors influencing deep reflection.

5.4. The Vulnerability of Deep Reflection

Deep reflection is vulnerable to reductionism, aside from superficiality. The practice of mentoring in relation to CBL is not without issues that encroach on the success of deep reflection. We cover three variations of reductionism that may thwart its success.

5.4.1. The Reductionism of Reflection to Spirituality

First, deep reflection is vulnerable to a reductionist view of the spiritual purposes of higher education. At first glance, this focus on rising proficiencies in competences may appear to conflict with the mission of Christian colleges, where the call for learning with the heart is pursued as mainly a spiritual matter. Could CBL—even aided by reflection exercises—do justice to the identities and innate qualities of Christian students? Is the heart not of supreme value compared to the hands?

This first reductionism is answered by the call to integral learning. This pious question is not wrong, but it is poorly constructed if the notion of being integral is left out. Yes, we may answer, knowing one's heart is important for budding professionals. But integral learning does not only involve the heart in the sense that once we involve the heart we attain wholeness. That would be a sorry reduction of head and hands to heart. Rightfully so, we need to avoid reductionism: head and hands also play a part in integral learning. Our answer may be that interrelating all these imaged qualities in learning helps us to gain a valued good. This is the good of being whole and coherent. Integral learning entails that the spirituality, morality, psychology, and even social condition of a learner are drawn together in a holistic way of gaining knowledge. Our heart may be the source of choosing a moral profile, yet integral learning is how we relate the source to other aspects of our being. Integral learning must be applied to avoid reductionism, even of the spiritual kind.

5.4.2. Pragmatism and Technicism in Reduction to Skills

A second reductionism to technicism threatens the acceptance of deep reflection in professional programs. This issue was raised in chapter 2 as the concern that involvement of heart in learning would lead us away from the higher goal of CBL: becoming professionally proficient.

A strong case against involving one's spirituality and morality in CBL was made by adherents to pragmatism in competency learning.[69] In their view, CBL is defined solely by the list of qualifications students are required to master. At most, the heart is involved through overemphasizing the psychological qualities of the student and devaluing the religious. A pragmatist asks, "Please, no spiritual hocus-pocus!"

Pragmatism is a very limited view of learning. It divorces students from using experientially all of their intelligences needed for gaining knowledge integrally.[70] The pragmatic objection boils down to the argument that gaining a certain competency masterfully does not come about through the exercise of morality or spirituality. If they are not needed, why use such messy, complex tools?

The basic supposition here is that other forms of integral learning (such as outright ethical learning in the liberal arts or Bildung), which require various types of normative thinking, will not fit into CBL unless they can be put into an instrumental relationship with outcomes-based education. Often professional schools will only accept moral formation if it is retooled as a means to the end of gaining specific practical competencies (for example, managerial capability).

Added to this is the efficiency argument. If there are no measurable effects of engaging in moral training, it is too costly to provide without obvious outcomes. On the simple assumption of a supposed lack of effectiveness, moral formation can be sidetracked.

This technicistic view of CBL is narrow yet potent, because it reveals a deeper, underlying belief that the outcomes of learning can (and thereby should) be value neutral. That is, learning outcomes should hold true for everyone despite their individual morality and spirituality. By this perspective, learning a competency amounts to employing a worldview-sanitized tool that anyone can use. It is our general observation that many professional schools adhere to this perspective.

From this vantage point, we see certain basic views on the nature of education. In section 3 of this chapter, we explored their differences in depth. For now, we argue that, where the neutralized view of CBL holds, it does damage to the student. If education is essentially nothing more than a fancy way to impart aptitudes for becoming skilled in dealing with knowledge, the aptitudes in CBL themselves will be the core concern, rather than the qualities of the person. In this neutralized strategy,

---

69. De Muynck and Roeleveld, *Competentiegericht*.
70. Kolb, *Experiential Learning*. See figure 2 below.

students concentrate mainly on becoming proficient for certain tasks. Their need to develop moral and civic values is left to other institutions in their personal lives, such as peers, friends, family, church, politics, or media. In terms of our metaphor of head, heart, and hands, the neutralized view claims that students may not use their hearts and certain elements of their heads in order to learn proficiently the use of their hands. In the effort to sanitize learning of any moral aspects, technicism in CBL amounts to a severe reductionism of all elements of the learning person to focus on only the methodical skills involved. The student is left to his or her own devices for gaining the necessary integral learning supposed in CBL. This discussion leads to the important question of how the moral formation involved in CBL can meet the objections raised by the technicists.

Before we reiterate our arguments in response, we recall the observation made in chapter 2 that moral education is essentially weak—perhaps too weak—in the way it is practiced at professional schools.[71] If moral formation is to be truly effective, its practice certainly must be intellectually rigorous and closely allied with powerful developments in society.

This objection to the weakness of moral formation, as held by a nonmoral and nonformative approach to CBL, also holds against the role of spirituality in moral formation (see chapter 4).

Certainly, moral formation as practiced by the mentor must not be wishy-washy. That is self-defeating. Still, even if a school cannot provide the highest standards of quality in moral education, the conclusion that a hands-off policy is best is still not warranted. Having no moral formation at all simply ensures that competency learning short-changes students and alienates them from morality. It is clearly best to make sure that moral competencies are studied as rigorously as other skills.

5.4.3. The Reduction of Experiential Learning in Reflection

A third reductionism is the piecemeal application of experiential learning theory and methods. One of the foremost sophistications in reflection exercises involves applying the theory of experiential learning. A focus on the theory of experiential learning points to the need for teaching and learning integrally. It also reveals that its practice is often quite partial and deficient.

Experiential learning involves many facets of the learner, in particular a direct encounter with the phenomena being studied rather than

---

71. Colby, "Whose Values."

merely thinking about the encounter, or only considering the possibility of doing something about it. It is not only talking about something, but talking with someone about something, including oneself. It is learning that is individual and personal for the learner. Experiential learning involves much personal reflection, which flows from a direct participation in the events of life. It is learning achieved through reflection upon everyday experience. Experiential learning is the way that most of us do our learning.

Experiential learning occurs when individuals engage in an activity, reflect upon the activity critically, derive some useful insight from the analysis, and incorporate the result through a change in understanding or behavior.[72]

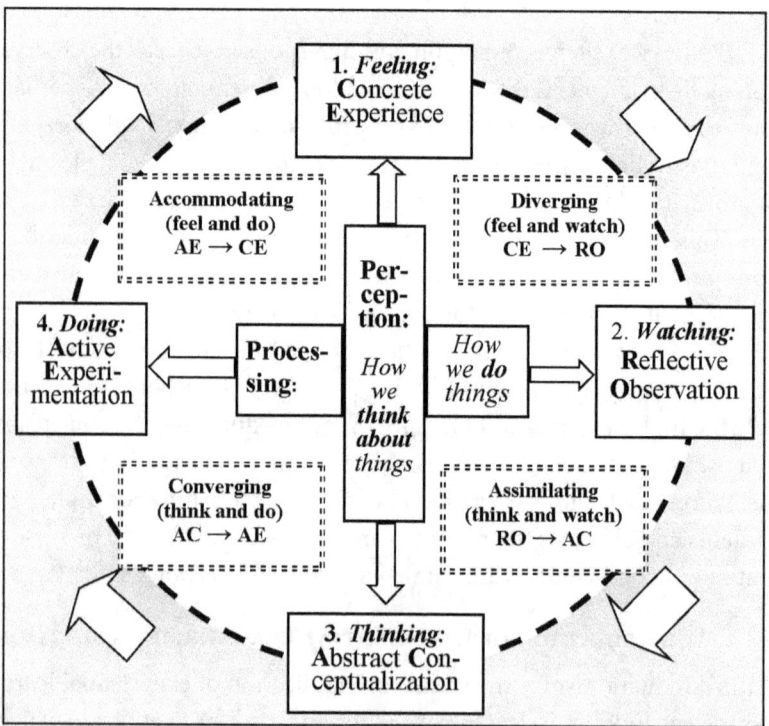

Figure 2. Experiential learning and Learning Style Inventory

David A. Kolb and Roger Fry (both at the Weatherhead School of Management, a private business school of Case Western Reserve University) developed the experiential learning model (see figure 2). The outer ring in figure 2 is composed of a cycle with four elements: (1) con-

---

72. Kolb, *Experiential Learning*.

crete experience, (2) observation of and reflection on that experience, (3) formation of abstract concepts based upon that reflection, and (4) testing of new concepts. These four elements are the essence of a spiral of learning that can begin with any one of the four elements but typically begins with a concrete experience. The model was developed predominantly for use with adult education but has found widespread pedagogical implications in higher education, including in the Netherlands.

David Kolb is also renowned in educational circles for his Learning Style Inventory (LSI). His model is built upon the idea that learning preferences can be described using two continuums: perception (active experimentation–reflective observation), and processing (abstract conceptualization–concrete experience). (See the cross in the inner ring of figure 2.)

The result of the combination of the spiral of learning and the learning preferences is four types of learners: converger (active experimentation, abstract conceptualization), accommodator (active experimentation, concrete experience), assimilator (reflective observation, abstract conceptualization), and diverger (reflective observation, concrete experience). Each of the types constitutes a learning profile that students are urged to choose for themselves in basic reflection practices.

The LSI is designed to determine an individual's learning preference. It is often applied as a basic reflection tool in the Netherlands in first cycle (bachelor) programs in professional schools. It appeals to the virtue of practical wisdom by embodying a spiral of learning that emulates practical wisdom. The learning model also promotes the virtue of authenticity by allowing each learner to adopt of the learner profiles for themselves. In section 4 of this chapter, we delved into the virtues of authenticity and practical wisdom presupposed in this model.

The experiential learning followed in most reflection practices is an effort to develop some form of practical wisdom. One of the most remarkable qualities of the experiential model of reflection is that virtues like wisdom, self-knowledge, and prudence are squarely situated within the selfhood of a person. In some respects, following the steps of the learning model and choosing a learning style comply with the call for integral learning. Kolb suggests that following all four steps will qualify the student to choose as well as implement the right course of action in concrete situations.

Piecemeal application of the model jeopardizes being integral, however. An initial choice of one of the preferred learning styles (see figure 2) could entail avoiding going through all four steps of experiential learning. In this way, application of the Kolb theory may be partial and deficient. Not engaging in all steps of experiential learning (see outer ring of figure 2) could lead to unduly emphasizing the role of the affections, to the detriment of cognition. We have observed this result. In terms of Kolb's model, students could run the risk of remaining stuck in, for instance, their choice of the profile of accommodator (feel and do) or of diverger (feel and watch) because these styles emphasize emotional intelligence and insights that do not require rigorous thought. Doing so could lead to serious neglect of the other forms of experiential learning that are more difficult (think and do, and think and watch). A similar choice limited to the learning style of assimilator and theoretical learning in phase 3 would be equally nonintegral because it avoids use of the hands. This choice also leads to deficient integral learning.

The Kolb model is designed to be applied holistically. This necessity raises a question about the requirement to be integral while engaged in experiential learning: must we always be integral? The rule is that we must. Despite our choosing an initial preferred learning style, we do not glean—neither from literature, nor from practice—any good reasons to believe that in fully experiential learning, the affective side of intelligence must dominate the cognitive side, or the other way around. In our estimation, experiential learning involves all steps of figure 2 in a balanced way. Why otherwise speak of experiential learning?

An example of this stipulation for an integral balance in reflection involving all steps of Kolb's learning styles is provided in sidebar 12.

> SIDEBAR 12. THE NEED FOR AN INTEGRAL BALANCE IN PROFESSIONAL LEARNING
>
> A study by Rene van Leeuwen and others of the learning effects in thematic peer-review discussion groups using experiential learning points out the need for the integration of cognitive skills in integral learning.[73] The effects of reflection on their provision of spiritual care by groups of nursing students were studied. The method of peer review is a form of reflective learning required as part of the

---

73. Van Leeuwen et al., "Spiritual Care"; republished in Van Leeuwen, *Towards Nursing Competencies*.

educational program on spiritual care in nursing for third-year undergraduate nursing students from two nursing schools in the Netherlands. The reflective journals kept by students (n = 203) throughout the peer-review process were analyzed qualitatively and grouped into themes. The analysis showed that students reflected on spirituality in the context of personal experiences in nursing practice. In addition, they discussed the nursing process and organizational aspects of spiritual care. The results show that the first two phases in the experiential learning cycle appear prominently, that is, the phase (1) *feeling*: concrete experience, and the phase (2) *watching*: reflective observation of that experience. The phases of (3) *thinking*: abstract conceptualization based upon the reflection, and (4) *doing*: active experimentation with behavior and testing the new concepts were less evident. The authors' conjecture is that the training of the students to apply the latter phases had been deficient. Also, they affirm the need for continuing guidance by tutors in demonstrating integral learning involving all phases of experiential learning. The tutor's role here is important, particularly with regard to providing content during the abstraction of experiences into general terms, as well as with regard to directing and testing alternative strategies in new conditions. The authors conclude that completing the whole reflection cycle seems essential for developing CBL, because students will then be capable of reaching the level of abstraction and testing alternative behavior necessary for adequate CBL.

We see here that a holistic application of experiential learning is useful in mentoring practical wisdom. The study by Van Leeuwen et al. affirms the importance of being integral in reflection exercises for CBL.[74] In order to properly train students to use their cognitive faculties, they are to engage in all phases of experiential learning in reflective exercises. Neglecting abstract conceptualization or active experimenting and testing also diminishes the likelihood that students will pick up on the need for practical wisdom. Clearly, the good life cannot be pursued if professional training adopts an aversion to conceptual analysis, logic, and argumentation theory. Students tend to opt for satisfying behavior

---

74. Van Leeuwen et al., "Thematic Peer Review."

instead of deeply examining their own thoughts and behaviors. Who monitors their reflections if their mentors do not?

These three vulnerabilities lead us to infer that deep reflection is highly challenged in professional programs. Our treatment of several issues regarding tensions between CLB and mentoring makes us question whether reflection practices in professional schools sufficiently counteract reductionism, pragmatism, and technicism in CBL, as well as the overemphasis on preferred emotional learning styles in experiential learning. Reflection practices on the one hand call for the condition of being integral. On the other hand, we have identified the vulnerability of deep reflection to reductionism.

6. CONCLUSION: BEING INTEGRAL

In summary, viewing moral formation from window I generates several perspectives which we adopt in this book:

- PISA requires integral learning.
- PISA requires coherence in the ethics of a curriculum.
- PISA combats fragmentation of morality in deep reflection.

In this chapter, we described deep reflection using the condition of I in PISA as a quality of moral education applied by learners in academia and by practicing professionals. We began by rediscovering the tradition of combining head, heart, and hands as precursor to achieving a moral profile no longer found in CBL. We found that recognition of the normativity of social practice can serve as a portal for understanding the normativity of vocational practices. The normative practices model of higher education shapes a student's consciousness of performing integrally in highly normative professional contexts. This discussion led to the maxim that the integral nature of both higher education and its practitioners helps train students to become integral—condition I. This integral nature allows the master to demonstrate to apprentices the narrative unity of life within practice.

We also discovered that modern mentoring and supervision attempt to establish unity of life in the way that students learn capabilities and practical virtues. But mentoring, when subject to reductionism, may readily fail in its integrative efforts. We draw the conclusion that the use of reflection tools ought to be refocused on being integral, rather than on the selfhood of the individual. An ethic of being responsible for one's formation is also drawn from this discussion.

A core instrument for engaging such ethics of responsibility is deep reflection on how one functions in social practices. Reflection requires knowledge of the moral self, as well as the development of practical wisdom. To be sure, the call for the virtue of authenticity can certainly clash with the call for the virtue of phronesis. The resolution of this conflict may be downgrading the importance of phronesis in developing a professional moral profile. From the perspective of deep reflection using PISA, phronesis serves as a central virtue in becoming professional. A person with the quality of phronesis is aware of the integral way values and norms figure and cohere in a situation. We believe that phronesis can be learned in the context of higher education. This belief presupposes that the person demonstrating phronesis is aware of the source of normativity and is willing and able to demonstrate phronesis in a given situation. In this respect, the ethic of demonstrating phronesis is one that includes going beyond just knowing and seeing what is good. It goes farther to apply these values in one's own life, while attending to how this is done. In our view, demonstrating phronesis is the proper way to meet the condition I in the practice of PISA.

The quest for integrity is demanding, and rarely, if ever, achieved. Even so, the basic motivation to aim for integrity lies in our spirituality, as we will explain further in chapter 4. We will explain that conceptions of who we are (or are not) as integral persons needs a substrate. We believe that this substrate concerns our spirituality, as we will explain further in chapter 5.

4

S: Being Spiritual

1. INTRODUCTION

OUR DISCUSSION OF THE PISA educational strategy continues with the letter S, which represents spirituality. Opening the window of spirituality in PISA allows us to see how faith, worldview, and deep feelings influence the moral formation of students in Christian higher education. Not only must their instructors gain insight into experiences and questions of meaning and purpose that motivate students to be moral, above all, students need this knowledge in order to make fitting career choices.

Spirituality is a trendy catchword that encompasses many traditions. To understand the phenomenon called spirituality, both book knowledge and experiential knowledge of a faith practice are important. Christians have their spirituality, as do Muslims and Hindus. The worldviews of New Age spirituality and secular humanism also express their own versions. One does not necessarily need to be a member of a religious institution to have spirituality. Nonreligious citizens have worldviews. We can study their abilities to reach the deepest desires of the human heart for meaning, purpose, and connection in their own communal sources of meaning. A well-known example of modern applications of spirituality is training in secular varieties of Buddhist-like spirituality as part of efforts in Western corporations to improve the wellness of their employees.

Students at most Christian colleges are currently take required courses on various religions, worldviews, and faith movements. As a result, their acquaintance with the ways people use spirituality in their daily lives is good. When used as a mirror to reflect on their own faith performance, such studies reveal to the student either the quaintness of their own spirituality, or its resemblance to others'. Students do well to respect the reality that non-Christians develop their spirituality as much as Christians do. This does not imply that Christian students should remain indifferent with respect to the content of other spiritualities. By studying how non-Christians live out their spiritualities, they gain insight on the depth and breadth of their own spirituality. This insight is a valuable element in Bildung.

In this chapter, we will not study various spiritualities to examine their many flavors and hues. As we tease out the elements of PISA, our attention is on the place of spirituality in the moral formation of students. Our focus is drawn sharply to the role of spirituality in the moral formation of professionals. This is not a microscopic analysis of what transpires in someone's faith life while working in a vocation. Our analysis is more like various video clips of someone's daily life as a spiritual person. Christians commonly call these faith practices, consisting of bits and pieces that could cohere into a meaningful way of life. We believe that students need to know how tradition, narrative, and roles regarding spirituality can influence how they are morally formed for the professions.

After characterizing spirituality, we illustrate from our own tradition of the Reformed Christian worldview and educational practice how spirituality functions in the sense of giving direction. From there, we examine in detail how certain narratives of spiritual profiles and moral profiles function in Reformed evangelical higher education. Next, we focus on social imaginaries and the specific roles involved in spirituality. The result is that we refresh our understanding of what traditionally has been termed a calling. Such an understanding prompts us to conclude that, from the standpoint of PISA, no moral formation can take place without the S of spirituality, and no moral profile can develop without vocational awareness.

2. SPIRITUALITY AND ITS FUNCTION

2.1. The Word Spirituality

Spiritual is a word defined in our dictionaries as an adjective, relating to, or affecting the human spirit or soul, as opposed to material or physical things.¹ The spirit itself is the nonphysical part of a person, which is the seat of emotions and character. We commonly call this the soul—where the deepest feelings, thoughts, and desires of the human person lie. Spirituality is then the noun that refers to what transpires in people when their spirit or soul is the object of attention. Obviously, this is the case in religious exercises where people celebrate their spirituality communally. It is also the case in hospital rooms and other care situations where chaplains and nurses competently address spiritual concerns of the patient. It is even the case in corporate human resources trainings that follow Eastern and New Age spirituality. In such cases, the inner quality of one's spirituality usually has an outer component shared with others of like mind and soul. Increasingly, people share their inner qualities in communications, thereby leaving the institutional confines of a more organized, religious spirituality to express their individual, spiritual souls. In this respect, they maintain their inner beliefs, while at the same time changing their outwardly perceived expression of that.

This vacillation between spirituality placed in the setting of organized religious practices and a highly individualized focus on the self as a spiritual person is part of current Western society. It is also very much part of Western education. The former stems from established religious conventions. The latter flows from what Charles Taylor has termed for us the ethics of authenticity (see chapter 3).² Many students become fascinated with the idea of drawing up their own version of spirituality, even if it leads them away from their original religious spirituality. They may also come to participate in political-cultural debates in classrooms where issues of spirituality and social justice are closely interwoven.³ Such participation helps them to develop their identities as politically aware, emerging adults, which Bildung requires of them (see chapter 1). As the language philosopher David Smith points out for the professional practice of language pedagogy, "Faith and spirituality may be pertinent to understanding personal identity, interpersonal interaction, institutional context, the effect of larger worldviews on pedagogical approaches, and the relationships between cultures constructed or evoked in the language learning setting."⁴ Any educator involved with immigrant students, which

1. *New Oxford Dictionary*, s.v. "spiritual."
2. Taylor, *Secular Age*.
3. Osborn, "Confronting the Zeitgeist," 3–11.
4. D. Smith, "Spirituality and Language Pedagogy," 23.

in Europe often includes students from strict Muslim and North African backgrounds, or Asian students with Confucian backgrounds, will know how influential the interrelationship of language and spirituality as part of a subculture can be. They also know how sensitive to the students' beliefs they must be when speaking on certain spiritualities. Spirituality is intricately involved in the language of communication. Hence, we see that spirituality has two sides: individual and cultural-lingual.

However, the focus in this volume is on the role of particular religious or spiritual beliefs in the manner whereby students are morally formed for vocations. We further examine the function of spirituality in the lives of students as religious persons in social practices. Our concern in this chapter is to analyze how people, individually and communally, use the spirituality they possess to guide their moral formation as professionals.

2.2. The Function of Spirituality

Our definition of spirituality flows from extensive research in care practices. We regard spirituality as "the religious and/or existential mode of functioning of a person including his or her experiences and how that person answers the question of meaning and purpose."[5] We use this definition to analyze the function of spirituality within social practices, such as education, business, and care, particularly regarding what people do with their spirituality when aiming to be moral. This behavior can be quite individual, but spiritual conduct can also be part of a broader faith movement. Our definition of spiritual functioning includes the practices that individuals use to be spiritual. At the same time, we recognize the importance of experiences as well as questions of meaning and purpose, and the ability of people to verbalize these.

Spiritual functioning entails a variety of functions. In religious circles, training in certain faith practices is standard fare. Training may include learning an inheritance of spirituality drawn from traditional sources, then applying these in well-established practices of faith. Such practices include catechism, youth groups, and discipleship training. Many regard

---

5. This definition of spirituality has been developed in the realms of medical ethics and nursing ethics by Jochemsen, *Ethiek van de Zorg*; Van Leeuwen and Cusveller, "Nursing Competencies for Spiritual Care"; Van Leeuwen and Cusveller, *Verpleegkundige Zorg en Spiritualiteit*; see for oversight and application of this development Van Leeuwen, *Towards Nursing Competencies*, 18, 80, 111.

the function itself as a significant part of doing their spirituality. One comes to possess a spirituality as part of enculturation but also as a result of applying it in practice. Such training can be extended to (and developed somewhat differently) in higher education. Choosing a college where one can develop one's spirituality is a very popular motive.

The function of spirituality is demonstrated in many types of ministries that foster spiritual formation in educational institutions and churches. Involvement in long- and short-term ministries, in and outside of churches, even internationally, are examples of how spirituality is put to work. Certainly becoming involved in faith-based organizations by doing good works is a very serviceable way of expressing one's spirituality, while, at the same time, service learning is known for being highly formative. Students strongly desire such experiences, because service learning emphasizes being integral in addition to being spiritual.

Service learning ministries relate spirituality to practical and concrete good works to achieve integrity. Other ministries achieve integrity by promoting the influence of spirituality in everyday practice. Christian colleges bring students, faculty, and staff together in communal public worship, linking them in a shared spirituality. Many Christian colleges in the Netherlands and North America have campus ministry programs held on campus. These may include campuswide worship services, small group Bible studies, musical worship programs, leadership development programs, or outreach programs.

Concerted efforts to engage in character development on the explicit basis of spiritual growth is often an explicit curricular activity at colleges. For instance, in North America, the John Templeton Foundation's College and Character Initiative,[6] and the Council for Christian Colleges and Universities (CCCU), in partnership with Cencentus, offers the Furnishing the Soul Project.[7] In sections 2.6 and 5 below, we return to a discussion of faith formation, but we do recognize that spirituality balances between something we do (the function) and something we possess (the content).

James Smith provides an example of the importance of doing spirituality. He writes:

---

6. See for information on the John Templeton initiative: http://www.collegeandcharacter.org/.

7. See for the CCCU their website (http://www.cccu.org) and for the Furnishing the Soul Project, their website (http://cccu.furnishingthesoul.com).

> Instead of turning to texts, doctrines and the theoretical articulations of theologians, we will consider what Christians do—or more specifically, what the church as a people does together in the "work of the people" (*leitourgos*).[8]

His central thesis is that liturgies—whether sacred or secular—shape and constitute our identities by forming our most fundamental desires and our most basic attunement to the world. A liturgy functions as a spirituality because:

> they prime us to approach the world in a certain way, to value certain things, to aim for certain goals, to pursue certain dreams, to work together on certain projects. In short, every liturgy constitutes a pedagogy that teaches us, in all sorts of precognitive ways, to be a certain kind of person. Hence every liturgy is an education, and embedded in every liturgy is an implicit worldview or understanding of the world.[9]

We agree that implicit understanding is of great importance in learning spirituality. But this does not mean (as we argued in chapter 1) that explicit understanding (that is, formalized knowledge in texts) is defunct.

Smith's vision for the Christian university is that it become a place where students and faculty learn to properly love the world. We believe that this project requires both implicit and explicit understanding of spirituality. We see in many liberal arts colleges demonstrations of this in ecclesial learning, that is, in campus worship, where the function of spirituality meshes with spiritual content.

> Insofar as Christian teaching, learning, and scholarship are to be formed by a Christian social imaginary, the rhythms and rituals of campus worship provide welcome opportunities to continue to form and reform our imaginations.[10]

We agree that such worship practices certainly may provide rich spiritual nourishment, and may even stimulate reflection. We doubt, however, whether liturgies as liturgies sufficiently educate us in professional training without the necessary coaching. Our simple reason is that it has never been shown convincingly that experiential learning can replace knowledge gained by more cognitive methods.

8. J. Smith, *Desiring the Kingdom*, 134.
9. J. Smith, *Desiring the Kingdom*, 25.
10. Ibid., 225.

If our liturgies take into account the conditions of being practice-minded and being integral (P and I of PISA), our liturgical consciousness may flourish, for the simple reason that spirituality needs a normed community. In terms of PISA, the S needs to adjust to the P, I, and A of PISA. We will point out later in this chapter that a liturgy of spirituality needs to be adjusted within a succinct moral formation strategy for any formation to take place. Simply handing over the sacramental keys of the church to students is not wise. Nonetheless, we share with James Smith a view of education as fundamentally a matter of formation.[11] We regard his approach to liturgies as supportive of our focus on the function of spirituality within moral formation.

Because we are interested primarily in how spirituality is used in the moral formation of professionals, we will stay close to home to explore the way spirituality works in higher education and in related professional practices. Our analysis of the religious and existential modes of how persons function allows us to focus on the norms and values of practices (the P) and thus on the way spirituality (as experiences and questions of meaning and purpose) is carried out in a strategy of moral formation.

We start with an example of how spirituality can function in the practice of teaching. In his research on the spirituality of teachers working in Christian primary schools in the Netherlands, Bram de Muynck found five ways that spirituality figures in the professional identity of teachers in practice.[12] First, spirituality concerns transcendence—that is, experiences that transcend commonplace reality. Second, spirituality involves inspiration, or bringing zest and courage into one's vocation. Third, spirituality is characterized by a process of searching to connect the experiences of inspiration and transcendence with commonplace practice (in his study, the vocational practice of teachers). Fourth, the methods of spirituality connect with the regular attention one gives to this searching process (for instance, in prayer and scripture reading). Finally, spirituality concerns sources, which are understood to be those documents crucial to the tradition in which the teacher stands. We con-

---

11. Ibid., 26.

12. The study was on two types of orthodox-Protestant schools belonging to two distinct communities of practice of orthodox-Reformed denominations in Christian education: the associated community of the experiential Reformed and the single community of the Reformed Church of the Netherlands (liberated).

clude from examining this study that the experiences and questions of meaning and purpose (or the second part of our definition of spirituality) figure prominently in the practice of teachers.

As seen from looking at these five aspects together, understanding the way spirituality functions in professional identity requires understanding the motives and beliefs on the basis of which a teacher conducts him- or herself. These beliefs must relate integrally to the teacher's experiences of pedagogical and religious inspiration and transcendence, the teacher's sources of inspiration, barriers to inspiration, and the conditions holding for the rise of inspiration. In other words, understanding the religious and/or existential mode of the functioning of a person can be very difficult if we do not understand how that person undergoes experiences and questions of meaning and purpose, how the person receives inspiration, and their view of the nature of transcendence.

At the same time, spirituality is not necessarily religious, even for religious persons. In this respect, two ways of regarding how spirituality operates integrally are helpful to our understanding. De Muynck puts forward a distinction between two types of spirituality in the vocational practice of the teacher in primary schools.[13] His research indicates that two types of spirituality in vocation interrelate and are expressed as beliefs. He differentiates between religious spirituality (as nourished by religious beliefs) and vocational spirituality (in which sources of inspiration and other conditions hold generically for teachers). Both types of spirituality coincide. De Muynck found through empirical research that religious spirituality sometimes clearly overlaps with vocational spirituality in those moments of inspiration in which pedagogical and religious transcendence coincide. De Muynck points out that the religious spirituality of teachers may reinforce their vocational spirituality. Such enforcement becomes manifest in the motives and the beliefs of teachers. Because teachers experience their responsibility in relation to God, they take their duties seriously. They transform their deep concern for the future of their students into activities for their formation. This interrelationship between the types highlights the role of beliefs in spirituality. His findings bring De Muynck to regard spirituality as "the manner in which one—by orienting oneself on sources—relates beliefs and experiences of inspiration and/or transcendence, more or less methodically, to

---

13. De Muynck, *Goddelijk Beroep*.

the actual practice of life."[14] These beliefs or narratives allow the practitioner to find integration between religious spirituality and vocational spirituality. We may then expect practitioners to express their vocational spirituality in terms of their beliefs. For practitioners to do so methodically is within the very context of the profession of education.

From the perspective of PISA, this study demonstrates how, through their beliefs, practitioners involve their spirituality (S) in their vocation, that is, in the normative practice of education (P), while at the same time aiming to be integral (I) in their efforts. We assume at this point that the beliefs of Christian teachers have religious backing. So far, we have treated what most Christian educators can recognize as their daily fare in practice.

This observation begs the question, is an explicit religious spirituality required for vocational spirituality to function in valid ways? The narratives of the beliefs that practitioners have about their vocational spirituality interest us much here. Such narratives bring to the foreground the question of whether these beliefs need to be explicitly religious. If a vocational spirituality could be reliable without a religious spirituality, then, from the perspective of the function of spirituality, what constitutes spirituality?

To analyze this question, we pose the following five questions on the function of spirituality:

1. Spirituality is functional, but how does it relate to sources, community, or tradition? We go further into this in section 2.3.

2. Spirituality is functional, but how does it relate to existential inspiration? We go further into this in section 2.4.

3. Spirituality is functional, but how is it understood in terms of roles? We go further into this in section 2.5.

4. Spirituality is functional, but how does it relate to faith formation? We reference here the issue of faith formation and treat this in section 2.6.

5. Spirituality is functional, but how does it relate to having a calling? We treat this in section 2.7.

---

14. Ibid., 406–9.

The result of this discussion will be that we caution against a self-governing type of vocational spirituality and advise maintaining the link with religious spirituality. Professionals need religious spirituality.

2.3. The Relations of Spirituality

Spirituality always functions in a specific environment. As Christians we readily recognize the ecclesiastical realm but also vocational practices like educational practice, or practices of business, care, and farming. We now are dealing with the context holding for religious spirituality (as nourished by religious beliefs) and the context holding for vocational spirituality (in which sources of inspiration and conditions hold generically for practitioners).

The context of religious spirituality and the context of vocational spirituality may overlap, as for instance in the work of the Salvation Army. Or the contexts can also be starkly differentiated, even leading to two separate areas: the private and the public. Because this can amount to dualism, we look for ways whereby practitioners may combine both.

Here the I in PISA comes to our aid. Being integral about spirituality means being able to balance the two contexts and types. We do not deal here with the clashes between opposing realms: the religious versus the nonreligious, the private versus the public, or even church versus state. We observe how professionals (in our latest example, teachers) are able to balance integrally their specific religious spirituality with their vocational spirituality.[15] This is far from a pious acrobatics; it is the very essence of the identity of the Christian professional. We may call this the ability to relate meaningfully, or the ability to be relational, to one's spirituality. The Christian professional may engage with others in common liturgies to do so communally.[16]

Relating to one's spirituality refers in this case to the function of relating to traditions, sources, and practices. For instance, one may follow devotionals and liturgies to celebrate a religious heritage. We call this feature of spirituality the relational quality of spirituality. Spirituality entails being in touch with something, near or far. Many definitions of spirituality include the factor of transcendence. For many Christians, being relational is having a relationship with God, with the other, with

---

15. De Muynck, *Goddelijk Beroep*.
16. J. Smith, *Desiring the Kingdom*.

the environment, and with oneself. Spirituality guides our being relational by pointing to a transcendental source of meaning. The sacred and doctrinal texts of religions are strong traditional sources of spirituality. These sources are taught to us, so that we come to understand their basic meaning and purpose. Such sources guide us in all of the aspects of being relational: personal, communal, and universal.[17] Along these same lines, we see our students exercising their spirituality as the living tradition of faith bequeathed to them by parents, instructors, and church authorities, as their instruction relates to distinct sources. This does not discount that media, political parties, student organizations, and peers play an instrumental role in revealing the value of spiritual sources. These elements are the social imaginaries of our spirituality.

What we mean by the relational functions of spirituality is that it is something people do relationally in terms of bringing spirituality into practice. People do so by living an integral life and by relating to fundamental sources and communities in ways applicable in their vocations. The deepest sources of meaning within themselves and beyond themselves are brought into their daily work. Because current practices of spirituality are not limited to belief content, but center more in the self and the self's transcendent relationship with sources of meaning, we see the reflective side of spirituality gaining prominence. By engaging in all sorts of reflection, people practice their spirituality and thereby gain transcendence. Such practices can take the form of a common liturgy that may be extensions of the Christian Sunday practices, but the practice of spirituality is essentially personal.

2.4. The Personal Aspect of Spirituality

Spirituality has an unmistakable existential aspect. Spirituality is about our interiority, and thereby reflects our existential beliefs regarding the deepest meaning of our lives. Spirituality connects our inner sources to resources of ultimate meaning that lie outside ourselves. Again, this is not a dichotomy between the private and the public; it is being integral and wholesome in one's core identity as a Christian professional.

We readily recognize spirituality in the personal contributions by students in communal gatherings to worship, such as campus ministry. We also recognize it in their willingness to be spiritual in their career

---

17. De Muynck and Kalkman, *Perspectief op Leren*.

choices. One instance of the latter is when a student adopts the maxim of justice for the marginalized in society as a personal calling (we go into this in detail below) by seeking employment in social work among the homeless in order to serve God. This type of spirituality goes beyond the worldview model of formation[18] to become an experiential matter for the student.[19] We will demonstrate from our analysis of narratives that Christians need such personal spirituality in order to position themselves correctly in the broader realms of society and thereby gain a moral profile. We expand on this in section 4 below.

For young adults, spirituality is the dynamic functioning of a person in deep self-examination along questions such as: Who am I? Why do I live? How am I living? These questions on spirituality are not merely about the self. They are more about the experience of the self in touch with a transcendental source, which is, for the Christian, God and God's revelation. For young adults, this can be an intense experience that defines how they see themselves introspectively. To be guided adequately in their quest for true spirituality, they need clear reference points. Yet, we do not assume a simple one-to-one accordance, as if their particular spirituality (for example, evangelical charismatic) would automatically bring them to spiritual growth.

Our focus here is on how spirituality provides an intrinsic motivation to work in a certain practice, as well as to choose to be moral in that profession. Because of this focus on our motivation for performance, we return to the inner qualities of being spiritual, particularly in its in-depth quality. The question becomes, just how does spirituality relate to one as a person? To respond, we must abandon an exclusively religious analysis to also bring in existential or experiential considerations. We define spirituality as having to do with a fundamental component of our human-being-ness, rooted in human desires, longings, and hungers of the human heart.[20] Spirituality is more than emotion; it requires a contemplative consciousness,[21] and, with that, a certain enthusiasm to apply one's spirituality in all areas of life. In some cases, we view this as an experiential aspect, because it is based on experience in everyday life.

---

18. Examples are Wolters, *Creation Regained*; Plantinga, *Engaging God's World*; and Garber, *Fabric of Faithfulness*, yet the spirituality in these works is very strongly "understood" in these models as part of a worldview.

19. Borst, *Temptatio et Gaudium*.

20. Jochemsen and Hegeman, *Ethiek van de Zorg*, 1.

21. Borst, *Temptatio et Gaudium*, 37.

It comes close to the type of moral sanity we covered in the previous chapter called *sophrosyne*.

The inner qualities of spirituality is not limited to the religious, of course. Anyone who is earnest about experiencing spirituality within the boundaries of their spiritual practices experiences such inner qualities. But it would be wrong to emphasize here only the question of whether nonreligious spirituality would not have the same earnest experience as religious spirituality. The issue of interest is not how superficial one is or is not; it is how earnestly one relates one's inner experiences to performance in practices.

Below, we return to this aspect in two ways. We deal with religious spirituality in section 3 of this chapter, and with vocational spirituality in chapter 5.

2.5. The Roles in Spirituality

As discussed in chapter 2, spirituality works functionally in terms of the roles carried out by participants. We also found that such roles are part of practices. An example of a role in spirituality would be the way a person engages in daily devotions and personal piety. These can be done individually but also communally. In this chapter, we recognize the force of liturgies as social imaginaries. A social imaginary is an implicit knowledge shared by people when they carry out their spirituality socially.[22] In other words, spirituality is what people do together, in terms of a social imaginary in communities. In this section, we focus on the communal aspects of carrying out certain roles whereby we learn our spirituality. In the context of higher education, we elucidate two examples of spirituality in community: (1) engaging in faith formation and moral formation, and (2) learning how to deal with the spirituality of others in professional care practice.

First, we treat extensively the role of faith formation and moral formation in section 2.6 and section 5 of this chapter. Our objective is to analyze the faith formation or moral formation of students, seeing as such formation is a cherished goal of many educators. We observe that the manner whereby faith is expected to progress differs by setting. Although empirical studies show that the rate of progress is not high during the college years,[23] we still conclude that spirituality does function as part of Bildung for students.

22. J. Smith, *Desiring the Kingdom*.
23. Edgell, "Preparing Business Students."

A second discussion track in this chapter is how to deal with the spirituality of others. In professional schools, certain departments, like nursing, develop the role of spirituality in the profession. A specific example would be of a nurse working from a Christian perspective who is prompted to cooperate with non-Christians in a hospital ward. Nurses serve the spiritual needs of patients and thereby must provide committed and skilled care in this area. As part of their training, student nurses must learn to deal with the spirituality of others and of themselves.[24] Such competence can be understood as the capability to be sensitive about the spirituality of others (both patients and colleagues). At the same time, it means being aware of one's own spirituality and how it relates to one's personal development and performance. Also, in the professional curricula of social work of the CHE, study career mentors (Dutch: *studieloopbaanbegeleiding*) aid students to develop their moral profiles in a worldview learning thread (Dutch: *levensbeschouwelijke leerlijn*) toward the goal of becoming full-fledged professionals in dealing with spirituality.[25] Spirituality in this context is knowing how to deal with one's own and others' spirituality (including worldviews) in a relational way. We return to this subject in section 5.

2.6. Spirituality and Its Function in Faith Formation

This is the first discussion track to hone in on faith formation. For the purposes of this book, faith formation is understood to be a way of exercising spirituality toward personal faith development and moral development. In education, the manner in which spirituality functions in the faith formation and moral formation of students is of great concern. Faith formation occurs at the nexus of context (school or religious institution), personal focus of spirituality, and the specific roles students play in becoming formed. Faith formation is a broad term encompassing moral formation. In this book, moral formation is defined as the process of gaining the morality required by one's spirituality and ethics. It is treated here as development based in ethical knowledge, skills, and attitudes for becoming moral in practice. The term *faith formation* is intended to do justice to our tradition, which places faith commitments before moral commitments.

---

24. Van Leeuwen and Cusveller, "Nursing Competencies"; Van Leeuwen and Cusveller, *Verpleegkundige Zorg*; Van Leeuwen, *Towards Nursing Competencies*.

25. Borst, *Temptatio et Gaudium*.

Recent empirical research is based in a review of five streams of literature on student faith formation:[26] the Christian pastoral stream, the Christian worldview stream, the Christian empirical stream based on Christian theory, the Christian empirical stream based on secular theory, and the general empirical stream based on secular theory. Our analysis of this literature review points out reasons why secular models of formation may not fit our students. At the same time, our analysis recognizes the function of secular models of student spiritual development.

2.6.1. FIVE STREAMS OF LITERATURE

Three of five streams of literature on student faith formation are explicitly Christian. The first could be termed the *pastoral literature*. Normally found in the ministry sections of seminary libraries, this stream of literature flows from theology and (mostly anecdotal) pastoral experience. Second, the Christian worldview literature has contributed significantly to faith integration in the business discipline, especially in sketching lines of metatheory. Integration of worldview theory into business thinking by Shirley Roels, Bob Goudzwaard, Jacques Ellul, Brian Walsh, and others has contributed to a biblical understanding of business. Worldview literature tends to be more conceptual than empirical, citing cases of companies or individuals rather than statistical studies.

Denise Daniels, Randall Franz, and Kenman Wong bring the worldview discussion of spirituality and management into a business education setting by developing implications of worldview for both management practice and pedagogy.[27] They use worldview analysis to frame four contrasting lenses through which a student or businessperson views the world. Under such a frame, a student ascribes to one or more worldviews. How the student arrives at this view is not analyzed. For Margaret Edgell's empirical study, multidisciplinary worldview theories formed the philosophical foundation of the third model tested—the extensive model illustrated in sidebar 17.[28]

Two other Christian streams are empirically based. CCCU scholars in psychology have developed a body of empirical work on the faith integration process over the past twenty-five years, many in the journal

---

26. Edgell, "Preparing Business Students."

27. Daniels, Franz, and Wong, "Classroom with a Worldview."

28. Clouser, *Myth of Religious Neutrality*; Van Brummelen, *Steppingstones to Curriculum*; Greene, *Reclaiming the Future*.

Research in Christian Higher Education.[29] Some conceive new conceptual frameworks and instruments, based on their Christian experience of faith formation. Edgell terms this stream of literature *empirical Christian innovation*. These inventors may refer to secular theory but do not explicitly root their theory in secular thought.

A second group of Christian scholars in psychology form a fourth stream of literature. They dig deeply into the dynamics of spiritual growth by utilizing classic spiritual and moral development theories from the secular academy. The journal *Research in Christian Higher Education* publishes on average at least one high-quality empirical study a year. More importantly, these scholars evidence biblical purposes and principles throughout their theory making. In order to appreciate their contribution, it may be helpful to review some of the secular theories they drew upon, which constitute the fifth and dominant stream of faith formation literature.

To find formal theories of faith formation that have been tested empirically, Christian scholars often look to the secular academy, where student development theory has matured. The classic, empirically based theoretical models of student spiritual development study the general student population, rather than targeting Christian students. Even so, there are hints of Christian background in at least some of the more recent classic theorists, such as James Fowler and Sharon Parks.[30]

2.6.2. Definitions: Faith Formation and Moral Development

Moral development is the prevalent term in the secular literature. In many studies, it has been narrowed down extensively to moral reasoning exercises. Not a few theorists neglect to define the term. Roels not only critiques several definitions but states why she prefers Charles Shelton's definition.[31] She compared definitions of "moral development" by Lawrence Kohlberg, Arthur Chickering, and Charles Shelton and decided that Shelton's definition was the most comprehensive.

According to Roels, Shelton defined the morally developed student as one who can answer the following questions: "1) To what am I committed? 2) Why am I committed to it? 3) How important is this commitment to me? 4) Do my behaviors manifest this commitment? and

---

29. Y. Smith, "The JBIB."
30. Fowler, *Stages of Faith*; Parks, *Big Questions*.
31. Roels, *Moral Development*.

5) Am I still growing in this commitment?"[32] By speaking of the need for being fully committed as part of faith formation, we do justice to our tradition, in which the individual places faith commitments before moral commitments.

For the purposes of Edgell's study, Shelton's definition of moral development was preferred, due to its comprehensiveness, clarity, and applicability to Christian experience.[33] Because CCCU student life professionals tend to use the term *faith formation* more than the secular term *moral development, faith formation* is the preferred term for Edgell's study. We follow that use and regard faith formation as a broader category than moral formation.

2.6.3. THE SECULAR STUDENT DEVELOPMENT CLASSICS

In the extensive body of literature on the development of students that has grown since Chickering's original study, *Education and Identity*,[34] the work of William Perry Jr. is central to any discussion of moral development.[35] Others typically expand upon and critique his work. Perry's work documents the ways that cognitive processes tie into moral development. His model of expected growth has aided pedagogy design.

Besides Perry, there are other important names in the field of secular student development, whose work we will now review. Kohlberg delineates six stages of development of moral judgment observed in individuals from childhood into adolescence and adulthood.[36] His sequential, cognitive-developmental approach arose from comparing the work of Jean Piaget, Erich Fromm, James Mark Baldwin, and others. His work is not based in a higher-education setting, and normally only the last three stages would apply to college-age subjects. However, Kohlberg's work is one of the key theories from which any study of student moral development would benefit.

Fowler, a Christian minister and theologian doing research on spiritual development, developed a theory on "growth in faith."[37] He describes faith in a way similar to H. Richard Niebuhr, as the individual's quest to

---

32. Shelton, *Adolescent Spirituality*, quoted in Roels, *Moral Development*, 3.
33. Roels, *Moral Development*.
34. Chickering and Reisser, *Education and Identity*.
35. Perry, "Cognitive and Ethical Growth."
36. Kohlberg, "Moral and Religious Education."
37. Fowler, *Stages of Faith*.

trust a center of value and authority in ways that transcend, integrate, and ground the individual. Fowler's theory is based on comparing the individual development theories of Erikson, Piaget, and Kohlberg.

Parks builds an addition onto Fowler's house.[38] She adds a phase during the young adult stage specifically to reflect the college years. She feels that Fowler's model makes an abrupt jump from adolescence to adulthood, so she inserts a young adult stage between adolescence and adulthood. Like Fowler's, her theory is based on not only traditional student development theory but also on her own experience as a minister, teacher, and counselor to young adults.[39]

A more recent but well-advanced line of student development theory springs from the work of Marcia Baxter Magolda and Jane Pizzolato.[40] Pizzolato is working along the lines of previous research by Baxter Magolda in the identity theory branch of student development theory. Pizzolato researched how at-risk students developed self-authorship and found that student growth into defining self-identity was spurred by provocative experiences, which are more commonly described as defining moments.[41]

> **SIDEBAR 13. APPLICATION IN THE BUSINESS DISCIPLINE: MORAL MANAGEMENT DEVELOPMENT IN THE SECULAR MANAGEMENT LITERATURE**
>
> Discussion of spirituality and business has recently become widely accepted in the secular, popular press. Such discussions are in their early stages in the secular scholarly literature, which is more descriptive and anecdotal than empirical. Theories of spiritual and moral development set in the context of management education benefit from the heightened interest in spirituality in business. Business ethics courses enjoy renewed interest in the era that began with the Enron fraud scandal. Scholarly work is nascent in this area, and tends to be descriptive and untested.[42]

38. Parks, *Big Questions*.

39. Chickering et al., *Encouraging Authenticity*.

40. Baxter Magolda, "Integration of Relational and Impersonal Knowing"; Pizzolato "Developing Self-Authorship."

41. Pizollato, "Developing Self-Authorship."

42. Barnett et al., "Learning to Learn"; Bell and Taylor, "From Outward Bound"; Dehler and Neal, "Guest Editors' Corner"; Marcic, "God, Faith, and Management Education."

This review of research in the secular academy reveals that this approach contains a thin concept of morality—one in which the primacy of commitments depends overmuch on the individual's own moral reasoning.

2.6.4. CONCLUSION: SPIRITUALITIES CLASH

Edgell's literature review concludes that secular theories clash with Christian experience.[43] Despite their usefulness, theories rooted in secular sources often clash with Christian thought and experience from the outset in their definition of terms. Because secular attempts to define faith or spirituality are universalistic, they inevitably miss crucial particularities of Christian experience. For example, Patrick Love, a prominent scholar of student spiritual development, separates spirituality from religion. According to Love, spirituality is a search for meaning, wholeness, and purpose in life, whereas religion ultimately involves doctrine and dogma.[44] Kohlberg, Fowler, and Parks theorize that maturity is a process of moving from dualistic thinking to an inclusion of paradox, then to a universalistic spirituality.[45]

Such a universalistic ideal is antithetical to Christian theology and hence problematic for the study of Christian faith formation. Interestingly, secular-based studies, including Pizzolato's,[46] noted contrary results for respondents with high religiosity or strong Christian beliefs.[47] Not surprisingly, in Edgell's pilot test of these classic models, a Christian student faced with the binary choice of accepting or rejecting the model as reflecting his own growth had to reject it on the basis of the universalist acme.

In response to Edgell's study, we posit that the capacity of persons to be moral cannot be reduced to merely having specified ethical knowledge, or to making decisions according to universalistic models that emphasize moral reasoning. Too often, the attainment of mere skills in moral reasoning is considered a sufficient indication of being moral. We

43. Edgell, "Preparing Business Students."
44. Love, "Comparing Spiritual Development."
45. Kohlberg "Moral and Religious Education"; Fowler, *Stages of Faith*; and Parks, *Big Questions*.
46. Pizzolato, "Developing Self-Authorship."
47. Jane E. Pizzolato in personal conversation with Margaret Edgell, March 22, 2005.

term this a *thin view* of morality, which supposes that having certain dispositions and aptitudes will do the trick. We therefore regard moral development as necessarily part of a broader framework. Such a framework recognizes the worldviews, social imaginaries, and virtue theory involved in faith formation. It also must recognize what Christian educational philosophy tells us to expect of moral performance at Christian educational institutions. We acknowledge in this respect the embedding of morality within social practices, as these are found in most Christian colleges and universities. Moral development, in our view, requires a thick or rich interpretation of morality, where we may expect the tradition, roles, and narratives belonging to a high-level moral context to impact moral development.[48]

Recent studies show how students can achieve high moral reasoning skills (by achieving a thin morality) and even demonstrate moral sensitivity in class, yet make a dramatic misuse of these moral competencies in actual practice.[49]

This brings us to the question, what is the differentiating quality of faith commitment that has a thick concept of morality versus a secular model that has a thin concept of morality? Our response follows our focus on practices (P) and being integral (I). It brings us back to the fundamental aim we have—to be a fully committed, faithful person in a specific professional moral practice.

2.7. Calling, Vocatio, and Spirituality

Our finding that secular spiritualities and Christian spiritualities clash within the process of faith formation, which led us to question the need for religious spirituality, led us further to examine whether a functional approach to spirituality undermines the very importance of religious spirituality. Or, stated more actively, how can we avoid undermining the importance of religious spirituality? In the following, we argue that having a calling as part of one's vocational spirituality is necessary. We believe that religious input is crucial to calling, but the veracity of this statement depends on how one defines calling.

In chapter 1, we introduced the notion of *vocation* as a strong feeling of suitability for a profession. The *New Oxford Dictionary of English*

---

48. Vos, *Tussen Vage Waarden*.

49. Berkowitz and Bier, *What Works*; Bok, *Underachieving Colleges*; Wallage, *Achtergrond*.

S: Being Spiritual 173

defines *vocation* as "a strong feeling of suitability for a particular career or occupation." We hold, in agreement with Timothy Wineberg,[50] that this is a matter of deep reflection on one's identity. Above, we used the term *vocational spirituality* to describe how spirituality functions in a vocation. In the next section, we show how calling, vocation, and spirituality interconnect. Readers of Cornelius Plantinga's *Engaging God's World* will recall his reference to "learning as a spiritual calling: properly done, it attaches to God"[51] and will also recall the prominent role of the notion of calling in the final chapter on "Vocation in the Kingdom of God." In Plantinga's words:

> A Christian's main vocation is to become a prime citizen of the kingdom of God—and this is true of every Christian, of artists and engineers as well as ministers and evangelists. All are called to mesh their kingdoms with those of other citizens in order to work together inside the Kingdom of God.[52]

It is the function of religious spirituality in relation to calling that interests us here. Calling, or the Latin term *vocatio*, is a central concept in the Christian tradition. It reveals basic spiritual motivations. We read in 1 Pet 2:9, "But you are a chosen generation, a royal priesthood, a holy nation. His own people, that you may proclaim the praises of Him who called you out of darkness into His marvelous light" (NKJV). Here the Apostle Peter tells us that all believers are called to bear joyful witness to the saving acts of God. The Reformer Luther taught that this calling is not to be limited—as was practiced in the Middle Ages—to monastic life, but broadened to all facets of our lives as Christians, whereby "your calling becomes your vocation and your vocation becomes your calling."[53] The *vocatio* thus encapsulates the spiritual urge one experiences for and in one's responsibilities in life. In a Reformed evangelical mindset, calling and occupation are much the same idea.

Yet, religious spirituality and vocational spirituality need not be identical. A key aspect of calling is the clear implication that someone calls another. In religious terms, it can be said that God calls us to a pro-

---

50. Wineberg, *Professional Care*.
51. Plantinga, *Engaging God's World*, xi.
52. Ibid., 108.
53. Buijs, "Vocatio."

fession, as spelled out by Luther and Calvin.[54] The professional practice that most certainly requires a calling is theological ministerial practice. Ideally, individuals experience a calling to seminary. After becoming a full-fledged practitioner, the minister is called to a specific congregation. In this example, the practitioner is literally called to do something at each stage. Any discussion of calling begs the question, how can individuals be certain of their calling?

It becomes necessary for potential ministers and their mentors to distinguish between a clear confidence about a calling and the lack thereof. In a recent dissertation on the calling of Dutch ministers in the Protestant Church of the Netherlands, Johan van Holten studied ministers' conception of their role and their vocational awareness related to calling.[55] His research revealed that the biblical notion of calling is not always clear for ministers. Some feel called by God, yet they have a poor vocational awareness. Conversely, others have not distinctly experienced God's call, yet they function quite well as ministers. Van Holten attributes the confusion to the fact that the concept of calling does not have a clear theological structure in the Bible, which reduces calling to "a certain confidence based on one's spirituality."[56] Calling turns out to be a very subjective and personal matter.

It is also necessary to distinguish vocational awareness from the belief in having a calling; although the two are related, they are not the same. To begin with, the phenomenon of vocational awareness does not match exactly the sense of having a calling in its original meaning. Van Holten claims that vocational awareness involves the individual consciousness of someone who experiences a calling. It always involves a personal interpretation of, and a need to respond to, a spiritual or nonspiritual experience that may elude the perception of others. It is mainly an experiential and personal matter.

It is obvious that we are facing here a phenomenological as well as a conceptual problem. Apparently, not every Christian will experience a distinct call from a God personally. Even so, they may have a *vocatio*, or an awareness of being suitable for an occupation. Another consideration is that, given that not everyone has a distinct religious spirituality, we run the risk of making the *vocational spirituality* (a generic reliance on

54. Plantinga, *Engaging God's World*.
55. Van Holten, *Rol en Roeping*.
56. Ibid., 3.

certain sources that provide meaning) into a secularized alternative to what can be seen as a higher type of calling—the *religious calling*. We intend here to distinguish between the two types of calling but not to separate them. Both are needed in order to remain integral in professional practices.

In our view, if we want to preserve the normativity of calling as portrayed by Plantinga, then we would do well to assume that a religiously inspired calling remains the norm. We term this a *calling1*. Seen in this way, a calling has distinct religious and spiritual qualities that arise from a definite recognition of having been called by God to a particular vocation. We will give an extensive treatment of this type of calling in sections 3 and 4 of this chapter. Calling1 may be regarded as a high calling, but we will point out in section 3 the fallacy of this supposition.

If we want to preserve the phenomenological aptness of a vocation—a strong vocational awareness—then we also do well to distinguish a second type of calling also related to spirituality, which we term *calling2*. Seen in this way, a calling2 is having a distinct vocational spiritual quality, which amounts to a confidence that one is suited for a vocation on the basis of one's spirituality. Most secular approaches to spirituality in occupations work with this notion.[57]

We recognize that most secular formation practices (see section 2.6 above) may assume that having a vocational awareness (calling2) is more than sufficient. Yet, for Christians, it is very important to bring the interrelationship between calling1 and calling2 into practice. This interrelationship ought to be taught by default in faith formation. To be sure, both callings should be taught not only in those professions where the religious spirituality and the vocational spirituality are expected to mesh completely, as described above by De Muynck, but also in all professions, as we argued in chapter 3 on being integral.

Still, most Christian practitioners will vacillate between the two types of calling, or drop the first, because the spiritual urge involved inherently in vocational spirituality is often considered to be more than sufficient. By dropping calling1, Christians divorce their religious spirituality from their strong feeling of fittingness for the development of their professional identity, thus losing confidence that their religious spirituality matters. Such a divorce violates the integral quality of one's calling as a Christian.

---

57. As does Wineberg, *Professional Care*.

Here we raise an explicit concern regarding the context of the tradition of spirituality. By *tradition*, we mean the place of the calling. Each individual fits into a tradition by filling a role in a certain social practice in a specific organizational culture. If calling is integral in nature (see chapter 3) and practical, religious spirituality must inform vocational spirituality, although it must be acknowledged that maintaining the integral quality of calling1 and calling2 is far from easy.

At this point in our discussion, we will only use the traditional term *calling* (in the sense of calling1) to indicate that persons actually receive a call as understood from religious spirituality. We gave examples in sections 3 and 4 of this chapter. Our use of calling1 fits well with Plantinga's description of calling as an experiential confidence that one is called to a vocation, grounded in one's religious spirituality. On the other hand, we will use the term *vocatio* (in the sense of calling2) to indicate a deep-seated urge to be involved in a vocation. We assume that this vocational awareness involves strong self-knowledge of one's character and capabilities. This second type of calling is treated in chapter 5. We acknowledge that, for many people, vocational awareness even when spirituality is involved may not be narrated religiously. Nonetheless we recommend that Christians combine their religious calling1 with their *vocatio*, or calling2.

To summarize, we defined calling and vocation, although their relatedness makes any distinction between them necessarily messy. It is far from easy to differentiate and recombine these two aspects: having a religious spirituality and a related calling (calling1) and having a vocational spirituality and a related awareness of *vocatio* (calling2). It is the nature of spirituality to evade simplistic analysis. The next section examines how religious spirituality functions in the context of higher education to influence personal calling and generate specific roles in formation. We hope to show how the functions of spirituality and calling mesh together rather than combine to form a mess.

3. THE CONTEXT OF CHRISTIAN SPIRITUALITY

3.1. Spirituality in Practice

Spirituality in practice reveals how people function in both religious and existential modes. Their behavior follows what has been inherited and applied by others before them. As is the case in most Christian colleges with which we are acquainted,[58] aspects of a specific spiritual tradition are manifested in educational practices. For instance, Reformed evangelical spirituality is a tradition but also a communal experience. It reflects the very intricate ways in which we organize our spirituality in education, often via the ways in which teacher practitioners understand their specific *vocatio* within the practice of higher education. If we apply this insight to the issue of moral formation, we see in the broad Reformed evangelical tradition the strong role of Calvinism in basic aspects of spirituality. We will trace certain beliefs enacted over history that have come to define Reformed spirituality in higher education.

3.2. Reformed Spirituality and the Pedagogical Motive

In this section, we limit our analysis of the influence of traditional spirituality to the question of which basic precepts of Calvinist Reformed spirituality led educators over the centuries to aid learners to develop a certain moral profile.[59] We shall demonstrate that the profile it generates is the calling. Calling includes a vocational awareness for realizing God's order in all facets of life, commonly referred to in Reformed circles as being a citizen of God's kingdom. Because this profile is related integrally to Calvinist spirituality, we must explain the context and the experience of calling.

The summons to learning in the Reformed tradition flowed directly from the recognition the first Reformers had of the learning needs of those who had formerly belonged to the Roman Catholic tradition. John Calvin emphasized the abilities of all people to learn. In many respects, his major publication (*The Institutes of the Christian Religion*) was written as an introductory text on the Protestant faith and as such embodied a strong pedagogical aim.[60] The overarching theme of the book—and Calvin's greatest theological legacy—is the idea of God's full sovereignty, particularly in salvation and election. But the power of God does not erase the ability of humans to exercise understanding, to which Calvin attributed great significance.

---

58. Three Dutch universities for higher professional education: Christelijke Hogeschool Ede, Gereformeerde Hogeschool Zwolle, and Hogeschool Driestar-Educatief in Gouda; Calvin College in the USA.

59. Bratt, "What Can the Reformed Tradition Contribute" serves well as an oversight of this development.

60. Calvin, *Institutes of the Christian Religion*. For English, we used the translation by Henry Beveridge; in Dutch the translation by Alexander Sizoo.

According to Calvin, all people were created to learn in a way that reflects the image of God within them.[61] We may term this the *love of learning about God's world*. Calvin did not say this lightly, being a foremost scholar of ancient and contemporary philosophy. The aspect of humanity that Calvin focused on was the ability of people (read: laypeople as well as clerics) to perceive God's will. In the new Reformed congregation, congregants sought the Holy Spirit for understanding of what God called every person to do in every walk of life. Each individual should do so by the grace of God.

Calvin then reasoned that the source of all truth lies in understanding the Word as guided by the Holy Spirit. The workings of the Holy Spirit are sovereign, to the extent that—if God deemed fit—heathens could receive revelation of the truth, even where Christians failed to comprehend. The radical implication was that anyone within the church could possibly receive truths imparted to him or her by the Holy Spirit. Remarkably, it also meant that non-Christians could be singled out by the Holy Spirit to receive certain truths on created reality and even on God, the *sensus divinitatis*. Calvin thus warned against looking down on non-Christian authors.

This remarkable point of view went beyond trusting the epistemology of knowing truths or logic, for which Calvin was renowned. Granted, the non-Christian was expected to need knowledge of the Word and the Holy Spirit to truly know the real truth. Nonetheless, the image of God, to some extent still reflected in the non-Christian as well as in the believer, could reveal much truth. Both Christian and non-Christian, in Calvin's view, need much instruction and aid from the Holy Spirit in order to discern truth from distortion of truth. The importance of this insight to the moral profile of humans is great. It means that all learning falls under the authority of the Holy Spirit. Hence, serious effort must be taken by those within the Protestant faith who want to emulate the quality of knowledge of other Christians and even of non-Christians. As we point out later, this love of learning means exercising humility by subjecting oneself to God's rule and to the workings of the Holy Spirit in the way God distributes learning.

A second pedagogical principle advanced in the Reformation was the teaching that Christ Jesus rules.[62] Followers of Christ Jesus may,

---

61. Col 3:10.
62. *Heidelberg Catechism*, Lord's Day 19.

through his grace, belong to his kingdom, but even for those who reject him, Christ still rules. Given that a common person in the church can come to know this truth experientially, then all in the church must demonstrate their personal indebtedness to the King for knowledge of his sovereignty. This gratitude has motivated millions of Christians to serve him, including in the field of education. Out of love for their King, educators put their full professional weight behind the optimal development of potential subjects of their King (understood as citizens of the kingdom). These subjects—having the innate capacity to learn—receive a calling (now in the sense of a confidence based on their spirituality) to display the value pattern of the King in their own lives, in their communities, and in their societies.

In these ways, Christian education has become a resourceful practice where the love of learning and the love for the King flow together in the formation of young members of the kingdom of God in their moral calling to serve the King. We term this the citizenship of the kingdom calling. In the classical sense of calling, someone—the King—is calling us to obedience.[63] As we point out below, this manifests itself in the profile of demonstrating love to the Ruler and his rule. Our short list of attitudes that compose this basic spiritual attitude in life includes orderliness, propriety, and (eventually) civility in the kingdom.

3.3. Reformed Spirituality and the Calling of Kingdom Citizens

In the following, we delineate five themes in the spirituality of Reformed evangelical thinking that influenced how educators came to advance a calling to be a kingdom citizen. Each of these themes has significance for the way educators view their students and also for the way they view themselves. We deal with the following themes: the glory of God, the Fall and Redemption, common grace and special grace, atonement and the law, and, finally, authority and responsibility.

3.3.1. THE GLORY OF GOD

Those of the Reformed stripe are known for advancing their causes with the express aim to glorify God. Others may wonder why they can be so confident in glorifying God. Nevertheless, they believe that within education their telos is found in Rom 11:36: "For of Him and through Him

---

63. Our focus is here on the "calling" to be kingdom citizen as a basic spiritual attitude in life.

and to Him are all things, to whom be glory forever. Amen" (NKJV). Knowledge of reality around us leads us back to God in order to make God's majesty shine. The figure of Christ Jesus is found at the root of this aim. Christian learners, including teachers, attempt to apply the doxology of Col 1:15–20 to the grandeur and glory of Jesus Christ. The image of the invisible God becomes visible in their lives of faith. Often this is called the profile of imitating Christ. For Paul, belief in the deity of Christ was practical in that Jesus rules in real life, in real time. Early Reformers learned that his rule has to do not only with personal redemption, but also with creation. In this way, the image of Christ prevails as Creator, Redeemer, and risen and glorified King. They taught that he prevails over the evil forces that Christians encounter, even though we may not recognize sufficiently his intervention.[64]

Three aspects of this spirituality are important for moral formation. First, the concern to share the knowledge that Jesus is more than Creator and Redeemer—he is also the upper Ruler of our present reality, here and now—makes us more aware of our current membership in his kingdom. His glory is to be our aim in all we do in his kingdom. All Christians hold responsibility to bring this about.

A second point is that deep, empirical knowledge of our present reality (or God's creation) is requisite for achieving kingdom aims and thus the glory of God. Obviously, knowledge of this world cannot be achieved without substantive scientific practice, scholarship, and professional performance.

A third consequence of Reformed spirituality is that the faithful have been taught for ages that we are not godlike but only created in the image of God. Coming close to the angels (Ps 8) does not take away our createdness, sinfulness, and dependence on redemption. We see the significance of this issue today when we encounter claims in New Age spiritualities and postmodern philosophies that cause modern people to usurp the glory that accrues only to Christ Jesus. We counter these movements with the statement that humans are only to be (re)created by the Spirit of God and renewed to the ultimate moral profile of true humanity before God and their fellows. The Spirit renews us in our humanity and brings us to this creational goal, which is to glorify God in higher education.[65]

---

64. Heb 2:12–18.

65. Noordegraaf, *Meer Dan een Formule*.

3.3.2. The Fall and Redemption

Many Christians hesitate to profile themselves morally, even as citizens of the kingdom of Christ. And for good reason: human depravity is one of the Christian dogmas most readily verified empirically. In the Reformed understanding,[66] humankind is enslaved to sin to the extent that the perversion of our being is the magnifying power of all sin. This evil force downgrades all of creation. It renders the levees blocking out sin porous. All this rot comes from what Christians refer to as the Fall.[67]

If then all of our being and doing is tainted by sin, so also are our profiles of ourselves. This reality implodes any high views we may have of ourselves. Because this is undeniable, our learning or logical prowess is to be distrusted. No spheres (not even the higher spheres) of our humanity are exempt from the all-pervasive virus of corruption. This means that in all we do, no matter how well-intentioned we are, we may insult instead of honor God.

For these cogent reasons, we must never forget that we have lost sight of our high calling. Never may we forget that we may delude others and ourselves in what otherwise are noble efforts to mirror the will of our Creator in our lives. Our profiles are always questionable as to their authentic spiritual quality and moral integrity.

This has led certain Christian ethicists to once again posit the moral gap.[68] Reformed evangelicals confess that a chasm exists between God and humans. With all of our spirituality and morality, we cannot bridge this gap ourselves. We can try by exaggerating our own capacities, as atheistic scientists increasingly tell us to do.[69] We can erect another false bridge by lowering our moral standards, as evolutionists and naturalists urge us to do, arguing that we cannot but follow our DNA-determined instincts, therefore making us less culpable.

A serious Christian avoids such gap-reducers by asking the question: "How can we become *other* men and not merely *better* men?"[70] This

---

66. Belgic Confession (or Dordrecht Confession), article 14.
67. Gen 3.
68. Hare, *Moral Gap*.
69. An example of the efforts to bridge the gap is demonstrated in the debate between theologian Douglas Wilson and atheist Christopher Hitchens, author of *God Is Not Great: How Religion Poisons Everything* (Twelve Books), on the web (http://www.christianitytoday.com/ct/2007/juneweb-only/122-52.0.html). Another example is the work of Richard Dawkins.
70. Hare, *Moral Gap*, 66, 99, 203.

is the core question found at the root of our struggle with the effects of the Fall and the need for redemption. Christians must learn that they cannot bridge the moral gap without the assistance of God through the redeeming work of Christ Jesus. This realization makes them dependent on and humble before God. In sidebar 14, we read about how certain students make this a reference point in their spirituality.

> **SIDEBAR 14. THE PERSONAL RELATIONSHIP WITH GOD**
>
> The theme of having a personal relationship with God comes strongly to the foreground in the experiential Reformed spirituality found at CHE. The experiential Reformed students experience a longing for piety also found in the Second Reformation or the *Nadere Reformatie* in the Netherlands. This movement emphasizes the *sola gratia* formulated by the initiator of the first Reformation, Martin Luther. Each person is expected to know whether he or she is graced (or not) by a redemptive relation with God and to strive to live a life *coram Deo*. The grace achieved through a personal relationship with Christ Jesus has a special place in the spirituality of the Second Reformation.
>
> The influence of this pietistic spirituality in Christian higher education has been and still is today that students may aim to study and prepare themselves for a vocation by seeking an obedient communion with God. A study conducted by Hans Borst on the spirituality of experiential Reformed students at CHE indicates how they try to achieve this in their study and professional work.[71] The core beliefs the students hold are Reformed evangelical with a strong emphasis on piety and an earnest lifestyle. The Lord wants to be worshiped in loving obedience. Humankind, however, is naturally inclined to disobedience yet does have the choice of being obedient or not. Even today, we have the choice of eating from the tree of good and evil, but our inclination to make the wrong choice must be taken into account. The true believer, therefore, wants to be obedient to all of God's commands. This means literally listening to the voice of the Lord and being responsive to that voice at all times. A deep reverence for God is the resulting ethos.
>
> The students interviewed expressed their trust in God's redemption. The Lord promises restoration of humanity through

---

71. Borst, *Temptatio et Gaudium*, 137.

grace and mercy. Redemption is possible for us again. Toward this end, we are called to have a personal relationship with God in obedience and personal communion. The respondents stated their beliefs that God speaks to them, influences their lives, clarifies issues for them now or later, and gives them perspective on all matters of life. For them, God is a relational reality. These students seek a relationship with God that brings them to seek a satisfactory, authentic religious life based on a concept of an obedient life before the face of God. They may call God Father, Surety, Guide, Comforter, Rock, Source, or Friend. Being called to worship God involves listening to God's voice and wanting to be obedient to God integrally. Engaging in this experiential side of faith means to experiential Reformed students having such a personal relationship with God that the relationship can be qualified as being close to or familiar with God.[72] In their witness of their personal relationship with God, they may use the words *nearness, practical, intimate,* or *personal*.

The study in sidebar 14 found among students a distinct disavowal of a human ability to choose a moral profile without the assistance of the Holy Spirit. Inasmuch as it follows the classic account of redemptive history through the Creation, Fall, and Redemption, the experiential Reformed spirituality emphasizes the immense impact of the Fall of humankind into sin. The Fall destroyed the image of God in humans and broke humankind's relationship with God. A gap exists between God and us that we of ourselves cannot bridge. Humankind's innate gifts, talents, and possibilities do remain. Yet they are so seriously tainted by natural sin that only a personal relationship with God provides sufficient capacity to know the truth and become saved in God. Experiential Reformed spirituality is a God-infused piety. Only through God's Spirit does the prospect of a moral profile come into view.

The result of this belief concerning the dark side of humankind has been that many Reformed evangelical students (as well as many charismatic evangelicals) may not accept the inherent goodness in moral profiles stemming from other than authentically biblical sources. From a positive perspective, only the choice of a biblical profile having the right spirituality is warranted. This very heavy demand on choosing

---

72. Ibid., 137.

the right moral profile leads to a stringent analysis of human behavior. Alternatively, it may lead to an unintended superficiality by avoiding the issue of humanity's brokenness altogether.

3.3.3. COMMON GRACE AND SPECIAL GRACE

The beliefs that humankind is innately sinful and that a gap exists between God and us that can only be bridged by the grace of God brought Calvinists to formulate a distinction between two types of grace. The first is common grace, general grace, or general revelation. We call it common because it comes to everyone through being alive in God's world. The natural order proves that there is a mighty and majestic Creator.[73] Paul affirms that the goodness of the Creator is evident in all of us,[74] such that the demands of God's law are apparent to every human conscience.[75] This allows us to presume that we all receive the capacity to acknowledge the existence of a gap.

The second type, special grace or special revelation, is the disclosure in one's heart and acceptance of Jesus as Savior of sinners, which includes the regeneration of the new birth.[76] The new birth is the supernatural work of the Holy Spirit wrought in us, changing our dispositions and inclining our hearts to God. The fruit of special grace is faith and good works. Special grace is the basis for believing that the moral gap between God and us can be bridged.

The distinction Calvinists make between common and special grace impacts the moral profiles Christians aim for in education. The realization that all men receive common grace in effect downsizes their conceit, self-importance, pride, hubris, and even their virtues in learning. Common grace cuts away any basis for thinking that Christians are the only ones graced, an attitude termed triumphalism. Given also our sinfulness, we not only distrust our capacities but certainly also our moral profiles. We are to submit our capacities and our profiles completely to the custody of God's Word and will and ultimately to the authority of Christ Jesus.

The concept of common grace prompts Reformed Christians to seek traces of God's grace in others so that we recognize the work of

73. Ps 19:1; Rom 1:19–21; Acts 17:28.
74. Rom 2:4.
75. Rom 2:14–15.
76. John 3:3.

the Holy Spirit in them as well. As manifest in Calvinist doctrine,[77] the Holy Spirit through divine providence prevents moral chaos. This last point implies that the impact of specific Christian spirituality on moral profiles is dependent on God's work in us. Only through God's special grace, as revealed in the Gospel, are we called to be the salt and the light of the world.[78] This spiritual profile entails a very high calling.

3.3.4. Atonement and the Law

The atonement brought about by Christ Jesus has implications for education in an indirect way. As previously pointed out, the work of the Holy Spirit was assumed to be so pervasive that one could come to believe that God works in all individuals, not only believers. One factor of God's handiwork here is the use of the Law (the Decalogue). The Reformers taught that God's law had distinct functions for all of our lives, with impacts on all of society. The Calvinist triad of three functions of the law is well-known: spiritual, civil, and moral.

The first function of the law is like a mirror reflecting to us both the perfect righteousness of God and our own sinfulness and shortcomings. The second function is how civil authorities use the law to restrain evil (which falls under common grace). The third function of the law is to urge believers to obedience and to the joy of doing good works. This third function was not meant to promote legalism, since Calvin strongly emphasized living "under the law toward Christ" as a rule of life.[79] Believers were expected to follow all three functions of the law as demonstration of their love for Jesus.[80]

The strong emphasis on living under the law in love for Christ emphasizes what above has been called common or general grace, which is the second function of the law. The impact of this on Christian education has been great, for if God uses law to create and maintain order, then the world must be orderly and not chaotic. It was a conviction (which persists today) that the law of God fits the way God created us and nurtures us. It was also a belief in God's providence that God uses the law to conserve our lives.[81]

---

77. Belgic Confession, article 13.
78. Matt 5:13–14.
79. 1 Cor 9:21; Gal 6:2.
80. Calvin, *Institutes of the Christian Religions*.
81. Jochemsen, *Ethiek van de Zorg*.

Calvinists viewed natural regularities as evidence of the dependable will of God for creation. Therefore, rational analysis (science) and the professional rule (government) of God's creation became very legitimate ways of understanding God's will for our lives. Moreover, Reformed educators sought to disclose God's patterns of atonement in ordinary life as well. They found, catalogued, and described these as doxologies to God's care. Much emphasis was placed on truly knowing what life is about, as well as knowing why God wants values and norms to guide this life. The philosopher Herman Dooyeweerd taught that the order of life could be known to such an extent that we can come to know—to some degree—the fundamental normativity lying at the basis of reality.[82] At the same time, Dooyeweerd warned that, if humanity's knowledge of that order did not coincide with that order, then this thinking would clearly violate the call to intellectual humility. Nonetheless, a pattern of orderliness became a basic feature in Calvinist views of reality and of humanity's image as knower of that reality. Calvinists profiled the believer as one loving and seeking God's whole-scale order in life, which leads to shalom.

3.3.5. Authority and Responsibility

The type of authority Reformed evangelical Christians may long for certainly is one of well-designed rulership. To be sure, such authority was placed under God's order or rule. Calvinist anthropology taught that God's image was sufficiently left in humans to be recognizable as such. A search for harmony and restoration of unity, or shalom, characterizes much of Reformed thinking. We may call this a type of organic philosophy, but that would not diminish the results of the efforts that many Reformed educators undertook to develop a grand narrative of how all of Creation is held together by the Creator and the Creator's providential rule. The rise of Reformed philosophy in the early twentieth century[83] can be attributed to this quest for orderliness, particularly in social, political, and economic organizations. At the same time, these philosophies considered the creational order as feasible, and, in its concrete manifestation, dependent on historical and cultural circumstances. A believer was to observe and understand this order and give it shape in concrete situations as a form of shalom.

---

82. Van Woudenberg, *Gelovend Denken*.

83. See the works of Vollenhoven, Dooyeweerd, and Van Til in Clouser, *Myth of Religious Neutrality*; and Van Woudenberg, *Gelovend Denken*.

3.3.6. Our Overview of the Reformed Evangelical Calling in Education

We now summarize our analysis of the spirituality of calling commonly found among Reformed evangelicals in education. An essential component of this spirituality is a belief in the necessity of an order of social organizations in an orderly society (based on the created natural order and Word-bound normative order). This belief includes an implicit image of a human being as an orderly person. Accordingly, the purpose of a Reformed education was to reflect this basic belief in God's order of the world. The motive of being subject to Christ's rule encapsulates these beliefs and purposes. The reconciliation of individuals, brought about by Christ Jesus, could not do other than lead to reconciliation in the order of social relations, bringing their citizenship in the kingdom to fruition. The faithful were thereby given a mandate to carry on the personal identity they received in their "house" to others in society. Their goal was to demonstrate the orderly rule of Christ's kingdom in all facets of their social lives, as true citizens of the kingdom. At the same time, they were to be aware of the restrictions of their capacities to know and determine that order within the dynamics of historical reality.

The high calling to bear witness as citizens of the kingdom to God's rule in all facets of society, as well as to be continually aware of one's limitations in knowing and being, forms the background of the Calvinist ethic of responsibility. In chapters 2 and 3, the basic normativity of God's created order has been dealt with as the philosophy of normative practices. We now focus mainly on the spiritual roots of the concept of being responsible before God, as found in Reformed spirituality.

A basic premise in Reformed evangelical education is that all partakers of the social practice of higher education are accountable to God, each other, and themselves to be citizens of the kingdom. A true citizen cannot be other than responsive to the basic normative order the King has determined for us to live by.[84] Each learner is to know what the natural and normative order of reality is and why God wants us to behave in a certain way in that order.

The ethical side of this spiritual reality is love as motive for meeting the demands of being responsive to God. It forms a type of cohesive identity of oneself as a person having a deep troth to one's King.

---

84. Hegeman, "Stewardship and Integral Learning."

Reformed ethics, therefore, may be regarded as one of the best-known expressions of the deep Reformed evangelical longing to answer to our awareness of what God wants from us.

The calling (calling1) of being a citizen in the kingdom of Christ is a basic spiritual attitude we find in Reformed evangelical spirituality, which is still advanced by educators today. In the following, we point out how it is used in several spiritual profiles in more practical terms. In doing so, we enter the field of vocational awareness (calling2).

4. SPIRITUAL PROFILES AND MORAL PROFILES

4.1. The Direction of Spiritual Profiles in Moral Profiles

Much of our Christian spirituality concerns the "spiritual orientation, the longing for fulfillment of one's life according to the purpose or will of God"[85] —what we refer to as calling1. Christians in the past have developed excellent models for spiritual orientation. It is not only a matter of feelings but a matter of the work and life to which one is called. Its fulfillment takes the form of vocation, or calling2. We will demonstrate how these two types of calling intermesh. We distinguish three established spiritual profiles that are found generally in Reformed evangelical education in addition to two newer models. The established profiles are those of being a disciple, being a steward, and being a sojourner. Newer models are the prime-citizen profile and the shalom-seeker profile. There are, of course, other profiles, but these suffice to demonstrate how important it is to have a spiritual profile in PISA.

Discussion of each of these profiles demonstrates that the inner qualities of a person (or the personal aspects of spirituality) and the outer aspects of behavior and conduct (the way spirituality is expressed) are connected. On the inside, we find Christian views, confessions, motives, ethos, habitus, meaning, etc. These matters all concern the core of our Christianity and our deepest motives. On the outside, we find what we actually do, such as the spiritual sources we use, the role we take on, and the liturgies and practices in which we engage. We assume here that a certain congruency between what is inner and what is outer is attempted when students choose a profile. In this way, the spiritual profile gives direction to the choice of a moral profile.

---

85. Van der Plas et al., *Dagelijks Leven*.

4.2. The Profile of the Disciple

Being a disciple means living according to the will of our Master. God continually tests our character, our faith, our obedience, our love, our virtues, and our loyalty to make us grow in them.[86] A disciple follows the Master, as the theologian Dietrich Bonhoeffer taught regarding complete surrender to God while bringing faith into practice.[87] The apostle Paul also speaks of this complete dedication of himself to Christ.[88]

Within education, it is less easily said that we are to become disciples with the aim of following Jesus. Speaking of teachers or learners as disciples implies a dependency relationship between the master and the disciple. Given that a disciple is someone who wants to become like the master,[89] what does this mean for the student? It means that the student wants to become a follower, a friend, a confidant, someone who cherishes the teachings of the master and brings them into practice. If discipleship is part of a spiritual growth program, then teachers certainly must meet the grade of being good disciples of Jesus. If not, it is conceivable that students may miss effective role modeling.

We urge teachers to serve as disciples of the Master. Further, they must create favorable conditions for the discipleship of students. Such conditions include open discussions on the profile of being a disciple in education as well as in professions. Discipleship certainly does not mean complete abandonment of critical faculties as much as it means truly knowing that one wants to follow the great Teacher, Jesus. Many evangelical churches and colleges engage in discipleship training. This training shows that aiming to become a disciple is quite possible, and it can form an attractive moral profile for students. In this training, there is much emphasis on character training and on disciplining the inner side of our spirituality.

4.3. The Profile of the Steward

The steward in this profile is not the vocation of airline attendant; it is the profile of someone who administers very prudently the matters entrusted to his or her care. The Bible tells us that we are stewards over

---

86. Warren, *Purpose Driven Life*, 43.
87. Bonhoeffer, *Cost of Discipleship*.
88. 1 Cor 4:16; 11:1; Eph 5:1; Phil 2:5–8; 3:17; 1 Thess 1:6; 2:14; 2 Thess 3:7, 9; 1 Tim 4:6; 2 Tim 3:10–11; Heb 3:7.
89. See 2 Pet 3:18; Gal 4:19; Eph 4:13.

everything the Lord gives us: "The earth the Lord's, and all its fullness."[90] Particularly in the current global climate crisis, we become more aware of our care for all of creation.[91] We have received a mandate to govern nature and culture as if we are stewards in the name of God. Here is a clear expectation that someone with the distinct duties of being a steward will aim consistently and truthfully to make sure that the outer display of spirituality is done with the right motives in mind.

The profile of steward corresponds with orderliness (see above) as part and parcel of a Reformed worldview. A steward is someone with a clear conception of overall responsibility (both individual and collective) in the practical affairs of the kingdom, who is able to organize this responsibility well. In particular, a steward is virtuous and faithful in serving others.[92] This includes the conviction that we are to be responsive to normativity (see chapter 2) and answerable for our deeds before God, now and at Christ's return.[93] In this sense, being a steward is more than a job, it is knowing how to narrate how we serve God in what we are entrusted to do. The more God gives us, the more God expects of us,[94] and the more we are dependent on God.

The profile of a steward in education has not been fully deployed for the reason that such a type of responsibility often is not fully recognized and practiced while learning. The same holds for a related profile, that of being a servant,[95] which is often used in the sense of being a steward. Being a steward or servant fits more the authenticity and faithfulness in the actual conduct of persons in a social practice rather than what transpires in a learning environment. Nonetheless, service learning[96] and stewardship learning[97] are actuated, often quite effectively, to

90. Ps 24:1, NKJV.
91. Gen 1:26; 2:15.
92. 1 Cor 4:1–2.
93. Luke 16:11.
94. Luke 12:48b.

95. The concept of being a servant is well known through the success of Robert Greenleaf's book *Servant Leadership: A Journey into the Nature of Legitimate Power and Greatness* and its use in leadership training (see for the Netherlands, http://www.servantleadershipcenter.net). An orthodox Protestant equivalent in the Netherlands is Leidraad (http://www.driestar.nl/Leidraad). The sense we use the term "servant" in this book is more in line with the biblical sense of a spiritual profile. An application is given by Hegeman, *Christelijk Dienen*.

96. Gunst Heffner, and DeVries Beversluis, *Commitment and Connection*.
97. De Muynck and Van der Walt, *Call to Know the World*.

fill this gap. Hegeman describes a new morality of service orientations that accompanies this basic notion of serving God dutifully.[98] We may see much exploration of this spiritual profile within the so-called newer learning (chapter 2).

4.4. The Profile of the Sojourner

In early European Christianity, a sojourner or pilgrim followed a religious practice of traveling away from home, not always aware of the destination, but in complete trust in God's providential care. Filled with the spirit of pilgrimage (*peregrinatio pro Christo*), the missionary Willibrord, a monk from the Abbey of Ripon in Northumbria, traveled to hostile Friesland in the year AD 690. His arrival marked the beginning of the Christianization of the Frisian people in Northern Europe, later followed by the efforts of Bonifacius in AD 716.

Pilgrims not only travel; they are also aware of their temporary stay on earth. They long to enter their ultimate destination in heaven. This profile of "being in the World, but not of the World"[99] means that the believer does not attach to earthly goods but is en route, a traveler, a visitor, a passer by. This has nothing to do with being a tourist. A pilgrim follows deliberately the path that God sets before him or her. Famous in this respect is the allegorical novel *The Pilgrim's Progress from This World to That Which Is to Come* by John Bunyan (published 1678), which is a classic read by many Christians today. The inner qualities of spirituality achieves great weight in this profile.

Pietistic Christians, particularly the experiential Reformed, may be very fond of the profile of the sojourner. This profile emphasizes the need for a certain foreignness in not becoming attached to the world and its sinful value patterns. A sojourner is also aware that in all facets of life one needs sanctification. The image of the sojourner also provides much consolation in the face of the many disappointments inherent in being foreign to the world. This profile points the believer toward the expectation of eternal life and the fulfillment of God's kingdom. This profile may also liberate Christians from much frenetic dutifulness in aiming at improving on this world, without losing sight of the call to obedience and the cloak of servanthood.[100] At the same time, the profile

---

98. Hegeman, "Stewardship and Integral Learning."
99. Ps 119:9; 1 Pet 1:17.
100. Van de Beek, *Hier Beneden*.

of being a sojourner can be abused in a dualistic fashion by withdrawing oneself from exercising responsibility for so-called worldly matters. In this way, the sojourner profile requires much nuanced insight into personal spirituality.[101]

The image of being a sojourner is explicitly followed by some orthodox Christians in higher education, even where students prepare themselves for jobs in the vocational sphere.[102] The sojourner profile is quite valuable for reminding us of the limitations of other moral profiles that may come into conflict with our basic spiritual habitus as sojourners. At the same time, it must not be applied dualistically with the ill effect of legitimizing a split identity (a problem we deal with in chapter 5).

4.5. The Profile of Being a Prime-Citizen of the Kingdom

The truly gifted work by Cornelius Plantinga Jr., *Engaging God's World: A Christian Vision of Faith, Learning and Living*, applies the basic Reformed concept of having a calling1, as explained above. He employs a central metaphor of going beyond being just a citizen of the kingdom to strive toward being an excellent or prime one. Given that most Christian students adopt the essential biblical truths (shalom, Creation, the Fall, Redemption), Plantinga argues that a student must aim for the profile of becoming a prime citizen in the realm of spirituality. He or she does this within the practice of what Plantinga calls learning as a spiritual calling that "properly done, . . . attaches us to God. In addition, the learned person has, so to speak, more to be Christian with."[103] This learning is directed toward a vocation in the kingdom of God. We read:

> Let's call a person who accepts Jesus' commission a good citizen of the kingdom of God, and let's call a person who accepts this commission with enthusiasm a prime citizen of the kingdom. A good citizen likes the kingdom of God just fine, but a prime citizen passionately yearns for the kingdom. A prime citizen has been redeemed far down in her spirit, way downtown in her heart, so that she deeply loves God and the things of God. She relishes God's Word. She rejoices in God her Savior. She finds that the things of faith—repentance, forgiveness, hope in God—seem sweet to her. Her pulse quickens at the prospect of blessedness such as "no eye

---

101. Borst, *Temptatio et Gaudium*, 142.
102. Borst, *Temptatio et Gaudium*.
103. Plantinga, *Engaging God's World*, xi.

has seen, nor ear has heard, nor the human heart conceived" (1 Cor. 2:9). In her best moods she longs not just for happiness, but for joy; not just for joy, but for God; not just for God, but also for the kingdom of God. Because of her enthusiasm for the kingdom, she doesn't merely endorse justice in the world; she hungers and works for it. She doesn't merely reject cruelty; she hates and fights it. She wants God to make things right in the world, and she wants to enroll in God's project as if it were her own. She "strives first for the kingdom" in order to act on her passion.[104]

Plantinga points out to us that the image of prime citizen of the kingdom is a strongly normative calling in the classical sense of being called by someone. It goes beyond the common profile of being a kingdom citizen (see above). He means thereby that a Christian's main vocation is "to prepare to add one's own contribution to the supreme reformation project, which is God's restoration of all things that have been corrupted by evil."[105]

Becoming a prime citizen entails a clear normative profile that embodies spirituality, on the premise that such a profile can fit education. Plantinga specifically sees this happening in individual learning, which involves knowledge, skills, and virtues (see the last chapter of his book). This profile figures as a candidate for the S in PISA, in the sense that it can be adopted by a person wanting to apply this vision in any vocation, even that of learning. At the same time, we are reminded by the pietistic Reformed spirituality that our talk of becoming a prime citizen must be infused with the right humility.

The qualities of Plantinga's model are evident. It is an exquisite presentation of the integral nature of faith applied to learning. Conditions I and S of PISA are very well treated. However, the difficulties with the prime citizen profile stem from the lack of its inclusion in the demonstrated faith practice of students in the vocational realm. Here we raise the question, just how can the innerness and the outerness of the prime citizen of the kingdom connect within the learning process in general and with the professional situation in particular? We simply do not yet know. Also, the concrete moral choices flowing forth from this profile in education are not yet evident, aside from the brilliantly written notion of longing for shalom (in Plantinga's chapter 1) as an Augustinian type of telos. We also do not know as yet how this approach can mesh with

104. Ibid., 108.
105. Ibid., xii.

learning outside of the highly complex context of an institution with a holistic Christian worldview. This last concern holds for professional studies in particular.

Applying this profile assumes that students have a spiritual vitality that will manifest itself through faith in action. The belief that one can authentically be a prime citizen of God's kingdom assumes that there is an inner holiness, a personal revival, or an experience of God that will result in a distinctive life that fits the profile. This kind of Christian commitment can be termed a very strong directional imperative. It requires much earnest attention by learners and their teachers.

Applying this spiritual profile requires much effort, including in professional studies. When the emphasis changes from getting all of the cognitive pieces together (worldview formation) to going out and living the life, we encounter many questions to explore about its involvement in moral formation. The accountability for performance as a prime citizen is thus a new area to explore in PISA.

4.6. The Profile of Seeking Shalom

In several philosophical works, Nicholas Wolterstorff has developed the fundamental notion of shalom, designed to guide higher education, and Christian higher education in particular.[106] This concept, also used by Cornelius Plantinga, has authentic biblical roots. In the Old Testament, shalom (peace, justice, wholeness, harmony, and spiritual wellness) contributes to the kingdom of God by restoring what was damaged by sin. By aiming for shalom, the believer pleases God. This all-encompassing notion is found in the Bible as a synonym for the ultimate end (or telos) for which believers live. Even more than that, shalom is also a way of life. In the New Testament, shalom also has the meaning of the presence of the kingdom itself. Since believers have (or should have) the telos of shalom, they are to live that shalom to the benefit of others. Wolterstorff argues that shalom ought to hold for learning as well. By pursuing shalom, education adopts the aim of reforming society. Wolterstorff's call to Christian educators is that "the Kingdom will not come without our efforts."[107] The work of the Christian educator stands in the kingdom-wide struggle to bring true shalom to a broken and sinful world. Higher education can be no exception.

---

106. Wolterstorff, *Until Justice and Peace Embrace*; Wolterstorff, *Educating for Life*; Wolterstorff, *Educating for Shalom*.

107. Wolterstorff, *Educating for Shalom*, xiii.

We see in Wolterstorff's educational philosophy how the integral nature of faith practice as assumed in the worldview approach is put into practice. Where Plantinga's model stops short of social involvement, there Wolterstorff's model continues. There is also the presumption that Christians wanting to do God's bidding are expected to always have this disposition. A shalom-seeker must internalize shalom. They must think about it, pray about it, study it, teach others about it, as well as do it. This is an active association of oneself with God's purpose on earth. Shalom in this conception is a spirituality that requires a connection between the inner as well as the outer aspect. It is a way of life.

Applying this spirituality to the moral formation of students is not easy. To start with, the shalom ethic is strongly imperative. The root words point this out. Words describing justice, such as *tsedeqah* in Hebrew and *dikaio'sune* in Greek, refer not only to the concept of what is right but also to the setting right of what is broken.[108] This implies that God commands us to aim at doing God's will. Wolterstorff repeatedly points out to us that shalom is not so much a matter of knowing but of doing. It is bringing the Decalogue into practice; it is beginning to practice the Sermon on the Mount. Shalom requires action, and that in two ways.

The central concept here is *dikaio'sune*, and we recognize two meanings of this word. In the broad sense, we may regard *dikaio'sune* as the quality that God expects to reign in a certain situation. Justice is to be done in a certain time and place so that peace and harmony come about. In the narrow sense, *dikaio'sune* also has the meaning of being righteous or justifiable, having virtue or purity of life, being righteousness in thought, word, and deed. In the latter sense, we see the just person appearing, of whom Jesus Christ is the supreme example. According to Wolterstorff, both aspects of *dikaio'sune* cohere within shalom.[109]

The complexity of this fully biblical moral profile makes us question its scope and utility. The demands placed on an individual wanting to live out shalom take on the contours of what the Anabaptist philosopher Kraybill calls realizing the upside-down kingdom in a lifestyle where values are so inversed that a new community is needed.[110] Realizing shalom in the double sense of the word is a high standard. Much like

---

108. Rom 3:21–26.
109. Wolterstorff, *Educating for Shalom*.
110. Kraybill, *Upside-Down Kingdom*.

the prime citizen of the kingdom profile, it is strongly normative, but the sheer immensity of its practical realization could be staggering for a single individual. It requires a moral formation whereby various moral competencies are understood in relation to communal effort. It is a social ethic that requires much thought and care to apply in one's life. Plantinga makes this very clear in a brilliant chapter on the longing for shalom.[111]

Given these profound qualities of the shalom profile, we see possibilities for mentors to emphasize the reference to Christ as the one whose character is the determinant of morality and ethics, and even the one in whom all things hold together, for "in Him all things consist."[112] It is the sheer immensity of aiming for public justice as well as becoming just that makes us quite aware of the need for humility and acceptance of God's sovereignty in life and faith as guiding virtues, so that it becomes a dependency relationship on God. As was the case with the profile of prime citizen, incorporation of the profile of shalom seeker in moral formation (including PISA) is a new area for educators and professionals to explore.

5. DOING SPIRITUALITY: TWO EXAMPLES

How do students apply their spirituality during education? We treat two ways whereby students learn to deal with their spirituality and that of others. The first is the practice of faith formation; the second is the practice of spiritual care. Both are examples drawn from Christian institutions, and both are carried out in higher education.

5.1. Faith Formation: A Case of Business Students

5.1.1. Introduction

In this section, we report the results of an empirical study of the faith formation of business students as carried out by Margaret Edgell.[113] In a survey of business students at a Christian university in the United States, she tested three models of faith formation by indicating which aspects of these models best reflected perceived experience. The first model (the

---

111. Plantinga, *Engaging God's World*.
112. Col 1:17b, NKJV.
113. Edgell, "Preparing Business Students."

classical model) was derived from classic secular theory. Defining moments, a cutting-edge model from the secular literature, offered a second model. A third model (the extensive model) was derived by Edgell from an explicitly Christian philosophy of education. Because the author's version of the extensive model was verified the most strongly of the three models, we will explain how this model serves to best understand the integration of spirituality and moral formation in PISA.

This empirical study by Edgell is used to understand how the mission of faith integration plays out in the area of moral formation, specifically in student faith formation. The study's main focus was on the spirituality of Christian students, meaning those who self-identify as Christian. In order to study highly applied approaches to faith formation in a professional discipline, a population of business students in a CCCU college in North America was the population of interest for this study. Edgell undertook an analysis of the actual working models of growth in faith, as evidenced in the population of students examined.

5.1.2. The Analysis of Working Models of Faith Formation

Edgell's general research question was, how closely do our working models of growth in faith in the disciplines reflect actual student experience? This question was approached using two strategies. First, three explicit models of faith formation were selected, two from the literature, and one from the author's understanding of a Christian philosophy of business education, to represent the three basic vectors of a metatheory of faith integration. Model 1 (the classical model) focuses on cognitive development. Model 2 (the defining moments model) is based on identity formation. Model 3 (the extensive model) exemplifies faith integration that is learned in practice. Second, the general research question was divided into two subordinate questions:

1. Do business students at the college that was studied progress over the college years into higher stages of development?

2. Are any of the three models a reliable measure of faith formation for the business student population studied?

The first question tests the assumed developmental nature of all three models. The second question leads to a test of the models against students' perceived experiences of faith formation. Each of the three models tested is described in the survey instrument via a short vignette, or personified development narrative. Each vignette also illustrates how a person chooses a certain spiritual profile.

5.1.2.1. Model 1: Classical

The classical model is illustrated by a vignette (see sidebar 15 below). John's story describes Parks's model of young adult growing in faith. Her model is the latest in a classic line of research in the general academy that has been validated for the general student population. Termed here the *classical model*, it is grounded in the work of Kohlberg, Fowler, and Parks.[114]

> **SIDEBAR 15. JOHN'S STORY: JOHN FINDS HIS CALLING**
>
> As a teenager, John read his Bible often and prayed. His prayers began to include requests for guidance regarding a vocation in business. His ideas of vocation in business were what he gained from parents, family, church, and Christian schooling. As he grew more mature, he began to critique and analyze the faith he had inherited. At times, he resisted the complete authority of his inherited belief system in the business world. He began to view other faiths as at least partially valid in how they related to the business world.
>
> A major step in maturing his faith was to own it for himself. He wanted to be recognized for who he was and who he was becoming. He had support from mentors, old and new, in developing his own convictions about how to conduct business. He made a commitment to his new view of himself as a Christian in business. He preferred to associate with others of similar belief, so he joined a Christian Business Breakfast Club. His openness to the people of other faiths was only within the boundaries defined by his Christian faith.
>
> As John matured even more, he became comfortable associating with people outside his faith. He joined Rotary Club, where he was very active. He became able to cope with ambiguities and paradoxes in the Christian faith, while still keeping his convictions.

5.1.2.2 Model 2: Defining Moments

The defining moments model is also illustrated by a vignette (see sidebar 16 below). Mike's story describes a defining moments model of student

---

114. Chickering et al., *Encouraging Authenticity*.

development. This model is based in student identity theory.[115] Pizzolato found that student growth into defining self-identity was spurred by provocative experiences. Such experiences "disrupted students' equilibrium such that they felt compelled to consider and begin to construct new conceptions of self."[116] This defining-moments approach resonates with a Christian approach called *work as ministry*, developed by Randy Kilgore.[117]

> SIDEBAR 16. MIKE'S DEFINING MOMENT
>
> Mike benefited from Christian schools and college in terms of much food for thought on faith integration in business. He thought about the person he would become and mulled over his choices.
>
> But he did not own faith integration in business for himself until he was faced with a decision with only two choices: either comply with his boss and falsify sales reports, or lose his job. In this defining moment, he had to decide which fork in the road to take. He had support from mentors, but he had to analyze the implications and choose for himself. This choice provoked him to decide which person he would become.
>
> He made his choice and committed to it. This defining-moment choice determined the way he operated in the business world from then on.

5.1.2.3 Model 3: Extensive Model

The extensive model is illustrated by a vignette as well (see sidebar 17 below). Susan's story describes the model devised by Edgell, which derives from what Richard Mouw would term *extensive faith formation*, which flows naturally from both a popular evangelical metaphor for faith formation and from a Kuyperian philosophy of education. This model sees Christian development as an ever-widening and deepening advance of a distinctly Christian worldview into all aspects of reality. The evangelical aspect of the extensive model derives from a popular tract entitled "My Heart, Christ's Home." This tract describes faith formation as the progressive invitation of Christ into further rooms in the house that rep-

---

115. Baxter Magolda, "Integration of Relational and Impersonal Knowing"; and Pizzolato, "Developing Self-Authorship."

116. Pizzolato, "Developing Self-Authorship."

117. Kilgore, *30 Moments*.

resents a Christian's life. For example, I may begin by inviting Christ into the front door and the living room, but it may take time for me to realize that he must also inhabit my kitchen and bedroom. This metaphor assumes that the Christian aims for the presence of religious spirituality in all areas of life.

The Kuyperian aspect of the extensive model is grounded in the work of Clouser and Van Brummelen.[118] The following vignette, "Susan's Legacy," is an attempt to express Mouw's concept of extensive growth in the form of fictional narrative.[119] The dynamic of this model is territorial, along the lines of Abraham Kuyper's claim of the world for Christ: "There is not one square inch of the entire creation about which Jesus Christ does not say, 'This is mine! This belongs to me!'" Like the Reformed tradition that Kuyper represents, this model is intended to exemplify progressive, personal victories for Christ—in essence, the process of sanctification, or dedicating one's life to God.

> SIDEBAR 17. SUSAN'S LEGACY
>
> Susan made a commitment to Christ by accepting salvation. More and more, she wanted Christ to matter in different areas of her life, including her business life. She decided to apply biblical thought to her business life, first, by avoiding sin and second, by feeling the need to share the gift of salvation with coworkers. Some of her initial efforts went well, some did not. She also focused on charitable giving from her earnings. She began to want to live all of her business life for God's purposes. She became concerned that her company did not always have values that matched her own, and Susan tried ways to navigate that difference. She desired more and more to mature throughout her lifetime in her faith in her business life. She began to find ways to change her company for the better, in ways that reflected her inner convictions. She matured to the point that she was looking for ways to pass on to the next generation what she learned.

---

118. Clouser, *Myth of Religious Neutrality*; Van Brummelen, *Steppingstones to Curriculum*.

119. Mouw, "Maturity Mandate."

5.1.3. Test of the Working Models

In this section we portray the main results of Edgell's study. We will conclude that the extensive model matches settings where a homogeneous spirituality exists, but that this moral climate may not necessarily lead to measurable moral development.

The test of the three faith development models done by Edgell focused on (1) progress of faith formation during education as described by the choice of three models, and (2) the fittingness of the three models used. In this population of business students, Edgell did not find evidence that significant growth in faith formation took place in the four years during which the students followed the curriculum. Student responses to all statement items contained in all three models varied very little by class. Edgell's first major conclusion is that measurable development in faith and moral formation is difficult to determine. In fact, it is very difficult to discern responses changing significantly with maturity over the college years.

Edgell comments further that she expected to observe measurable development using the classical model, because Parks focuses her stages of development in the college years. However, the general literature on spiritual and moral development of students indicates that longitudinal studies usually need to include five years after college to show statistically significant changes over time. Other considerations regarding slow development include gender differences,[120] and the maturity that occurs outside college experience,[121] especially as students increasingly take time off from college. Edgell was not surprised to see little change in defining moments factors because experiential influences from business settings are much more prevalent after graduation.

The second research item addressed the question of which of the working models fit the experience of the students the best. Edgell examined whether the three models provided a reliable measure of faith formation for the business student population studied. Vignettes representing the three models were presented to respondents who could then choose the model that fit their experience. Edgell's conclusion is that the secular models are a poor fit for the population of students studied. Edgell therefore holds that customizing extant models of student spiri-

---

120. Gilligan, *Different Voice*.
121. Chickering et al., *Encouraging Authenticity*.

tual development[122] to fit a Christian population has very little promise. In her estimate, the extensive model is the best fit. A model of spiritual development that springs from an extensive Christian worldview, without dependence on classic or recent secular theories is the best fit to the studied business student population. This does not discount that some aspects of the other models, in particular the defining moments model, closely approximate student experience.[123]

The extensive model deserves consideration in our discussion of moral formation in the professions. It portrays a strongly homogenous population that reflects quite positively on having gained spiritual and moral competencies but that may remain quite limited in its propensity to develop during the college years. The image is one of a high and thick shared collective morality along with a low level of skills in actual formation. It resembles a survey study done in the Netherlands by Nicolien de Jong and Tirza van Laar on the morality of students and faculty of a

---

122. Kohlberg, Fowler, and Parks; Baxter Magolda and Pizzolato.

123. A significant result of Edgell's study is that the secular models have a low reliability. The results were ambiguous, in that the highest mean (or highest agreement) was seen for the defining moments vignette, but it also had a significantly wider standard deviation than the other models. Statement items representing each of the three models were placed in four groupings: (1) statements representing the Kohlberg, Fowler, and Parks models; (2) statements representing the Baxter Magolda and Pizzolato models; (3) statements representing the extensive model; and (4) statements or "free-writes" representing various comments made by business students studied, collected by Edgell. The extensive model grouping showed the highest mean. Standard deviations did not vary significantly, aside from the low standard deviation for the classic model grouping. Because the standard deviation for the highest-mean grouping is close to the standard deviations of most of the other groupings, the results for the groupings by model are less ambiguous than the results for the vignettes. Based on the highest mean, it appears that respondents agreed most with the extensive model. The extensive model grouping then had the highest reliability. Hence, the statements of the extensive model reliably represent the studied business students' perceptions of their faith formation. The next-highest alpha was for "free writes," a loose grouping of student statements collected by Edgell, although three items were negatively correlated. Lower alphas for statements based on classical and defining moments models indicate that elements of these models do not reliably represent the perceived experiences of this population. Subsequent factor analyses were performed on all four groupings to see if elimination of the weakest-fitting statement items improved the reliability of any model to a statistically significant degree. Reliability of the extensive model did not improve with elimination of any items, such that the model's reliability has solid statistical significance. Elimination of items in the "free-writes" grouping brought it to a slightly more statistically significant reliability. Elimination of items in the classical and defining moments groupings did not improve their reliabilities, nor were their reliabilities enough to rate statistical significance.

Christian university.[124] The respondents at this school clearly appreciated the Christian university as a warm and secure setting that contributes to all kinds of social-emotional aspects of moral formation, such as growth in autonomy and empathy. High scores on self-reported moral sensitivity and moral focus (two main variables in morality) correlated strongly with an appreciation of moral upbringing and experiencing moral community. The low incidence of reported immoral behavior complements this picture, also given the fact that these incidences decreased as students approached the maturity of their senior year. At the same time, moral reasoning skills remained on a low, conventional level. The basic conclusion by De Jong et al. is that a thick and rich moral community is highly appreciated by students and staff in almost equal measure and strength, but moral development is low. This is another indication that Christian colleges would do well to examine the background variables in moral development that may contribute to the rather limited impetus for growth.

5.1.4. Implications for PISA

The results of this study by Edgell tell us that despite the limits of this study to the business student population of the (unnamed) college, we do well to question standard models of spiritual development. There is ample reason to assume that the model where students undergo an extensive exposure to a Christian worldview, the extensive model, may be a better fit for understanding the spirituality of students as experienced by them. It is precisely this fact that interests us, for it allows for a thick concept of moral formation. At the same time, the likelihood that a thick and rich moral climate might just stifle moral formation should also be considered. It calls in any case for a distinct view on just what moral formation and growth is expected to be.

Despite the fact that such fittingness could depend on the religious tradition and context of the population of Christian students involved, we recognize the consistent and extensive role of spirituality in the extensive model as better fitting the need for vocational spirituality and having a distinct spiritual calling. It comes closer to the vocational realm of the practitioner than the classical model or the defining moments model.

---

124. De Jong et al., "Morality at a Christian University."

The extensive model, which closely approximates the educational philosophy of this book, assumes less certain stages or moments of faith, more an orderly progression of faith. The spiritual background of such an orderly process of faith maturation is described in section 3 of this chapter. Edgell characterizes this as "a lateral and territorial expansion of their faith understandings into more areas of their lives."[125] We duly note that expansion of faith understandings includes into vocational practices.

Also of significance is the result that none of the models tested—even the classical model, which has been verified extensively in the general student population—showed significant step-wise progress in the four years of college for the population studied. Edgell regards this as an indication that the models that we would expect to serve best the design of curriculum and pedagogy for faith integration may not fit students' own view of their maturation process. The final implication is that faculty who apply their own working models of student faith formation, which are often highly customized to characteristics of local populations, may find them to be reliable indicators for understanding the spiritual growth of their students.

Edgell's extensive model is also a functional model, which complies with our functional approach to spirituality. The implications for PISA of Edgell's study lie in the area of what to expect in terms of the spirituality of students as they practice it. The functional approach to spirituality introduced in this chapter takes the actual practice of faith as a point of departure. This approach complies with the idea Edgell suggests, that working models by faculty members could be more valid in their guidance of moral formation than the theoretical models. It stands to reason that a closer fit of the practical working model leads to more reliable learning practices.

The extensive model also fits with the idea of having moral competencies. This idea of having a valid working model of faith formation complements strongly the focus on moral competencies in PISA. Moral education is meant to be transformational. It focuses on the necessary changes in instruction and environment that must accompany the transformation of the learner. The interaction with the environment implies that educators must create learning environments that foster appropriate ethical intuitions. In addition, learning must proceed from the novice

---

125. Edgell, "Preparing Business Students."

level to that of the master in moral competencies, as required in PISA. The idea that human nature is cooperative and self-actualizing addresses the specific contexts for moral growth. This idea requires educators to affirm community as part of learning. Educators must also foster self-regulation. The latter idea affirms the social practices environment, put forward in PISA. In PISA, we focus on the actualization of a moral profile that aims for more than what the self wants. It aims to seek what the person considers to be his or her calling within the normativity of practice, spirituality, and integrity. PISA focuses on normative learning. The extensive model provides a good pedagogical portrait of what actually happens in higher education.

At the same time, the use of a working, functional model of spirituality—of which the extensive model is an exemplar—without the normative reference found in a clear belief structure (see section 3 above) may, despite its educational utility, lead to the fragmentation so common to modern times. Fragmentation can also arise for the simple reason that there are many rooms that require incorporation in one's house of faith. We urge teachers and students, therefore, when applying the functional approach in a working model, to take into account the needed normativity regarding one's house of faith. We see three ways of doing this within PISA.

First, we examine the role of what we termed the interrelationship between a worldview or spirituality and pedagogy on the level of theological depth and philosophical support. Working models of faith formation need a frame of reference that is distinctly bound to explicit faith practices and traditions, so that their manifestations comply with conditions P and I of PISA. Our term of reference in this respect is section 3 of this chapter, where we covered the Reformed evangelical spirituality and its focus on pedagogy. Without the direction given by such a body of thought, the functional working model could unintentionally reinforce individualistic tendencies. This working model also requires the use of deep reflection as a tool to ensure that educators as well as students understand the fundamental role of worldviews in their moral formation. We go into this in the next chapter.

Second, our examination of the role of spiritual profiles (see section 4 of this chapter) tells us that spiritual profiles can be part of the way students image themselves as Christians in order to gain confidence in the efficacy of their religious spirituality for their vocational spirituality. Above, each of the models' exemplars (John, Mike, and Susan) portrayed a certain spiritual profile, which we may assume fits their identity as Christians and the way that they perceive themselves. Edgell's study points out that choices of the classical model and the defining moments model were also clearly present. Therefore, the choice of a certain profile and related spirituality could vary in a student population, and educators must respect this. Another example could be that pietistic students often narrate their religious spirituality as a longing to divorce themselves from the sinful world. This longing may take the form of an extreme dualism. Christian educators employing PISA would be concerned that an extreme dualism would have negative impact on their vocational spirituality.

The final issue is how the choice of profile (for John, Mike, or Susan) matters for practice. Each choice of spiritual profiles is of course individual. Varying degrees of directional force are possible, as we stated above. The question becomes not so much whether the spiritual profiles can be applied within professional performances but to what extent. We already know that serious and earnest people follow these high profiles, but how extensively? The sobering message of Edgell's study is that Christian students may only gain very implicit faith formation. We conclude that deep reflection on one's faith formation is not only prudent and wise; it requires explicit attention. We return to this subject later in chapter 6.

5.2. *The Competency in Spirituality Role*

We focus now on empirical research dealing with the spirituality of clients and patients from the understanding of one's own spirituality. Another example of the function of spirituality in education is provided by Dutch nursing scientists. Rene van Leeuwen coordinated a module entitled "Nursing Care and Spirituality" for third-year nursing students. Building on the model of Henk Jochemsen,[126] and following empirical research done by himself and Bart Cusveller, spirituality in this module is regarded "as a function in human conduct, to which each person adds his own meaning in his own way."[127] This approach ties in well with the context of Dutch health care, where caregivers are confronted with care seekers having various spiritual backgrounds. Van Leeuwen et al. primarily studies the individual needs of religious patients for whom

---

126. Jochemsen, *Ethiek van de Zorg*.

127. Van Leeuwen and Cusveller, "Nursing Competencies"; Van Leeuwen and Cusveller, *Verpleegkundige Zorg*.

certain religious practices are important (prayer, fasting, visits to church or mosque), and also the needs of those patients who name their spirituality in nonreligious terms (meditation, silent periods, or contact with nature).[128] This approach focuses on the anthropological structure in which humans function spiritually, as well as their relationship to issues of meaning:

> In this spiritual function, the beliefs, practices, and lives of human beings express their relationships to that which transcends the physical, mental, and social. It involves activities, convictions, and attitudes relating to fundamental features of human existence, such as death, suffering, vulnerability, dependency, the inevitability of choices and the sacred.[129]

In this approach, both caregivers and care seekers are involved in spirituality. This implies that each person is able to have a relationship with "that which transcends." We regard this as the human capacity to go beyond the immediate experience of reality to a higher—or deeper—source of meaning, such as religion or worldview.[130] In their research on the ability of the nurse to engage his or her own spirituality as well as the spirituality of the patient or care seeker, Van Leeuwen and Cusveller developed a competence-based profile consisting of three core domains and six core competencies, which served as indicators of performance in their study.[131] Their designed profile is displayed in sidebar 18.

SIDEBAR 18. COMPETENCIES FOR NURSES PROVIDING SPIRITUAL CARE

1. Awareness and self-handling:

- Handles own values, convictions, and feelings in their professional relationship with patients of different beliefs and religions.
- Addresses the subject of spirituality with patients from different cultures in a caring manner.

---

128. Van Leeuwen and Cusveller, "Nursing Competencies"; Van Leeuwen and Cusveller, *Verpleegkundige Zorg*.

129. Jochemsen, *Ethiek van de Zorg*; Van Leeuwen and Cusveller, "Nursing Competencies," 235.

130. Cusveller, *Met Zorg Verbonden*.

131. Van Leeuwen and Cusveller, "Nursing Competencies."

2. Spiritual dimensions of the nursing process:
- Collects information about the patient's spirituality and identifies the patient's need.
- Discusses with patients and team members how spiritual care is provided, planned, and reported.
- Provides spiritual care and evaluates it with the patient and team members.

3. Assurance and quality of expertise:
- Contributes to quality assurance and improving expertise in spiritual care in the organization.

At the core of this approach is the idea that the spirituality of the caregiver and the care receiver intermesh in a certain professional way. On the side of the caregiver, certain conditions hold that impinge on being a professional regarding spirituality. A core condition is that "caring for the spirituality of a patient means for nurses a confrontation with their own values and beliefs . . . a confrontation with their own spirituality. . . . The personal values of the nurse are regulative for the way she regards herself being a professional."[132] This consciousness of one's own spirituality and how it regulates one's conduct is, according to Van Leeuwen and Cusveller, a key factor that impacts positively on patient care. Nurses who can demonstrate their personal faith in performance apparently can deliver spiritual care on a deeper level than those lacking this aptitude.[133] The authors point out that engaging in a certain spiritual self-diagnosis and spiritual self-awareness via reflection are essential preparations for becoming spiritually competent in caring.

Van Leeuwen and Cusveller describe a profile for the spiritually competent nurse with the following characteristics: "They are spiritually (or religiously) involved, have the necessary experience in life and work and are also influenced positively by an upbringing where concern for aspects of spirituality existed."[134] They emphasize that nurses with such a profile also feel a distinct responsibility for spirituality.

---

132. Ibid., 70–71.
133. Ibid., *Verpleegkundige Zorg*, 72.
134. Ibid., *Verpleegkundige Zorg*, 73.

This profile contains a clear moral indicator. It concentrates on the willingness and also the ability to feel a responsibility for the spirituality of the care seeker. The capacity to be moral in this respect assumes at the same time a competency to act prudently. Van Leeuwen and Cusveller point convincingly toward the interwoven character of being a good professional as well as being a responsible person toward the spirituality of others. Having a high professional aim as well as being able to work with one's own spirituality apparently go quite well together, at least for highly competent Dutch nurses.[135]

6. CONCLUSION: BEING SPIRITUAL

To summarize this chapter, we state that viewing moral formation from the window S generates several perspectives:

- PISA follows worldview education and social imaginaries.
- PISA monitors faith formation and moral formation.
- PISA requires narratives on the choice of a moral profile.

The condition S is a wide view on spirituality that allows us to take into regard the context of spirituality as manifest in spiritual traditions, personal profiles in spirituality, and the roles undertaken to deal with spirituality. Spirituality seen in this way is how beliefs and experiences of inspiration and transcendence are related to the actual practice of life. Students may already be involved in faith formation when learning worldviews, as well as when engaging in faith formation. The next chapter follows up on this chapter by studying how PISA helps students come to learn how to use their spirituality in their choice of a vocation.

Spirituality has been treated in this chapter as a broad concept, including religious as well as nonreligious human conduct, related worldviews and doctrines, social imaginaries, liturgies, community practices, faith formation, and methods in professional learning. The condition S amounts to a broadly conceived human functioning whereby the abilities to exercise contemplative consciousness or transcend to ultimate levels of meaning are understood.

We also differentiated religious spirituality from vocational spirituality. We find a clear-cut distinction difficult to maintain, particularly when trying to understand how Christians follow their calling or their

---

135. Cusveller, "Cut from the Right Wood."

vocation. Yet, in practice we find people with a religious spirituality and a related calling, as well as people having a vocational spirituality and a related vocational awareness. The first type of calling requires a solid grasp of one's worldviews; the second type of calling, a solid grasp of one's desires to follow this worldview in practice. We believe that both senses of calling must intermesh, so that one gains a strong feeling of being suitable for a certain occupation (calling2) that is supported by warranted religious spirituality (calling1).

Next, we examined the tradition and practice of Reformed evangelical spirituality in terms of a pedagogical worldview. Here we found a determined focus on ensuring that one's basic commitments comply with the standards of God. We saw that this may concentrate itself in the notion of having a classical calling, or a confidence based on one's spirituality whereby one experiences a distinct call. This is certainly the case for Reformed evangelical learning, where being a citizen of the kingdom is a basic spiritual attitude in life, which we all are called to follow. Adopting this spirituality entails choosing a certain spiritual profile to express this. We covered several profiles (disciple, steward, sojourner, shalom seeker, etc.). We observed that a choice of profile requires making manifest what transpires in the heart and mind of the believer. We believe that choice of profile strengthens what we termed vocational awareness, that is, a necessary confidence of being suitable for a vocation specifically from the confidence of one's spirituality. In this way, spirituality can lead to strong feelings of true, intrinsic motivation to pursue a profession. Deep reflection helps us to discover these feelings.

Students, for whom educators bear pedagogical responsibility, may use different models in their quests of their faith formation. We covered three models (classical, defining moments, and extensive). The extensive model closely approximates student experience; it fits the rich and thick notion of morality at Christian colleges; and it fits PISA best. At the same time, we caution against having excessively high expectations of progress in formation. We say in faith that much depends on the working of the Holy Spirit in the lives of students.

Our conclusion is that the condition of spirituality functions in PISA as a willingness and confidence to exercise a calling in line with one's faith or worldview. In our approach, we believe that making evident before oneself and others which specific spiritual profile one adopts is necessary for displaying one's willingness to be moral. Our treatment of several profiles—disciple, steward, sojourner, prime citizen, and shalom-seeker—points this out. Each spiritual profile calls upon us to be moral and confident that our faith supports our choice.

One's choice of a specific spiritual profile to live for helps make one's telos in life manifest. The direction that one takes in professional performance thus becomes clearer. We believe this is necessary for making a proper choice of one's professional moral profile. At the same time, we recognize that many Christians involved in the secular world find it quite difficult to publicly portray their spiritual profile. This implies that they need to learn how to be answerable—the next step in PISA.

5

A: Being Answerable

1. INTRODUCTION

THE LAST CONDITION IN deep reflection with PISA is the letter A—the condition of being answerable. In being answerable, we are required to explain or justify our actions. The student who is answerable in PISA chooses willingly to be a responsible, accountable professional. The student's willingness implies that he or she chose a moral profile after reflecting deeply on being answerable. Clearly, this process requires guidance, which derives from an ethics of accountability.

The prominent rise of reflection in professional training indicates that becoming a professional increasingly requires knowing who you are and what you want to become. Professionals must be able to account for their behavior in a given practice. We hold this to be a moral issue, which is complicated. Prominent ethicists agree with us that the formation of professionals has a moral aspect. In this way, they confirm our view of the ethics of normative practices (see chapter 2). We will explain this in terms of ethical profiles found in society in this chapter. Professional training is moral also because exploring psychological depths by reflecting deeply on the self is a moral matter. In chapter 3, reflection is defined as the interpretation or reinterpretation of experience and knowledge. In this chapter, we will point out its normative qualities. We will conclude that deep reflection needs an ethical standard to direct it.

Being answerable is defined here as the willingness and ability to be responsible in a professional practice. We use the condition A of being answerable to plumb the moral foundations of reflection. Being answerable is another word for wanting earnestly to be responsible in your job. By requiring answerability for a professional, we require the willingness and the ability to be responsible within a practice. The willingness to be responsible can be determined by a clear answer to the question:

"Rebecca, why do you want to be a good nurse?" The ability to be responsible is a matter of exercising moral competencies. Here we might ask, "You say you want to be a good nurse, Rebecca, but do you know of yourself that you can meet the moral grade?" If Rebecca wants to be a good nursing professional, then she must know whether or not she's got what it takes in terms of professional knowledge and skills, which includes having a moral backbone in a well-chosen moral profile. This emphasis on her willingness and her ability to be held morally accountable is the A in PISA.

In deep reflection with PISA, we aim for high accountability from students. We would not require it if we didn't believe that it is possible. In this chapter, we start by reviewing several prominent ethical approaches to moral identity that call for personal accountability. We explore how mainline ethicists require solid practices of moral development in the form of narratives with a particular focus on moral profiles. This review clarifies the moral basis of having a profile but also the fact that a profile need not necessarily be moral. This exercise will make it clearer how having an identity and choosing a moral profile can be combined.

We then proceed to ask what it means for one's psychological identity to have a certain moral answerability. How deep must a person's reflection go into his or her identity in order to arrive at ethical responsibility? This is the core task of mentoring Christian students: helping students to realize how deep and far their development should go as responsible people. In this chapter, we concentrate on two sides of such a challenge.

First, we spell out what it is that Rebecca is required to do beyond showing a capability to be responsible. She must answer, what makes me unique? and, what makes me who I am? She needs to reflect deeply on her identity in relation to what she wants to become. This is the essence of supervision and coaching.[1] Being answerable requires knowing one's self. What exactly about the self counts toward being answerable? We discuss this further in this chapter.

---

1. In this chapter, we will deal with the role of spirituality in moral formation. One of the issues by Christian supervisors is the role of spirituality in developing a professional profile. Basically, two approaches will be followed in this chapter that to our knowledge have not yet been distinctly pursued by supervisors: (1) the role of spirituality itself in supervison and reflection; for a Dutch example, see Borst, "Spiritualiteit ter Sprake in Supervisie"; (2) the specific manner of addressing spirituality of others; see Fitchett, *Assessing Spiritual Needs*. Both approaches return at various points in this chapter.

Second, we take a strong normative stand on how the identity and morality of the student can and must develop. Rebecca must also answer, who do I want to become? and, do I have it in me to realize that? We will point out that her mentors and coaches must know how mainline psychology takes into account the reflection on one's identity, and how such reflection figures into choosing a moral profile.

Throughout this chapter, we will discuss one of the major issues in student career mentoring. We refer here to the correlation between having a moral identity and choosing a moral profile. This correlation is found in the core mentoring question, does a student have the right dispositions to become a good professional? If we applied this question to Rebecca's case, we would ask, is what Rebecca believes she is as a moral person (her dispositions) connected to what she aims to become (a good professional)?

Our conclusion will be that we need an ethics of deep reflection to guide educators and students in order to bring students into the right learning situation (which we call Bildung) for choosing the right moral profile.

2. MODERN PROFILES IN ETHICAL THEORIES

2.1. Introduction

The awareness that moral identity must be guided by the right ethical choice is advanced by four recent writers on ethical formation: Alasdair MacIntyre, Johannes van der Ven, Sabina Lovibond, and Albert Musschenga.[2] Each scholar puts forwards a theory on the choice of a moral profile. We conclude our literature review with an analysis of the role of moral profiles in current ethical theories of an ethics of deep reflection. We concentrate our review on the manner in which being answerable is treated.

2.2. MacIntyre and the Profile of the Excellent Practitioner

Alasdair MacIntyre tells us that, to become fully answerable, we need to become excellent social practitioners. We consider MacIntyre's profile to correspond to the profile of the normative practitioner or, more

---

2. Not only by these authors, in practice it is a recurrent issue. A good example for nursing is Hatrick Doane, "Am I Still Ethical?" Our focus is now primarily on the ethical basis for being answerable.

simply, the practitioner. This profile is found in professional studies in line with the normative practices model (see chapter 2 of this book). Alasdair MacIntyre successfully popularized the philosophy of the virtuous practitioner.[3]

The most important quality in the profile of the practitioner is his or her ability to focus on the telos of that practice. The practitioner also needs the accompanying ability to be a coherent incarnation of virtues required to achieve the telos of that practice. The image emerges of a robe worn by the "master" in the ancient guild. The moral cloak that belongs to the practice is accepted by the practitioner, so to speak. Acceptance of this moral cloak cannot be understood (as demonstrated in chapter 2) without the help of tradition and community. In this section, we limit our attention to the moral profile involved and its relation to being answerable.

As MacIntyre tells us, for a practitioner to be called a practitioner, the person embodying that role must be identified within a narrative of how the practice came about, how it functions, and how it intends to develop. A simple example is the ministry of a pastor in a church. The ministry represents the social practice. The minister is the practitioner. The focus of the practitioner on the moral self takes place in a concrete community—in this case, the community of the liturgical churches, synagogues, and mosques. To be a moral self in such a community is "to be accountable for the actions and experiences which compose a narrative-able life within a community."[4] Thus, for the minister, his or her moral profile is achieved by being part of the best traditions of that community, including the virtues which accrue to it.

> The virtues find their point and purpose not only in sustaining those relationships necessary if the variety of goods internal to practices are to be achieved . . . but also in sustaining those traditions which provide both practices and individuals' lives with the necessary historical context.[5]

In short, we cannot divorce the moral profile of a practitioner (for instance, the minister) from the values, norms, and direction of a certain social practice in a certain historical context. Being an excellent professional in a virtuous practice entails being part of such a legacy.

---

3. MacIntyre, *After Virtue*; see also MacIntyre and Dunne, "MacIntyre on Education."
4. MacIntyre, *After Virtue*, 217.
5. Ibid., 223.

2.3. Van der Ven and the Profile of the Moral Communicator

Johannes van der Ven tells us that, to become fully answerable, we need to become moral communicators of truth. Narratives function centrally in the achievement of moral profiles. Moral formation does not succeed without the ability to dialogue from one's point of view. A special ability in this respect is moral communication, the Dutch Roman Catholic philosopher of religion tells us. In his *Formation of the Moral Self*, he draws from the narrative philosophy of Paul Ricoeur to focus on the search for truth and the rationality of morality within a religious context.[6] For purposes of explaining moral formation, he chooses an "interactionistic" approach for defining the relation of the moral agent to his community.[7] The moral agent should enjoy ample freedom within this communal setting, where he or she is taught to exercise varied (mainly social-cognitive) skills for dealing with others.

We see certain benefits to the concept of the moral communicator. Van der Ven's theory applies well in a multicultural setting, adjusts well to the call for argumentation of one's profile in modern society, and is well-designed philosophically to support moral development in post-Kohlberg fashion in cognitive as well as emotional development.[8] Foremost, it is an effective account of the search for truth in moral development that maximizes the role of communication.

Our analysis of Van der Ven's theory is that it is communitarian in the sense that the moral agent is not only counteractive but also proactive. Not only does the environment orchestrate the individual, the individual also orchestrates, conducts, and even creates the environment, albeit not from nothing. The competency to narrate one's interaction with that environment is remarkably prominent. By actively and passively, narratively and argumentatively participating in this multidimensional communication, "the self tells and is told its own story, spins and is spun its own web of meanings, from which character emerges."[9] In other words, the agent becomes a moral communicator of the self within a certain context.

---

6. Van der Ven, *Formation*; Van der Ven, *Morele Zelf*.
7. Van der Ven, *Morele Zelf*, 8–118.
8. See also Gibbs, *Moral Development and Reality*.
9. Van der Ven, *Morele Zelf*, 43.

Van der Ven's moral profile of the moral communicator emphasizes strongly the ability of a mature moral agent to find his or her way in a plethora of traditions, including a religious one. Because his model highlights the interaction of the moral agent with tradition, we find that it agrees with our conceptualization of the moral profile.

2.4. Lovibond and the Profile of Virtuous Author of One's Self

Sabina Lovibond contends that, in order to become fully answerable, we need to become authors of our own social representation in society.[10] British philosopher and feminist, Sabina Lovibond provides a study of moral formation that discloses traditional sources in relation to what she calls "naturalist" idiom.[11] In her book, *Ethical Formation*, she introduces the moral profile of becoming an author of one's social virtues. This moral profile requires the ability to engage in self-representation of one's moral identity within a social context. Authorship is, according to Lovibond, a clear variation of being answerable, which arises as a result of a naturalist upbringing (a definition of naturalist ethics is introduced below). This type of nurture involves adjusting to one's second nature, as well as one's social environment.

Lovibond's authorship profile takes as its starting point the classic Greek idea that moral virtue is the outcome of a successful process of formation (see our coverage of phronesis in chapter 4). Western civilization has adhered to this Greek concept of formation until now. Such an approach explores the ethical question, "What does it take to qualify as a person who can be relied on, so far as humanly possible, to do the (objectively) right thing?"[12]

In Lovibond's social system, authorship occurs when ethically formed persons adopt relevant values and principles as their own, so that their behaviors are predictable. Thus, they can be held accountable for their behaviors. In this regard, they are able to be the author of a moral judgment, which is to speak as one person, self-consistent over time in their desires, beliefs, and habits of judgment.[13] This ability is "authorship." Authorship produces acts of moral expression by serious

---

10. Lovibond, *Ethical Formation*.
11. Ibid., xi, 25.
12. Ibid., 9.
13. Ibid., 86–110.

authors, who represent the "second nature." [14] Authorship is a reflection of the social representation of the self within the social system.

Authorship is thus a manner of being answerable. Authorship represents a paradigm in terms of the full capacity of being a self-representing subject—a fully autonomous subject of moral thought and speech. This paradigm complements the cognitive learning found in traditional practical wisdom. The goal of formation, as envisaged in Lovibond's view, is to bring about a psychological condition in which self-representation is possible. She finds this condition to be crucial, for it is characterized by serious, not merely opportunistic, moral narratives. It results in "the ability to represent, or answer for, ourselves authoritatively to others."[15] Authorship is then a manner of being answerable, but in terms of enacting what we say. In this way, it complements the profile of the moral communicator.

We recognize the call for authorship or moral self-representation as paradigmatic for modern life (including for feminist views on moral development).

We determine that the moral profile Lovibond describes is also naturalist in its ethics in the sense that moral formation takes place in the tension between the inner being and the cultural context. At the same time, it is naturalist in its call for self-formation, or the development of one's second nature. Her concept of authorship implies strongly a do-it-yourself approach to moral formation. It also implies that it is possible to continually redesign one's moral profile.

2.5. Musschenga and the Profile of Having Personal Integrity

The ethicist Bert Musschenga has written a major work on integrity.[16] Musschenga points out that, to become fully answerable, we first need to become persons having personal integrity. Before that, he published a leading study on the education of moral integrity.[17] Remarkable in his work is his emphasis on integrity as a psychological construct. He points out that the rise of concern about integrity is closely associated with the cultural and social structural results of modernization. Given the

---

14. Ibid., 121.
15. Ibid., 159.
16. Musschenga, *Integriteit*.
17. Musschenga, "Education for Moral Integrity."

social, cultural, and moral fragmentation in modern society, there is a greater need to accurately assess the reliability of persons, as well as the predictability of their conduct. In many respects, integrity is the result of the exercise of practical reason (phronesis). In chapter 3, we introduced this virtue in our treatment of condition I—becoming integral. In Musschenga's work, we see a stronger emphasis on the coherence and consistency of a person's judgments and behavior. Musschenga's work thereby complements what was termed in chapter 4 the ethic of authenticity. The difference is that Musschenga's conceptualization entails a concerted effort to be authentic.

Achieving integrity as a moral profile is not a direct consequence of the effort to be authentic, however. Many adults achieve authenticity without moral integrity. By this we do not imply that they are necessarily immoral—we simply mean that personal integrity is not the same as moral integrity. One can aim to be real, authentic, and reliably so, and yet be immoral.

Musschenga demonstrates that having integrity as a profile can mean two things. In the first place, he demonstrates that there is a core in the personality of each person that needs to be protected against infringement. This is what Augusto Blasi calls the core of the self.[18] In the second place, if we say that someone has integrity, we mean that there is internal coherence and consistency between his or her various convictions, and external consistency between what that person professes and what he or she actually does. The emphasis is on the whole range of the person's projects, convictions, and actions and not just on carrying out a specific role.[19] In Musschenga's view, personal integrity means having a profile with a distinctive character. We would say of a man with personal integrity that "he says what he thinks," or that "he is consistent and coherent in his judgment," or that "he does what he says." He is virtuous in this respect, but he is not necessarily moral.[20]

Moral integrity presupposes that a person of integrity has identified him- or herself with social moral values and principles. Musschenga agrees with Blasi that persons of moral integrity have shaped their identities around moral concerns, such that morality has become constitu-

---

18. Blasi, "Emotions and Moral Motivation."

19. Musschenga, "Education for Moral Integrity," 222; Musschenga, *Integriteit*, 16, 196.

20. Musschenga, "Education for Moral Integrity," 226; Musschenga, *Integriteit*, 16, 145–66.

tive of their identity.[21] In this way, material moral values are internalized so that a person's social morality will usually coincide largely with that of the community. In judging a person's moral integrity, one starts from the substantive virtues, principles, and values considered essential for the diverse social roles that people normally fulfill in a society. Moral integrity is determined by a person manifesting in his or her conduct the values to which that person claims to adhere. The average moral person may be committed to moral values, but only those persons who have made these commitments part of their moral identity have moral integrity.

We also consider the person who has amoral personal integrity. An amoral personal integrity can mean that a person has personal integrity because he or she aims at more consistency, coherence, and correspondence with values, but this condition alone does not yet make the person's conduct moral. The fact that people even aim at being truthful and dependable does not yet mean that their integrity is moral; it can be amoral. We take the simple example of a teacher who demonstrates integrity in carrying out his classroom duties well, with fairness in examining and assessing his students, but he does not care about the impact of his teaching conduct on students, simply for the reason that he believes it is entirely their own business how they learn. We could then say that this teacher is incompetent in the sense that he does not meet the moral grade of being a good teacher (condition P in PISA). Nevertheless, this teacher could well be a very kind and considerate person, true to his very limited sense of having personal integrity. Although his kindness does not spill over into his work, thereby violating condition I of being integral, still we could not say that he does not possess personal integrity. He is obviously incompetent, but he is not necessarily an unreliable person lacking authenticity. If he does not make his incompetence a moral issue, we say that he lacks the moral profile of being answerable for his performance as a teacher in an integral way. In that sense, he lacks moral integrity for his particular job, but he does not lack personal integrity.

Musschenga comes to the conclusion that the profile of a moral self should not contain the ideal of unity in the self of the person (as does MacIntyre; see above). To have a moral self, one must identify oneself with moral values, possess character virtues that bring one to aim at

---

21. Blasi and Glodis, "Development of Identity," in Musschenga, "Education for Moral Integrity."

these values, and demonstrate awareness as a moral person, and conduct oneself accordingly.[22] A person having moral integrity has a self that is constituted by socially shared, moral identity–conferring commitments.[23] The emphasis lies more on the attachment to morality and less on the unity of the self. In this manner, a moral profile depends more on adherence to morality than on the unity of the self.

2.6. Properties of Moral Profiles in Ethical Theories

Four scholars, each prominent in their fields of philosophy, ethics, and theology, have provided us cursors concerning the properties of moral profiles. Each scholar we consulted asserts that, in order to become fully answerable, we need to become someone with a certain moral profile. By examining the four moral profiles of social practitioner, moral communicator, the virtuous author of the self, and the person of integrity, and understanding these from the perspective of being answerable, as we have done, we can draw the following conclusions.

2.6.1. Profiles Need to Be Moral

None of the four moral profiles dealt with here is explicitly ethical. The moralities of the profiles examined are found in the mingling of many moral values with our humanity and our social condition. Here we emphasize the importance of being integral, or condition I. We see this in the carrying out of different social practices (according to MacIntyre), the ability to participate and communicate in various forums of truth finding (per Van der Ven), the ability to adjust well to social nature as the author of one's life (according to Lovibond), and the ability to develop into a well-adjusted person having psychological integrity (per Musschenga). All of these aspects support a moral profile, but none of them flows forth from an explicit substantial morality or moral value, as was the case with spiritual profiles (see chapter 4).

Christian morality, seated as it is in spirituality, flows from an explicit morality. Hence it reaches deeper than these four moral profiles. Because most Christians assume that the basis of morality lies in spirituality, it is no surprise that the morality found in the profiles discussed

---

22. Musschenga, *Integriteit*, 156.
23. Musschenga, "Education for Moral Integrity," 223.

here is the result of what one chooses, based on a deeper level of contemplative consciousness.

For this reason, Christian students need to delve deeper via deep reflection. We keep in mind here that morality has a distinct function, which is a far cry from mere moralism. In order to guide the moral emotions, we need explicit cognitions in moral development.[24] This calls for a deep reflection on the beliefs one has concerning adopting a profile. By deep reflection, we mean the normative learning accruing from a focus on one's experience. A budding professional must undertake a thorough analysis of the necessary moral characteristics in order to choose the right moral profile. Knowledge of the explicit moral content of each profile is needed to maintain the moral self-sufficiency, moral unity, and integrity of one's moral identity.[25]

2.6.2. MORAL PROFILES DEMAND CONSIDERABLE EFFORT TO REALIZE

In all four studies cited here, we see that the effort to develop a moral profile is a long and strenuous process. The explicit moral formation on conventional and higher levels conducted by the individual into the young adult years later becomes a matter of lifelong moral learning. We also see that certain models[26] argue that explicit educational effort must be undertaken to achieve a higher level of morality, which complies strongly with theories of character building and even moral cognition.[27] Lovibond emphasizes the importance of applying practical reason (phronesis) along with a stringent analysis of phronesis in what she calls a "determinate critique."[28] We later call this kind of analysis deep reflection (see conclusion). Clearly, gaining a moral profile is a serious business.

All four profiles assume answerability relating to a telos, although each emphasizes a different aspect of moral integrity. In all of the profiles studied, the requirement of a willingness to be answerable is absolute. The

---

24. Blasi, "Emotions and Moral Motivation"; Gibbs, *Moral Development and Reality*.

25. Musschenga, *Integriteit*.

26. Meant are models by Van der Ven, *Formation* and Lovibond, *Ethical Formation*.

27. Kohlberg, "Moral and Religious Education"; Van der Ven, *Formation*.

28. Lovibond, *Ethical Formation*, 140–44.

importance attributed to being answerable flows mainly from a recognition of the importance of the telos that is inherent in spiritual profiles (chapter 4). More common is the call for self-discipline, sometimes with an ascetic quality.[29] Virtuousness is sought explicitly in excellence of the practitioner,[30] in finding and communicating truth[31] in phronesis while aiming for self-representation,[32] and in aiming for personal, moral, and professional integrity.[33]

From the perspective of psychology, much effort goes into moral formation. This effort requires goal-oriented development that takes place in phases. This conceptualization is strongly emphasized by Van der Ven in his treatment of the stages of moral development. Van der Ven's conceptualization is similar to the models of other moral philosophers.[34] We return to this issue in section 4.3 of this chapter to study how the moral identity of a person needs guidance in development. Yet, this discussion of the effort of moral formation may run the risk of losing sight of the telos of moral formation.

2.6.3. Moral Identities May Differ Considerably

These four profiles vary widely in their valuation of moral identity and in their reliance on moral psychology. The treatment of moral profiles varies greatly in the literature examined. This variation is due to differing views on moral identity. MacIntyre and Van der Ven warn us more explicitly than Lovibond and Musschenga do to avoid moral fragmentation, in order to maintain the unity of the moral identity. Lovibond adjusts to differences in moral identity by theorizing that moral psychology is a reflection of social nature. Musschenga does not regard it to be necessary for a person aiming for personal integrity to also seek moral integrity. The differences between their concepts of moral identity are vast.

We conclude that moral psychology is a weak basis for achieving a moral profile. At the same time, our study of moral formation cannot do without a proper understanding of moral psychology. Our analysis

---

29. Lovibond, *Ethical Formation* and Van der Ven, *Formation* agree on this.
30. MacIntyre, *After Virtue*, 190.
31. Van der Ven, *Formation*.
32. Lovibond, *Ethical Formation*.
33. Musschenga, *Integriteit*.
34. Particulary Kohlberg, "Moral and Religious Education"; Gibbs, *Moral Development and Reality*.

of reflection practices points to the need for a normative analysis of this problem.³⁵ In section 4 below, we discuss how the rise of naturalist ethics relates to moral psychology. We subsequently argue that moral psychology must be given its rightful place in moral formation.

2.6.4. No Moral Profile without Narratives

Our fourth conclusion is that all four approaches give prominent place to narratives. Stated simply, we compose much of our moral profile by talking about it. We seek to understand our moral identity by talking about it with others. Van der Ven's moral communicator is a narrator. Lovibond emphasizes that we develop authorship through community interaction.

This conclusion that narratives are necessary agrees with the PISA model, in that becoming answerable means being able to narrate one's moral choices. Narrating moral choices in professional communities requires explicit training. This requirement highlights the communal character of moral development, of which Lovibond and Van der Ven remind us, and which MacIntyre takes as given. The need for training in narrating moral choices confirms the above conclusion that gaining moral profiles requires explicit effort.

We will discuss in the next section how narratives depend on the stages of moral development. Each stage may involve a different type of communication. Such differentiation between stages implies that the student also needs to discern the requirement to be answerable at each stage. To this matter we now turn.

3. THE REQUIREMENT TO BE ANSWERABLE

3.1. Defining What It Is

Being answerable and having a moral profile presuppose each other. The requirement to be answerable is not only ethical, it is also a matter of moral psychology. Our treatment of being answerable in reflection practices will demonstrate the connections with moral psychology. The step from ethics to moral psychology is important here. In the context of moral formation, the concept of being answerable is taken broadly to mean an ability and a willingness to be accountable for those matters

---

35. Van Leeuwen, *Towards Nursing Competencies*; Hunink et al., "Moral Issues."

and conduct for which one is responsible.[36] Answerability assumes that a person demonstrates a certain competency in situations where he or she carries responsibility. Even so, answerability is more than a skill or a performance. It is the willingness to account for one's conduct within a certain practice.[37] The requirement to be answerable, then, presumes a full-fledged, complex competency held by a person who is fully aware of his or her identity in a certain situation. The quality of being fully aware requires some explanation.

There are two ways to focus on this aspect of the moral psychology involved: the will and the ability to be answerable.[38] First we explore how students use their feelings about being answerable for becoming a professional (the I and S in PISA). Then we analyze how they can meet certain standards of being answerable in practices (the P in PISA).

3.2. What Is the Willingness to Be Answerable?

We provide an example to refresh our normative consciousness of the condition to be answerable. Sidebar 19 details a case where the willingness to be answerable is obvious, but is it real?

> SIDEBAR 19. PERSONAL BRANDING: HOW CAN I BEST SELL MYSELF?
>
> Personal branding is the process whereby people and their careers are marketed as brands. This is also called "self-packaging." Business guru Tom Peters states, "There is literally no limit to the ways you can go about enhancing your profile."[39] A personal brand is the strong impression or established image that comes to mind when people think of you. By personal branding, professionals can create an image of themselves and profile how unique they are in their market.[40] Os Guinness describes the shadow side of this phenomenon. He writes:

---

36. Hoogland et al., *Professioneel Beheerst*.
37. Jochemsen and Glas, *Verantwoord Medisch Handelen*.
38. Our emphasis is on the informal side of responsibility, which involves psychology and morality. Other aspects, such as the formal juridical, social, and ethical aspects have been treated in other studies, for instance: Hoogland et al., *Professioneel Beheerst*; Hegeman, *Christelijk Dienen*; Jochemsen and Glas, *Verantwoord Medisch Handelen*.
39. Peters, *Brand Called You*, 83.
40. Kwakman, *Personal Branding*, 10.

> In such a world of appearances, character loses significance, "face value" becomes all important, and the door is opened to the "makeover era" of spin doctors and plastic surgeons. . . . Character was traditionally understood as the inner form that makes anyone or anything what it is—whether a person, a wine, or a historical period. It is therefore deeper than, and different from, such outer concepts as personality, image, reputation, and celebrity. Character was the deep selfhood, the essential stuff a person is made of, the core reality in which thoughts, words, decisions, behavior, and relationships are rooted. As such, character determined behavior just as behavior determined character. Character was who we are when no one sees us—but God. . . . The emphasis now is on surface, not depth; on possibilities, not qualities; on glamour, not convictions; on what can be altered endlessly, not achieved for good; and on what can be bought and worn, not gained by education and formation. To be a person is therefore to be a project. It is up to each of us to create and wear our own "designer personality"—carefully crafting ourselves with résumés, skills and appearances all chosen with the expertise and care of a Paris couturier designing a dress for a Hollywood actress on an Oscar night. Character may be its own reward, but personality is what wins friends, gets jobs, attracts lovers, catches the camera's eye, and lands the prize of public office.[41]

Personal branding is, according to Guinness, a symptom of a crisis of truth and character. This crisis does not pass by the student.

Believing that one can manage and control the way one is perceived by people is a modern concept. Os Guinness warns us of its pitfalls. Personal branding builds on the social rituals in which we engage to determine our identity. Identity is formed as we ask ourselves, how do I want others to perceive me? Does my image or persona have a consistency that establishes instant trust and immediate credibility? In plain language, are all of the components of my appearance in sync? In this book, we call this identity formation the quest for a profile.

How do I present myself (or sell myself) as completely unique, as well as thoroughly real? In this chapter, we examine how phenomena like personal branding require being answerable. I can certainly sell myself as different, but is my differentiating quality really me? When a professional puts him- or herself forward as a personal brand, we need to

41. Guinness, *Time for Truth*, 44–47.

know whether the image the professional portrays is real. Os Guinness's description of the devaluation of this social ritual by personal branding (see sidebar 19) cuts to the core of moral formation.

So, the question becomes, can students learn to present themselves properly, that is, with integrity? The PISA model is useful to tackle this concern, even though we may not fully resolve it. As explained in previous chapters, we first ask the question whether the professional's personal brand complies with what we expect of professionals in a certain practice (under condition P). We then continue to inquire if there is consistency between one's personal brand and what one does in that practice (under condition I). All in all, we would like to know what makes someone tick, or why a person engages in personal branding. Our questions for them are, why go to such lengths to tediously create a crafted image of yourself and to market that image of yourself? and, when doing so, do you reflect on what you want out of life (which would be an application of condition S)? However, we cannot elicit a full answer to the question, are you for real with your personal brand? without also having asked the personal brander to self-identify as a responsible person. If the brander is willing to narrate his or her responsibility to us, we call that being answerable (condition A). Condition A is one condition in the PISA model, but it does not stand alone.

Professional practice demands that personal branding includes being answerable. On the surface, condition A sets a positive tone because it assumes that if professionals are involved in personal branding, they are eager to be held accountable to others for their personal brand. Applying this condition entails that professionals choose a moral profile with a corresponding moral identity. Condition A and its ancillary requirements ought to be part and parcel of personal branding by professionals—but expecting such thorough consideration by personal branders is highly optimistic. There is the case of the professional who does not openly admit the validity of the legitimate standards of a practice. In other cases, a professional will admit their legitimacy but will not comply with the standards on occasion. We argue that in neither case is such an individual a true professional. If one is self-consciously involved in name branding, then one must be able and willing to give a true account of oneself as being a responsible person. This requirement includes the hard questions of whether (as Os Guinness reminds us) the choice of a profile is merely a choice to be a type of person who is all surface, skills, and résumé—and no character. We expect at least some soul-searching about being authentic. In this way, one's personal brand cannot be properly appraised without having exercised the P, I, S, and A of PISA. Personal branding, which at first blush sounds highly attractive, actually turns out to be a significant test of the DNA of one's moral fiber.

The reason why we investigate the difficult issue of personal branding is that all professional studies hold the (oft implicit) assumption that professionals are what they profile themselves to be: dependable, trustworthy, and having integrity. It is essential to professional training that students discover whether their actual identities actually comply with the demands of a professional profile. They must at least have learned at some point in their studies what it is to be completely answerable or authentically willing to be held accountable for being a professional. In the same way, they show that they are willing and able to know and observe the standards of their practice. These assertions are supported by the career-mentoring concept that we develop below.

3.3. Reflection in the Practice of Higher Education

First, we return to our discussion of the nature of reflection. In chapter 3 (section 5), we dealt with the organization of reflection practices, where we made a distinction between it and the personal use of reflection. We now continue to examine the personal use of reflection, this time in the context of higher education, as follows. We begin by introducing student career mentoring services (SCM) and supervision. Next, we explore a widely used approach to personal reflection called the core reflection model. Last, in reviewing these, we discuss the value of involving moral psychology in deep reflection.

Student career mentoring services (SCM), such as student coaching or mentoring (Dutch: *studieloopbaanbegeleiding*) are becoming central elements in professional training. In chapter 3, we introduced the basic forms of mentoring and supervision in our study of reflection practices. We characterized student mentoring as the responsibility to assess whether or not the student increases in proficiency, thereby climbing from the foundation (Dutch: *propedeuse*) to the bachelor level and from there to professional master for not only one particular capability but integrally in all capabilities belonging to the competences profile. We return to this phenomenon to focus more on the nature of reflection as carried out by students in the mentoring practices of SCM.

In this book, we assume that deep reflection can be a component of all forms of student mentoring, with particular emphasis on career mentoring and supervision as they are focused on professional performance. Taking a broad view of mentors and supervisors, we see them reflected in the following case of deep reflection, taken from a landmark study by Benner et al.:[42]

> In both interviews and survey responses, advanced-level students and beginning nurses frequently described how their sense of mission, or calling, made it possible for them to withstand the rigors of learning for practice and gave them the courage to enter high-stakes situations, where the consequences of a mistake can be enormous. The students claim that this understanding of the significance of their work and their identification with nursing practice were what kept them focused through terrifying clinical situations, heavy or conflicting academic demands, and competing family and work responsibilities—any of which might have led them to drop out. They cite classmates who were performing well but who did not identify themselves with the significance and relevance of nursing practice and consequently chose to drop out of the program. Students describe finding what [Charles] Taylor calls "a moral source": "Coming to clarity about [our motivations] why we are doing this can help identify and neutralize other extraneous motives . . . which may muddy action and lead us away from our goals. And it [moral sources] will characteristically also inspire us to strengthen our resolve. A motivation which has this kind of potential to empower I want to call 'a moral source.'"[43]

In this citation, and also in Taylor's work introduced in chapter 3, we see a merging of the importance of practice (P), a sense of mission and a moral source based in a given spirituality (S), and a distinct need to be answerable (A). In the following, we explore how mentoring via SCM negotiates these steps in the development of a proper moral profile.

SCM is a learning process that is a component part of competence-based learning. Via SCM, the students gain insight into their own learning process, govern it, and thereby become responsible for their personal development. This development by students in their professional studies has as the goal their achievement of professional competence. By this we

---

42. Benner et al., *Educating Nurses*, 178. For a European example, see Dierckx de Casterlé, *Verpleegkundig Beroep*.

43. Taylor, *Secular Age*, 673; cited in Benner et al., *Educating Nurses*, 178.

do not mean low-level competencies that merely qualify them for a job. Rather, we mean the high-level, "royal" attainment of personal identity, which carries for Christians a responsibility to become a professional in society. We argue that the latter should be the distinct, Bildung-related aim of SCM.

A core element in SCM is reflection under supervision. We define reflection under supervision broadly as the ability to look back on one's own behavior and then to use such knowledge to improve one's performance. The highest standards for reflection are found in the practical science of supervision as developed for professionals.[44] This agogic learning system, held in and for organizations, is known as staff supervision, training supervision, student supervision, or training supervision.[45] In Dutch professional schools, supervision is a required element in most curricula.

In the next section, we focus on the role of reflection in supervision and in particular on its effect on moral development.

3.4. Reflection and Supervision

We take as our reference point the definition of supervision as a didactic method aimed at the improved learning of professional conduct in sectors where the goal-directed aspects of the relationship between practitioner and client are the focal point, as in the caring professions.[46] The agogical process of supervision requires: (1) a supervisor or coach, and (2) a supervisee (receiving supervision). The supervisor coaches the supervisee, so that the latter can integrate his or her work experience based on reflection and personal choice. In supervision, which closely accompanies learning on the job, the supervisee learns to perform in an integrative manner based on autonomous learning. The aim is to improve professional performance.

44. Supervision is a practical science of recent origin. Our attempt to describe it as a learning tool does not have the pretence of giving a full-fledged account of it. For its development in the Netherlands, see Coenen, *Onderzoek naar de Ontwikkeling*.

45. Ruijters, *Liefde Voor Leren*. Supervisors in professional education engage in supervision with students as a form of professional counseling, serving the assurance and development of the quality of communication and cooperation in professional contexts. For the character of supervision in the Dutch and European contexts, see the website of the Association of the National Organisations for Supervision in Europe (ANSE): http://www.anse.eu/.

46. Siegers, *Handboek Supervisiekunde*, 31–32.

> SIDEBAR 20. DO WE WANT AMORAL SUPERVISION?
>
> Emphasis on morality in supervision and reflection practices may strike a dissonant cord for some. In his book, *The Death of Character*, the American sociologist James Davison Hunter argues that the task of instilling enduring moral commitments and ideals within young people is a failing effort.[47] Our problem, Hunter argues, is not an absence of morality, but rather the emptying of meaning, significance, and authority from the morality that is advocated in education. Morality is reduced to the thinnest of platitudes and is severed from its social, historical, and cultural rationales. Modern psychology has taken over the role of character education. Psychology limits itself to strengthening dominant moral emotions and to building a strong sense of self-worth or self-esteem.

Moral psychology is not adequate for supervision. If we are limited to moral psychology, our critical question becomes, can self-esteem sanction morality, or does it ultimately reduce to self-serving hedonism?[48] This critical question also arises at Christian colleges in the Netherlands because explicit discussions of morality and spirituality have been found to be notably absent from supervision and reflection practices.[49] This can be seen as evidence of the predominance of psychology in moral development. Such trends provide good reason to listen for how purely the notes of morality and reflection are played in the educational orchestra.

Reflection is the core process in supervision. Although the supervision process requires a working experience involving working conduct, it has at its core the reflection process. By way of reflection, the supervisee learns to handle various facets of the required skills, so that he or she achieves higher levels of learning in the work place. Reflection, defined broadly, links cognition and affection at its highest levels. To be sure, reflection is not restricted to supervision. In a majority of the current organizational literature, we find that the reflection process is assumed to embody a type of learning also found in most modern organizations.[50] The special quality of reflection is that it allows us to draw upon deeper

---

47. Hunter, *Death of Character*.
48. Meriwether, "Can Self-Esteem Sanction Morality?"
49. Hunink et al., "Moral Issues."
50. Ruijters, *Liefde Voor Leren*.

levels of consciousness in well-defined levels and in situations in which we relate to others. These sociological qualities make it a situated learning involving others. Siegers characterizes this broader view of reflection as "the ability to retrace the understanding of an experience, making this explicit and attributing new meaning to that experience."[51] On the highest level of such reflection, there is an explicit link between cognition and affection as they concern conduct.

From the outset of reflection, a student must bring an extant observing self to the exercise. Thus, the integral experience is taken as the point of departure for reflection. For this reason, the measure to which a professional (whether in training as a student or as a professional in advanced development) is able to develop an observing self is crucial to reflection. There must be a type of inner dialogue, an intrapsychic process. If professional performance is to improve, the innerness of reflection must connect to the outerness of conduct. The identity or self-image of a practitioner is the essential starting point for reflection.

3.5. Core Reflection

In order to describe the core reflection model, we begin with the question, how does the practitioner (undergoing supervision) see him- or herself? Dutch scholars of education Fred Korthagen and Angelo Vasalos developed a widely adopted reflection model representing the "inner dialogue" in reflection (see figure 3).[52] They call their model the core reflection.

---

51. Siegers, *Handboek Supervisiekunde*, 159, 177.

52. Korthagen, *Waar doen*; Korthagen, "Essence of a Good Teacher"; Korthagen and Vasalos, "Niveaus in Reflectie"; Korthagen and Vasalos, "Levels of Reflection"; Korthagen and Lagerwerf, *Leren Van Binnenuit*.

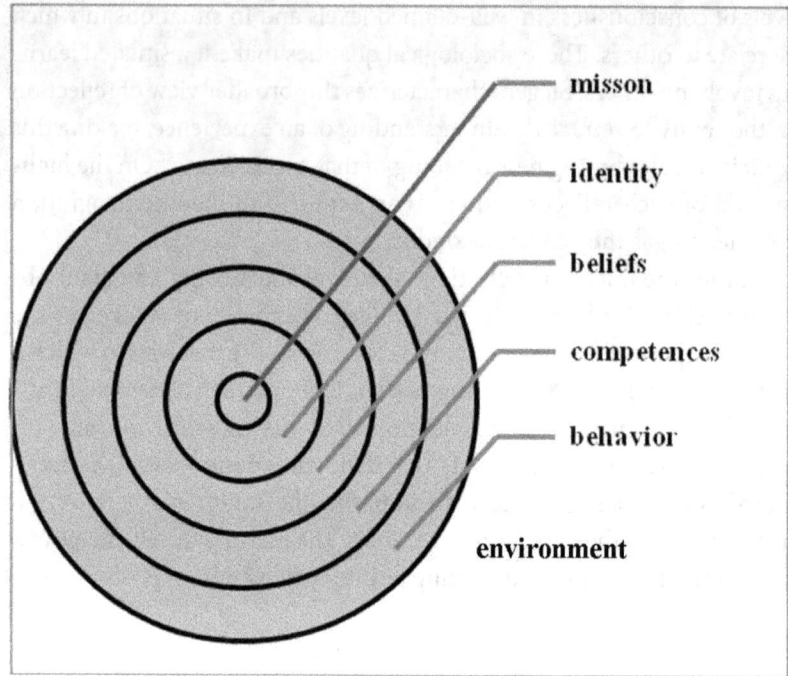

Figure 3. Core reflection

SIDEBAR 21. CORE REFLECTION

Core reflection is a fundamental form of reflection on the "inner core" of a professional. The model in figure 3 above shows various levels that can influence the way a professional functions. The idea behind the model is that the inner levels determine the way an individual functions on the outer levels, but also that there is also a reverse influence (from outside to inside). The most inner circle is the self.

The next inner layer is one's mission, defined and described as follows: reflection on the level of mission evokes such issues as why the person decided to become a professional, or even what a person sees as his or her calling in the world. According to Korthagen and Vasalos, this level is concerned with what inspires us and what gives meaning and significance to our work or our lives.[53] This is a transpersonal level, since it involves becoming aware of the mean-

---

53. Korthagen and Vasalos, "Niveaus in Reflectie"; Korthagen and Vasalos, "Levels of Reflection."

ing of our own existence in the world and of the role we see for ourselves in relation to our fellows.

Interesting dynamics occur at the core. Getting in touch with the inner levels (self and mission) has a very practical significance. For example, on the level of identity, a beginning teacher may be so focused on surviving in the classroom that he or she takes on the role of a police officer. This kind of teacher has quite a different influence on the class from one who is always conscious of the interests and needs of the pupils and whose actions are sincerely rooted in a pedagogical ideal (on the level of mission). Where the first teacher may invite a power struggle, the second often succeeds in creating an atmosphere of togetherness, so that the pupils also consider it important to work together in a pleasant and productive atmosphere. When reflection extends to the two deepest levels in figure 3 (the core of the personality), Korthagen and Vasalos consider core reflection to be taking place. This model has reached general audiences in a book by Korthagen and Lagerwerf.[54]

In the core reflection model, identity is layered and is also observed and experienced in layers. One aspect of the core reflection model is the representation of various levels in people. Think in this respect of an onion. In the model, these levels can be influenced and changed. Only the outer levels (environment and behavior) can be directly observed by others. Those levels near the inner core (beliefs, identity, and mission) are aspects of the inner self of the practitioner. Focusing reflection on the inner aspects means coming closer to one's personal relationship to one's competencies.

The core reflection model is applied in SCM in ways that reach the core of the self as professional. This model is widely used in supervision and in SCM as a model to assess work-related performance, as well as the student's reflection on his or her performance. Through the development of their portfolios, students are expected to develop a professional identity, understood as "an unconscious body of needs, images, feelings, values, role models, previous experiences and behavioral tendencies, which together create a sense of identity."[55] However, these are not yet the

---

54. Korthagen and Lagerwerf, *Leren Van Binnenuit*.
55. Korthagen, "Essence of a Good Teacher," 15.

heart of the matter. The innermost core is that of mission or spirituality. Korthagen explains that the core deals with "highly personal questions as to what end the teacher wants to do his or her work, or even what he or she sees as his or her personal calling in the world. In short, the question of what it is deep inside us that moves us to do what we do."[56]

Our critique of the core reflection model found positive and negative elements. Our affirmative assessment is that this model is quite useful when addressing the role of the inner core. In the supervision of practitioners, the main idea (in this case, supervision of student teachers) is to aim at discovering the core qualities. These become apparent when dealing with the core of a student's personality. Core reflection aims at more than just cognitive insight. Its goals are to arrive at questions of identity and of the spirituality or calling that guides one, which in Korthagen and Vasalos's model is called one's mission. Thinking, feeling, and wanting are all important aspects of taking new action based on a core quality. Examples of core qualities are trust, courage, creativity, sensitivity, candor, decisiveness, spontaneity, and flexibility.[57] These core qualities are to be reflected on and chosen between, in the manner in which we choose a moral profile. Finally, it is at the inner core where we can find the willingness to be answerable.

Yet, application of this model also points to its limitation of being too focused on the inner orientation, Vos and De Muynck argue.[58] In their critique of this model, they point out that reflection on professional performance only concerns the personhood of the professional. Its standard of quality is found only in the person. For this reason, they think that the emphasis is too much on introspection and retrospection on personal performance and personal biography. Because the focus remains too much on the innerness of the subject, significant elements of professional practice cannot be sufficiently addressed in this model. It contains the bias of the pure core of the individual person that merely would have to adjust itself to the inner flow. In the case of teaching, Vos and De Muynck argue that external elements that should be addressed are the content of the teaching practice, the overall pedagogical philosophy, the tradition, the organizational setting, and perceptions of roles

---

56. Ibid., 16.
57. Korthagen and Vasalos, "Levels of Reflection."
58. Vos and De Muynck, "Hoe Vormend," 66.

involved in the social practice of teaching.[59] In the core reflection model, the relationship between moral or spiritual principles and personal beliefs and convictions remains too internal to the person.

When the core reflection model is compared to the PISA model, the elements of I (being integral) and P (relating to practice) are missing. Although the inner core is referred to as being transpersonal because it concerns one's consciousness of one's own existence in the context of professional performance, we still miss the condition I of being integral. Being integral in this respect must not be confused with adjusting to the inner flow. Criteria belonging to a suprapersonal level or normative assessment are not part of the core reflection model. This is the condition P in PISA. In the area of teaching, Vos and De Muynck find this a serious drawback. Transpersonal issues like, what is good teaching? or, what makes a good teacher? which are put forward from broader normative frameworks (such as actual professional practice or tradition) are not addressed sufficiently in this model. Even if core reflection concerns the entire domain of professional performance, such reflection still takes place only from the internal point of view of the supervisee. The basic notion of the importance of the context of one's performance, exemplified by a professional practice, is not part of core reflection. Because it misses this external orientation, core reflection needs to be buttressed by the use of moral formation strategies, such as PISA.

The goal of this analysis is to highlight how the PISA model connects the core (rather than the more superficial outer layers) to moral formation. In this chapter, we argue that an expanded and operational version of core reflection is needed, particularly in those areas involving the context of work (P), the relation between the individual and practices (I) and spirituality (S). We believe that the stronger notion of being answerable, condition A, is also needed here. Core reflection needs to connect to moral formation, especially in the way students account for their formation. Our ideal in this connection is that reflection practices address the integral sense of the self. Thus, the supervisee meets conditions I and A of PISA. One's perception of one's moral identity is therefore an essential element of supervision. Without this deeper look into one's identity, reflection using the so-called onion model could easily remain superficial.

---

59. Vos and De Muynck, "Hoe Vormend."

Superficial reflection in supervision entrenches the status quo. Empirical analysis tells us that this ideal of in-depth reflection on being answerable is not typically realized.[60] Reflection as conducted at professional schools in the Netherlands is often limited to professional know-how. In daily practice, knowledge is often used without reflection.[61] The student or supervisee focuses only on an action strategy and its consequences for the workplace environment. When goals, values, frameworks, and, to a significant extent, strategies are taken for granted (e.g., the way we use language: we do not think of the rules of grammar, even if we know them), this suggests that we are stuck in single-loop learning. Consequently, a great number of students may encounter the danger of merely adapting to customs. This is the situation in supervision and reflection whereby student apprentices become aware of the need to adjust to customs rather than to change them.

Thus, reflection can be limited to learning ways of doing things that may be suitable for maintaining oneself within a hostile environment but are not optimal for living a Christian lifestyle. This kind of superficial reflection is much like avoiding style errors without learning the grammar involved. We acknowledge that reflecting on, for example, a best practice is potentially quite beneficial to professional practice. Merely learning how to adjust oneself to the practice, however, ought not be our highest standard. We may instead need to work toward change.

Reflection, including in the PISA model, should lead to the development of best practices. Reflection exercises are meant to help professionals become aware of what they have been doing, share that with colleagues, receive feedback, and reflect on it together. The purpose of such reflection is to evaluate particular actions in the light of what should be considered best practice (encompassing evidence-based practice). Such reflection and evaluation will always, consciously or subconsciously, take place in the light of the professional knowledge, the experience, and the basic convictions (the spirituality, or condition S) of the participants on what constitutes a best practice.

---

60. Van Leeuwen, *Towards Nursing Competencies*.

61. The various loops are treated in chapter 3, section 5.2. See this for the treatment of the organization surrounding reflection and supervision and the place of deep reflection regarding these loops of reflection and other forms.

3.6. The Rising Challenge of Moral Psychology

How can we interpret the perceived lack of depth in supervision and reflection? One explanation is that fundamental notions of agency are increasingly challenged by the rise of moral psychology and, in particular, the dominance of naturalized ethics. We think that the growing superficiality of supervision can be traced to the rise of moral psychology and naturalized ethics.

By *naturalized ethics*, we mean the approach "that takes certain facts about human nature as starting point for virtue theory."[62] It seeks to ground ethical theory in what is known about human motivation, the nature of the self, the nature of human concepts, how our reason works, how we are socially constituted, and how our minds operate.

We have two main concerns with naturalized ethics. Our first concern is that naturalized ethics legitimizes the dominant strategy in modern moral education to emphasize the importance of feelings as a guide to one's values. This dominant strategy leads to an emphasis on individual choice and the centrality of self-regard or self-esteem in the student's moral maturation.[63] Our second concern is the other side of the coin—what self-esteem is replacing. Naturalized ethics may very well be used to keep reflection practices clean of spirituality because it bolsters the role of emotions and the central role of the will. In naturalized ethics, moral psychology and ethical theory reach a common juncture, but we question seriously the ethics involved.

Under a naturalized ethics, self-esteem also replaces virtues. This dominant ethic takes the metaphor of flourishing and combines it with the most important presumed fact about humans—that they construct their own characters.[64] At first, we may be attracted by the notion that young people are expected to construct their characters. Such a construction appears nicely linked to the pursuit of both personal happiness and social virtue. However, here the explicit naturalistic account of human flourishing may take the place of the possession of virtues.[65] The development of the self under naturalized ethics relies more on dispositions

---

62. Lapsley and Power, *Character Psychology*, 2.
63. Hunter, *Death of Character*, 86–87.
64. McKinnon, "Character Possession," 36–66.
65. Ibid., 48.

that young people have already accepted and endorsed for themselves (connected with self-esteem) and with which they come to identify.[66]

Our final critique of naturalistic ethics is that students are assumed to be able to form their own moral characters naturally. The upshot of this approach is that students will be expected to assess their character development according to the success of how far they progress by themselves in their reflection. The assumption that students can do this naturally may even sound good to us.

> SIDEBAR 22. DIFFICULTIES IN IDENTIFYING MORAL ISSUES IN REFLECTION
>
> In research on reflection practices of nursing students in the Netherlands, remarkable difficulties were found for students in intermediate and advanced levels of the program in their abilities to reflect on morality.[67] Hunink et al. arrive at the following diagnosis and recommendations.
>
> The characteristics of nursing practice indicate that the moral formation of nursing students is significant for nursing education. In their moral formation, practitioners aim at a competence to demonstrate adequate moral behavior in all nursing situations. This requires in turn a competence to identify the moral dimension of everyday nursing care and to deal with it in a way consistent with the moral principles of the profession and of the professional as a person. An important question in this context is whether students are able to identify the moral dimension in everyday decisions and whether nursing education helps them to deal sufficiently with such decisions. In order to answer these questions, Hunink et al. quantitatively and qualitatively investigated texts written by students in the context of mentoring situations at several professional universities in the Netherlands. The results indicate that students rarely identify moral issues. These results imply that there is little conscious moral reflection and deliberation in dealing with everyday situations.
>
> Their main recommendation for improvement is to increase the moral quality of reflection. With additional instruction and training of supervisors concerning the field of moral issues, Hunink

---

66. McKinnon, "Character Possession," 50.
67. Hunink et al., "Moral Issues."

et al. expect them to coach students more adequately in mentoring situations. The same holds for trainers on the job. They could become better role models for students in handling moral issues in practical conduct. The results of this analysis show that much time is lost to discussing procedural matters. By implication, too little time is available in sessions to deal with emerging ethical issues. This consequence runs the risk of missing the goals of intervision (i.e., peer mentoring) as well. A type of action research is recommended by Hunink et al. By way of video monitoring and/or participant observations, the conduct of a mentoring session is discussed with students, in order to determine whether moral aspects that were not dealt with properly need added attention. Such expanded study also allows more insight into the role of the supervisor.

The question we raise in this book is whether the naturalized ethics currently applied in reflective practice is leading us away from virtue approaches—particularly the neo-Aristotelian and related Christian ethics. In these virtue approaches, reflection is on whether one's life aims at some telos or end of human flourishing, or some spirituality that ties in with truth beyond human choice (see chapter 4). We question seriously the wisdom of emphasizing subjective notions of character that are gaining priority over given sources of morality (spirituality) and also over standards of professional conduct. As sidebar 22 reveals, mentors involved in supervision will have to undertake much more effort to ensure that students learn to better identify moral issues in reflection.

Most accountability structures in mentoring are based on the assumption found in naturalized ethics that the descriptive account of character construction takes on normative force. We see very little evidence of an ethic of responsibility in mentoring practices, whereby moral profiles are used (see sidebar 22).

The result of a naturalist mentoring practice is a neutered mentoring that is legitimized by naturalized ethics. Naturalism also generates the assumption that if students do not choose a moral profile, they apparently do not need it (naturally).

3.7. Conclusion

To summarize, we put forward being answerable, or meeting condition A, as a basic requirement in moral development. We determined that moral identity is dealt with actively in reflection exercises, so that students come to choose their own moral profiles while trying to understand how their own moral identities fit their choices. Here we find a gap between what actually transpires and what we aim for.

Deep reflection goes beyond a simple reflection on one's inner core. When superficial reflection is compared to deep reflection in the PISA model, superficial reflection lacks the conditions of being properly attuned to practice (P) and of being integral in that practice (I). Because supervision practices encompass all aspects of a person's identity and character, we therefore argue that educators are required to be actively involved in open and substantial guidance on the issue of moral development.

We acknowledge that a significant gap exists between our standard and current naturalist practices in supervision that overemphasize psychology. We examine next how the issue of having a certain moral identity is dealt with in current Christian higher education. In doing so, we examine how having a certain moral identity (under moral psychology) is related to ethics. In the next section, we continue to explore the relationship between having a moral identity and choosing a moral profile.

4. FROM IDENTITY TO PROFILE

We saw above that, in student career mentoring (SCM), a great deal of attention goes to what is called the self-identity issue. Students are expected as members of Western society to define as much as they can their own identities. This expectation is part of the neoliberal aim of personal autonomy. We question these theoretical assumptions. In the following section, we point out that it is important to understand that one's moral identity needs to be connected to one's moral profile. Here we examine the process of moving from identity to profile. We go beyond the focus on identity as such to emphasize fidelity with one's core self.

4.1. Social-Psychological Profiles of Students

During the past two decades, a subdiscipline of psychology has formed around devising psychological labels to categorize college students. John L. Holland categorizes students as realistic, investigative, artistic, social,

A: Being Answerable 243

enterprising, or conventional.[68] In more general terms, Bayard Baylis has already thoroughly categorized Christian students in North America using the following labels: nonconformist, success and sports, Christian leader, academic liberal, confident academic, and creative individual.[69] An almost identical list of profiles has been provided by Asten: hedonist, leader, social activist, scholar, status striver, and artist.[70] These profiles have a strong social-psychological basis. They receive much attention as colleges try to describe the general profiles of their student populations. They are what we may call *social profiles*. It is doubtful, however, whether students will adopt these in their explorations of their own personal self-identities.

Paramount in this fixation on social-psychological profiles is the influence of social constructivism[71] and naturalized ethics (see above). These two postmodern perspectives emphasize how individuals develop despite their environment, or in conflict with that environment. The rise of self-identity theories, in particular that of James Marcia, relates to these perspectives by supporting the ideology that this is exactly what students ought to do in their moral formation.

4.2. Self-Identity Statuses

To understand the development of student self-identity theory, commentators typically refer to the theory originally drawn up by Erik Erikson and further developed by James Marcia and others. The concepts of commitment and exploration are held to be the main dimensions for understanding spiritual identity development. *Commitment* stands for the psychosocial bonds that young people experience at the end of adolescence. *Exploration* describes how these adolescents search for and weigh alternative identities before making commitments to an identity, which usually occurs during a crisis. Both of these variables are intuitively recognizable in the lives of young people. Identity theory brings us close to one of the original meanings of Bildung (as the phi-

---

68. Holland, *Making Vocational Choices*, 151.

69. Baylis, *CCCU*. Through a FIPSE grant, Bayard Baylis and his research team interviewed several thousand evangelical students at Christian universities within the CCCU (first and fourth years, same cohort). They also videotaped interviews of three thousand students at the beginning of their college experience and one thousand (those remaining) during their senior year.

70. Astin, "Empirical Typology," as cited in Baylis, *CCCU*.

71. Hegeman, "Stewardship and Integral Learning."

losopher Gadamer reminds us), whereby a sense of alienation is crucial for achieving one's image (*Bild*) of oneself (see chapter 1). We can recognize Bildung in terms of identity commitments in the lives of students, at one stage or another.

Based on the above two variables, Marcia also identified four identity statuses, one being the ideal. Each status represents a particular style of coping with the task of identity achievement.[72]

TABLE 2. MARCIA'S FOUR IDENTITY STATUSES RELATED TO EXPLORATION AND COMMITMENT

	No Commitment	Commitment
No Exploration	D: Identity diffusion	F: Identity foreclosure
Exploration	M: Identity moratorium	A: Identity achievement

The utility of Marcia's theory is that it pinpoints an ideal condition that must exist if a young adult is to make a good choice on what the psychologist John Holland calls vocational identity.[73] This is portrayed in table 2 as status A. Having the identity status of achieved (A) assumes implicitly that the student has explored and committed to his or her ego identity. It expresses what the psychologist Holland terms a level of comfort or satisfaction with the current identity status, thus indicating a level of readiness to explore his or her identity in relation to career development.[74]

Such development has been validated, although such development is not complete for many students. The validity of the development of identity status has been established in many studies. We can expect young adults to generally move from the status of diffusion (D) to that of identity achievement (A), although there are indications that progress in development is more the exception than the rule and that about 50 percent of young adults will not reach the achievement identity status

72. Marcia, "Development and Validation."
73. Holland, *Making Vocational Choices*.
74. Ibid., 56.

(A).⁷⁵ This does not mean that the student has an incomplete identity but that a certain cognitive sophistication has not come about. As Marcia himself points out, "Advanced identity formation is associated with advanced reasoning ability. It seems that adolescents and adults who can take multiple perspectives on themselves and others also have a firmer and more flexible sense of who they are."⁷⁶ Becoming "achieved" requires competencies, which apparently not all young adults attain.

The Dutch educational researcher Gerdien Bertram-Troost finds that the model of identity statuses is not explicit enough to be used as a developmental theory.⁷⁷ Empirical research does not univocally confirm that there is a development of all young adults via a direct order of identity statuses to a final status. Furthermore, Bentram-Troost points to a second defect of identity theory: describing identity development using identity statuses does not pay enough attention to the relationship between developing individuals and environmental factors that influence their development.⁷⁸

This second critique echoes the condition P in PISA, but other factors negate its conditions I and A, as follow: First, Marcia's theory is not considered applicable to female development (the case being that many young women apparently are predisposed to foreclosure). The initially cognitive model does not explain the difference between boys and girls for the reason that women (more than men) adjust themselves to the context in which they develop. Marcia's theory does not acknowledge this factor sufficiently.⁷⁹ This is a theoretical condition that rebuffs condition I in PISA. The conclusion is warranted that determining one's identity status can be useful in student mentoring, but, for the purposes of the PISA model, seeking an identity status ought to be normatively guided for ensuring condition A. We caution against urging students to become identity-achieved and postcrisis with commitments. Given also that a certain identity regression is not part of the original model,⁸⁰ we must avoid using the identity status model as an ideology for identity development. Without recognizing the importance of context involving

75. Bosma, "Identiteitsontwikkeling," 138.
76. Marcia, "Treading Fearlessly," 133.
77. Bertram-Troost, *Geloven in Bijzonder Onderwijs*, 25, 35.
78. Ibid., 42.
79. Bosma, "Identiteitsontwikkeling," 139.
80. Bertram-Troost, *Geloven in Bijzonder Onderwijs*, 32.

moral and spiritual values (conditions P, S, and I) we may fall into the trap of overemphasizing natural development over against normed development (see above our critique of naturalized ethics).

We must look for an additional support in psychology that allows us to pinpoint the manner in which students choose to be moral, thereby influencing their own identity.

4.3. The Theory of the "Agentic Self"

The approach by Augusto Blasi and others caught our attention. They describe the role of responsibility of the person for his or her own moral identity.[81] This approach is called the agentic self or the responsible self approach in moral psychology. We introduce the agentic self approach at this point to demonstrate a close connection between having a moral identity and aiming for a moral profile.

4.3.1. BEING RESPONSIBLE FOR A MORAL IDENTITY

The theory by Blasi et al. regarding moral identity maintains that our moral conduct cannot be divorced from our emotions. As a psychologist, Blasi holds that emotions should be controlled and regulated, the degree to which differs according to psychologists and philosophers, but they all agree that our emotions fall under the responsibility that we feel for what we do. Our cognitions and beliefs govern our identity, and thereby our psyche. Blasi et al. call this the "agentic approach" to regulating emotion.[82]

The agentic self theory has two important aspects that concern us. The first aspect concerns the specific core content around which a moral identity is developed. It is the content of the conception of the self. For instance, this can be a belief that a person has concerning him- or herself: "I am good at sports." It can also be a normative belief, such as "becoming a follower of Christ is worthy," or "I should not want to become an authoritarian leader," etc. This core belief has a certain objective function, that is, it can be shared with others and is not necessarily person bound. Others may also hold such conceptions of self. In this respect, we can think of ourselves as practitioners in a certain profession: "I am a

---

81. Blasi and Milton, "Sense of Self"; Blasi and Glodis, "Development of Identity"; Blasi, "Emotions and Moral Motivation"; Blasi, "Moral Character."
82. Blasi, "Emotions and Moral Motivation," 10.

nurse," or "I am a religious worker." A certain judgment of responsibility concerning one's identity ensues.

The second aspect is the experience one has concerning one's identity, for instance, a belief that "maybe I should work harder to be athletic," or "I don't feel I can become a good disciple all by myself," or "being a nurse is the greatest thing I have experienced in my life." This subjective side is emotion bound and quite important to our motivation to become what we hope to be.

Blasi goes on to point out that the objective side (the known) and the subjective side (the knower) need to flow together in one moral identity. In line with others,[83] Blasi emphasizes that persons need to become moral adults. Within the agentic self approach, this is gaining a certain fidelity to one's core self:

> Subjective identity maturity also entails an increasing sense of agency over one's self, such that the identity contents one cares most about are actively appropriated into one's core self. This is coupled with a heightened sense of possession or ownership over one's identity and actualizing it in daily life. In other words, with mature subjective identity there is a greater desire for self-consistency; fidelity with one's core self is seen as a necessity, and self-inconsistency elicits intense negative affect.[84]

The central focus on the ethos of "fidelity with one's core self" by the agentic self means that the growth toward maturity cannot be loosened from normative conceptions of the self (or profiles of persons). These profiles may contain certain values, goals, personality characteristics, and emotions. Individuals adopt profiles for themselves as figurations of what they see as the core of their selves. Simultaneously, they reject other features. The process of adoption and rejection of a moral profile generates feelings of ownership over those aspects that are considered the core of the self. For instance, people identify themselves with a theme or issue, such as animal rights, pacifism, nationalism, or care for the homeless. Young adults can defend their choices in this respect with a vehemence that reveals the deep emotional need served. Of interest to us here is the measure to which they succeed in doing so.

---

83. See Van der Ven, *Formation*; Lovibond, *Ethical Formation*; Gibbs, *Moral Development and Reality*.

84. Hardy and Carlo, "Identity," 236; see also Blasi and Glodis, "Development of Identity."

4.3.2. Moral Backbone

This process is special, Blasi tells us, because it coincides with our beliefs regarding a certain duty to or commitment to our selves.[85] Such beliefs form the core of a moral identity. They also protect it and ensure its realization. Blasi explains that people make very personal and specific choices for certain moral values. They integrate these with their beliefs and personal values in order to create a coherent sense of self. The result may be "I am an animal rights activist," "I am antimilitaristic," or "I am a follower of Jesus." By exercising fidelity to their own choices, they create a certain fortitude and thus feel accountable for what they have created. This attempt at empowerment of their subjective sense of self in a moral profile concerns what we call being answerable.[86] We can also say then that they demonstrate moral backbone.

The importance of agentic self theory is that it connects having a moral identity to the commitment that people experience in doing so. Without a narrative and evidence of this commitment, it is difficult to speak of being answerable. This display of moral backbone demonstrates motivation. Once a person defines for him- or herself a committed moral identity, then we may expect that person (so Blasi tells us) to adhere to this as an objective. We can expect the person to avoid betraying his or her own commitment and damaging his or her self-image. The values that a person chooses and his or her commitment flow together into a consistent moral profile, according to Blasi.

4.4. Conclusion

Following the theory of the Agentic Self, we determined that attention given to psychological factors of one's identity certainly does not exclude morality, including a longing to maintain one's moral identity and thereby live consistently. We may conclude that becoming aware of having a moral identity implies a certain awareness of the ethics involved. This is an important factor when determining one's identity status. Certainly reflection—particularly in supervision—will make one aware of the "greater desire for self-consistency; fidelity with one's core self," which according to Hardy and Carlo's interpretation of Blasi's theory is a necessity for our

---

85. Blasi, *Moral Character*.
86. See Hardy and Carlo, "Identity," 237.

moral identity.[87] Knowledge of one's identity status must include a commitment of fidelity to oneself in order to attain moral backbone.

An important support for this commitment is a good sense of ethics, a matter to which we now turn.

5. PISA AND DEEP REFLECTION IN PRACTICE

5.1. Review of Deep Reflection

Deep reflection, when conducted in the two loops of supervision, makes evident the importance of accountability. We have proposed in this book a form of reflection that digs deeper than the ordinary reflective practice—a form that we call deep reflection. We characterized this as normative learning involved in the interpretation or reinterpretation of experience and knowledge. In this type of reflection, the process includes two layers or loops found in regular supervision practice, whereby we expand on what has been termed "core reflection." We will explain in this section that deep reflection allows us to learn better the importance of the willingness and the ability to be held morally accountable, as required by the A in PISA.

The first loop is common reflection as practiced in ordinary supervision and coaching. In this primary reflection model, the basic values and beliefs that function as standards are presupposed and accepted silently or adapted to as normative. Such single-loop reflection evaluates practice in the light of those shared, commonly accepted beliefs. This type of reflection does not require supervisors or supervisees to draw upon their personal motivations and beliefs. Single-loop reflection often does not penetrate the layers of moral identity. Expressing a narrative of one's moral profile is often avoided as well.

In chapter 3, section 5, we pointed out that deep reflection requires going deeper than single- (and even double-) loop reflection to explore the integration of deeply held beliefs with one's professional practice. In deep reflection, students' personal spiritual beliefs need to be expressed and discussed with respect to their implications for their practice. Students should be able to explain them and to relate them to their practice, especially to the values implicitly or explicitly embodied in their practice. This information may lead to an adaptation of their personal

---

87. Ibid., 236.

beliefs and values. However, it can also result in a change in the value system of that actual practice or in a mutual fine-tuning.

5.2. PISA, Deep Reflection, and Teaching Ethics

In the following sections, we point out how PISA using deep reflection can also be used in the actual practice of teaching a curricular course. We aim to show that our strategy of moral formation can be used to design coursework and also to interconnect mentoring and coursework. In this discussion, we wrap up some loose ends, particularly those dealing with questions like, just how do I do it? and, what does it mean on the work floor?

In this way, we also emphasize that deep reflection is not limited to a mentoring context. There are no restrictions on engaging in deep reflection outside of mentoring, even though much of present educational practice applies deep reflection in mentoring. Because we have belabored so strongly the connection between mentoring and deep reflection, we do not spell out a specific strategy. Instead, we note how instructors can become aware of the link with mentoring.

5.2.1. Applying PISA and Deep Reflection in Course Work

Our example is course work in ethics as found in professional education at a Christian school. Choosing this example has the disadvantage that we may unintentionally overemphasize the ethical side of PISA. We engage in deep reflection in other courses without necessarily calling upon an ethical perspective—for instance, sociology, organization sciences, philosophy, and accounting. Obviously, other disciplines, such as theology, philosophy, worldviews, and pedagogy can be connected fruitfully to deep reflection. Our illustration of the application of PISA in ethics courses is thus meant heuristically.

In the following, we therefore illustrate what is possible in ethics courses. We urge educators to explore the use of deep reflection in their own courses. We take examples from courses in the ethics of business and social work to illustrate how PISA and deep reflection can be used by instructors.

5.2.2. Background Issues and PISA

A curriculum that allows for Christian content in its courses relates well to PISA. We are thinking here of courses that have an explicit knowledge base in Christian literature. At the same time, there may also be informal knowledge practices involving the liturgical formation of the imagination as popularized by James Smith—see the final chapter of his *Desiring the Kingdom*.[88] Against this background of ecclesial practices, PISA and deep reflection can flourish. Because such an environment is not always present at professional schools, we aim a bit lower to focus mainly on what transpires in professional courses.

As a strategy, PISA calls for worldviews in a curriculum. Our choice of ethics courses to demonstrate PISA also has the advantage that ethics covers much of the territory belonging to worldviews, such that the range of human conduct covered is broad, allowing more illustrations. A special note regards the Christian ethics we would choose. We recommend following the philosophical ethics of John E. Hare, because, like Hare, we hold ethical theory to be historically and also philosophically theistic.[89] The Belgian theologian Patrick Nullens also provides us a theistic understanding of the three major approaches in ethics.[90] We are grateful to be able to access such knowledge for educational purposes. This theistic background provides us with much material for deep reflection. But, rather than making practicing ethics easy, it actually requires the educator to think in terms of ethics against the background of Christian worldviews, imaginaries, and philosophy. It could therefore be advantageous for ethics educators to piggyback on courses in the curriculum where worldviews and social imaginaries are already learned, so that a rudimentary understanding of worldviews is in place.

Christian education represents an already extant opportunity to engage in deep reflection. In such a setting, students can exercise their beliefs to gain a good grasp of worldviews. Excellent grounds for learning include explaining your own beliefs as they are relevant to your practice, along with their basis in the Christian faith and how faith functions in everyday life. We see here also an excellent opportunity to develop narratives, as described above. Explaining one's own beliefs falls under the condition of answerability within PISA. This implies that the professional is willing to accept in concrete situations the validity of the norms and values that are acknowledged as valid. Such willingness entails the virtues of honesty and responsiveness. Dealing with these virtues is the stuff of mentoring, but such learning can be enfolded into course work as well.

---

88. J. Smith, *Desiring the Kingdom*, 215–30.
89. Hare, *Moral Gap*; Hare, *God's Call*; Hare, *Why Bother*; Hare, *God and Morality*.
90. Nullens, *Verlangen Naar het Goede*; Nullens and Michener, *Matrix*.

PISA as strategy also directs us unmistakably toward practices. Our portrayal of ethics education is oriented on ethics in professional situations. In our experience of ethics education, we call this the ethics of responsibility. Based on earlier studies of the applied ethics of responsibility in professional performances,[91] we outline how ethics teaching could take place in professional education.

Most ethics courses in professional curricula have strong overtones of applied ethics. We cannot treat any of these in detail, but PISA allows us to make the following determinations. The PISA model does not follow a decisionistic ethics that teaches a thin morality. Such a thin ethics takes place on the fringes of human practices, where practitioners encounter a collapse of regular performances, and where they no longer feel that they can carry out their roles responsibly. In this usage, thin ethics is no more than a highly proficient way of solving almost all kinds of nasty quandaries. In most cases, an expertise foreign to the practice itself must be interjected in order for decision making to take place. Cusveller points that that much of professional health care ethics adheres to this thin concept of morality because much depends on taking peremptory decisions.[92] Thin ethics are even more evident in so-called dilemma analyses that take logical steps for solving quandaries. Thin ethics gives the impression that, beyond these instances, morality is not relevant. A very meager professional learning is the result.

The PISA approach offers a thick and rich concept of ethics. Much in line with our Dooyweerdian approach, we hold that ethics is one aspect of our created reality. It has always existed to be known and understood by humans. The result of our philosophy is that we are highly attentive to various moral issues that arise in the performance of professional practice.[93] Happily, this philosophy is also applied often in professional learning and has shown proficiency there in determining what the moral point of view means for practices taken in their entirety. Cusveller in his treatment of such an ethics reminds us of the rich basis of Christian care

---

91. Hegeman, *Christelijk Dienen*; Jochemsen and Glas, *Verantwoord Medisch Handelen*; Cusveller, *Met Zorg Verbonden*.

92. Cusveller, *Met Zorg Verbonden*.

93. Our position is not unique for seeking integral ethics in formation practices; see for instance, Narvaez, "Integrative Ethical Education." However, it is unique for placing the moral issues within the normativity of practice (see chapter 2, our normative reflective practitioner model) and seeking deep reflection that meets the demands of philosophical ethics as well as being practicable.

practices where ethics is a way of discussing the moral properties of the entire care practice of nursing, for instance, loyalties and dependency relations of vulnerable people and colleagues.[94]

It is clear that our approach to ethics is broad, built on the bases of Bildung, Christian worldview, and Christian philosophy. This is one clear result of following the PISA strategy of moral formation.

Another aspect of our approach is the way a rich and thick view of normativity is taught and learned. Our approach involves paying attention to a wide range of ethics. We recognize here the three major categories of ethical thinking: (1) consequentialist or utilitarian ethics as found in the context of learning, (2) deontological or rule-bound ethics as found in the role of learning, and (3) virtue ethics as found in the person engaged in learning.[95] To be clear, we do not want to emphasize the theories as such. We focus only on how deep reflection relates to these three approaches, as discussed below.

We note finally that we limit our portrayal of ethics mainly to applications in the actual practice of ethics in the courses and modules of professional schools. This limitation curtails any discussion of the philosophical or theological merits of our approach that may be pursued in other academic settings.

In the following discussion, we employ three approaches to learning ethics (in a module) using PISA and deep reflection:[96]

- Teaching ethics regarding the context of practices
- Teaching ethics regarding the professional's role in learning
- Teaching ethics regarding the personhood of the practitioner

5.2.3. Teaching Ethics regarding the Context of Practices

Using PISA, we find of great importance the context of learning of the practices involved, in particular two main practices: higher education and the vocational field. We examine how these are positioned in the

---

94. Cusveller, *Met Zorg Verbonden*.

95. Other major types, such as axiological theories, have not been studied at this point for their use in deep reflection. We claim no exclusion of other categories but focus on the presence and integrative use in deep reflection.

96. We are following here the approach initiated in the Netherlands for professional medical ethics and ethics of care by Jochemsen and Glas, *Verantwoord Medisch Handelen*. See also for general application Hegeman, Kole, and Jochemsen, *Hoofd, Hart en Handen*.

social, cultural, political, and historical situation at hand. From our treatment of practices (in chapters 2 and 3), we understand that practices have a distinct telos, or an ultimate goal that is the expected aim of practitioners. We concentrate on that now for the sake of brevity.

It is a good learning exercise to identify the common telos, structure, and normative principles in one's practice. PISA unmistakably requires knowledge of context, and in particular the normativity of practices, traditions, and roles. Professionals act as if the core value of their practice really matters. They pose ideas and questions about the principles and norms that must be observed in order to realize the core value of their practice. Mutual recognition of the virtues of integrity and practical reason in the way professionals perform in a practice may be a profitable starting point for learning virtues. This often provides an opportunity for deep reflection in the classroom. Practitioners involved in course work, field trips, or projects can also engage with these ideas.

An instructor following PISA in teaching an ethics course does well to apply a Christian teleology. A Christian teleology is a theory that all things are designed for or directed toward a final result. Our approach follows the teleology of Augustine, whereby we hold that God will spell out for us what our telos is in God's Word. Because the concept of normative practices (see chapter 2) is partly based on teleology, we can adapt this to learning by recognizing the thought patterns of final causal thinking to be part of our created reality.

It should be clear at this point that deep reflection following PISA requires a good grasp of normativity. For deep reflection on the context of learning, knowledge of the structure of reality, understood as the normativity of reality, is imperative. A professional may go so far as to require knowledge of the historical and moral situation of its practices (or condition P). For the student of business, this could take the form of knowing a firm's big picture: customers, competitors, industry trends, and best practices. All of these form a part of the context of the learning person. Such learning requires a student to be proficient in knowledge of what the properties of that business are, its purpose, and how various disciplines are involved in realizing that purpose. As a different example, a course on the ethics of the social worker entails knowing what is involved in care for imprisoned clients (for instance, the incarcerated delinquents in a correctional institute in which the social worker is involved). Clearly, the social work student doing an internship in a prison also must have a very good understanding of the normativity of that situation, so that interventions with incarcerated clients fit legal and moral expectations.

In an ethics course, we may regard this approach to be *consequentialism*—the theory that we should evaluate the rightness and wrongness of actions by the goodness and badness of their consequences in each given circumstance. Our theistic ethics approach (described above) tells us that it is possible to believe that God has a route for each one of us toward our final good. Theistic ethics helps us to see how these routes could be coordinated in ways that allow them to reach the final goal of the whole of creation.[97] The implication for ethics in a certain professional practice is that we are open to ways in which people, collectively or individually, aim for certain consequences and use their reasoning to achieve these aims.

Exercising deep reflection means that students place their awareness of the reality of humanity's abilities within the context of worldviews and anthropology. How does this relate to the student's own view of his or her self? Of others being able to reason morally? How are the student's views accepted in professional situations? Deep reflection calls for the development of a moral profile, which means, in a nutshell: Can I swing it? Do I want to be involved in what smacks so much of hedonism? Such issues are the fuel for deep reflection.

What does the moral profile of the student look like at this juncture? We illustrate this from the framework of an ethics course in terms of the challenges it presents to students. The framework is based on moral logic; many students find this a great difficulty, although others may excel at it. Many students' experiences with moral logic resemble a math block. Mentors may have a role, by offering support and tutoring. We do not treat student mentoring services in any detail here, but we do welcome the involvement of student services.

By following a syllabus in consequentialist ethics using PISA, the student gains the requisite knowledge of the teleology of the practices involved, as well as the consequentialist morality of practitioners. In order for a student to learn how to conduct him- or herself morally, the student must attain knowledge of highly proficient patterns of moral reasoning. This includes learning the patterns of thought structured in terms of moral ends, utilities, and consequences. The teleology or finality of the context of professional performance not only must be known but

---

97. Hare, *God and Morality*, 274; see Nullens, *Verlangen Naar het Goede*, 71.

also must be argued both for and against. In most practices, the finality is known by studying the intrinsic aims of a practice and also the extrinsic aims as found in institutions in related practices, as in corporate mission statements and fundamental policies. The instructor must then provide judiciously the relevant values and norms and require students to engage in moral reasoning to achieve these. After all, in this type of ethics, much depends on being able to reason well, which is a key proficiency for professional students.

Obviously, practitioners involved in these situations must have the requisite knowledge of the pertaining values and norms of a context, but deep reflection requires more than a cursory awareness. For a student practitioner, proficiency entails being familiar with the rudimentary nature of the organizations and professions involved, at least on the level of having a good command of single-loop learning and making good progress in double-loop learning. Their CBL must be on a certain par for deep reflection to take place. This requirement requires the instructor to pinpoint the specific proficiencies needed by the student in order to understand what is the case. Without such knowledge, the student will have difficulty knowing how to position him- or herself morally in certain situations. Deep reflection presupposes certain fundamental knowledge of the P of the practice involved and its normative foundations. Because of this, it requires the instructor to understand the practice in its entirety.

Consequential ethics is not easy to learn. With sufficient knowledge of how it is used in practice, however, it may not be all too difficult to portray in professional courses. The reason is that much of professional conduct can be understood in terms of practical logic, goals, objectives, and ends. This sounds very much like the phronesis or practical logic, as treated in chapter 3. In this respect, many courses in professional curricula highlight the consequential type of ethical thinking, which calls for much practical reason. This involves the moral competency of knowing when, where, and how ethical skills (sensitivity, judgment, focus, and action) are needed—as well as how this can be utilized for improving on one's practice.

In this regard, we offer two examples of deep reflection on consequential ethics in professional learning projects. Our first example is the issue of hidden discrimination by businesses of physically handicapped people. In this hypothetical case, the discrimination is structural in character, disqualifying handicapped people through performance standards. Suppose a human resources student encounters this kind of discrimination while engaged in her main internship. She could undertake deep reflection on this issue by writing an academic essay about her perspective on discrimination in the workplace of her internship. We assume that she brings in case studies of handicapped exclusion, which she analyzes by applying the ethical theory of public justice in the workplace. She not only applies the requisite ethical analysis; she also examines her position on this issue from the standpoint of the ethics of responsibility. Through this process, she is well aware of her position, which is her moral profile in this context. A second example is of a social work student on location in a correctional institution in an internship. He is writing a memo for his supervisor about solving a moral dilemma on the work floor. The dilemma focuses on the requirements for handling whistle blowing under the pressures of time and stress and with limited means. His memo explores the responsibilities of all parties involved. After his analysis, he is well aware of the position he has, which is his moral profile in this context. This student must also undertake an in-depth reflection on what transpires, but he may have to postpone doing this until the situation is resolved.

Both cases call for students to write on morality. The first case of the business student may well require reflection on general knowledge of responsibilities. The case of the social work student involves decision making in a very concrete situation. The decision process entails emotional and thorny issues like personal security and accountability. We believe that deep reflection applies to both types of situations. This is because it requires a thorough normative understanding of the nature of the problem, as well as of the roles of the persons involved.

Students engaged in deep reflection question the structure and direction of a certain professional situation. By doing so, the learner moves into an appropriate learning posture for being open to morality. Deep reflection on the contextual variables calls for understanding much of what in ethics is called utilitarian or consequentialist ethics, but the emphasis can be on the specific type of moral reasoning involved. On a rudimentary level, this means that the student has a sufficient grasp of the moral consequences of certain practices that he or she is getting involved in, whether analyzing it or performing in it. Without such knowledge, the student does not have sufficient moral competencies to understand the situation. As has been repeatedly pointed out in this book, having competencies on a professional level is an accepted standard. There is no reason to assume that it is diluted by the inclusion of moral competencies as part of understanding the ethical properties of professional practices.

The moral formation of the student also depends on networks in his or her professional context, through which the student learns to communicate morally. These networks are valuable avenues for engaging in deep reflection. Instructors and mentors help a student through informal moral guidance. We see clearly in many professional practices how masters help apprentices and journeymen to gain tacit knowledge of the intricacies of professional ethics. It is crucial that such learning take place within the pertaining context where morality is encountered so that an immediate effect can be felt personally. Deep reflection addresses the need for the normative knowledge that devolves from networks.

We summarize here how deep reflection following PISA aids instructors and students in an ethics course where the focus is on the context of learning. PISA requires attention to context, in particular to the way moral logic is applied in practices. An ethics instructor knows that this is an issue that interests mentors. It requires consultation between instructor and mentor. Second, PISA aids students in understanding how specific consequences of their own thinking play out in practices. PISA further allows students to compare such consequences to the ultimate goals and purposes expressed in our Christian worldviews. PISA brings about a strong normative understanding of life and professional practices. In particular, it gives utilitarian thinking a normative bedding.

5.2.4. Teaching Ethics of the Professional's Role in Learning

An instructor following PISA in an ethics course does well to apply *deontology*—a theory that judges the morality of an action based on the action's adherence to a rule, duty, or obligation. The instructor can apply deontology by referencing the moral commands drawn from a Christian worldview, social imaginary, or ethos. But the instructor does not do well to apply these by rote. The components of morality that center in rights and obligations are naturally linked, Hare reminds us, to commands, including "the deep, historically-based resonance between obligation or moral law and the notion of being commanded by God."[98]

Again, the fundamental choice of theistic ethics does not make deep reflection easy. PISA requires a proficiency in being integral (condition I) that presupposes being aware of how various moral values and norms

---

98. Hare, *God and Morality*, 261.

cohere. It also presupposes being answerable (condition A), which means being aware of the manner in which one's spirituality (condition S) figures in one's choices. Applying these conditions requires an active involvement with rules, duties, and other moral codes, including when these have no basis in Christian command theory. Christian philosophers do not want to remove the theological premises from a command theory, for then we are left with society as the source of the command. This tension must be addressed in ethics studies. The focus on PISA aids these efforts.

Our experience is that students learn ethics best by analyzing their roles in certain practices. After all, professional morality is mostly about doing the right thing. In applying PISA, the roles involved in learning call upon the highly normative network of values and norms found in the practices themselves, in particular, understanding which values and norms apply authoritatively. In current teaching and learning practice, we often find the focus on the roles that students engage in when learning.

By *role*, we mean behavior and activities directed toward learning excellent performance. This is knowledge pertaining to codes, rules, and regulations, as well as a good understanding of the principles supporting them. In many curricula for professional studies, we see roles adequately represented in CBL. Although roles are sometimes vague, as a didactical instrument, roles work well.

Using PISA as a strategy for moral education, the student gains by focusing on their role, which offers requisite knowledge regarding the norms of professional conduct. The next question to explore is, how much social proficiency is needed to engage in ethical expertise? Deep reflection can aid students in understanding the basic normative values inherent in roles, their purposes, and the coherence of performing a role within the normative structure of a practice. This includes the patterns of thought that guide one's rule-governed behavior in the conduct of performance. For these reasons, the deontology of the role must be known.

For instance, in setting up a business ethics course, the role behavior of the learning person (or workplace competencies) can be used to understand how to deal with moral issues. This can be achieved by asking, for example, if I perform according to the required workplace competencies, just how does this affect the moral issue? In this approach, learning is oriented toward how a certain proficiency (communication and collaboration skills, creative thinking and problem-solving skills, technological literacy, global business literacy, leadership, or career self-management), as exercised well by the student, affects moral issues. A specific example would be how the social work student treats the incidence of violence that he or she witnesses in an internship in a prison. If the student explores how this moral issue relates to a sense of being responsible for this in terms of communication proficiencies, the question requires the student to place the incident and his or her role within the framework of rules for communicating proficiently in a certain light. Because certain rules, rights, and obligations have specific authority and legitimacy, they must be understood and used to determine the student's responsibilities. Such an experience serves as excellent training in the morality involved.

Therefore, a good knowledge of roles accompanies a proper exercise of moral knowledge of deontology. If the instructor of the ethics course follows PISA, deep reflection can be focused on having certain knowledge of the values and norms regarding roles, as carried out in practice. This requires the knowledge gained through applying deontological ethics in learning. Such application should not fixate on certain rules but should instead explore the integral way that roles relate to codes of moral conduct as part of the normative structure of society.

Learning roles via deep reflection challenges students to see the relevance of CBL. Deep reflection opens up awareness of the higher purposes of CBL. A moral role in practice is the ethical behavior that can be expected from a person who holds a certain position. This gives a framework to CBL. Here the I of PISA figures saliently because this role behavior must meet the standards of coherence and integrity and is clearly the stuff of mentoring. The integration of various low-level performance indicators in the concept of a role is therefore necessary. Aiming for this standard requires much and thorough reflection on the part of students. It also requires students to be able to account for their calling in following a role, which pertains to their deepest motivations (condition S) and also to their ability to be answerable (condition A).

Because roles are often comprehended tacitly, they are made explicit in exercises called ethical dilemmas. Much of modern ethics (of the thin variety) consists of rules, protocols, and strict argumentation that apply to roles in specific cases. Such cases emphasize a very limited way of reasoning according to only one or two principles. Much of professional ethics is highly technical and, in that sense, bound by strict, rationalist rules. Typical professional teaching and learning makes great use of so-called ethical dilemma solving, by using the dilemma-solving technique or the regulatory cycle to resolve so-called moral quandaries. Students using this technique follow previously designed questionnaires and protocols, and they are closely monitored for their compliance with specified rules.

From the perspective of PISA, training based on such dilemma solving runs the risk that students gain only a very limited view of the morality of professions. Deep reflection following PISA avoids the pitfall of a severe reduction of professional conduct entailed in a purely technical approach to moral problems. Without deep reflection, we see that the moral role of responsibility is often left out because it fits a thick and rich view of morality. The reason we need the fuller view is because the normative context of the social practice can be determinative. For instance, the visits undertaken by pastoral workers defy technicism. So does spiritual guidance by a nurse for terminal patients. Such a provision of the highest quality of care in the role of pastor or nurse cannot be reduced to techniques and protocols. A pastoral worker can, through an excellent exercise of his or her role as spiritual advisor, contribute the defining edge to the well-being of patients by being aware of the moral role responsibility involved. This goes far beyond solving dilemmas with a decision-making instrument. Very little excellent professional performance flows automatically forth from solving so-called dilemmas with technique and without deep reflection. Students would certainly be malformed without going deeper.

We can summarize how PISA aids instructors and students to address deontological ethics and the roles of students following deontological ethics. Clearly, it aids them to acknowledge the most authoritative values drawn from theistic ethics, worldviews, social imaginaries, and ethos, especially as these pertain to roles and conduct in dilemma situations. It emphasizes the integral nature of moral reasoning. It makes students aware of the strong influence of codes that figure in the context of learning. PISA brings about a strong normative understanding of individual and collective performance. In particular, it gives deontological thinking a strong place in assessing the rightness of moral authority.

5.2.5. Teaching Ethics of the Person of the Practitioner

In most moral training, the perspective of the person concerns virtue ethics. An instructor of an ethics course following PISA does well to apply *virtue theory*. Virtue theory holds the individual character of the person to be the proper moral object of concern.[99] The normative practices model (treated in chapter 2) follows much of the virtue ethics of MacIntyre.[100] The condition of being integral in the practice of higher education was discussed in chapter 3 as the need for the virtues of phronesis and authenticity, both of which are well adjusted to the demands of being integral. We also explained the need for a range of practical virtues in practices and also in CBL (in chapter 2). Thus, we hardly need to argue now that virtues matter.

From the perspective of PISA, moral formation concerns not only character of the person but also worldviews, social imaginaries, and ethos—the S of spirituality. The learning of virtues can only take place if there is a clear engagement of the learner with transcendental sources of meaning.

In our approach, we also lean heavily on theistic virtue theory, which states that God is the ultimate good that is drawing us towards itself.[101] We acknowledge that much of what passes today for virtue theory drops God out of the account of virtue. We agree with Hare that this leaves us with a definition of virtues that is either derived from human nature or socially constructed.[102] We acknowledge that much of what passes for virtue must be assessed against the background of our theistic view of being virtuous.[103]

In Christian higher education, the individual's ethos and worldview form a swivel for directing a personal choice to follow professional ethics. In developing a professional attitude, deep reflection transcends the identity (person) and the ethos (motivation based in beliefs) to involve learning how to choose a moral profile. (Much of this was covered in depth above.)

The core concept of deep reflection in relation to virtues concerns the student. The student is the subject engaged in knowing a certain context. The student can reflect on his or her own knowledge processes concerning objects and can be held accountable for the roles carried out. In other words, having virtues as such does not suffice. Just having empathy does not make a good nurse.

99. Vos, *Tussen Vage Waarden*.
100. Seminal is MacIntyre, *After Virtue*.
101. Hare, *God and Morality*, 252.
102. Ibid., 259.
103. Vos, "After Duty."

The student learns in deep reflection to understand him- or herself as a whole person who carries out a role in a certain context. In deep reflection on roles, it is important to motivate the student to think in terms of the normative side of excellent professional role conduct. Once that is accepted, it is possible to explain which attitudes, professional ethics, and other norms are required for professional behavior. For achieving ethical goals, knowledge of learning skills must be adjusted to personal characteristics. The manner in which students carry out such assignments is personal because it concerns their role identification. In this way, in PISA, virtues are mostly studied and learned in relation to the performance of the student as a professional.

We refer to previous points as relevant to make our case for the importance of the person in role identification. In PISA, this requirement (regarding the learning person) has been extensively covered. In the setup of a course on the ethics of business or social work, the focus on the learning person coalesces into the notion of choosing a moral profile. For the business student, such a choice may, for instance, be called developing corporate citizenship. In this concept, the learning is oriented on the values, vision, and culture of the corporate organization, so that virtuous conduct advantageous to the business corporation is advanced. In professional education, such citizenship becomes known as professional attitudes and bearing. Similar learning can be undertaken in a course for social workers.

5.2.6. Summary of Applying PISA in Teaching Ethics

Applying PISA as a strategy of moral formation clearly calls for the embedding of courses (in our example, ethics courses) in a curriculum that assumes a rich and thick normativity. Our critical stance on improving professional performance can only be possible if we have the right normativity at hand. The instructor must then think integrally, be as close to the values of the professional practice as possible, and must be in touch with mentors and professionals from their respective vocational fields. This all calls for a thick and rich normative environment for learning.

We have demonstrated that deep reflection can be a relevant element in courses (in our example, an ethics course). In our treatment of three types of ethics in professional schooling, we showed that deep reflection has two functions. First, it can make the student quite aware of the values and norms that serve in the normative understanding of reality in any type of ethics. Second, it can also make the student aware of the moral profile that he or she needs to perform with moral proficiency.

Normative learning as advanced in PISA requires a good learning environment. Realizing this aim requires a concerted effort by management, instructors, and mentors. In this section, we have not fully addressed the involvement of management. For instructors and mentors to interact in the interest of students requires a good governing structure. In the final chapter, we address this issue in depth.

6. CONCLUSION: BEING ANSWERABLE

Viewing moral formation from window A generates several perspectives:

- PISA leads to stewardship of learning through accountability.
- PISA requires deep reflection as part of professional development.
- PISA evaluates moral performance.

How does a student know whether he or she has the right dispositions to become a good professional? In this chapter, we have explored ethical theory, mentoring practices, and psychological theories to arrive at an answer. Our answer has two parts: choose a moral profile, and engage in deep reflection about it.

Our treatment of the condition A of being answerable converges on the various reflection practices used to become answerable. Without proper reflection, no serious attempt at becoming answerable can be expected. We focused on one appropriate quality of reflection, namely that a student narrates being answerable for choosing and aiming for a moral profile in what commonly is called *core reflection* but which we name *deep reflection*.

We raised in this chapter the concern that in our Christian professional training we run the risk that reflection sessions often concentrate on the social and psychological aspects of how students experience a case. We pointed out that naturalized ethics may come to legitimize a minimal concept of reflection on answerability. Doing so would fail to teach Christian students to become professionally aware of the proper way to integrate their morality and spirituality with their professional conduct. To achieve this, it is important to make the right choice of the proper moral profile. With reference to the PISA model, you employ it to achieve a right profile.

Our study of the formal ethics of moral formation tells us that a profile, professional or not, is often not explicitly moral. Nonetheless, a student cannot do without one when exercising the moral competencies required in a professional field. Choosing a moral profile requires considerable effort on the part of students and their coaches, which entails an explicit training of moral competencies that coincides with the moral profile.

Each moral profile has different characteristics. We reviewed four dominant ones in the literature: the social practitioner, the moral communicator, the virtuous author of the self, and the person of integrity. These basic moral images are part of Western culture and will influence personal choices for being moral. Because no moral profile can be chosen well without talking about them extensively, we need to engage in narrative practices that help us make the proper choice. We have also discussed psychological and ethical theories that aid us in determining the relationship between having a moral identity and aiming at a moral profile. We have discovered that up-to-date psychology and modern ethics point us to the central role of forming a moral identity from a normed conception of the self. Accordingly, we determined that a moral identity and choosing a moral profile must be strongly connected. We have come to realize that, without an ethic of responsibility, we could run the risk of adopting the current naturalized ethics, according to which our profiles are subject to our own ideas of our moral identity.

In order to avoid psychologizing pitfalls, we need to take an explicit normative stand on being answerable. To guide students who want to enter a professional field, we urge them to choose a moral profile and to engage in deep reflection on it. Our reasons to do so are buttressed by scholarly studies on moral formation.

The evidence calls for deep reflection in the practice of mentoring and supervision. This reflection has a relationship to various ethical perspectives. Open discussion on the choice of a moral profile by reflecting from various ethical perspectives is very useful. These discussions will aid students to avoid a designer personality and to gain moral competencies in dealing with their own conduct. In this way, they will achieve Bildung.

6

Putting PISA into Practice

1. INTRODUCTION

Our aim in this final chapter is to provide clear steps for implementing PISA. PISA implementation is designed to aid colleagues in reviewing and revitalizing current educational strategies in their institutions of higher learning. PISA implementation is also recommended for practitioners in professional supervision and students involved in self-assessment, but we address here mainly educators working in institutions of higher education. Application of the PISA strategy occurs on three levels: macro, meso, and micro. Such application leads to three concrete products that are interdependent: beliefs, policy, and performance, realized on the macro, meso, and micro levels.

The macro level is that of the institution or department. We examine the practices that manifest themselves in education at the institutional level. On this level, we find the objectives and boundary conditions that hold for moral formation. We review how administration regards moral formation. This review leads to the determination of educational beliefs, that is, updating views on professional education, the pedagogy of educators, and the interrelationship between faith and learning on an institutional level. The core question at the institutional level is, just how much is moral formation desired at this institution?

The meso level involves the curriculum and the role of educators involved in curriculum. On this level, we look at the policy regulations for moral formation as carried out in modules and mentoring practices. We review how educators facilitate, engage, and monitor moral formation. This review directs the formulation of policy in order to reconsider the utility of the moral formation curriculum. At the curricular level, the core question is, just how feasible is moral formation in the curricula of this department?

The micro level focuses on how the student is involved in learning the role of a professional in practice. On this level, we find the actual conduct of moral formation. We see what students do in moral formation and what the results are. This leads to the product of student performance in terms of achieving the right moral proficiencies. The core question at the student level is, just what does it all add up to?

On each level, we treat the impact of PISA on improving moral formation strategies. We term these impacts *PISA perspectives*. They are found in the conclusions of the above chapters.

At this juncture, we cannot prove that using PISA as proposed here leads to the expected results. At most, PISA is a heuristic that leads us to ask relevant questions about all facets of moral formation. Using the four main conditions of PISA and its perspectives, we have developed thirty questions for managers, curriculum developers, educators, mentors, and those students interested in their moral formation. To gain an overall view of the validity of a program, we recommend following this checklist at each level. The result could be a working document for further deliberation by a department on its quality of education in terms of beliefs, policy, and actual performance. It also provides students with a frame of reference to understand their vocational formation.

2. APPLYING PISA ON THE INSTITUTIONAL LEVEL: BELIEFS

The most important criterion on this level concerns beliefs or philosophies concerning moral formation at an institution. Such beliefs are often considered objectives for worldview education, while the justification for related moral formation is only implicit. Our quest here is to determine why the institution should engage in moral formation altogether. The second type of criterion concerns the boundary conditions present in the institution. These are the factors that underpin the realization of institutional objectives. Boundary conditions include the historical, economic, and legal measures needed for education, and in particular the involvement of institutional belief traditions. Without adequate beliefs representing a living tradition through narratives, much moral formation may just remain a pious wish.

PISA brings into view certain perspectives regarding the institutional level or departmental level. The first is the role of PISA in rethinking the role of practitioners and practices in educational philosophy. The second is the influence of PISA on devising a normative framework for CBL. The third is the role of PISA in furthering education in worldviews and spirituality. Application of these PISA perspectives leads to renewed belief in the legitimacy of moral formation in education at an institution.

2.1. Perspective: Focus on Practitioners in PISA Qualifies Practices

Chapters 2 and 3 introduced a model of practices that emphasizes the normativity of practices and the role of practitioners. This model entails a philosophical and ethical view of the reality of practices and the normativity required to guide them. This model has the advantage of reorienting the basic types of professional performance at institutions of higher learning. Along these lines, we ask:

1. Who practices what and why? Where in the institution does the role of practices and practitioners come into focus? Does the institution have a policy on their interrelationship?

   Answers may lead to clarification of the norms and values of normative practices. Examples of normative practices are those carried out by educators, the practices of professionals, and other practices, as in sports. Results may lead to a reassessment of educational philosophy regarding realities of normative practice, the need for appropriate learning conditions, and how normative practice can be built into pedagogy.

2. How do educators and students fit into a view of practice? How do departments offering curricula handle students' demand for vocational preparation of professional practices? How do educators qualify in this educational endeavor?

   Answers may clarify the standards the institution maintains on the Bildung of students, as well as standards for proficiency level requirements for entry into certain vocations. The result may be an overview of principles regarding the learning conditions of students and the teaching conditions of faculty regarding normative practices.

2.2. Perspective: PISA Follows Worldview Education

An important application of PISA inquires how faith practice and educational practice coalesce in teaching worldviews that are applied in the vocational practice. Worldview teaching is one of the main strategies for bridging the gap between faith and learning. Moral formation using deep reflection is the manner whereby worldviews are learned integrally and put to use in normative practices. The importance of spirituality in PISA was treated in chapter 4. Seeing PISA as a necessary follow-up to worldview education has consequences for an overall formation strategy at an institution of higher learning. The pertinent questions become:

3. How is moral formation perceived at the institution as part of worldview education? In the existing process of moral formation at our institution, how are educators and students involved in accounting for their moral choices and their spirituality in the processes of reflection on their performances? How is spirituality treated in relation to morality?

    Note here that we are not yet examining actual practice (please see below) but only expectations at this point. These questions address how highly an institution regards following up on worldview and spirituality education in the curriculum. Answers to these questions hit on institutional views on moral formation and spirituality and how these are implemented. The result may be an analysis that clarifies where the strengths and weaknesses lie in the institution's educational philosophy on moral formation.

Our next question is:

4. Are educators motivated? Do students have qualified educators motivated to teach them the proper knowledge, skills, and attitudes? Are educators motivated to mentor them in gaining the requisite morality and spirituality for entering vocational practice?

    An answer to this question specifies the required attitudes and proficiencies of educators for coaching students in areas of morality and spirituality at an institution. The result may be an argument for ethical and agogical upgrade, or for training certain educators in relation to practices.

Of course, we are interested in whether PISA can be applied on this level to make improvements in the area of moral formation. We are interested in how knowledge from this book is applied. We inquire:

5. Which arguments are given for the conditions of PISA? Which sources and warrants are used to underwrite the existing practices of the four elements of PISA: P: practice minded; I: integral, S: spiritual, and A: answerable?

6. How are the challenges to an ethics of moral formation met in terms of institutional philosophies of education?

   Answers require delving into principled views on what takes place in the lives of students. The result here may be a statement of the importance of a strategy of moral formation, its objectives, and its underpinnings.

2.3. Perspective: PISA Provides a Normative Framework for CBL

The newest challenge for professional colleges in terms of being integral is that competence-based learning (CBL) requires students to make hard choices on who they want to be in a vocation, often right off the bat in their curriculum. In some colleges, the CBL framework is not used, but related concepts such as core qualities (see chapters 2 and 5) are employed instead, entailing similar concerns for measureable output of student proficiencies.

7. How are the outcomes of education qualified? Does the institution have a normative framework for learning of proficiencies and related output? How is this implemented in school policy?

   In this book, we have repeatedly held that Christian colleges need adequate formation strategies to compensate for the diminishing influence of faith practices during the rise of CBL. An answer to question 7 will lead to fundamental views on learning proficiencies in curricula.

8. How do faith- and outcome-based education (CBL) mix? Which sources of norms followed by the institution provide the leading values and norms in the formation of students? How are these inculcated in terms of a formation strategy?

   Answers will drive at the reliance on sources other than those determined by worldview and spirituality for uncovering core qualities of students (see role of being integral in PISA). Responses will also point to the reformulation of beliefs on the legitimacy of CBL. The result will be a statement on the importance of a principled view on outcome-based education.

Answers to the above questions may generate (or regenerate) beliefs relating to moral formation. These beliefs provide the warrant for moral formation on the curricular level.

3. APPLYING PISA ON THE CURRICULAR LEVEL: POLICY

Policies spell out the means needed to achieve desired effects in specified time frames and under the right conditions. Several PISA perspectives address the organization of moral formation on the departmental or curricular levels. The first is the role of PISA in monitoring what already takes place in the area of moral formation in each curriculum of the department. The second is that PISA aims for coherence in moral formation in each curriculum of a department. The third is the overall view of stewardship of learning implied thereby. These perspectives lead to new (or renewed) guidelines on moral formation in each curriculum of the department.

3.1. Perspective: PISA Monitors Moral Formation

Implementation of PISA fosters the right conditions, in the context of the curriculum, for a student to choose a moral profile. PISA also assesses what has already taken place. PISA serves in this respect as a grid of criteria that each curriculum must meet. Each element of the curriculum requires assessment as to how effectively it leads to the four conditions of P, I, S, and A. Along these lines, we inquire:

9. What constitutes moral formation as carried out?

    This question addresses the matter of how knowledge of ethics and spirituality (or worldviews) in terms of theories, skills, and aptitudes are learned by students. The result brings into focus the nature of learning modules and also how well mentoring is performing.

10. How are mentoring practices organized? In these practices, what is the role of deep reflection?

11. How is faith formation planned and carried out?

    Answers may show where the moral formation in a curriculum is expected or not expected to take place, as well as what actually takes place. The next questions examine which quality assessments might be needed:

12. What is the quality of existing moral formation? Does the practice of moral formation in modules and mentoring meet the conditions of P, I, S, and A?

13. Does it work? Do existing practices of moral formation in each curriculum lead to effective output on each condition of PISA?

    Answers may show the strengths and weakness of efforts at moral formation already undertaken. The practice and output of moral formation is thereby assessed.

The above questions may be difficult to answer without a clear qualitative analysis of courses or modules, buttressed by surveys held in the group of students involved, and followed up by focus groups. The involvement of quality assessment experts is advised.

3.2. Perspective: PISA Requires Coherence of Ethics in a Curriculum

Using PISA entails coordinating various educational practices and subpractices within a curriculum so that a concerted effort on moral formation comes about in each curriculum. The main instrument of coordination is courses or modules. By *modules* we mean any concerted effort (curricular or extracurricular) to create learning conditions leading to certain learning outcomes. Within the whole body of modules in a curriculum, a coherence in ethics is needed.

14. Which modules are to contribute to moral formation? Can the modules be differentiated as to the type of moral formation (element of PISA)?

    Responses specify expectations for moral formation in the curriculum so that modules explicitly aimed at formation (or ethics) and mentoring can be given more weight than those delivering support (thematic courses, philosophy, etc.).

15. Which modules are interrelated or interdependent?

    This question addresses how ethics, spirituality, and worldviews (in terms of theories, skills, and aptitudes) are learned by students. It also addresses the relationship this has to learning in other courses, such as philosophy, etc. The result brings the exact function of modules in a curriculum into focus.

16. Does consensus exist on quality standards? To what extent do the views held on moral formation by all those responsible for curriculum actually cohere in the curriculum? To what extent do they not? What are the mechanisms used to find common ground and devise practical policies?

Answers to these questions make visible the existence of (or lack of) a community of morality in a department.

3.3. Perspective: PISA Leads to Stewardship of Learning through Accountability

In this book, we aim to revitalize stewardship by educators. Stewardship in education is the virtue of tending to the needs of learners. It begins with the vocational awareness of being a true pedagogue (see chapter 1). As educators become true stewards, students gain ownership of their own moral formation. We found that, in the moral formation process, educators (including coaches and mentors) are as accountable as students are. Engaging PISA as a moral formation strategy trains students as well as educators to be stewards of learning. Posing the following questions in a department hits at both its Bildung efforts and its sense of moral community.

17. Are educators stewards of moral learning by students, and, if so, how? Do educators have a vocational awareness to guide students on their quest?

    This question may be differentiated for various types of educators: instructors, coaches, mentors, supervisors, or professional supervisors involved in training practitioners, inside and outside of educational institutions.

18. Do students (or practitioners seeking training) become stewards of their own moral learning, and, if so, how? Have students gained ownership of their own learning?

Answers to these questions lead to an assessment of how moral formation in a curriculum fits into the need for Bildung as an overall formation strategy. It requires an assessment of the effectiveness of the pedagogical strategies involved.

3.4. Perspective: PISA Requires Integral Learning

The traditional quest to bridge the gap between faith and learning is rapidly changing into that of faith and professional performance. As explained in chapter 3, this holistic aim has to do with head, heart, and hands as part of modern educational developments, such as constructivism and CBL. Such trends lead to major concerns about whether curricula are sufficiently integral, in particular where the role of faith is concerned. For these reasons, we ask:

19. Is learning integral? How do types of normative learning cohere in moral formation?

    Responses may be complex because they may reveal many types of normative learning. PISA requires that learning a worldview and performing morally in practice form an integral whole. At the same time, the answer to these questions hits at the heart of the matter of which profile students choose for themselves (an issue on the micro level). Students run the risk that their choice of worldview in class is a poor match with their choice of moral profile gained during field trips and from mentors' perceptions of the performance profile required in their profession. An institution or department must therefore create learning environments whereby all manners of learning can be connected. The answer to this question may entail specifying the range of learning practices found. Hence, it requires detailed knowledge of actual learning processes.

20. How is integral learning put into practice? In which curricular or extracurricular experiences at our institutions do students learn to integrate all of the desired profiles authentically?

    Answers to this question create an overall view of how learning to become integral can mesh with moral formation efforts on the curricular level. This data may lead to an assessment of internal coherence in a curriculum—a difficult issue. We recommend qualified assistance from experts in the area of quality assessment in education to determine the nature of integral learning.

Answers to the above questions may (re)generate policy for moral formation. These policies are to be implemented and assessed for their utility in bringing about the proper performance.

4. APPLYING PISA ON AN INDIVIDUAL LEVEL: PERFORMANCE

Moral formation is something engaged in by students and by faculty members in the process of student formation. There are two main products of moral formation: narratives by students and assessments by educators of the manner whereby students arrive at their narratives.

We see several PISA perspectives that require attention on this micro level. The first is the actual practice of deep reflection. The second perspective is determining the specific vocational awareness of individuals that flows from their spirituality. The third is the role of PISA in combating the fragmentation that individuals undergo in practice. The fourth is whether students can account sufficiently for how their choice of a moral profile came about. Using these perspectives leads to accurate knowledge of actual performance by students in their quest for a moral profile and how they arrive at their narrative.

4.1. Perspective: The Practice of Deep Reflection

The strategy, ethics, and tool of deep reflection have all been treated extensively in this book. We regard it to be the best tool for students to monitor how moral formation takes it course during a period of learning. It requires a relationship of trust between a teacher or mentor and the student, but more so, it requires clear and workable opportunities to do so. Regarding deep reflection, we ask:

21. How is deep reflection organized? What are the facilities and boundary conditions for engaging in deep reflection?

    In many colleges, there will be mentoring practices available that may carry out the bulk of implementation of this tool. Answers will lead to the identification of people, places, and circumstances for deep reflection.

22. Is the practice of deep reflection part of an integral moral formation strategy? Without the full PISA framework, deep reflection may remain a fragmented endeavor.

    Answers will lead to coordination between various mentors and teachers.

23. Who supervises the practice of deep reflection? This question addresses the need for monitoring the diverse and separate applications of this tool.

    Answers may lead to protocols, particularly concerning the role of intimacy and other factors requiring transparent and safe practices commonly found among mentors and pastors.

4.2. Perspective: Narrative on the Choice of a Profile

PISA requires that one's calling is chosen, reflected on in terms of vocational awareness, and worked out in a narrative. In this book, we have termed this the choice of a moral profile for a certain vocation. We pointed out that each element of PISA is involved in this choice. An important factor is that students must learn that modern occupations must be seen as vocations where calling leads to vocational awareness, which leads to the choice of a moral profile. Following this development pattern will help students to serve their clients or patients well. The result will be a strong and deliberate assurance of one's suitability for working in a particular career or occupation. This belief in one's efficacy is essential when choosing direction in a practice. It requires a student narrative expressing this belief. To assess this PISA perspective, we might inquire:

24. What is the specific vocational awareness of each student for which practice? How is this awareness translated into a moral profile chosen for a certain practice?

    Responses will be highly individual. They must be addressed by mentors and teachers, and by supervisors in reflection and supervision exercises. This question concerns a specific choice the individual student must make and their level of commitment and confidence in that choice.

25. How does the choice of a moral profile fit a student's spirituality? This question is a core question when engaging PISA on the individual level.

    An answer will be a sizeable part of the personal narrative of the individual student, which can include this answer and the above concerning vocational awareness.

26. Which narrative is used? How have students learned to be answerable to what they consider to be their worldview-led calling?

    An answer can be contained in a (preferably) written narrative, but digital versions are increasingly common (e.g., youtube.com). Both versions become very significant contributions to student portfolios.

Answers to these questions are best treated in mentoring but may be undertaken in certain courses on ethics, philosophy, or spirituality as part of exercises in drawing up proper narratives.

4.3. Perspective: Combating Fragmentation in Practice with Bildung

The choice of a moral profile is not made without cognizance of how it figures into a broader political and social context. And because we are interested in excellence in the matter of this choice, we do not avoid confrontation with those who are skeptical of the need for a specific spiritual choice. We acknowledge the sad fact that contemporary Western culture works actively against establishing a coherent moral view of life. Because of this, moral formation runs the risk of becoming overly compartmental, economic, and instrumental, which makes it subject to forces of bureaucracy and the market. This we call the problem of fragmentation. As we explain in this book, moral formation will then turn into bits and pieces of well-meaning but ineffective concern. Several questions can be posed to establish whether the problem of fragmentation is addressed properly.

27. How does one's vocational awareness fit into a coherent moral view of life?

    An answer requires command of both worldview and relevant practices. It is best formulated after engaging in deep reflection.

    A related, important factor is that even Christian higher education may involve several types of social practices types, each having its own normativity: the faith practice, the educational practice, and the vocational practice (for instance, jobs), and perhaps other relevant practices, such as sports, music, or political involvement. Each practice has an ideal of what it is like to be a good reflective practitioner in that practice. This may contribute to the problem of fragmentation. Fragmentation may prompt dilemmas requiring deep reflection.

28. What detracts from being integral? How does one's choice of a moral profile (calling or vocational awareness) relate to various practices one is involved in? How do these other profiles detract from one's choice of a moral profile?

>An answer will give form to the way the student has developed an integral perspective in his or her narrative.

The answers to these questions are clearly personal items that are part of each student's portfolio. In student mentoring, these narratives are often not shared with educators or peers. Nonetheless, monitoring of these artifacts is important for establishing the quality of moral development.

4.4. Perspective: Evaluating Performance

Much attention in PISA goes to the boundary conditions holding for moral formation: beliefs and policies. Yet, the actual student performance is what it is all about. Therefore, it makes sense to ask each student:

29. How effective is one's moral education? How does one's moral education influence the choice of one's calling, and the quality of vocational awareness?

>Responses should establish the significance attributed to various elements of moral formation. We do not discount the possibility that factors such as the charisma of certain teachers tend to lead students to attribute their education positively. But not inquiring means not knowing. Ratings by students are very valuable data that must be translated into knowledge for the department.

A similar approach should be taken by the educators involved. Ratings by teachers, mentors, and others regarding the actual performance of students are important to know. Hence we ask:

30. How efficient is your program of moral education? How well does the education received by students contribute to moral formation?

>This final question inquires about the costs of the means used to realize certain performances. Responses to this question are crucial for improvement of the quality of moral formation.

Answers to the above questions may provide empirical information about the actual performance of students in their moral formation. They may also provide a form of assessment.

6. THE REPORT: ARE WE PISA PROOF?

Answers to the above thirty questions should lead to accurate assessments of the quality of education for moral formation. We ask, tongue in cheek, "Are we PISA proof?" At the same time, we realize how deeply we also must reflect as educators on what is ultimately our deepest belief—that we need the guidance of the Holy Spirit in all of our work, as well as in our assessments.

Bibliography

Arend, Arie J. G. van der. "De Verpleegkundige als Patient Advocate" [The nurse as patient advocate]. *Tijdschrift voor Gezondheid en Ethiek* [Journal for health and ethics] 13, no. 3 (2003) 71–75.

Argyris, Chris. *Knowledge for Action: A Guide to Overcoming Barriers to Organizational Change.* San Francisco: Jossey-Bass Wiley, 1993.

Argyris, Chris, Robert Putnam, and Diana McClain Smith. *Action Science: Concepts, Methods and Skills for Research and Intervention.* San Francisco: Jossey-Bass, 1985.

Argyris, Chris, and Donald A. Schön. *Organizational Learning II: Theory, Method, and Practice.* Reading, MD: Addison-Wesley, 1996.

Astin, Alexander W. "An Empirical Typology of College Students." *Journal of College Student Development* 34, no. 1 (1993) 36–46.

Baart, Andries. *Een Theorie van de Presentie* [A theory of presence]. Utrecht, NL: Lemma, 2001.

Baart, Andries, and Annelies van Heijst. "Inleiding: Een Beknopte Schets van de Presentietheorie" [Introduction: A short review of presence theory]. *Sociale Interventie* [Social intervention] 12, no. 2 (2003) 1–4.

Baart, Andries, and Majone Steketee. *Wat Aandachtige Nabijheid Vermag: Over Professionaliteit en Present-zijn in Complexe Situaties* [What being close means: About being professional and present in complex situations]. 2003. http://www.verwey-jonker.nl/doc/participatie/D2109331-5_014E.pdf.

Baets, Walter R. J., and Gert van der Linden. *The Hybrid Business School: Developing Knowledge Management through Management Learning.* Amsterdam: Pearson Education Uitgeverij, 2000.

Barnett, Carole, Terence Krell, and Jeanette Sendry. "Learning to Learn about Spirituality: A Categorical Approach to Introducing the Topic into Management Courses." *Journal of Management Education* 24, no. 5 (2000) 562–79. doi:10.1177/105256290002400504.

Baxter Magolda, Marcia B. "The Integration of Relational and Impersonal Knowing in Young Adults' Epistemological Development." *Journal of College Student Development* 36, no. 3 (1995) 205–216.

Baylis, Bayard. *CCCU Collaborative Assessment Project.* Paper presented at the AAHE Conference on Assessment and Quality. Miami Beach, FL, June 11–15, 1997. http://www.cccu.org/filefolder/CCCU_Collaborative_Assessment_project.rtf.

Beek, Bram van de. *Hier Beneden is Het Niet: Christelijke Toekomstverwachting* [No seeking of salvation below: Christian expectations of the future]. Zoetermeer, NL: Meinema, 2005.

Bell, Emma, and Scott Taylor. "From Outward Bound to Inward Bound: The Prophetic Voices and Discursive Practices of Spiritual Management." *Human Relations: Studies Towards the Integration of the Social Sciences* 57, no. 4 (2004) 439–66. doi:10.1177/0018726704043895.

Bennamar, Karim. *Reflectietools*. Amsterdam: Boom, 2006.

Benner, Patricia. "Using the Dreyfus Model of Skill Acquisition to Describe and Interpret Skill Acquisition and Clinical Judgment in Nursing Practice and Education." *The Bulletin of Science, Technology and Society* 24 (2005) 188–199. doi:10.1177/0270467604265061.

Benner, Patricia, Molly Sutphen, Victoria Leonard, and Lisa Day. *Educating Nurses: A Call for Radical Transformation*. The Preparation for Professions Series of the Carnegie Foundation. San Francisco: Jossey-Bass, 2010.

Berkowitz, Marvin W., and Melinda C. Bier. *What Works in Character Education*. Washington, DC: Character Education Partnership, 2006. http://www.characterandcitizenship.org.

Bertram-Troost, Gerdien D. *Geloven in Bijzonder Onderwijs: Levensbeschouwelijke Identiteitsontwikkeling van Adolescenten in de Voortgezet Onderwijs* [Faith and private education: Worldview and the development of identity of adolescents in preparatory education]. Zoetermeer, NL: Boekencentrum, 2006.

Blasi, Augusto. "Emotions and Moral Motivation." *Journal for the Theory of Social Behaviour* 29, no. 1 (1999) 1–20. doi:10.1111/1468-5914.00088.

———. "Moral Character: A Psychological Approach." In *Character Psychology and Character Education*, edited by Daniel K. Lapsley and F. Clark Power, 67–100. Notre Dame, IN: Notre Dame Press, 2005.

Blasi, Augusto, and Kimberley Glodis. "The Development of Identity: A Critical Analysis from the Perspective of the Self as Subject." *Developmental Review: Perspectives in Behaviour and Cognition* 15, no. 4 (1995) 404–433. doi:10.1006/drev.1995.1017.

Blasi, Augusto, and Kathy Milton. "The Development of the Sense of Self in Adolescence." *Journal of Personality* 59, no. 2 (1991) 217–42. doi:10.1111/j.1467-6494.1991.tb00774.x.

Boele, Kees P. *Overtuigend Anders* [Being authentically different]. New Year's Speech held January 10, 2007. Internal publication. Ede, NL: Christelijke Hogeschool Ede.

Boersma, Kees, Jan van der Stoep, Maarten Verkerk, and Ad Vlot, eds. *Aan Babels Stromen: Een Bevrijdend Perspectief op Ethiek van Techniek* [Residing at Babel's streams: A liberating perspective on ethics of technique]. Series Verantwoording 19. Amsterdam: Buijten & Schipperheijn, 2002.

Bok, Derek C. *Our Underachieving Colleges: A Candid Look at How Much Students Learn and Why They Should Be Learning More*. Princeton, NJ: Princeton University Press, 2006.

Bonhoeffer, Dietrich. *The Cost of Discipleship*. New York: Touchstone, 1995. First published 1937 by Christian Kaiser Verlag.

Borst, Hans. "Spiritualiteit ter Sprake in Supervisie" [Spirituality raised as issue in supervision]. In *Supervisie in Onderwijs en Ontwikkeling: Delen en Helen* [Supervision in education and development: Sharing and healing], edited by Sytze de Roos, 43–50. Houten, NL: Bohn Stafleu Van Lochem, 2010.

———. *Temptatio et Gaudium: Aanvechting en Vreugd; Een Onderzoek naar de Bevindelijk-Gereformeerde Spiritualiteit onder Studenten SPH*. [Temptatio et Gaudium:

Temptation and joy; Research on spirituality of Reformed-pietistic students of wocial work]. Series Dixit 3. Amsterdam: Buijten & Schipperheijn, 2006.

Borst, Hans, and Frans van der Veer, eds. *Christelijke Hulpverlening, Ons een Zorg? 25 Jaar Opleiding SPH in Ede.* [Christian care, do we care? 25 years of social work education in Ede]. Ede, NL: Christelijke Hogeschool Ede, 2005.

Bosma, Harke. "Identiteitsontwikkeling" [Development of identity]. In *Psychologie van de Adolescentie: Basisboek* [Psychology of adolescence: Standard work], edited by Jan de Wit, Wim Slot, and Marcel van Aken. 23rd ed. Baarn, NL: HB Uitgevers, 2004.

Boyer, Ernest L. *The Basic School: A Community for Learning.* Princeton: The Carnegie Foundation for the Advancement of Teaching. San Francisco: Jossey-Bass, 1995.

———. *Collected Speeches, 1979-1995.* Princeton: The Carnegie Foundation for the Advancement of Teaching. San Francisco: Jossey-Bass, 1997.

———. *College: The Undergraduate Experience in America.* Princeton, NJ: The Carnegie Foundation for the Advancement of Teaching. New York: HarperCollins, 1988.

Bratt, James D. "What Can the Reformed Tradition Contribute to Christian Higher Education?" In *Models for Christian Higher Education: Strategies for Success in the Twenty-First Century,* edited by Richard T. Hughes and William B. Adrian, 125-40. Grand Rapids, MI: Eerdmans, 1997.

Brush, Silla. "Fixing Undergrad Education." *U.S. News and World Report*, February 26, 2006. http://www.usnews.com/usnews/news/articles/060306/6qa_2.htm.

Buijs, Govert J. "De Vocatio van de CHE" [Calling of the CHE]. *Lezingen Identiteitsdag CHE 2007* [Speeches on Day for Identity CHE 2007]. Internal publication. Ede, NL: Christelijke Hogeschool Ede, February 7, 2007.

Burgan, Mary. "In Defense of Lecturing." *Change Magazine* 38, no. 6 (2006). Princeton, NJ: The Carnegie Foundation for the Advancement of Teaching. http://www.carnegiefoundation.org/change.

Burggraaf, Maarten. *Christelijk Onderwijs Vandaag* [Christian education today]. Reformation series 13. Kampen, NL: Kok, 1985.

Calvin, John. *Institutes of the Christian Religion.* 1536-1560. English language translation by Henry Beveridge. Peabody, MA: Hendrickson, 2008. Dutch language translation by Alexander Sizoo. Zoetermeer, NL: Meinema, 1994.

Carr, David. "Moral and Personal Identity." *International Journal of Education and Religion* 2, no. 1 (2001) 79-97.

Chickering, Arthur W., Jon C. Dalton, and Liesa Stamm. *Encouraging Authenticity and Spirituality in Higher Education.* San Francisco: Jossey-Bass, 2006.

Chickering, Arthur W., and Linda Reisser. *Education and Identity.* 2nd ed. San Francisco: Jossey-Bass, 1993.

Claessens, Patricia, and Bernadette Dierckx de Casterlé. "Skilled Companionship: Verpleegkundige Zorg Vanuit een Zorgethisch Perspectief" [Skilled companionship: Nursing care from an ethic of nursing care]. *Tijdschrift voor Gezondheidszorg en Ethiek* 13, no. 3 (2003) 76-80.

Clouser, Roy A. *The Myth of Religious Neutrality.* Rev. ed. Notre Dame, IL: University of Notre Dame Press, 2005.

Coenen, Bert. *Een Onderzoek Naar de Ontwikkeling van Supervisie in Nederland: Een Illusie van Voltooidheid* [An analysis of the development of supervision in the Netherlands: An illusion of completion]. Soest, NL: Nelissen, 2003.

Colby, Anne. "Whose Values Anyway?" In *Bringing in a New Era in Character Education*, edited by William Damon, 149–71. Stanford, CA: Hoover Institution Press, 2002.

Commissie Kwalificatiestructuur. *Gekwalificeerd Voor de Toekomst: Kwalificatiesstructuur en Eindtermen voor Verpleging en Verzorging* [Qualified for the future: Structure of quality and end terms for nursing and care]. Zoetermeer and Rijswijk, NL: Ministerie van OC&W / Ministerie van VW&S, 1996. http://www.bigregister.nl/doc/pdf/05.%2520Gekwalificeerd%2520voor%2520de%2520toekomst_tcm18-11677_20522.pdf.

Cusveller, Bart S. *A-Module: Moreel Beraad in de Ethische Commissie*. [Module A: Moral deliberation in ethical committees]. Internal publication. Ede, NL: Christelijke Hogeschool Ede; Zwolle, NL: Gereformeerde Hogeschool, 2005.

———. "Cut from the Right Wood: Spirituality and Pluralism in Professional Nursing Practice." *Journal of Advanced Nursing* 25 (1998) 266–73. doi:10.1046/j.1365-2648.1998.00782.x.

———. *Met Zorg Verbonden: Een Filosofische Studie Naar de Zindimensie van Verpleegkundige Zorgverlening* [Connected through care: A philosophical study on meaning dimensions of nursing care]. Series Lindeboom 14. Amsterdam: Buijten & Schipperheijn, 2004.

Cusveller, Bart S., ed. *Zorg Dragen: Naar een Christelijke Visie op Zorg* [Caring for: Towards a Christian perspective on nursing]. Series Lindeboom 8. Amsterdam: Buijten & Schipperheijn, 1998.

Cusveller, Bart S., Anja van den Heuvel, Eline van den Broek, and Grietje van Maanen. "Competenties van Verpleegkundigen in Ethische Commissies" [Competencies for nurses in ethics committees]. *Verpleegkunde, Nederlands-Vlaams Tijdschrift voor Verpleegkundigen* 20, no. 1 (2005) 8–17.

Dalton, Jon C. "Career and Calling: Finding a Place for the Spirit in Work and Community." "The Implications of Student Spirituality for Student Affairs Practice," edited by Margaret A. Jablonski. Special issue, *New Directions for Student Services* 95 (2001) 17–25. doi:10.1002/ss.19.

Daniels, Denise, Randall S. Franz, and Kenman Wong. "A Classroom with a Worldview: Making Spiritual Assumptions Explicit in Management Education." *Journal of Management Education* 24, no. 5 (2000) 540–61. doi:10.1177/105256290002400503.

Dean, Cornelia. "Believing Scripture but Playing by Science's Rules." *New York Times*, February 12, 2007. http://www.nytimes.com/2007/02/12/science/12geologist.html.

Dehler, Gordon, and Judy Neal. "The Guest Editors' Corner." *Journal of Management Education* 24, no. 5 (2000) 536–39.

DeVries Beversluis, Claudia. *Community as Curriculum*. Fall Faculty/Staff Conference Address held September 3, 2003, at Calvin College, MI, USA.

Dierckx de Casterlé, Bernadette, Elizabeth Darras, and Koen Melisen. *Het Verpleegkundig Beroep In Crisis? Een Onderzoek Naar het Professioneel Zelfbeeld van Verpleegkundigen*. Centrum voor Ziekenhuiswetenschap en Verplegingswetenschap Katholieke Universiteit Leuven, 2003. http://www.czv.kuleuven.be/project/6/Belimage_rapport.pdf.

Doornenbal, Robert J. A. "Klassieke oudheid en vroege kerk: De Beroving der Egyptenaren" [Classics and the early church: Spoiling the Egyptians]. In De Muynck, *Perspectief op Leren*, 31–55.

Dreyfus, Herbert L., and Stuart E. Dreyfus. "The Ethical Implications of the Five-Stage Skill-Acquisition Model." *Bulletin of Science, Technology and Society* 24, no. (2004) 251–64. doi:10.1177/0270467604265023.

Dunne, Joseph. "Arguing for Teaching as a Practice: A Reply to Alasdair MacIntyre." *Journal of Philosophy of Education* 37, no. 2 (2003) 353–69. doi:10.1111/1467-9752.00331.

Edgell, Margaret. "Preparing Business Students to Be Salt and Light: Three Models of Faith Formation in Business Tested Head-to-Head." *Christian Business Academy Review* 5, no. 1 (2010) 63–71.

European Commission. *Action Plan on Adult learning: It Is Always a Good Time to Learn.* Communication from the Commission to the Council, the European parliament, the European Economic and Social Committee and the Committee of the Regions. COM(2007) 558 final. Brussels, October 27, 2007. http://eur-lex.europa.eu/LexUriServ/LexUriServ.do?uri=COM:2009:0558:FIN:EN:PDF.

European Network for Universities of Applied Sciences (UASNET). *Eight In-depth Country Surveys and General Report BaLaMa Project.* 2007. http://www.uasnet.eu.

Fish, Stanley. All in the Game. *Chronicle of Higher Education.* http://www.chronicle.com.

———. "Conspiracy Theories 101: Op-ed." *New York Times,* July 23, 2006.

———. "Why We Built the Ivory Tower." *New York Times,* June 1, 2004.

Fitchett, George. *Assessing Spiritual Needs: A Guide for Caregivers.* Augsburg, MN: Fortress, 1993.

Floyd, Shawn D. "Could Humility Be a Deliberative Virtue?" in Henry, *The Schooled Heart,* 155–70.

Fowler, James W. *Stages of Faith: The Psychology of Human Development and the Quest for Meaning.* San Francisco: Harper & Row, 1981.

Gadamer, Hans-Georg. "Education Is Self-Education." *Journal of Philosophy of Education* 35, no. 4 (2001) 529–38. doi:10.1111/1467-9752.00243.

———. *Kleine Schriften* [Brief notes]. Vol. 1. Tübingen: JCB Mohr, 1967. In Jan B.M. Vranken, *Kritiek en Methode in de Rechtsvinding* [Critique and method in law]. Deventer, NL: Kluwer, 1978.

———. *Truth and Method.* Translation from original *Wahrheit und Methode: Grundzüge einer philosophischen Hermeneutik* revised by Joel Weinsheimer and Donald G. Marshall. 2nd ed. London: Continuum, 2004.

Garber, Steven. *The Fabric of Faithfulness: Weaving Together Belief and Behavior.* Downers Grove, IL: InterVarsity, 1996.

Geudens, Frans. "Via Reflectie Naar Expertise: De Rol van Stage bij de Ontwikkeling van Kennis" [From Reflection to expertise: The role of internship for the development of knowledge]. *Onderwijs en Gezondheidszorg* 21, no. 5 (1997) 86–91.

Gibbs, John C. *Moral Development and Reality: Beyond the Theories of Kohlberg and Hoffman.* Thousand Oaks, CA: Sage, 2003.

Gilligan, Carol. *In a Different Voice: Psychological Theory and Women's Development.* Cambridge, MA: Harvard University Press, 1982.

Glanzer, Perry L., Michael Beaty, and Larry Lyon. "Moral Education at Religious Research Universities: Exploring Faculty Attitudes." *Religious Education* 100, no. 4 (2005) 386–403. doi:10.1080/00344080500308546.

Green, Jocelyn C. "Research Illuminates Students' Spiritual Search." *CCCU Advance* 1, no. 14 (2005) 2, 14–15.

Greene, Albert. E. *Reclaiming the Future of Christian Education: A Transforming Vision*. Colorado Springs, CO: Purposeful Design, 2003.

Greenleaf, Robert. *Servant Leadership: A Journey into the Nature of Legitimate Power and Greatness*. New York: Paulist, 1997.

Gremmen, Bart. *The Mystery of the Practical Use of Scientific Knowledge*. Enschede, NL: Febodruk, 1993.

Griffioen, Sander. *Moed tot Cultuur: Een Actuele Filosofie* [Called to engage culture: An actual philosophy]. Series Verantwoording 20. Amsterdam: Buijten & Schipperheijn, 2003.

Guardini, R. *Vrijheid, Genade, Lot* [Freedom, grace, fate]. Translated by Jean Duprés. Hilversum, NL: Paul Brand, 1963.

Guinness, Os. *Time for Truth: Living Free in a World of Lies, Hype, and Spin*. Grand Rapids, MI: Baker Books, 2000.

Gunst Heffner, Gail, and Claudia DeVries Beversluis, eds. *Commitment and Connection: Service-Learning and Christian Higher Education*. Lanham, ML: University Press of America, 2002.

Halawah, Ibetsam. "The Impact of Student-Faculty Informal Interpersonal Relationships on Intellectual and Personal Development." *College Student Journal* 40, no. 3 (2006) 670–78.

Hardy, Sam A., and Gustavo Carlo. "Identity as a Source of Moral Motivation." *Human Development* 48, no. 4 (2005) 232–56. doi:10.1159/000086859.

Hare, John E. *God's Call: Moral Realism, God's Commands and Human Autonomy*. Grand Rapids, MI: Eerdmans, 2001.

Hare, John E. *God and Morality: A Philosophical History*. Chichester, UK: Wiley-Blackwell, 2009.

Hare, John E. *The Moral Gap: Kantian Ethics, Human Limits, and God's Assistance*. Oxford: Clarendon, 1996.

Hare, John E. *Why Bother Being Good? The Place of God in the Moral Life*. Downers Grove, IL: InterVarsity, 2002.

Hatrick Doane, Gweneth A. "Am I Still Ethical? The Socially-Mediated Process of Nurses' Moral Identity." *Nursing Ethics* 9, no. 6 (2002) 623–35. doi:10.1191/0969733002ne556oa.

Hegeman, Johan H. *Christelijk Dienen: Een Verantwoordelijkheidsethiek voor Leidinggevenden* [Christian service: An ethics of responsibility for leaders]. Amsterdam: Buijten & Schipperheijn, 1994.

———. "Stewardship and Integral Learning," in de Muynck, *The Call*.

Hegeman, Johan H., and Henk Jochemsen. "Direction Discernment and Moral Formation," in De Muynck, *Bridging the Gap*.

Hegeman, Johan H., Issac A. Kole, and Henk Jochemsen. *Hoofd, Hart en Handen: Integrale Morele Vorming in Christelijk Hoger Onderwijs* [Head, heart, and hands: Integral moral formation in Christian higher education]. Series Herkenning 14. Ede, NL: Christelijke Hogeschool Ede, 2004.

Heidelberg Catechism. (1563) 2009. http://www.reformed.org/documents/.

Henry, Douglas V., and Michael D. Beaty, eds. *The Schooled Heart: Moral Formation in American Higher Education*. Waco, TX: Baylor University Press, 2007.

Higgins, Christopher. "MacIntyre's Moral Theory and the Possibility of an Aretaic Ethics of Teaching." In *Journal of Philosophy of Education* 37, no. 2 (2003) 279–92. doi:10.1111/1467-9752.00326.

Hill, Alexander, and Ian Stewart. "Character Education in Business Schools: Pedagogical Strategies." *Teaching Business Ethics* 3, no. 2 (1999) 179-93. doi:10.1023/A:1009846123335.

Holland, John L. *Making Vocational Choices*. 2nd ed. Odessa, Fl: Psychological Assessment Resources, 1992.

Hollinger, Dennis P. *Head, Heart, and Hands: Bringing Together Christian Thought, Passion and Action*. Downers Grove, IL: InterVarsity, 2005.

Holten, Johan H. 2009. *Rol en Roeping: Een Praktisch-Theologisch Onderzoek naar de Rolopvatting van Aanstaande, Beginnende en Oudere Predikanten Gerelateerd aan Hun Roepingbegrip* [Role and calling: A practical-theological research regarding the role conception of preparatory, beginning, and older ministers as related to the vocational concept]. Zoetermeer, NL: Boekencentrum, 2009.

Hoogland, Jan, and Henk Jochemsen. "Professional Autonomy and the Normative Structure of Medical Practice." *Theoretical Medicine and Bioethics* 21 (2000) 457-75.

Hoogland, Jan, Johan J. Polder, Sytse Strijbos, and Henk Jochemsen. *Professioneel Beheerst* [Professionally managed]. Report of the Prof. Dr. G. A. Lindeboom Instituut 12. Ede, NL: Prof. Dr. G. A. Lindeboom Institute, 1994.

Hoorn, Leo van, ed. *Onderwijsportaal* [Education portal]. Internal publication. Christelijke Hogeschool Ede, 2004.

Hunink, Gert, Rene van Leeuwen, Michel Jansen, and Henk Jochemsen. "Moral Issues in Mentoring Sessions." *Nursing Ethics* 16, no. 4 (2009) 487-98. doi:10.1177/0969733009104611.

Hunter, James D. *The Death of Character: Moral Education in an Age without Good Or Evil*. New York: Basic Books, 2000.

Jacobson, Douglas. "Theology as Public Performance: Reflections on the Christian Convictions of Ernest L. Boyer." Messiah College Presidential Scholars Lecture, February 17, 2000. The Ernest L. Boyer Sr. Archives and Memorabilia Collection, the Boyer Center, Messiah College, Grantham, PA, 2000. http://www.boyercenter.org/literary_resources.shtml.

Jochemsen, Henk. *Ethiek van de Zorg tussen Technische Beheersing en Professionele Hulpverlening: Een Cultuurkritische Beschouwing* [Ethics of care between technical control and professional care: A critical view of culture]. Published public lecture, Research Group Ethics of Care. Ede, NL: Christelijke Hogeschool Ede, 2003.

———. "Christian Medical Ethics and Current Ethical Trends." In *Health Care: What Hope?* edited by L. C. Steyn. Voorthuizen, NL: HCF-Nederland, 2003.

———. "Normative Practices as an Intermediate between Theoretical Ethics and Morality." *Philosophia Reformata* 71 (2006) 96-112.

———. *Opdat het Gras Weer Bloeie: Ontwikkeling, Levenswetenschappen en Religie* [May the meadows bloom: Development, life-sciences and religion]. Published public lecture at the Institution of the Chair of Christian Philosophy. Wageningen, NL: Wageningen University and Research Centre, 2009.

Jochemsen, Henk, and Gerrit Glas. *Verantwoord Medisch Handelen: Proeve van een Christelijk Medische Ethiek* [Responsible medical conduct: Test of a Christian medical ethics]. Series Lindeboom 10. Amsterdam: Buijten & Schipperheijn, 1997.

Jochemsen, Henk, and Johan H. Hegeman. "Connecting Christian Faith and Professional Practice in a Pluralist Society," in De Muynck, *Bridging the Gap*.

Jochemsen, Henk, and Johan H. Hegeman. "Ethiek van de Zorg: Domein, Activiteiten en Eerste Resultaten van een Lectoraat" [Ethics of care: Domain, activities and first results of a research group]. *Radix* 3, no. 2 (2005) 89–101.

Jochemsen, Henk, Martine Klaasse-Carpentier, Bart S. Cusveller, Ada van de Scheur, and Johan Bouwer. "Questions of Life and Death in the Terminal Phase: Towards Quality Criteria for Spiritual Care in the Terminal Palliative Care from the Patient's Perspective." In *Spirituality and Meaning in Health Care, a Dutch Contribution to an Ongoing Discussion*, edited by Johan Bouwer, 85–103. Leuven, BE: Peeters, 2008.

Jochemsen, Henk, Roel Kuiper, and Bram de Muynck. *Een Theorie over Praktijken: Normatief Praktijkmodel voor Zorg, Sociaal Werk en Onderwijs* [A theory regarding practices: The normative practices model for care, social work and education]. Series Dixit 1. Amsterdam: Buijten & Schipperheijn, 2006.

Jong, Nicolien de, Tirza van Laar, Jan Carel Vierbergen, and Johan H. Hegeman. "Morality at a Christian University in the Netherlands," in De Muynck, *Bridging the Gap*.

Kelly, Brighid N. "Preserving Moral Integrity: A Follow-up Study with New Graduate Nurses." *Journal of Advanced Nursing* 28, no. 5 (1998) 1134–45. doi:10.1046/j.1365-2648.1998.00810.x.

Kilgore, Randy. *30 Moments Christians Face in the Workplace*. Boston: Marketplace Network, 2003. http://www.marketplace-network.org.

King, Patricia, and Leo A. Fields. "A Framework for Student Development: From Student Development Goals to Educational Opportunity Practice." *Journal of College Student Personnel* 21, no. 6 (1980) 541–48.

King, Patricia M., and Matthew J. Mayhew. "Moral Judgement Development in Higher Education: Insights from the Defining Issues Test." *Journal of Moral Education* 31, no. 3 (2002) 247–70. doi:10.1080/0305724022000008106.

Klarus, Ruud. "Competentiegericht Opleiden" [Education for proficiencies]. In *Handboek Effectief Opleiden* [Handbook of effective education], edited by P. Schramade. Den Haag, NL: Delwel, 2000.

Koehn, Daryl. *The Ground of Professional Ethics*. New York: Routledge, 1994.

Kohlberg, Lawrence. "Moral and Religious Education and the Public Schools: A Developmental View." In *Religion and Public Education*, edited by Theodore S. Sizer, 171. Boston: Houghton-Mifflin, 1967.

Kolb, David A. *Experiential Learning: Experience as the Source of Learning and Development*. Upper Saddle River, NJ: Prentice Hall, 1984.

Korthagen, Fred A. J. "In Search of the Essence of a Good Teacher: Towards a More Holistic Approach in Teacher Education." *Teaching and Teacher Education* 20, no. 1 (2004) 77–97. doi:10.1016/j.tate.2003.10.002.

———. *Waar Doen We Het Voor? Op Zoek Naar de Essentie van Goed Leraarschap* [Why do it? Looking for the essence of good teaching]. Published public lecture, Utrecht University. Utrecht, NL: WCC, 2001.

Korthagen, Fred and Bram Lagerwerf. *Leren Van Binnenuit: Onderwijsontwikkeling in een Nieuwe Tijd* [Learning from the heart: Educational development in a New Age]. Soest, NL: Nelissen, 2008.

Korthagen, Fred and Angelo Vasalos. "Levels in Reflection: Core Reflection as a Means to Enhance Professional Growth." *Teachers and Teaching: Theory and Practice* 11, no. 1 (2005) 47–71. doi:10.1080/1354060042000337093.

Korthagen, Fred and Angelo Vasalos. "Niveaus in Reflectie: Naar Maatwerk in Begeleiding." *VELON: Tijdschrift voor Lerarenopleiders* [Journal for teacher educators] 23, no. 1 (2002) 29–38.
Kraybill, Donald B. *The Upside-Down Kingdom*. Scottsdale, PA: Herald Press, 2003.
Kwakman, Frank. *Personal Branding: Naam Maken als Professional* [Personal branding: Making a name as a professional]. Den Haag, NL: Academic Service, 2004.
Landelijk Opleidingsoverleg SPH. *De Creatieve Professional* [The creative professional]. Republished as *De Creatieve Professional: Met Afstand Het Meest Nabij* [The creative professional: Distant and yet the closest], edited by A. Stuur. Amsterdam: SWP, (1999) 2009.
Landelijk Overleg Opleidingen Theologie. *Een Professional met Diepgang: Domeincompetenties voor Bachelor of Theology* [A deep going professional: Domain proficiencies for bachelor of theology]. 2006.
Lapsley, Daniel K., and F. Clark Power, eds. *Character Psychology and Character Education*. Notre Dame, IN: University of Notre Dame Press, 2005.
Le Cornu, Alison. "The Shape of Things to Come: Theological Education in the Twenty-First Century." *British Journal of Theological Education* 14, no. 1 (2003) 13–26.
Lechner, Daniel. *Bildung Macht Frei: Humanistische en Realistische Vorming in Duitsland, 1600–1800* [Bildung liberates: Humanistic and realistic formation in Germany, 1600–1800]. Amsterdam: Aksant, 2003.
Leeuwen, Rene van. *Towards Nursing Competencies in Spiritual Care*. Dissertation, University of Groningen, 2008. http://dissertations.ub.rug.nl/faculties/medicine/2008/r.r.van.leeuwen/.
Leeuwen, Rene van, and Bart Cusveller. "Nursing Competencies for Spiritual Care." *Journal of Advanced Nursing* 48, no. 3 (2004) 234–46. doi:10.1111/j.1365-2648.2004.03192.x.
———. *Verpleegkundig Competentieprofiel: Zorg voor Spiritualiteit* [Nursing competency profile: Care for spirituality]. Report Prof. Dr. G. A. Lindeboom Instituut 17. Ede, NL: Prof. Dr. G. A. Lindeboom Institute for Medical Ethics, 2006.
———. *Verpleegkundige Zorg en Spiritualiteit: Professionele Aandacht voor Levensbeschouwing, Religie en Zingeving* [Nursing care and spirituality: Professional concern for worldviews, religion and meaning]. Utrecht, NL: Lemma, 2005.
Leeuwen, Rene van, Lucas J. Tiesinga, Doeke Post, and Henk Jochemsen. "Learning Effects of Thematic Peer Review: A Qualitative Analysis of Reflective Journals on Spiritual Care." In Van Leeuwen, *Towards Nursing Competencies*, 181–97.
Leeuwen, Rene van, Lucas J. Tiesinga, Doeke Post, and Henk Jochemsen. "Spiritual Care: Implications for Nurses' Professional Responsibility." *Journal of Clinical Nursing* 15, no. 7 (2006) 875–84. doi:10.1111/j.1365-2702.2006.01615.x.
Love, Patrick G. "Comparing Spiritual Development and Cognitive Development." *Journal of College Student Development* 43, no. 3 (2002) 357–73.
Lovibond, Sabina. *Ethical Formation*. Cambridge, MA: Harvard University Press, 2002.
MacIntyre, Alasdair. *After Virtue: A Study in Moral Theory*. 2nd ed. London: Duckworth, 1984.
MacIntyre, Alasdair, and Joseph Dunne. "Alasdair MacIntyre on Education: In Dialogue with Joseph Dunne." *Journal of Philosophy of Education* 36, no. 1 (2002) 1–19. doi:10.1111/1467-9752.00256.
Marcia, James E. "Development and Validation of Ego Identity Status." *Journal of Personality and Social Psychology* 3 (1966) 551–58. doi:10.1037/h0023281.

———. "Treading Fearlessly: A Commentary on Personal Persistence, Identity Development, and Suicide." *Monographs of the Society for Research in Child Development* 68, no. 2 (2003) 131–38. doi:10.1111/j.1540-5834.2003.00257.x.

Marcic, Dorothy. "God, Faith, and Management Education." *Journal of Management Education* 24, no. 5 (2000) 628–50. doi:10.1177/105256290002400507.

Martinez, Richard J. "Defining and Developing a Space for Business Scholarship in the Christian Academy." *Christian Scholar's Review* 34, no. 1 (2004) 55–75.

May, Larry. *The Socially Responsive Self: Social Theory and Professional Ethics*. Chicago: University of Chicago Press, 1996.

McDonald, William M., ed. *Creating Campus Community: In Search of Ernest Boyer's Legacy*. San Fransciso: Jossey-Bass, 2002.

McKinnon, Christine. "Character Possession and Human Flourishing." In *Character Psychology and Character Education*, edited by Daniel K. Lapsley and F. Clark Power. Notre Dame, IL: Notre Dame Press, 2005.

Meriwether, Nicholas K. "Can Self-Esteem Sanction Morality?" *Journal of Moral Education* 32, no. 2 (2003) 167–181. doi:10.1080/0305724032000072942.

Merriënboer, Jeroen J. G. van, Richard E. Clark, and Marcel De Croock. "Blueprints for Complex Learning: The 4C/ID-model." In *Competency-Based: A New Approach to Learning in Dutch Higher Education*, edited by José Eggink and Els van der Werf, 29–57. Groningen, NL: Hanse University, 2006.

Miller, David. "Virtues, Practices and Justice." In *After MacIntyre: Critical Perspectives on the Work of Alasdair MacIntyre*, edited by John Horton and Susan Mendus, 247–51. Notre Dame, IN: University of Notre Dame Press, 1994.

Morris, Jason. M., Albert B. Smith, and Brent D. Cejda. "Spiritual Integration as a Predictor of Persistence at a Christian Institution of Higher Education." *Christian Higher Education* 2, no. 4 (2003) 341–51. doi:10.1080/15363750390246105.

Mouw, Richard J. *The God Who Commands*. Notre Dame, IN: University of Notre Dame Press, 1991.

———. "The Maturity Mandate: A Sermon." In *Keeping Faith: Embracing the Tensions in Christian Higher Education*, edited by Ronald A. Wells. Grand Rapids, MI: Eerdmans, 1996.

Munk, Marian S. *Ethiek in Zorgopleidingen en Zorginstellingen: Achtergrondstudie* [Ethics in curricula of care and institutions of care: Background study]. Zoetermeer, NL: Centrum Gezondheid en Ethiek, 2005.

Musschenga, Bert W. "Education for Moral Integrity." *Journal of the Philosophy of Education* 35, no. 2 (2001) 219–35. doi:10.1111/1467-9752.00222.

———. *Integriteit: Over de Eenheid en Heelheid van de Persoon* [Integrity: Concerning the unity and wholeness of the person]. Utrecht, NL: Lemma, 2004.

Muynck, Bram de. *Christelijk Leraarschap Tussen Presentie, Vorming en Werkelijkheid* [Christian teaching between presence, formation and reality]. Published public lecture, Research Group Education and Identity, April 23, 2004. Gouda, NL: Hogeschool Driestar-Educatief, 2004.

———. *Een Goddelijk Beroep: Spiritualiteit in de Beroepspraktijk van Leraren in het Orthodox-Protestantse Basisonderwijs* [A godly vocation: Spirituality in the professional practice of teachers in Orthodox-Protestant primary education]. Heerenveen, NL: Groen, 2008.

Muynck, Bram de, Johan H. Hegeman, and Pieter H. Vos, eds. *Bridging the Gap: Connecting Christian Faith and Professional Practice*. Proceedings of the European

Conference of the European Chapter of the International Association for the Promotion of Christian Higher Education held April 20–23, 2009, in Biezenmortel, Netherlands. Sioux Center, IA: Dordt College Press, forthcoming.

Muynck, Bram de, and Bert Kalkman. *Perspectief op Leren: Verkenningen Naar Onderwijs en Leren Vanuit de Christelijke Traditie* [Perspective on learning: Reconnoitering education and learning from the Christian tradition]. Gouda, NL: De Groot Goudriaan, 2005.

Muynck, Bram de, and Evert Roeleveld. *Competentiegericht Leren, Opleiden en Begeleiden: Bezinning op een Denkwijze* [Proficiency directed learning, training and coaching: Reflections on a perspective]. Series Dixit 2. Amsterdam: Buijten & Schipperheijn, 2005.

Muynck, Bram de, and Hannes Van der Walt, eds. *The Call to Know the World: A View on Constructivism and Education*. Series Dixit International 1. Amsterdam: Buijten & Schipperheijn, 2006.

Nandram, Sharel S., and Karel J. Samsom. *Succesvol Ondernemen: Eerder een Kwestie van Karakter dan van Kennis* [The succesful entrepreneur: More a matter of character than of knowledge]. Breukelen, NL: Universiteit Nijenrode, 2002. http://www.klaever.nl/EditorPictures/34/2001-12-19-22-51-15_NY0100.pdf.

Narvaez, Darcia. "Integrative Ethical Education." In *Handbook of Moral Development*, edited by Melanie Killen and Judith G. Smetana, 703–732. Mahwah, NJ: Lawrence Erlbaum, 2006.

New Dictionary of Christian Ethics and Pastoral Theology. Edited by David. J. Atkinson, David H. Field, Arthur Holmes, and Oliver O'Donovan. Leicester: InterVarsity, 1995.

Nicholls, Gill. *Professional Development in Higher Education: New Dimensions and Directions*. London: Kogan Page, 2001.

Nijhoff, Rob. 2004. *Identiteit Onder Invloed: School Blijven met ICT en Media* [Identity under pressure: Remaining a school with ICT and media]. Amersfoort, NL: Instituut voor Cultuurethiek.

Noddings, Nel. *Educating Moral People: A Caring Alternative to Character Education*. New York: Teachers College Press, 2002.

———. "Is Teaching a Practice?" *Journal of Philosophy of Education* 37, no. 2 (2003) 241–51. doi:10.1111/1467-9752.00323.

Noordegraaf, Albert. *Meer Dan een Formule: De Betekenis van de Gereformeerde Grondslag voor Christelijke Organisaties* [More than a formula: The meaning of the reformed foundation for Christian organizations].Vijverbergserie 1. Kampen, NL: Kok, n.d.

Nullens, Patrick. *Verlangen Naar het Goede: Bouwstenen Voor een Christelijke Ethiek* [Longing for the good: Building blocks for a Christian ethics]. Zoetermeer, NL: Boekencentrum, 2006.

Nullens, Patrick and Ronald T. Michener, The Matrix of Christian Ethics: Integrating Philosophy and Moral Theology in a Postmodern Context. Milton Keynes, UK: Paternoster Press, 2010.

Olthuis, Gert, Wim Dekkers, Carlo Leget, and Paul Vogelaar. "The Caring Relationship in Hospice Care: An Analysis Based on the Ethics of the Caring Conversation." *Nursing Ethics* 13, no. 1 (2006) 29–40. doi:10.1191/0969733006ne848oa.

Osborn, Terry A., "Confronting the Zeitgeist: Social Justice, the Spirit of the People, and Language Education." In *Spirituality, Social Justice and Language Learning*, edited by David I. Smith and Terry A. Osborn, 3–12. Charlotte, NC: Information Age, 2007.

Pannier, Christine, and Jean P. Verhaeghe, trans. *Aristoteles: Ethica Nicomachea*. Groningen, NL: Historische Uitgeverij, 1999.

Parks, Sharon D. *Big Questions, Worthy Dreams: Mentoring Young Adults in Their Search for Meaning, Purpose, and Faith*. San Francisco: Jossey-Bass, 2000.

Pascarella, Ernest T., and Patrick T. Terenzini. *How College Affects Students*. San Francisco: Jossey-Bass/Wiley, 1991.

Perry, William G., Jr. "Cognitive and Ethical Growth: The Making of Meaning." In *College Student Development and Academic Life: Psychological, Intellectual, Social and Moral Issues*, edited by Philip G. Altbach, Karen Arnold, and Ilda Carreiro King, 48–116. New York: Garland, 1997.

Peters, Tom. "The Brand Called You." *Fast Company*, Mansueto Ventures, August 31, 1997. http://www.fastcompany.com/online/10/brandyou.html.

Pizzolato, Jane E. "Developing Self-Authorship: Exploring the Experiences of High-Risk College Students." *Journal of College Student Development* 44, no. 6 (2003) 797–812. doi:10.1353/csd.2003.0074.

Plantinga, Cornelius., Jr. *Engaging God's World: A Christian Vision of Faith, Learning, and Living*. Grand Rapids, MI: Eerdmans, 2002.

Plas, José van der, Harmen Talstra, and Johan Visser, eds. *Dagelijks Leven met God: Een Lees- en Werkboek over Christelijke Spiritualiteit* [Daily Living with God: A Reader and Workbook on Christian Spirituality]. Zoetermeer, NL: Boekencentrum, 2005.

Polder, Johan J., Jan Hoogland, Henk Jochemsen, and Sytse Strijbos. "Profession, Practice and Profits: Competition in the Core of Health Care System." *Systems Research Behavioral Science* 14, no. 6 (1997) 409–421. doi:10.1002/(SICI)1099-1743(199711/12)14:6<409::AID-SRES129>3.0.CO;2-I.

Puolimatka, Tapio. *Moral Realism and Justification*. Helsinki: Suomalainen Tiedeakatemia, 1989.

Reinders, Hans S. *The Future of the Disabled in Liberal Society: An Ethical Analysis*. Notre Dame, IN: University of Notre Dame Press, 2000.

Reynaert, Wouter, Dorien Admiraal, Magreet van Haasteren, Dick Mans, and Martin Reekers. *Studieloopbaanbegeleiding en Assessment: Spelen met Grondhoudingen* [Study mentoring and assessment: Playing with core attitudes]. Groningen, NL: Wolters-Noordhoff, 2006.

Roels, Shirley. *Moral Development in College Juniors and Seniors: A Case for Curricular Change*. Unpublished independent study, Michigan State University, Lansing, MI, 1990.

Ruijters, Manon. *Liefde Voor Leren: Over Diversiteit van Leren en Ontwikkelen In en Van Organisaties* [Loving to learn: About diversity in learning and developing in and by organizatons]. Deventer, NL: Kluwer, 2006.

Ruyter, Doret de, and Jim Conroy. "The Formation of Identity: The Importance of Ideals." *Oxford Review of Education* 28, no. 4 (2002) 509–522. doi:10.1080/03054 98022000013643.

Sanden, Johan M. M. van der. *Ergens Goed in Worden: Naar Leerzame Loopbanen in het Beroepsonderwijs* [Becoming good at something: Towards useful career paths in vocational education]. Published public lecture, Research Group Didactics of Vocational Learning. Eindhoven, NL: Fontys Hogescholen, 2004.

Schilling, Thomas. "The Presence Approach in New York: Two Intriguing Examples." *Sociale Interventie* 12, no. 2 (2003) 50–58.

Schön, Donald A. *The Reflective Practitioner: How Professionals Think in Action.* New York: Basic Books, 1983. Reprinted by Avebury: Ashgate, 1990.

Schuurman, Egbert. "Tussen de tijden," in Boersma et al., *Aan Babels Stromen*.

Schwartz, Lisa. "Is There an Advocate in the House? The Role of Health Care Professionals in Patient Advocacy." *Journal of Medical Ethics* 28, no. 1 (2002) 37–40. doi:10.1136/jme.28.1.37.

Shelton, Charles M. *Adolescent Spirituality: Pastoral Ministry for High School and College Youth.* Chicago, IL: Loyola University Press, 1983.

Siegers, Frans. *Handboek Supervisiekunde* [How to practice supervision] Houten, NL: Bohn Stafleu Van Loghum, 2002.

———. *Instellingssupervisie: Leren over Werk in de Context van Leiding, Begeleiden, Samenwerken* [Supervision in institutions: Learning about work in the context of leading, coaching and working together]. Houten, NL: Bohn Stafleu Van Loghum, 1995.

Smith, David I. "Moral Agency, Spirituality, and the Language Classroom." In Smith and Osborn, *Spirituality*, 33–50.

———. "Spirituality and Language Pedagogy: A Survey of Recent Developments." In Smith and Osborn, *Spirituality*, 13–29.

Smith, David. I., and Terry A. Osborn, eds. *Spirituality, Social Justice, and Language Learning*, Charlotte, NC: Information Age, 2007.

Smith, James K. A. *Desiring the Kingdom: Worship, Worldview and Cultural Formation.* Grand Rapids, MI: Baker Academic, 2009.

Smith, Yvonne. S., "The JBIB and the State of Faith/Business Integration: Accomplishments and Gaps." *Journal of Biblical Integration in Business* (Fall 2005) 154–65.

Taylor, Charles. *A Secular Age.* London: Belknap Press and Harvard University Press, 2007.

The New Oxford Dictionary of English. Oxford: Oxford University Press, 1998.

The Westminster Dictionary of Christian Ethics. James F. Childress and John Macquarrie, eds. Philadelphia, PA: Westminster, 1967.

Tillema, Harm. "Gericht Werken met Competenties in de Opleiding" [Purposively working with proficiencies in education]. *VELON: Tijdschrift voor Lerarenopleiders* [Journal for teacher educators] 25, no. 2 (2004) 28–34.

Unen, Chaim van. *De Professionals: Hulpverleners Tussen Kwetsbaarheid en Beheersing* [The professionals: Care givers between vulnerability and control]. Delft, NL: Eburon, 2003.

Unen, H. J. van. *Prodeonisme.* Muiderberg, NL: Pro Deo Pers, 1984.

Van Brummelen, Harro. *Steppingstones to Curriculum: A Biblical Path.* Seattle: AltaVista College Press, 1994.

Van Dyk, John. *The Craft of Christian Teaching: A Classroom Journey.* Sioux Center, IA: Dordt Press, 2000.

Vandamme, Ruud. *De Vork: Methodiek voor Persoonlijke en Maatschappelijke Ontwikkeling* [The fork: Method for personal and social development]. Utrecht, NL: Vandamme Instituut, 2009.

Ven, Johannes A. van der. *Formation of the Moral Self.* Grand Rapids, MI: Eerdmans, 1998.

Ven, Johannes A. van der. *Het Morele Zelf: Vorming en Ontwikkeling.* Kampen, NL: Kok, 1999.

Verbrugge, Ad. "De Vraag naar de Deugd in een Tijd van Onbehagen." [Enquiring after virtue in an age of discontent]. *Wapenveld* 54, no. 4 (2004) 4–12.

Verkerk, Maarten J., and Arthur Zijlstra. "Philosophical Analysis of Industrial Organisations." *Philosophia Reformata* 68 (2003) 101–122.

Verkerk, Marian, Hilde Lindemann, Els Maeckelberghe, Enne Feenstra, Rudolph Hartoungh, and Menno de Bree. "Enhancing Reflection: An Interpersonal Exercise in Ethics Education." *Hastings Center Report* 34, no. 6 (2004) 31–38.

Vermaat, Panc, Dingeman Quant, Jan van der Graaf, Willem H. Velema, and Maarten Burggraaf. *Vieren en Vasthouden: 1974 G.S.A.–1999 CHE* [Celebrating and retaining: 1974 G.S.A.—1999 CHE]. Series Herkenning 5. Ede, NL: Christelijke Hogeschool Ede, 1999.

Visser, Arie. *De School als Leer- en Leefgemeenschap: Een Schoolconcept voor Christelijk/ Reformatorisch Onderwijs.* [The school as learning and living community: A schooling concept for Christian/experiential Reformed education]. Deel 5. Ridderkerk, NL: BGS, 2000.

Visser, Max. "Deutero-Learning in Organizations: A Review and Reformulation." *Academy of Management Review* 32, no. 2 (2007) 659–67.

Vos, Pieter H. "After Duty: The Need for Virtue Ethics in Moral Formation," in De Muynck, *Bridging the Gap.*

———. *Tussen Vage Waarden en Strakke Normen: Kansen van een Deugdenbenadering in het Onderwijs* [Between vague values and strict norms: Possibilities for a virtue approach in education]. Published public lecture, Research Group Moral Formation. Zwolle, NL: Gereformeerde Hogeschool Zwolle, 2006.

Vos, Pieter H., and Bram de Muynck. "Hoe Vormend is de Leraar? Een Pleidooi voor Brede Vorming" [How formative is the teacher? A plea for broad formation]. *Radix* 31, no. 2 (2005) 55–70.

Vries, Maarten J. de. "Technologie en Ontwerpen in een Postmoderne Samenleving" [Technology and design in a postmodern society], in Boersma et al., *Aan Babels Stromen.*

Wain, Kenneth. "MacIntyre: Teaching, Politics and Practice." *Journal of Philosophy of Education* 37, no. 2 (2003) 225–40. doi:10.1111/1467-9752.00322.

Wallage, Philip. *Achtergrond Informatie Onderzoek Ethische Vorming Studenten* [Background research data on the ethical formation of students]. No pages. Also found in press release KPMG of June 21, 2009. KPMG, the Netherlands. Online. http://www.kpmg.nl/Docs/Corporate_Site/Publicaties/ achtergrondinformatie _onderzoek_ethische_vorming_studenten.pdf.

Warren, Rick. *The Purpose Driven Life: What on Earth Am I Here For?* Grand Rapids, MI: Zondervan, 2003.

Weigel, Van B. *Deep Learning for a Digital Age: Technology's Untapped Potential to Enrich Higher Education.* San Francisco, CA: Jossey-Bass, 2002.

Weinsheimer, J. C. *Gadamer's Hermeneutics: A Reading of Truth and Method.* London: Yale University Press, 1985.

Wenger, Etienne. *Communities of Practic:. Learning, Meaning, and Identity.* Cambridge: Cambridge University Press, 1998.

Westminster Shorter Catechism. (1647), 2008. http://www.reformed.org/documents/.

Wetenschappelijke Raad voor Regeringsbeleid (WRR). *Waarden en Normen en de Last van het Gedrag* [Values and norms and the burden of behaving]. Amsterdam: Amsterdam University Press, 2003.

Widdershoven, Guy. "Technology and Care from Opposition to Integration." In *Between Technology and Humanity: The Impact of Technology on Health Care Ethics*, edited by Chris Gastmans, 35–48. Leuven, BE: Leuven University Press, 2002.

Wineberg, Timothy. *Professional Care and Vocation: Cultivating Ethical Sensibilities in Teaching*. Series Professional Learning 5. Rotterdam, NL: Sense Publishers, 2008.

Wolters, Albert M. *Creation Regained: Biblical Basis for a Reformational Worldview*. Grand Rapids, MI: Eerdmans, 1985.

Wolterstorff, Nicholas. *Educating for Life: Reflections on Christian Teaching and Learning*, edited by Gloria G. Stronks and Clarence W. Joldersma. Grand Rapids, MI: Baker, 2002.

———. *Educating for Responsible Action*. Grand Rapids: Eerdmans, 1980.

———. *Educating for Shalom: Essays on Christian Higher Education*, edited by Clarence W. Joldersma and Gloria G. Stronks. Grand Rapids, MI: Eerdmans, 2004.

———. *Reason within the Bounds of Religion*. 2nd ed. Grand Rapids, MI: Eerdmans, 1984.

———. *Until Justice and Peace Embrace: The Kuyper Lectures for 1981 Delivered at the Free University of Amsterdam*. Grand Rapids, MI: Eerdmans, 1983.

Woudenberg, René, van. *Gelovend Denken: Inleiding Tot een Christelijke Wijsbegeerte* [Believing thinking: Introduction to a Christian philosophy]. Series Verantwoording Christelijk Wijsgerige Reeks 7. Amsterdam: Buijten & Schipperheijn, 1992.

Name Index

A

Admiraal, D., 292
Arend, A. J. G. van der, 90, 91, 281
Argyris, C., 10, 136, 281
Astin, A. W., 281

B

Baart, A., 94, 281
Baets, W. R. J., 10, 281
Barnett, C., 170, 281
Baxter Magolda, M. B., 170, 199, 202, 281
Baylis, B., 243, 281
Beaty, M. D., 37, 38, 285, 286
Bechtold, J., 31
Beek, A. van de, 191, 281
Bell, E., 170, 282
Bennamar, K., 9, 139, 282
Benner, P., 10, 72, 87, 88, 90, 230, 282
Bertram-Troost, G. D., 245, 282
Blasi, A., 220, 221, 223, 246, 247, 248, 282
Boele, C. P., 30, 42, 282
Boersma, F. K., 282
Bok, D. C., 14, 29, 30, 31, 32, 33, 34, 38, 103, 104, 107, 172, 282
Bonhoeffer, D., 189, 282
Borst, J. C., 25, 164, 166, 182, 192, 282, 283
Bosma, H., 245, 283
Bouwer, J. C., 288
Boyer, E. L., 31, 32, 33, 283
Bratt, J. D., 283
Bree, M. de, 294
Broek, E. van den, 284

Brush, S., 29, 283
Buijs, G. J., 173, 283
Burgan, M., 38, 42, 283
Burggraaf, M., 121, 283, 294

C

Calvin, John, 174, 177, 178, 185, 283
Carlo, G., 247, 248, 286
Carr, D., 283
CCCU, 157
Cejda, B. D., 290
Chickering, A. W., 169, 170, 198, 201, 283
Childress, J. F., 293
Claessens, P., 91, 283
Clark, R. E., 290
Clouser, R., 71, 167, 200, 283
Coenen, B., 283
Colby, A., 31, 32, 33, 47, 145, 284
Conroy, J., 292
Cusveller, B. S., 84, 115, 156, 166, 206, 207, 208, 209, 252, 253, 284, 288, 289

D

Dalton, J. C., 25, 27, 283, 284
Daniels, D., 167, 284
Darras, E., 284
Day, L., 10, 282
De Croock, M. B. M., 290
de Jong. See Jong, N. de
de Muynck. See Muynck, A. de
Dean, C., 102, 283, 284
Dehler, G., 284
Dekkers, W., 291

DeVries Beversluis, C., 23, 24, 34, 104, 190, 284, 286
Dierckx de Casterlé, B., 91, 283, 284
Doornenbal, R. J. A., 130, 284
Dreyfus, H. L., 285
Dreyfus, S. E., 285
Dunne, J., 110, 111, 112, 113, 121, 126, 216, 285, 289

E

Edgell, M., 17, 25, 50, 165, 167, 168, 169, 171, 196, 197, 199, 201, 202, 203, 204, 206, 285
European Commission, 285
European Network for Universities of Applied Sciences, 285

F

Feenstra, E., 294
Fields, L. A., 288
Fish, S., 36, 285
Fitchett, G., 214, 285
Floyd, S. D., 27, 285
Fowler, J. W., 168, 169, 170, 171, 198, 202, 285
Franz, R., 167, 284

G

Gadamer, H. G., 18, 19, 20, 21, 22, 23, 244, 285
Garber, S., 15, 23, 28, 32, 45, 119, 120, 285
Geudens, F., 138, 285
Gibbs, J. C., 217, 223, 224, 247, 285
Gilligan, C., 201, 285
Glanzer, P. L., 36, 285
Glas, G., 127, 226, 252, 253, 287
Glodis, K., 221, 246, 282
Graaf, J. van der, 294
Green, J. C., 285
Greene, A. E., 167, 286
Greenleaf, R., 286

Gremmen, B., 286
Griffioen, S., 6, 286
Guardini, R., 286
Guinness, O., 226, 227, 228, 286
Gunst Heffner, G., 23, 34, 104, 190, 286

H

Haasteren, M. van, 292
Halawah, I., 286
Hardy, S. A., 247, 248, 286
Hare, J. E., 26, 181, 251, 255, 258, 262, 286
Hartoungh, R., 294
Hatrick Doane, G. A., 215, 286
Hegeman, J. H., 49, 63, 104, 108, 110, 164, 187, 190, 191, 226, 243, 252, 253, 286, 287, 288, 290
Heijst, A. van, 94, 281
Henry, D. V., 37, 38, 286
Heuvel, A. van den, 284
Higgins, C., 84, 286
Hill, A., 19, 287
Holland, J. L., 242, 243, 244, 287
Hollinger, D. P., 104, 105, 287
Holten, J. van, 174, 287
Hoogland, J. J., 76, 226, 287, 292
Hoorn, L. van, 122, 287
Hunink, G., 25, 232, 240, 241, 287
Hunter, J. D., 232, 239, 287

J

Jacobson, D., 31, 287
Jansen, M., 287
Jochemsen, H., 11, 63, 76, 104, 127, 128, 156, 164, 185, 206, 207, 226, 252, 253, 286, 287, 288, 289, 292
Jong, N. de, 202, 203, 288

K

Kalkman, B., 163, 291
Kelly, B. N., 109, 288

Kilgore, R., 199, 288
Killen, M., 291
King, P. M., 33, 288
Klaasse-Carpentier, M., 288
Klarus, R., 54, 288
Koehn, D., 81, 288
Kohlberg, L., 169, 170, 171, 198, 202, 217, 223, 224, 288
Kolb, D., 144, 146, 147, 148, 288
Kole, I. A., 104, 253, 286
Korthagen, F. A. J., 233, 234, 235, 236, 288, 289
Kraybill, D., 195, 289
Krell, T., 170, 281
Kuiper, R., 288
Kwakman, F., 289

L

Laar, T. van, 202, 288
Lagerwerf, B., 235, 288
Landelijk Opleidingsoverleg SPH, 289
Landelijk Overleg Opleidingen Theologie, 289
Lapsley, D. K., 239, 282, 289, 290
Le Cornu, A., 289
Lechner, D., 19, 21, 289
Leeuwen, R. van, 25, 122, 148, 149, 156, 166, 206, 207, 208, 209, 225, 238, 287, 289
Leget, C., 291
Leonard, V., 10, 282
Lindeboom, G. A., 284, 289
Lindemann, H., 294
Linden, G. van der, 281
Love, P. G., 171, 289
Lovibond, S., 129, 130, 215, 218, 219, 222, 223, 224, 225, 247, 289
Lyon, L., 285

M

Maanen, G. van, 284
MacIntyre, A., 28, 49, 70, 72, 78, 79, 80, 84, 110, 111, 112, 113, 114, 121, 124, 126, 215, 216, 221, 222, 224, 225, 262, 285, 289, 290, 294
Maclain Smith, D., 10
Macquarrie, J., 293
Maeckelberghe, E., 294
Mans, D., 292
Marcia, J. E., 243, 244, 245, 289, 290
Marcic, D., 170, 290
Martinez, R. J., 290
May, L., 290
Mayhew, M. J., 33, 288
McClain Smith, D., 10, 136, 281
McDonald, W. M., 31, 290
McKinnon, C., 239, 290
Melisen, K., 284
Meriwether, N. K., 232, 290
Merriënboer, J. J. G. van, 290
Michener, R. T., 251, 291
Miller, D., 72, 290
Milton, K., 246, 282
Morris, J. M., 290
Mouw, R. J., 119, 199, 200, 290
Munk, M. S., 33, 290
Musschenga, A. W., 215, 219, 220, 221, 222, 223, 224, 290
Muynck, A. de, 25, 38, 57, 64, 94, 95, 110, 115, 123, 140, 144, 159, 160, 162, 163, 175, 236, 237, 288, 290, 291, 294

N

Nandram, S. S., 40, 291
Narvaez, D., 252, 291
Nicholls, G., 291
Nijhoff, R., 44, 291
Noddings, N., 108, 109, 291
Noordegraaf, A., 180, 291
Nullens, P., 251, 255, 291

O

Olthuis, G., 81, 291
Osborn, T. A., 155, 291, 292, 293

Name Index

P

Pannier, Ch., 127, 292
Parks, S. D., 168, 170, 171, 198, 201, 202, 292
Pascarella, E. T., 33, 292
Perry, W. G. Jr., 169, 292
Peters, T., 226, 292
Pizzolato, J. E., 170, 171, 199, 202, 292
Plantinga, C. Jr., 120, 173, 174, 175, 176, 192, 193, 194, 195, 196, 292
Plas, J. van der, 188, 292
Polder, J. J., 83, 287, 292
Post, D., 289
Power, F. C., 239, 282, 289, 290
Puolimatka, T., 75, 292
Putnam, R., 10, 136, 281

Q

Quant, D., 294

R

Reekers, M., 292
Reinders, H. S., 83, 292
Reisser, L., 169, 283
Reynaert, W., 292
Roeleveld, E., 57, 64, 140, 144, 291
Roels, S., 167, 168, 169, 292
Ruijters, M., 231, 232, 292
Ruyter, D. de, 292

S

Samsom, K. J., 40, 291
Sanden, J. M. M. van der, 292
Scheur, A. van de, 288
Schilling, T., 94, 95, 293
Schön, D. A., 10, 281, 293
Schuurman, E., 293
Schwartz, L., 90, 91, 293
Sendry, J., 170, 281
Shelton, C., 168, 169, 293
Siegers, F., 231, 233, 293

Smetana, J., 291
Smith, A. B., 290
Smith, D. I., 80, 155, 292, 293
Smith, J. K. A., 7, 8, 11, 125, 155, 157, 158, 159, 162, 165, 293
Smith, Y. S., 168, 293
Stamm, L., 283
Steketee, M., 94, 281
Stewart, I., 19, 287
Stoep, J. van der, 282
Strijbos, S., 287, 292
Sutphen, M., 10, 282

T

Talstra, H., 292
Taylor, C., 7, 8, 9, 20, 22, 124, 125, 128, 129, 130, 133, 155, 170, 230, 293
Taylor, S., 170, 282
Terenzini, P. T., 292
Tiesinga, L. J., 289
Tillema, H., 293

U

Unen, Ch. van, 293
Unen, H. J. van, 293

V

Van Brummelen. H., 167, 200, 293
van de Beek. *See* Beek, A. van de
van der Arend. *See* Arend, A. J. G. van der
van der Plas. *See* Plas, J. van der
van der Ven. *See* Ven, J. A. van der
van der Walt. *See* Walt, H. van der
Van Dyk, J., 293
van Heijst. *See* Heijst, A. van
van Holten. *See* Holten, J. van
van Hoorn. *See* Hoorn, L. van
van Laar. *See* Laar, T. van
van Leeuwen. *See* Leeuwen, R. van
Vandamme, R., 135, 293
Vasalos, A., 233, 234, 235, 236, 288, 289

Veer, F. van der, 283
Velema, W.H., 294
Ven, J. A. van der, 129, 130, 215, 217, 218, 222, 223, 224, 225, 247, 293, 294
Verbrugge, A., 41, 294
Verhaeghe, J. P., 127, 292
Verkerk, M. A., 294
Verkerk, M. J., 82, 282, 294
Vermaat, P., 121, 294
Vierbergen, J. C., 288
Visser, A., 294
Visser, J., 292
Visser, M., 137, 294
Vlot, A., 282
Vogelaar, P., 291
Vos, P. H., 15, 172, 236, 237, 262, 290, 294
Vranken, J. B. M., 285
Vries, M. J. de, 294

W

Wain, K., 294
Wallage, P., 13, 14, 33, 172, 294
Walt, H. van der, 38, 291
Warren, R., 189, 294
Weigel, V. B., 294
Weinsheimer, J. C., 21, 22, 294
Wenger, E., 107, 108, 109, 294
Wetenschappelijke Raad voor Regeringsbeleid, 41, 295
Widdershoven, G., 74, 295
Wineberg, T., 16, 17, 88, 89, 173, 175, 295
Wolters, A. M., 6, 71, 164, 295
Wolterstorff, N., 6, 194, 195, 295
Wong, K., 284
Woudenberg, R. van, 71, 186, 295

Z

Zijlstra, A., 82, 294

Subject Index

A

agentic self, 246
alienation, 22, 244
answerable, *See also* being answerable.
  See chapter 5, 213
  requirement to be, 225, 226
  willingness to be, 223, 226, 236
applying PISA. *See* chapter 6, 267
  heuristic for, 51
  in course work, 250
authenticity
  and balance with phronesis, 133
  and being integral, 133
  and deep reflection, 123
  and emotional balance, 131
  and LSI model, 147
  and practical wisdom, 101, 124
  and sophrosyne, 131
  and spirituality, 155
  call for in secular age, 124
  ethic of, 128
  focus on individual, 133
  gaining of in learning, 66
  of being steward, 190
  of young adults, 49
  popularity of, 131
  versus phronesis, 134, 151
  versus purpose, 22
  view C. Taylor on, 125
  virtue of, 133, 262
  without moral integrity, 220
authorship
  and being accountable for behavior, 218
  and communities, 225
  as moral self-prepresentation, 219
  as result of formation, 218
  as self-authorship, 24
  naturalist concept of, 219
  of at-risk students, 170
  view S. Lovibond on, 129, 218

B

being answerable. *See also* chapter 5, 213
  and authorship, 219
  and having personal integrity, 219
  and in-depth reflection, 238
  and knowing one's self, 214
  and moral profile, 225
  and narrating responsibility, 228
  and personal branding, 227
  and theistic ethics, 259
  as basic requirement in moral development, 242
  as needed in core reflection, 237
  definition of, 213
  demands by professional practice on, 228
  described by modern ethicists, 215
  in professional reflection, 213
  moral backbone in, 248
  need of proper reflection, 264
  PISA perspectives on, 264
  requirement defined, 225
  requires normative stand, 265
  view S. Lovibond on, 218
  view A. MacIntyre on, 216
  view A. Musschenga on, 221
  view J. van der Ven on, 217
being integral. *See also* chapter 3, 99
  about spirituality, 162
  and carrying out roles, 116

being integral–continued
    and CBL, 149, 271
    and core reflection, 237
    and deep reflection on virtues, 123
    and direction, 123
    and experiential learning, 145
    and integrity, 221
    and metaphor of head, heart, and hands, 104, 134
    and narrative unity of life, 134
    and phronesis, 128
    and social practices, 114
    and telos, 112
    as aim in supervision, 131
    as part of medieval guild, 106
    background studies of, 124
    characterized, 49
    definition of, 99
    difficult goal for students, 49
    examples in business studies, 111
    ideal of, 101
    importance of communities in, 107
    in core identity, 163
    in master-apprentice relationship, 120
    modern demand for, 130
    narrating of, 119
    or being dual, 101
    PISA perspectives on, 150
    practice in higher education, 109
    presupposed in being spiritual, 133
    relation to integrity, 99
    the call to be, 103
being practice minded. *See also* chapter 2, 53
    adoption of the ethics of professional practice, 86
    and applying NRP model, 81
    and authentic learning, 67
    and CBL, 54
    and engaging morality, 53
    and indicators for professional performance in labor situations, 60
    and liturgies, 159
    and moral profiles, 87
    and norms constituting normative practices, 71
    philosophical model of, 68
    PISA perspectives on, 96
being spiritual, 50. *See* spirituality. *See also* chapter 4, 153
    as part of PISA, 153
    PISA perspectives on, 209
being whole. *See* being integral
Bild, 45
    and calling, 46
    as part of identity achievement, 244
    choice of by way of morality, 87
    choosing the right one, 45
    normative origins, 46
    of Christ, 21
    of the master and image of wholeness in one's craft, 106
Bildung
    after applying PISA, 265
    and CBL, 58
    and combating fragmentation in practice, 278
    and spirituality, 25, 154
    and three learning tracks, 63
    Christian roots of, 21
    Christian version of, 24
    definition of. *See* footnote 26, 18
    in practice, 20
    influence by Humboldt on, 22
    modern forms of, 19
    pedagogical meaning of, 21
    tradition of, 18
buffered self, 124-126, 133
    and authenticity, 125

C

calling. *See also* calling1 and calling2
    ability of students to account for, 260
    and core reflection, 234
    and deep reflection, 138
    and narrative unity of life, 113
    and pedagogical paradox, 21
    and religious spirituality, 173
    and spirituality, 172
    and tradition, 176
    and vocatio, 62

and vocational awareness, 210
as being called by someone, 173
biblical notion of, 174
choosing of, 46
classical, 179, 193, 210
differentiating two types in, 175
example in ministerial practice, 174
example of John, 198
high view of, 181
how two types intermesh, 210
in nursing, 230
in Reformed worldview, 177
initial, 1
of Kingdom citizens, 179
Reformed evangelical version in education, 187
spirituality of, 50, 187
traditional view of, 176
within PISA, 205, 277
calling1, 175-176, 188, 192, 210
as being Kingdom citizen, 188
calling1 combined with calling2, 176
calling2, 175-176, 188, 210
as vocational awareness, 188
CBL (competence-based learning), 60
and being practice minded, 54
and Bildung, 65
and deep reflection, 140, 256
and experiential learning, 149
and generic competences, 77
and higher education, 55
and learning tracks, 64
and loops of learning, 137
and medieval guild, 105
and mentoring, 134, 141, 150
and normativity of social practice, 150
and pedagogical paradox, 15
and phronesis, 124
and reflection practices, 43
and rise of practical virtues, 39
basic to moral development professions, 54
challenge to being integral, 49
combines world of work with world of learning, 62
compensating drawbacks of, 68
conditions for, 97
deficiencies of, 60, 62, 143, 144, 145
described, 55, 56
double goods in, 110
integral learning in, 142, 149
learning relevance of, 260
legitimacy of, 271
mentoring in, 110
mix with faith education, 271
moral profiles in, 101
needed in the professions, 2
normative framework for, 68, 269, 271
personal proficiencies in, 141
requires authentic learning environments, 66
requires competencies, 57
requires holistic approach, 57
roles in, 259
taking constitutive and regulative sides into account, 86
technicistic view of, 144
test by PISA, 54
together with moral formation, 97
tuned to vocations, 57
challenges to moral formation in higher education
dealing with rise of reflection, 41
dealing with young adult learners, 42
feasibility of, 33
handling weaknesses of, 35
holding on to ideals of formation, 30
modern call for excellent schooling, 28
modern call for self-determination, 27
new educational developments, 38
rise of practical virtues, 39
classical model, 198
commitment, 244
as code word for moral formation, 32
in identity development, 243
communities
and authorship, 225
and construction of identity, 107
and moral integrity, 221

communities–continued
    and social practice, 216
    and spirituality, 159
    and stewardship, 274
    apprenticeship in, 108
    as part of learning, 205
    examples of spirituality in, 165
    moral qualities of educational, 203
    of practice (COP), 107, 108
    of practice and medieval guilds, 108
competence-based learning. *See* CBL
competencies
    constitutive side to, 77
    for business students, 141
    for nurses providing spiritual care, 207
competency in spirituality role, 206
condition A. *See* being answereable
condition I. *See* being integral
condition P. *See* being practice minded
condition S. *See* being spiritual
consequentialist ethics, 85, 255-256
    and PISA, 253
constitutive rules
    founding and conditioning practice, 75
contemplation, 89
control beliefs, 6, 8
core of the self, 220
core reflection, 229, 235-237, 249, 264
    and deep reflection, 237
    and inner dialogue, 233
    critique by PISA, 236, 237
    in SCM, 235
    model, 233

D

deep reflection
    and deep listening, 11
    and loops of learning, 136
    and organization in practice, 134
    and other forms of learning, 137
    and teaching ethics, 263
    and vocation or calling, 11
    as learning strategy, 2
    as meta-reflection, 11
    as part of professional development, 264
    assessing practice of, 276
    characterized, 11
    choice of moral profile in, 46
    definition of, 2
    drawing from spiritual and moral sources, 137
    fragmentation of morality in, 150
    going beyond core reflection, 242
    in course work, 250
    in mentoring, 134
    in practice, 249
    in professional context, 134
    on moral identity, 223
    requires virtues, 134
    review of, 249
    teaching ethics with PISA, 250
    vulnerability of, 143
    with PISA, 214
defining moments model, 198-199
deontological ethics and PISA, 253
determinate critique
    as deep reflection, 223
direction, 142
    and faith formation, 205
    and integral lattice of normativity, 123
    and learning virtues, 126
    and moral imagination, 10
    and narrative unity of life, 122
    and social practice, 216
    awareness by students of, 101
    choice of wrong, 14
    choosing of, 277
    commonly shared by teacher and student, 121
    depends on knowing proper worldviews, 8
    discerning of, 6, 9
    example of need, 13
    following regulative side of practice, 80
    function of spirituality in, 154
    in practice of teaching, 115
    in professional performance, 211
    influencing structure, 79

needs knowledge of regulative side
    to practices, 79
needs moral profiles, 55
normative direction for professional
    conduct, 89
of spiritual profiles in moral
    profiles, 188
regulates choices of practitioners,
    96
spiritual, 9
structure and direction in
    Reformational philosophy, 71
structure and direction of higher
    education, 109
structure and direction of practices,
    128
through beliefs, 5
through spiritual profile, 188
to professional conduct in practice,
    39
use social imaginaries in, 9
with worldview formation and
    moral formation, 5
double-loop learning, 136
double-loop reflection, 249

E

ethic of authenticity, 125, 128-133, 220
ethic of professional care, 17
ethical comportment, 10
ethical formation. *See* moral formation
ethics of a curriculum, 150
ethics of responsibility, 44, 48, 51, 101,
    151, 252, 257
ethics of vocation, 16
evaluating performance with PISA, 279
experiential learning.,150, 158. *See*
    figure 2, 146
    aims at practical wisdom, 147
    and being integral, 145
    and LSI, 146
    characteristics of, 145
    cycle of, 149
    example of nursing students, 148
    four steps of, 148
    need to be integral in, 148

reductionism in, 145
    theory of, 146
exploration, 244
    in identity development, 243
exploration and commitment. *See* table
    2, 244
extensive model, 199
    and moral competencies, 204
    Kuyperian aspect, 200

F

faith formation
    and integration of spirituality and
        moral formation, 197
    and moral development, 168
    and PISA, 203
    case of business students, 196
    classical model, 197-198
    defining moments model, 197-198
    extensive model, 197, 199
    five streams of, 167
    models tested, 201
    needs faith practices and traditions,
        205
    secular student development, 169
    working models of, 197
fidelity to one's core self, 247
foreclosure, 244, 245

H

head, heart, and hands, 4, 7, 105
    and being integral, 49
    and community, 106
    and deep reflection, 134, 136
    and mentoring, 140
    as Biblical standard, 104
    as metaphor, 104
    as not exclusively Christian, 106
    as required in CBL, 150
    assumes social practice, 106
    holistic aim in, 275
    in communities, 107
    knowledge management of, 108
    mutually reinforcement in, 105
    violations of, 145

higher education
    and being integral, 113
    double goods in, 110
    normativity of, 113

I

identity
    and moral answerability, 214
    going from identity to profile, 242
integral. *See* being integral
integral learning, 144
    and Bildung, 144
    and CBL, 142
    and narrative, 121
    and telos, 112
    as put into practice, 275
    as requirement in PISA, 150
    call to, 143
    current ideals of, 24
    in theory of experiential learning, 147
    normativity of, 102
    role of tutors in, 149
    supposed in CBL, 145

L

learning
    as a spiritual calling, 192
learning dependency, 110
learning style inventory model, 147
learning tracks, 63
life narrative and moral traditions, 84
LSI. *See* learning style inventory model

M

mentoring
    and deep reflection, 134
mission
    as innermost core, 236
moral backbone, 248
moral call for excellent schooling, 28
moral formation
    and age of learners, 42
    and commitment, 32
    and educational developments, 38
    as development, 2
    as noble calling for educators, 25
    as PISA strategy, 48
    challenges to in higher education, 26
    commitment to moral and civic ideals, 31
    feasibility of, 33
    ideals of, 30
    in higher education, 18
    of young business professionals, 13
    qualms have educators on, 37
    renewed strategy of, 44
    weaknesses of, 35
moral identity
    being responsible for, 246
moral profile
    and educators, 3
    and regulative side of practices, 87
    cannot do without narratives, 225
    demands considerable effort, 223
    directed by spiritual profiles, 188
    needs deep reflection, 223
    professional, 3
    quest for, 1
    review of properties in ethical theories, 222
    within practice, 4
moral psychology
    and reflection, 232
    challenge of, 239
moral source, 230
moral training, 14
morality
    moral sensitivity and moral focus, 203
    thick and thin, 172

N

narrative
    allows comparison with lives of others, 120
    and moral profile, 217, 225
    as part of practice, 120

Subject Index 309

function of, 119
   on choice of a profile, 277
narrative unity of life, 134
naturalized ethics, 239, 243, 264, 265
   and replacing virtues, 239
   critique of, 239
   in reflective practice, 241
   in relation to normed development, 246
   neutered mentoring, 241
   view on accountability in, 241
normative practices model, 114, 150, 216, 262, 288
   and vocational practice, 97
normative reflective practitioner, 86
normative reflective practitioner model. See NRP model
NRP model. See also figure 1, 70
   and intrinsic normativity, 86
   and role of moral profiles, 89
   bridges gaps between theory and practice, 86
   concept of professional practice, 71
   consequences for practices, 81
   constituitive rules as part of, 74
   limitation of, 121
   normative reflective practitioner model, 70
   relation with theory of practices, 114

P

pedagogical duty of the teacher, 112
pedagogical paradox, 14
   as calling for educators, 21
   as lead or let grow, 15
   challenges of, 15
   explains measure of difficulty for educators, 14
   in educational practice, 37
   pitfalls of, 45
   thin line of, 26
   unavoidable in professional schooling, 15
personal branding, 226-227, 229

personal integrity
   and authenticity, 221
   and moral integrity, 221
perspectives, 29
   normative, 75
   on learning, 100
   on reality, 74
phronesis
   absence of in education, 133
   and authorship, 130
   and being integral, 128, 133
   and good judgment, 132
   and integrity, 220
   and practical wisdom, 128
   as embedded in hermeneutics, 129
   as found in CBL, 124
   as part of one's profile, 128
   as part of professional proficiency, 128
   as practical logic, 256
   as practical reason, 223
   as second or social nature, 129
   as virtue, 127, 131, 262
   definition of, 127
   in ethics of profiles, 224
   in relation to sophia, 127
   limiting of in education, 131
   narrative aspect of, 128, 130
   versus authenticity, 134, 151
   versus sophrosyne, 132
PISA, 51. See also chapter 6, 267
   and background issues, 250
   and deep reflection, 249
   and generating beliefs, 268
   and generating performance, 276
   and generating policy, 272
   and integral learning, 275
   and stewardship, 274
   and teaching ethics, 253
   and thick morality or ethics, 252
   applying on curricular level, 272
   applying on individual level, 276
   applying on macro, meso, and micro level, 271
   calls for worldviews in, 251
   coherence of ethics in curriculum, 273

PISA–continued
    educating, training and analyzing, 51
    focus on practitioners, 269
    follows worldview education, 270
    four perspectives on moral formation, 48
    monitoring moral formation, 272
    normative framework for CBL, 271
    on institutional level, 268
    putting it into practice, 267
    strategy outline, 48
PISA perspectives, 268, 269, 272, 276
    on being answereable, 264
    on being integral, 150
    on being practice minded, 96
    on being spiritual, 209
    treated in chapter 6, 268
practical virtues
    in CBL, 40
practical wisdom, 149
    according to Aristotle, 127
    and authenticity, 101
    and authorship, 219
    and being integral, 99
    and the LSI, 147
    as framework for being authentic, 136
    indispensable in professional training, 149
    indispensable in reflection, 151
    mentoring of, 149
    older ideals of, 129
    reflecting on, 130
    required in professional schooling, 133
    return of, 126
    same as phronesis, 124
    violation of in reflection practices, 132
    virtue of, 126
practice. *See also* being practice minded
    and normative ethics, 85
    as socially established human activity, 72
    constitutive rules of, 74
    definition of by A. MacIntyre, 70
    regulative side of, 79, 80, 87
    standards of excellence for, 73
    telos of, 72
professional practice
    according to fundamental attitudes, beliefs, and motivations, 80
    as normative practice, 69
    normative structure of, 68
    regulative side of, 87
    willingness to accept morality, 86
profile
    and calling, 46
    and regulative side of professional practices, 87
    choosing of, 46
    definition of, 2
    how profiles regulate practice, 95
    in modern ethical theories, 215
    needs to be moral, but not always, 222
    of creative professional, 92
    of disciple, 189
    of entrepreneur, 40
    of excellent practitioner, 215
    of good pedagogue, 45
    of having personal integrity, 219
    of moral communicator, 217
    of patient advocate, 90
    of presence practitioner, 94
    of prime-citizen of the Kingdom, 192
    of seeking shalom, 194
    of skilled companion, 91
    of sojourner, 191
    of spiritually competent nurse, 208
    of steward, 189
    of teacher servant, 88
    of virtuous author of one's self, 218
    properties of in ethics, 222
    social-psychological versions of, 242
    spiritual, 188

Q

qualifying principle of practice, 74
    as telos, 75

quest, 1
  across the curriculum, 4
  and being whole in Bildung, 100
  and personal branding, 227
  and spirituality, 126
  as shared responsibility, 4
  avoided by educators, 27
  example of Reformed view on, 186
  example of quest for meaning, 92
  fitting the professional grade, 13
  for a moral profile, introduction, 1
  for integrity, 151
  for spirituality, 125
  in classic model of faith formation, 169
  involves other spheres in life, 26
  meeting five major conditions, 4
  meets challenges, 43
  needs guidance, 164
  of journeyman, 106
  practical examination of in PISA, 268, 274, 276
  requires knowledge of conditions holding for higher education, 47
  shared between teacher and student, 27
  spiritual, 14
  traditional, 275
  typical requirements for Christian, 1
  using deep reflection, 2
  within practice, 119

R

reductionism of reflection
  and experiential learning, 145
  and spirituality, 143
  and technicism, 143
reflection
  and deeper levels of consciousness, 232
  and direction, 10
  character of, 9
  common or first loop / level, 249
  deep. *See* deep reflection
  difficulties in identifying moral issues, 240
  double loops of, 10
  first level, 10
  in practice of higher education, 229
  in supervision, 232
  reduction of in experiential learning, 145
  reduction of to skills, 143
  reduction of to spirituality, 143
  rise of in education, 41
  second level, 10
  shallow practice of, 43
reflection tools, 9, 41, 139
  focus on being integral, 150
Reformed ethics, 188
Reformed spirituality
  and calling of Kingdom citizens, 179
  and pedagogical motive, 177
  and personal relationship with God, 182
  as pedagogical worldview, 210
  authority and responsibility in, 186
  experiential tradition, 182, 183
  in higher education, 177
  pietistic tradition, 193
  view of man, 180
regulative function of moral profiles, 89
regulative side. *See also* structural side
  characterized, 79
  combats conservatism, 81
religious spirituality. *See* spirituality, *also* Reformed spirituality
  as basis for calling, 173
  versus vocational spirituality, 210
role
  importance for morality of performance, 259
rules
  and virtues, 78
  belonging to practices, 76
  constellation of, 82
  constitutive, 74, 75, 76
  constitutive of a competency, 78
  constitutive side of church worker, 77

Subject Index

rules–continued
- constitutive, mastering of, 93
- founding and conditioning practice, 76
- of practice and competent performance, 85
- of practice as second nature, 84
- of the practice in NRP model, 73

S

salience, 88
SCM (student career mentoring)
- and reflection, 229
- and self-identity, 242
- as learning process, 230
- reflection under supervision, 231

self-determination in modern choice
- call for, 27

self-identity statuses, model of, 243
service learning, 20, 23, 33, 34, 104, 157, 190
single-loop learning, 136
single-loop reflection, 249
social imaginaries
- and deep reflection, 11
- and discernment, 7
- and liturgies, 7
- and spirituality, 154
- characterized, 8, 165
- critique of, 8
- force of, 165
- importance in spirituality, 209
- involved in ethics education, 258
- involved in faith formation, 172
- key part in discerning direction, 9
- limited view on, 8
- need complement of cognitive moral order, 8
- of buffered self, 125
- of spirituality, 163
- on campus, 158
- priority for Christian higher education, 7
- role in PISA, 209
- supports reflection practices, 9
- transcending of, 9

versus worldviews, 8
social profiles
- of students, 243
sophrosyne, 131
- versus phronesis, 132
spiritual function, 207
spiritual profiles
- in Reformed evangelical education, 188
spirituality
- and Bildung, 25
- and calling, 172
- and faith formation, 166
- and liturgies, 158
- and personal aspect, 163
- and relations, 162
- and vocational spirituality, 173
- Calvinist Reformed tradition of, 177
- clashes of, 171
- competency in, 206
- context of, 176
- definition of, 154-155
- functional definition of, 156
- in education, examples, 196
- in practice, 176
- pietistic, 182
- roles in, 165
- vocational, 203
stewardship, 7, 190, 264, 272, 274
structural side
- and regulative side, 79
- of practices, 79
structure and direction, 128, 257. See *also* direction
student career mentoring services. See SCM
supervision,
- amoral, 232
- and coaching, 214
- and core reflection, 233, 235
- and developing practical virtues, 49
- and one's mission, 236
- and reflection, 231
- and reflection tools, 140
- and unity of life, 150
- core process in, 232
- definition of, 231

Subject Index   313

double loops in, 249
in Dutch and European contexts, 231
in relation to mentoring. *See* footnote 64, 138
moral psychology in, 232
naturalist practices in, 242
need for morality in, 232
need for PISA, 242
perception of one's moral identity in, 237
role of spirituality in, 214
superficiality in, 238

T

teaching ethics
  with PISA, 253
technicism, 143, 145, 261
  in CBL, 150
teleological ethics and PISA, 254
telos, 44, 72-81, 193-194, 223-224, 241, 254
  and choice of a spiritual profile, 211
  and opinion and experience of users practices, 83
  and tradition of a practice, 121
  of a practice, 72
  of the practitioner, 216
  realized by professionals, 82
  role of, 112
theistic ethics, 255, 258, 261

V

virtue ethics and PISA, 253
virtue theory, 16, 27-30, 39, 172, 261-262
  and naturalized ethics, 239
virtues
  cultivation of in practices, 83
vocatio, 62, 174. *See* calling2
  as type of calling, 172
vocation
  as part of dream, 1
  definition of, 173
  ethics of, 16

view T. Wineberg on, 16
vocational awareness
  and calling, not the same, 174
vocational identity, 244
vocational spirituality, 175
  and calling2, 176
  and faith formation, 203, 206
  and having a calling, 172
  and identity of Christian professional, 162
  context of, 162
  integration with religious spirituality, 161, 162
  may supplant religious spirituality, 175
  must following calling1, 176
  narratives of, 161
  not identical to religious spirituality, 173
  secularized, 174
  versus religious spirituality, 160, 209
  view C. Plantinga on, 173

W

wholeness. *See* being integral
worldview
  and calling, 210
  and deep reflection, 5, 10, 137, 262
  and faith formation, 167-170
  and function in spirituality, 207, 262
  and liturgy, 158
  and model of formation, 2, 164
  and moral profile, 16
  and morality of community, 69
  and other than Christian, 153
  and sophrosyne, 132
  as part of PISA, 48, 251, 253, 268-270, 273, 275, 278
  Christian, 16, 17, 199, 202
  function of, 5
  interaction with norms of practice, 85
  used by practitioners, 79
  versus social imaginary, 8